THE OPINION OF MANKIND

The Opinion of Mankind

SOCIABILITY AND THE
THEORY OF THE STATE
FROM HOBBES TO SMITH

Paul Sagar

PRINCETON UNIVERSITY PRESS
PRINCETON & OXFORD

Copyright © 2018 by Princeton University Press

Published by Princeton University Press,
41 William Street, Princeton, New Jersey 08540

In the United Kingdom: Princeton University Press,
6 Oxford Street, Woodstock, Oxfordshire OX20 1TR

press.princeton.edu

All Rights Reserved

First paperback printing, 2019
Paperback ISBN 978-0-691-19151-5
Cloth ISBN 978-0-691-17888-2

Library of Congress Control Number: 2017945419

British Library Cataloging-in-Publication Data is available

This book has been composed in Miller

Printed on acid-free paper. ∞

Printed in the United States of America

*To Bob Hargrave, who taught me the art of philosophy,
and István Hont, who showed me the importance of history.*

As is the osprey to the fish, who takes it
By sovereignty of nature. First he was
A noble servant to them; but he could not
Carry his honours even: whether 'twas pride,
Which out of daily fortune ever taints
The happy man; whether defect of judgment,
To fail in the disposing of those chances
Which he was lord of; or whether nature,
Not to be other than one thing, not moving
From the casque to the cushion, but commanding peace
Even with the same austerity and garb
As he controll'd the war; but one of these—
As he hath spices of them all, not all,
For I dare so far free him—made him fear'd,
So hated, and so banish'd: but he has a merit,
To choke it in the utterance. So our virtues
Lie in the interpretation of the time:
And power, unto itself most commendable,
Hath not a tomb so evident as a chair
To extol what it hath done.
One fire drives out one fire; one nail, one nail;
Rights by rights falter, strengths by strengths do fail.

(WILLIAM SHAKESPEARE, *THE TRAGEDY OF CORIOLANUS*)

CONTENTS

Acknowledgments · ix

INTRODUCTION
1

CHAPTER 1
Sociability
27

CHAPTER 2
History and the Family
67

CHAPTER 3
The State without Sovereignty
103

CHAPTER 4
Rousseau's Return to Hobbes
139

CHAPTER 5
Adam Smith's Political Theory of Opinion
166

CHAPTER 6
Alternatives and Applications
211

Index · 243

ACKNOWLEDGMENTS

I HAVE INCURRED enormous intellectual and personal debts in the course of writing this work. Particularly important were the support and direction of my teachers during graduate study, when the foundations of this book were laid. Quentin Skinner at Queen Mary, and then István Hont at Cambridge, helped me to see (if not always fulfill) the tasks required for treating the history of political thought with the seriousness that it demands. My debts to István in particular are especially large, and it is a source of continual sadness that his early death meant that he never had the chance to tell me why the entirety of what follows is wrong. I am also deeply indebted to John Robertson for taking over the (not always enviable) task of supervising my PhD thesis in its later stages, and for offering me guidance and advice then and since.

A number of individuals were especially supportive over the course of writing this work, and deserve particular mention. Richard Bourke has been a permanent source of scholarly and personal support since my days at Queen Mary, and I would not be where I am without him. I am deeply grateful. Hallvard Lillehammer has long provided a refreshing change of perspective, a sense of proportion, and a sharp critical eye. Edward Hall has been one of my longest-serving readers, and a continual source of encouragement. Robert Jubb has been one of my most critical readers, and his willingness to hold me to account has been of immense value (numerous reflexive protestations notwithstanding). Robin Douglass has provided an unfailingly sharp eye, and his generosity (and speed) in returning his thoughts has helped me immeasurably. Nakul Krishna has been a long-standing source of intellectual stimulation and inspiration, as well as bastion of encouragement in the quest to advance a humanistic discipline. Bernardo Zacka has often been the reason I've kept going, not just through his personal encouragement, but via the example that his scholarship sets. Clif Mark and Waseem Yaqoob have helped to remind me that there is a life outside of the academy, usually when I most needed reminding. Tom Pye has been an excellent discussant of eighteenth-century political thought, and spotted important changes required at the final stages of this manuscript's preparation. Ben Tate has been an exemplary editor for this project, and his unfailing support and belief are greatly appreciated.

During my time at Cambridge I have been privileged to work alongside an astonishingly talented group of junior colleagues. Their presence created an intellectual environment of great fertility. I am accordingly grateful to Teresa Bejan, Jos Betts, Kenzie Bok, Greg Conti, Hugo Drochan, Katrina Forrester, Tom Hopkins, Sam James, Emily Jones, Dmitri Levitin, Kristen Loveland, Dom O'Mahony, Clara Maier, Ben Slingo, Sophie Smith, James Stafford, Hester van Hensbergen, Stephen Wertheim, and Sam Zeitlin for being where they were, at the various times that they were there.

I owe debts to many other colleagues at Cambridge. Duncan Kelly served as my doctoral examiner, and was a permanent source of advice and critical insight during the long writing of what became this book. In the Department of Politics, I am especially grateful to Duncan Bell, Chris Brooke, David Runciman, and Helen Thompson, each of whom has been continually generous in offering me support, direction, and encouragement. At King's College, Anna Alexandrova, Jude Browne, John Dunn, James Laidlaw, Perveez Mody, Mike Sonenscher, and Sharath Srinivasan have been the best of colleagues to work with and teach alongside. I am also grateful to Mike Proctor for helping make King's such a congenial place to live and work. In the Department of Philosophy, Clare Chambers and John Filling have been unfailing sources of intellectual engagement and encouragement. In History, I owe thanks to Annabel Brett, Joel Isaac, Chris Meckstroth, Magnus Ryan, Sylvana Tomaselli, and Damien Valdez.

Beyond Cambridge, debts are due to many others, not least my parents Keith and Francine, for their continuous love and support. In addition, thanks must go to Tom Adams, Ben Alston, Bob Arnold, James Arnold, Hollie Booth, Josh Booth, Anna Comboni, Louis Caron, Raph Cormack, Sam Davis, Abigail DeHart, Anne Marie Droste, Roisin Ellison, John Fahy, Ben Fairhurst, Mark Fisher, Ste Forshaw, Ste Gallivan, Nick Gooding, Angus Gowland, Ben Gray, Sam Greenbury, James Harris, Kinch Hoekstra, Jonathan Howard, Shaun Hurrell, Jeremy Jennings, Will Jones, Béla Kapossy, Mads Langballe Jensen, Graham Lean, Jay Levy, Anja Lindberg, Beth Lister, Nathan Masih-Hanneghan, Sarah Maule, Iain McDaniel, Roia McHugh, Ben Murphy, Isaac Nakhimovsky, Stuart Nistead, Ali North, Simon O'Donoghue, Johan Olsthoorn, Rob Parr, Phil Parvin, Ste Paweleck, Cady Pearce, Andrew Price, Ryan Rafferty, Paul Rimmer, Enzo Rossi, Matt Sleat, Dana Smith, Hattie Soper, Tom Stein, James Swire, Caighli Taylor, Mark Thakkar, Chris Thomson, Jonas Tinius, Chris Townsend, Richard Tuck, Georgios Varouxakis, Rosie Wagner, Ruth Watkinson, Calum Watson, Sarah Williams, James Wilson, Peter Wirnsberger, and Sophie Zadeh. Especial gratitude is reserved for Shamu and Hera.

Some parts of this work have appeared previously. Parts of chapter 2 were published as "Of Mushrooms and Method: History and the Family in Hobbes's Science of Politics" (*European Journal of Political Theory* 14, no. 1 [2015], 98–117). Chapter 3 appeared as "The State without Sovereignty: Authority and Obligation in Hume's Political Philosophy" (*History of Political Thought* 37, no. 2 [2016], 271–305). Both are reproduced here by permission of the editors and publishers.

THE OPINION OF MANKIND

Introduction

Hume, Smith, and the Opinion of Mankind

DAVID HUME'S ESSAY "Of The First Principles of Government" opened with the following declaration:

> Nothing appears more surprizing to those, who consider human affairs with a philosophical eye, than the easiness with which the many are governed by the few; and the implicit submission, with which men resign their own sentiments and passions to those of their rulers. When we enquire by what means this wonder is effected, we shall find, that, as Force is always on the side of the governed, the governors have nothing to support them but opinion. It is therefore, on opinion only that government is founded; and this maxim extends to the most despotic and most military governments, as well as to the most free and most popular. The soldan of Egypt, or the emperor of Rome, might drive his harmless subjects, like brute beasts, against their sentiments and inclination: But he must, at least, have led his *mamalukes*, or *prætorian bands*, like men, by their opinion.[1]

However "surprizing" this realization might have been to those with "philosophical eyes," it was not for Hume, at least by the time he published his essay in 1741, a new one. On the contrary, he had by that point already articulated a powerful and original political theory which put at its center an analysis of the "easiness with which the many are governed by the few." This easiness was chiefly oriented around what his later essays referred to as the opinion of mankind, and which Hume declared "all human affairs" to be "entirely

---

1. David Hume, "Of the First Principles of Government," in *Essays Moral, Political and Literary*, ed. E. F. Miller (Indianapolis: Liberty Fund, 1987), 32–33.

governed by."[2] This political theory was located in the second and third books of *A Treatise of Human Nature*, published in 1739 and 1740. Yet the *Treatise* was not a success in Hume's lifetime. In his own words, it "fell dead-born from the Press," and Hume's aim in many of his later essays, as well the 1748 *Enquiry Concerning Human Understanding* and the 1751 *Enquiry Concerning the Principles of Morals*, was to restate the philosophical arguments he had first published in the *Treatise* when still in his late twenties.[3] Yet, a significant consequence of the work falling "dead-born" was the submergence and general loss from historical consciousness of Hume's most sophisticated articulation of his political philosophy. For whereas the two Enquiries offered improved, as well as extended and sometimes new, articulations of Hume's epistemological and moral views, with brief restatements of his theory of justice in the second *Enquiry*, his political essays—owing to their short and accessible formatting, and their often being focused on relatively immediate political issues of concern to mid-eighteenth-century readers—did not recapitulate, let alone extend and improve, the deep political theory articulated in the *Treatise*.[4] Whilst Hume's philosophies of understanding and of morals in both the *Essays* and the *Treatise* have subsequently been recognized as contributions of the highest order, the status of his political philosophical writings remains far more equivocal. John Rawls, for example, taught his students that Hume wrote merely as an "observing naturalist," and that he was "not in general trying to answer the same questions" as Thomas Hobbes or John Locke had attempted before him, with the apparent implication that Hume's questions were of a lower order of political analysis than those of the great theorists usually afforded pride of place in the canon of Western thought.[5] This is unfortunate, if not—as I hope to show—entirely surprising. Hume was a political theorist of the first

2. David Hume, "Whether the British Government Inclines More to Absolute Monarchy, or to a Republic," in *Essays*, 51.

3. David Hume, "My Own Life," in *Essays*, xxxiv.

4. Regarding Hume's development and improvement of his epistemological positions, see Peter Millican, "The Context, Aims and Structure of Hume's First *Enquiry*," in *Reading Hume on Human Understanding*, ed. P. Millican (Oxford: Oxford University Press, 2002), 27–66, and also "Hume's 'Compleat Answer to Dr Reid'," Hume Conference, University of Koblenz, Germany, (Oxford: Hertford College, last modified December 16, 2011), http://www.davidhume.org/papers/millican/2006%20Hume's%20Answer%20to%20 Reid.pdf. On the second *Enquiry* as an improved version of Hume's moral philosophy, see Jacqueline Taylor, *Reflecting Subjects: Passion, Sympathy and Society in Hume's Philosophy* (Oxford: Oxford University Press, 2015), and "Hume's Later Moral Philosophy," in *The Cambridge Companion to Hume*, ed. D. F. Norton and J. Taylor (Cambridge: Cambridge University Press, 2009), 311–40. That Hume also reworked and improved his theory of the passions found in bk. 2 of the *Treatise* in his later essays and the short *A Dissertation on the Passions*, see Amyas Merivale, "An Enquiry Concerning the Passions: A Critical Study of Hume's Four Dissertations" (unpublished doctoral thesis: University of Leeds, 2014).

5. John Rawls, *Lectures on the History of Political Philosophy* (Cambridge, MA: Harvard University Press, 2007), 165.

rank, but appreciating the depth of his political engagement, and the direct continuities between his thought and that of his more illustrious predecessors, requires us to first understand the wider context of debate in which he was embedded. Yet, more than that, it also requires us to recognize that the final power of his arguments depends upon a shift in our understanding of what political philosophy is and can hope to achieve. Until these things are done—and they have so far largely not been done—we will fail to appreciate the depth and originality of Hume as a political thinker. Enabling and promoting such an appreciation is one of the central endeavors of this book.

Hume's deep political theory in the *Treatise* did not, however, go entirely unnoticed by his contemporaries. In particular, his close friend and intellectual successor, Adam Smith, read and absorbed Hume's arguments, and adapted them to his own purposes in the construction of a political theory that would move beyond the *Treatise*. Unfortunately, Smith never completed this political project, and had the manuscript he had long been working on, but never finished, incinerated shortly before his death in 1790. Whilst much of that theory can now be recovered from the student notes of Smith's Glasgow lectures of the 1760s, when these materials surfaced in the late nineteenth and mid-twentieth centuries Smith had been retrospectively anointed the founder of classical economics. The texts now known as the *Lectures on Jurisprudence* were for a long time read in that light, as well as part of the prehistory of a Marxist alternative to the mainstream. Similarly, whilst the *Theory of Moral Sentiments*—which contained some of Smith's most penetrating, albeit frequently submerged, political insights—sold well in his lifetime, its longevity did not much extend beyond the eighteenth century, and it is only relatively recently that it has again been recognized as a major work, although predominantly one of moral, not political, philosophy. The primary fate of the *Wealth of Nations*, by contrast, was to be retroactively decreed the urtext of modern economic theory. As a result, Smith, like Hume, largely passed into historical consciousness in virtue of intellectual achievements that lie predominantly outside of the realm of political thought.

Although we now have access to Smith's political theory, as well as to Hume's, the distinctive nature of their contributions remains obscured. At present, Hume is not widely regarded as a first-rate, or particularly important, political thinker in the Western tradition, periodic (often hostile) attention to his famous theory of justice as an artificial virtue notwithstanding. Certainly, whilst his stature as a major epistemological and moral philosopher is today in doubt by few, Hume's writings on politics are not typically ranked, even by his admirers, amongst the received major texts in the history of Western political thought, at least when compared with those of Plato, Aristotle, Aquinas, Hobbes, Locke, Rousseau, Hegel, Marx, and so forth. Indeed, and especially to his critics, Hume often figures as a mere sociologist of politics, a thinker who offers novel explanations of practical phenomena, but who fails to appreciate the fundamental normative implications of proper political theory: at best a critic of weak and vulgarized versions of Locke's arguments, at worst a legitimizer of mid-eighteenth-century prejudice and complacency.[6] Smith has fared slightly better in recent scholarship, with increasing attention paid to his political theory as recovered from the lecture notes, themselves understood as deeply connected to his powerfully articulated moral philosophy in the *Theory of Moral Sentiments*, with ever more widespread acknowledgement that the *Wealth of Nations* is also a deeply political book.[7] Nonetheless, the nature of Smith's political contribution has not yet been properly appreciated, owing precisely to the fact that doing so first requires a proper recovery of Hume's political theory. In any case, and despite the favorable scholarly attention increasingly paid to Smith's political thought, he, like Hume, still stands largely outside of the usual pantheon of great political thinkers taken to have articulated the most important visions of politics available in the Western tradition.

Against the prevailing assessment, this book aims to show that when it comes to political theory, Hume and Smith have been underappreciated, even by their admirers.[8] Furthermore, by recovering Hume's political theory, and seeing how Smith took over and extended it in turn, we are invited to ap-

---

[6]. See especially John Dunn, "From Applied Theology to Social Analysis: The Break between John Locke and the Scottish Enlightenment," in *Wealth and Virtue: The Shaping of Political Economy in the Scottish Enlightenment*, ed. I. Hont and M. Ignatieff (Cambridge, 1983), 119–36; P. F. Brownsey, "Hume and the Social Contract," *Philosophical Quarterly* 28 (1978), 132–48.

[7]. See most especially István Hont, "The Language of Sociability and Commerce: Samuel Pufendorf and the Theoretical Foundations of the 'Four Stages' Theory," in *Jealousy of Trade: International Competition and the Nation State in Historical Perspective* (Cambridge, MA: Belknap Harvard, 2005), 159–84; "Commercial Society and Political Theory in the Eighteenth Century: The Problem of Authority in David Hume and Adam Smith," in *Main Trends in Cultural History: Ten Essays*, ed. W. Melching and W. Velema (Amsterdam: Rodopi: 1994), 54–94; "Adam Smith's History of Law and Government as Political Theory," in *Political Judgment: Essays for John Dunn*, ed. R. Bourke and R. Geuss (Cambridge: Cambridge University Press, 2009), 131–71; István Hont and Michael Ignatieff, "Needs and Justice in the *Wealth of Nations*," in Hont, *Jealousy of Trade*, 389–443; but also, for example, Samuel Fleischacker, *On Adam Smith's "Wealth of Nations": A Philosophical Companion* (Princeton, NJ: Princeton University Press, 2005); Charles L. Griswold, *Adam Smith and the Virtues of Enlightenment* (Cambridge: Cambridge University Press, 1999), chaps. 6–7; Craig Smith, *Adam Smith's Political Philosophy: The Invisible Hand and Spontaneous Order* (Abingdon, UK: Routledge, 2006); Ryan Patrick Hanley, "Commerce and Corruption: Rousseau's Diagnosis and Adam Smith's Cure," *European Journal of Political Theory* 7 (2008), 137–58.

[8]. With regard to Smith in particular, most assessments of his political writings focus on his warnings about unintended consequences and his skepticism about governmental interference in the workings of the economy. Although these are certainly features of Smith's thought—and important ones—what I will try to bring out below is the extent to which they are more or less surface manifestations of Smith's commitment to a much deeper form of political theorizing, taken over from Hume.

preciate a mode of political theorizing that not only stands as a major historical achievement in and of itself, but presents possibilities for how we can think about politics today. In order to make this ambition clearer, it will be helpful to specify more explicitly some of my intellectual points of departure, thereby also supplying a rationalization for my focus on Hume and Smith that goes beyond their considerable intrinsic merits as individual thinkers, and which may even help to persuade readers who are initially skeptical of turning to them for insight. The rest of this introduction supplies that wider background.

The Theory of the State and the History of Political Thought

In recent decades, several of the most important frameworks for understanding the history of political thought in the early modern period, and in particular for understanding the origins and nature of the modern state, have assigned a central role to the political philosophy of Thomas Hobbes. Quentin Skinner has argued that the idea of the modern state came into being when politics transitioned from the status of the person of the prince—especially in Italian Renaissance political thought, but also with regards to the monarchomach, or "king-killing," Calvinist resistance theorists of the sixteenth century—to the state *as* a person, epitomized in the theory of representative sovereignty that Hobbes outlined in *Leviathan*. Skinner has urged us to recover Hobbes's idea of state personhood as a way of making sense of present political predicaments, especially in relation to public debt, whilst also arguing that Hobbes is the source of a modern (albeit fallacious) understanding of liberty that underpins the contemporary liberal state form.[9] John Dunn, by contrast, has long argued that Hobbes's political theory represents an inadequate prudentialism that cannot supply sufficient reasons why the state can make legitimate claims regarding the obedience of subjects. Dunn sees John Locke as the only theorist to have fully grasped the inadequacy of Hobbes's picture. But Locke's own solution was theistic all the way down, and thus (Dunn thinks)

---

9. Quentin Skinner, "The State," in *Political Innovation and Conceptual Change*, ed. T. Ball, J. Farr, and R. L. Hanson (Cambridge: Cambridge University Press, 1989), 90–131; "From the State of Princes to the Person of the State," in *Visions of Politics*, vol. 2, *Renaissance Virtues* (Cambridge: Cambridge University Press, 2002), 368–413; "Hobbes on Persons, Authors, and Representatives," in *The Cambridge Companion to Hobbes's Leviathan*, ed. P. Springborg (Cambridge: Cambridge University Press, 2007), 157–80; *Hobbes and Republican Liberty* (Cambridge: Cambridge University Press, 2008); "A Genealogy of the Modern State," *Proceedings of the British Academy* 162 (2009), 325–70. On the long prehistory of the emergence of the modern state in Hobbes, see Quentin Skinner, *The Foundations of Modern Political Thought*, 2 vols. (Cambridge: Cambridge University Press, 1978). See also David Runciman, "What Kind of Person is Hobbes's State? A Reply to Quentin Skinner," *Journal of Political Philosophy* 8, no. 2 (2000), 268–78, but also Paul Sagar, "What is the Leviathan?" *Hobbes Studies* (forthcoming).

is not an option in our disenchanted world. Nobody, according to Dunn, has yet found a way of getting past Hobbes without Locke's unacceptably theistic grounding. Hobbes thus remains central, as both a rebuke to our incapacity to do better, and representing a positive proposal that we cannot honestly embrace if we are committed to the divided-sovereignty democratic politics of the modern world.[10] Richard Tuck, by contrast, has argued that Hobbes's moral and political theory was an attempt to defuse earlier incarnations of ethical skepticism, particularly as put forward by Michel de Montaigne and Pierre Charron, and which was achieved by Hobbes's taking over Hugo Grotius's emphasis on the ineliminable natural right of self-preservation as the foundation of an antiskeptical theory, and which stands at the origin of the emergence of the modern state. Similarly, István Hont has argued that the modern state is a fusion of Hobbes's idea of representative sovereignty with an acceptance of commercial activity as a now unavoidable feature of politics. The "modern republic," or what we now call the liberal democratic state, is a trading entity predicated upon politics as organized through the matrix of representative sovereignty—which has its origin in Hobbes.[11]

These four scholars, typically considered part of a "Cambridge school" in the history of political thought, certainly disagree about the precise nature of Hobbes's importance. Nonetheless, there is clear agreement amongst them that Hobbes *is* of central importance, and all articulate some version of a claim that his centrality rests upon the articulation of a vision of the modern state, one with which we must still reckon if we ourselves are to achieve an adequate grasp of that entity, and hence of modern politics. Yet, these "Cambridge" scholars are hardly unique in placing a heavy emphasis on Hobbes's importance to the development of Western political theory, and his enduring presence in making sense of our current situation. Leo Strauss, a very different kind of scholar, emphasized the centrality of Hobbes to the emergence of modern political theory, as have many of his students and followers.[12] John Rawls, a philosopher of a very different stripe again, taught his students that

---

10. John Dunn, *The Political Thought of John Locke: An Historical Account of the Argument of the "Two Treatises on Government"* (Cambridge: Cambridge University Press, 1969); *Western Political Theory in the Face of the Future* (Cambridge: Cambridge University Press, 1979); "What Is Living and What Is Dead in the Political Theory of John Locke?" in *Interpreting Political Responsibility: Essays 1981–89* (Padstow, UK: Polity, 1990), 9–25; "The Politics of Imponderable and Potentially Lethal Judgment for Mortals: Hobbes's Legacy for the Understanding of Modern Politics," in Thomas Hobbes, *Leviathan*, ed. I. Shapiro (New Haven: Yale University Press, 2010), 433–52.

11. István Hont, "Jealousy of Trade: An Introduction," and "The Permanent Crisis of a Divided Mankind: 'Nation-State' and 'Nationalism' in Historical Perspective," in *Jealousy of Trade*, 1–156, 447–528.

12. Leo Strauss, *The Political Philosophy of Hobbes: Its Basis and Genesis*, trans. E. M. Sinclair (Oxford: Clarendon Press, 1936); *Natural Right and History* (Chicago: Chicago University Press, 1965).

Leviathan was the "greatest single work of political thought in the English language," and placed it in a "social contract" tradition that his own political theory was in part an extension of.[13] Raymond Geuss, perhaps Rawls's most scathing critic in contemporary political theory, nonetheless similarly maintains that modern Western political theory begins with Hobbes.[14] Others, such as Jeremy Waldron, see Hobbes's political writings as an important foundation of contemporary liberal political theory, and of the form of justification for the use of coercive force that a specifically liberal politics mobilizes.[15] More generally, and when it comes to the construction of traditions of thought that span multiple thinkers and across extended periods, libraries abound with volumes with titles like *The Social Contract from Hobbes to Rawls*.[16] Yet what if a privileged emphasis on Hobbes is liable to generate mistaken, partial, and distorted appraisals of both the history of political thought and the forms that political theory may take? In particular, what if an overemphasis on Hobbes blinds us to theoretical alternatives in the historical record that stand in marked opposition to his manner of theorizing politics? And what if those alternatives should turn out to be superior? These are the possibilities taken seriously in this book, attempted primarily via a recovery of the idiom of political theory exemplified in the work of Hume and Smith, which I hope to convince the reader make for a finally more plausible and satisfying vision of politics than that which stays with Hobbes, or continues to work in Hobbesian vein.

Of course, work that starts with Hobbes—or at least takes Hobbes to be at the start of something important—need not necessarily stay with him, and

---

13. Rawls, *Lectures*, 23. It should be noted that Rawls did immediately qualify this statement by making clear that for him *Leviathan* didn't come "the closest to being true," nor did he think "that it is the most reasonable"—nonetheless, he still identified it as the greatest when taken on balance, and overall. This book aims to disrupt the coherence of such a judgment: that if we abandon Hobbesian ways of thinking, the sheer and undeniable intellectual power of Hobbes's conceptual edifice may not be enough to support Rawls's verdict. More generally, if Skinner is right that Rawls is a "gothic" theorist in explicitly Hobbesian mold, then Rawls's own remark about the significance of *Leviathan* may be particularly telling: Skinner, "Machiavelli on *Virtù* and the Maintenance of Liberty," in *Renaissance Virtues*, 161.

14. Raymond Geuss, *Philosophy and Real Politics* (Princeton, NJ: Princeton University Press, 2008), 21.

15. Jeremy Waldron, "Hobbes and the Principle of Publicity," *Pacific Philosophical Quarterly* 82, no. 3-4 (2001), 447–74.

16. David Boucher and Paul Kelly, eds., *The Social Contract from Hobbes to Rawls* (London: Routledge, 1994). Other examples include Jean Hampton, *Hobbes and the Social Contract Tradition* (Cambridge: Cambridge University Press, 1986); Patrick Riley, *Will and Political Legitimacy: A Critical Exposition of Social Contract Theory in Hobbes, Locke, Rousseau, Kant and Hegel* (Cambridge, MA: Harvard University Press, 1982); Jody S. Kraus, *The Limits of Hobbesian Contractarianism* (Cambridge: Cambridge University Press, 1994); Mark E. Button, *Contract, Culture and Citizenship: Transformative Liberalism from Hobbes to Rawls* (University Park, PA: Pennsylvania State University Press, 2008).

important and interesting alternatives can and have been developed in that way.[17] Indeed, this book ought itself to be read as an attempt at such a thing: the sheer level of attention and detail given over to Hobbes in what follows is proof enough that I too assign him a central place in the history of political thought. Nonetheless, I hope to show that much can be gained in an explicit attempt to get out from under Hobbes's shadow, even if we must first spend a considerable amount of time in the shade. Hobbes is, without doubt, important—but we should nonetheless aspire to leave him behind. Hume and Smith show how this might be done, and we stand to learn a great deal from them accordingly.

What follows is intended as a dual intervention—in both the history of political thought and contemporary political theory. That this should particularly be so with regard to the theory of the state is given by the fact that although the state remains the central unit of analysis in both domestic and international politics, its basis, nature, purpose, and normative authority are subjects of protracted disagreement and confusion. This is certainly so in the history of political thought, not least because of the competing accounts that scholars supply of the state's leading historical theorizers, but also because of the manner in which theory interacts with practice in the historical instantiation of institutional structures. By contrast, in the majority of contemporary anglophone political theory the *nature* of the state is frequently assumed as being relatively unproblematic from a conceptual point of view, and hence standardly taken as given or simply left unconsidered, with far more attention focused upon the normative ends to which the power of organized rule should be directed, particularly with regard to the realization of the values of liberty and equality.[18] This, however, is an awkward state of affairs, insofar as the confusion generated by controversy in the history of political thought ought to impinge upon the confidence of contemporary normative theorizers. If we do not have a clear grasp of what the state is, including especially what its central functions and justifications are, then we cannot proceed with an adequate degree of confidence, let alone intellectual authority, when it comes to attempting to stipulate the normative constraints and goals that should govern its activities, either at home or abroad. In this sense, the history of political thought rightly acts as a *disruptive* influence on contemporary normative theorizing. By insisting that we do not have an adequate grasp of one of our most fundamental political concepts, it demands that we re-examine and make secure the foundations of our theoretical enterprises, before presuming to build upon them.

---

17. For a provocative and singular example, consider Richard Tuck, *The Sleeping Sovereign: The Invention of Modern Democracy* (Cambridge, Cambridge University Press, 2015).

18. For an indictment of this state of affairs, see Jeremy Waldron, "*Political* Political Theory: An Inaugural Lecture," *Journal of Political Philosophy* 21, no. 2 (2013), 1–23.

An aim of this book is ultimately to offer a different way of thinking about whether there are "foundations" to be had in theorizing the modern state, and what follows from getting clear on that. To this end, it will be helpful to situate my argument as being an alternative to the framework for understanding the modern state articulated by István Hont, which may be summarized as follows: On Hont's account, Hobbes is a paradoxical figure. Due to his lack of any theory of the economy, Hobbes stands as the last of the Renaissance, or premodern, theorists of politics. Nonetheless, it was a fusion of Hobbes's idea of "union" as the foundation of the state through an act of artificial representation with the post-Hobbesian emergence of "commercial society" in the eighteenth century that together "created the modern representative republic, our current state form."[19] Hont identifies "the modern doctrine of sovereignty" as central to this process, something which "started with Bodin in France and reached its classic formulation in the work of Thomas Hobbes." This "doctrine" claimed that "the survival and greatness of a political community required the creation of an ultimate decision-making agency whose task was to devise adequate responses to external challenges and stop infighting at home with an iron hand."[20] Originally a response to the religious wars of early modern Europe, and a rejoinder to theories of divided sovereignty and monarchomach theory, this idea could only become functional for the eighteenth century (and after) when it was married to the acceptance of commerce as an ineliminable feature of advanced human societies, and hence of advanced human politics. Thus, whilst Hobbes can be credited with "the self-conscious theoretical invention" of the "modern republic," his "invention" could become fully functional only after "late-eighteenth-century revisions."[21] Hont chiefly credits the achievement of such revisions to the French Revolutionary pamphleteer and constitutionalist Emmanuel Sieyès. For it was Sieyès, Hont claims, who inherited Hobbes's ideas through Jean-Jacques Rousseau's "appropriating" many aspects of the Englishman's political theory, yet rejected Rousseau's inbuilt fusion of representation and absolutism which the Genevan saw as "a vehicle for despotism."[22] Sieyès broke with Rousseau by allowing the permissible representation of sovereignty back into the theoretical framework, but also departed from Hobbes because he "explicitly anchored the modern representative republic in the economy."[23] Whilst Hont's view of Sieyès is ultimately equivocal (his thought is "not sufficiently original to warrant regarding him as the creator of democratic or civic nationalism in Europe," for it is "Hobbes's originality, mediated in part by Rousseau, which shines through Sieyès's

---

19. Hont, "Introduction," 21.
20. Hont, "Permanent Crisis," 464.
21. Hont, "Introduction," 128, 125.
22. Ibid., 470.
23. Ibid., 133.

thought"[24]), he nonetheless states that "Sieyès's Hobbesian constitutionalism effectively laid the foundations for the dominant state form of the contemporary era. Democracy today means a representative republic embedded in a commercial society."[25]

We might certainly question Hont's use of the definite article when talking of "the modern doctrine of sovereignty." But his framework serves as a useful critical foil for the present study. This is because even if we grant that such a thing as "the modern doctrine of sovereignty" exists—in the singular, and originating with Hobbes—Hume and Smith are best understood as operating outside of it. Once we see this, we are also in a position to better understand Hume and Smith's place in the history of political thought more generally, as well as in contrast to how they have been placed by other important interpreters.

For example, recent work by Richard Tuck has claimed that one of the most central divisions within the history of modern political thought can be understood as being between thinkers who accepted the sixteenth-century French jurist Jean Bodin's distinction between "sovereignty" and "government"—a group including especially Hobbes, Rousseau, and the Girondins of the French Revolution—and others who resisted or elided it, most notably Grotius, Samuel von Pufendorf, and Sieyès. Tuck sees Hobbes as crucial in articulating that idea of a sovereign power that is "sleeping," an innovation picked up by Rousseau, who insisted in turn that whilst government should not be democratic, sovereignty—the more fundamental site of authority—must by necessity be so, upon pain of forfeiture. Tuck claims that Rousseau thereby made "modern" democracy possible: insofar as democracy was no longer considered a feature of government, feasibility constraints associated with direct popular rule in large-scale commercial states could be bypassed. A democratic sovereign could license a nondemocratic government to rule on its behalf, which is how Tuck believes contemporary national democratic arrangements now operate (at least approximately). However, entirely neglected in Tuck's account—despite an entire chapter on "The Eighteenth Century"—is the alternative suggested in particular by Hume and Smith, and explored in detail by this book: that lying behind "government" there is no final, philosophically identifiable, and stable foundation of "sovereign" authority, but only the constant and contested changing swirl of opinion. As with Hont's "modern doctrine of sovereignty," so with Tuck's suggestion that modern democracy rests upon a sovereignty-government distinction: even if these claims about the grand trajectory of the history of political thought in (especially) the eighteenth century are true, Hume and Smith must be under-

---

24. Ibid., 134.

25. Hont, "Permanent Crisis," 486. The ambiguity of Hont's claim here is itself rather problematic.

stood as standing outside of this line of development, insofar as they eschew the theory of sovereignty in favor of that of opinion.[26]

By operating outside of the language and conceptualizations of sovereignty theory, in particular as traceable to Hobbes, Hume and Smith forged a way of thinking about politics that was distinctively their own. To appreciate this, however, we must first get to grips with their alternative vision of how and why human beings could live in large and lasting societies over time. In the period under analysis in this book, questions of human sociability and the analysis of the modern state were understood as being inextricably intertwined: one could not hope to understand the latter without taking a detailed position on the former. Hume and Smith took importantly different positions from Hobbes (and also from Bernard Mandeville, Rousseau, and Immanuel Kant) on the question of human sociability, and doing so enabled them to clear a conceptual space upon which to build a different theory of the state. Accordingly, this book excavates rival accounts of human sociability in considerable detail, because doing so is the only way to properly understand and appreciate the theories of politics that supervened upon this conceptually prior debate. Showing how Hume and Smith, in particular, innovated in these regards in turn enables us to understand their thought at a deeper, more integrated, and more far-reaching level than has typically been managed thus far.

What I take to be the consequent originality—and, in turn, power—of Hume and Smith's political thought has likewise generally been underappreciated in existing scholarship. This has largely been because of a tendency to excessively reduce the distinctive nature of their interventions, usually by interpreting them as more or less direct products of established predecessor discourses, rather than as new and relatively independent insights in their own right.[27] I

---

26. Again, see Tuck, *Sleeping Sovereign*. For doubts as to whether Tuck's account *is* true, see Robin Douglass, "Tuck, Rousseau, and the Sovereignty of the People," *History of European Ideas* (forthcoming); Paul Sagar, "Of the People, for the People," *Times Literary Supplement*, June 17, 2016, 12.

27. Examples of presenting Hume and Smith as primarily innovators within established approaches, rather than forgers of new ones, include J.G.A. Pocock's claim that they were "commercial humanists," e.g. "Virtues, Rights, and Manners: A Model for Historians of Political Thought," in *Virtue, Commerce, and History: Essays on Political Thought and History, Chiefly in the Eighteenth Century* (Cambridge: Cambridge University Press, 1985), 37–50. Duncan Forbes and Knud Haakonssen opposed the view that Hume and Smith were primarily modifiers of the seventeenth-century natural-law tradition, e.g. Duncan Forbes, *Hume's Philosophical Politics* (Cambridge: Cambridge University Press, 1975), chaps. 1–2; "Natural Law and the Scottish Enlightenment," in *The Origins and Nature of the Scottish Enlightenment*, ed. R. H. Campbell and A. S. Skinner (Edinburgh: John Donald, 1982); Knud Haakonssen, *The Science of a Legislator* (Cambridge: Cambridge University Press, 1981); "What Might Properly be Called Natural Jurisprudence?", in Campbell and Skinner, *Scottish Enlightenment*; *Natural Law and Moral Philosophy: From Grotius to the Scottish Enlightenment* (Cambridge: Cambridge University Press, 1996); "Natural Jurisprudence

aim instead to show that Hume and Smith were major and original innovators in the history of political thought, best understood as forging their own theoretical approach, rather than primarily taking over and adapting (even if in important and novel ways) pre-existing theories or discourses.

Accordingly, much of my argument is dedicated to showing how and why the political thought of Hume and Smith must be taken on its own terms, in order to properly understand the nature and sophistication of their interventions. But in the process another sort of question is raised. Namely, that if Hume and Smith were indeed working within a new idiom forged largely without precedent, were they *right* to do so? Did they succeed in getting further than relevant alternatives, or simply end up confused and travelling down a stagnant backwater? The majority of this book attempts the relatively less ambitious task of showing that Hume and Smith were operating in an original, in particular non-Hobbesian, idiom of political theory. I also believe, however, that they were right to do so. For the most part I do not argue directly for this latter claim: my hope is to present Hume's and then Smith's arguments in such a way that their power and merits stand out of their own accord, leaving

---

and the Scottish Enlightenment," in *Philosophy and Religion in Enlightenment Britain: New Case Studies*, ed. R. Savage (Oxford: Oxford University Press, 2012). For the wider architectonic of Pocock's thought and his seminal statement of it, *The Machiavellian Moment: Florentine Political Thought and the Atlantic Republican Tradition* (Princeton, NJ: Princeton University Press, 1975); for an extended working-out of Smith's thought as influenced by Pocock, see John Robertson, "The Scottish Enlightenment at the Limits of the Civic Tradition," in Hont and Ignatieff, *Wealth and Virtue*, 137–78, and "Scottish Political Economy Beyond the Civic Tradition: Government and Economic Development in the *Wealth of Nations*," *History of Political Thought* 4, no. 3 (1983), 451–82. Against the civic humanist reading of Hume in particular, see especially James Moore, "Hume's Political Science and the Classical Republican Tradition," *Canadian Journal of Political Science* 10, no. 4 (1977), 809–39. Against the natural-law reading, see James Moore, "Hume's Theory of Justice and Property," *Political Studies* 24, no. 2 (1976), 103–19; "Natural Law and the Pyrrhonian Controversy," in *Philosophy and Science in the Scottish Enlightenment*, ed. P. Jones (Edinburgh: John Donald, 1988), 6–19; and Pauline C. Westerman, "Hume and the Natural Lawyers: A Change of Landscape," in *Hume and Hume's Connexions*, ed. M. A. Stewart and J. P. Wright (Edinburgh: Edinburgh University Press, 1994), 83–104. More generally, the civic-humanist and natural-jurisprudence readings of Hume and Smith have been displaced by the more recent literature's emphasis on an "epicurean" nature of Hume's thought (in particular) and his indebtedness to the controversy between Mandeville and Francis Hutcheson in moral theory, as well as growing interest in Smith's relationship to Rousseau (in the case of the younger thinker). Details of these debates are provided where relevant in what follows. Although neither the civic-humanist nor natural-law reading of Hume and Smith is widely held at present, the tendency to present Hume as merely innovating within established approaches continues: Hume's most recent intellectual biographer ultimately presents his moral and political thought as little more than a synthesis of the prior ideas of Mandeville on the one hand, and Shaftesbury and Hutcheson on the other (see James Harris, *Hume: An Intellectual Biography* (Cambridge: Cambridge University Press, 2015), 35–77, 121–42).

readers to decide for themselves who has the best of things. The exception is the concluding chapter, where I offer support for some of what I see as the most important—but also the most likely to be misunderstood, or unfairly received—aspects of Hume's and Smith's thought.

With these preliminaries in place, two final preparatory matters must be covered before the analysis proper begins. First, the place that I myself must assign to Hobbes. Second, the question of the historiographical approach that I have adopted in what follows.

Hobbes's Proper Place

Despite urging that we ultimately move away from an emphasis on Hobbes and his ways of thinking in our attempts to understand the modern state, and in turn the predicaments and possibilities wrestled with by political theory, it is nonetheless necessary to devote considerable attention to Hobbes's work in what follows. This is because in order to fully appreciate Hume's, and in turn Smith's, alternatives, we must have a clear picture of the Hobbesian structure to which both were in large part providing an alternative. Once we recognize Hobbes as important for understanding Hume's and Smith's distinctive contributions, then we will be in a position to follow them out of his theoretical shadow.

In the introduction to the *Treatise,* Hume famously proposed that in order to achieve "success in our philosophical researches," we must "march up directly to the capital or center" of all the sciences, "to human nature itself." By concentrating on Hume's insistence upon the priority of a "science of man," we can begin to better bring into focus the fundamental nature of his political project. After establishing a central science of man, Hume tells us, we may in turn "extend our conquests over all those sciences, which more intimately concern human life. . . . In pretending therefore to explain the principles of human nature, we in effect propose a compleat system of the sciences, built on a foundation almost entirely new, and the only one upon which they can stand with any security."[28] Hume continues:

> And as the science of man is the only solid foundation for the other sciences, so the only foundation we can give to this science itself must be laid on experience and observation. 'Tis no astonishing reflection to consider, that the application of experimental philosophy to moral subjects shou'd come after that to natural at the distance of above a whole century; since we find, in fact, that there was about the same interval betwixt the origins of these sciences; and that reckoning from

---

28. David Hume, *The Clarendon Edition of the Works of David Hume: A Treatise of Human Nature,* ed. D. F. Norton and M. J. Norton (Oxford: Oxford University Press, 2008), T.I.6, SBN xvi.

THALES to SOCRATES, the space of time is nearly equal to that betwixt my LORD BACON and some late philosophers in *England*, who have begun to put the science of man on a new footing, and have engag'd the attention, and excited the curiosity of the public. So true it is, that however other nations may rival us in poetry, and excel us in some other agreeable arts, the improvements in reason and philosophy can only be owing to a land of toleration and liberty.[29]

The "late philosophers in *England*" are given in a footnote as "Mr. *Locke*, my Lord *Shaftesbury*, Dr. *Mandeville*, Mr. *Hutcheson*, Dr. *Butler*, &c."—and at least two things here are puzzling.

First, that despite Hume's insistence (repeated in the "Abstract" of the *Treatise*) that these five authors have "begun to put the science of man on a new footing," they in fact share no common approach to philosophical matters, and certainly not any "experimental method" of "experience and observation."[30] Second, that although it is perhaps unsurprising that attention has typically been focused upon what a "science of man" founded on "experience and observation" might consist of, this distracts from Hume's claim that the five authors have begun to put it on a *new* footing. Why, after all, should they be putting it on a new footing, rather than simply establishing it afresh? Who had presented a science of man before the five authors?

It may be that Hume's wording is simply loose, his appeal to the five authors shallow. There is a heavy hint of national chauvinism in these passages; not just the elevating of Francis Bacon to the status of founder of modern science, but the panegyrics to the final superiority of a land of "toleration and liberty." Having recently returned from France, Hume was well aware of the accomplishments of European thinkers, recommending René Descartes, Nicolas Malebranche, George Berkeley, and Pierre Bayle to his friend Michael Ramsay as preparation for an attempt at the *Treatise*.[31] Accordingly, his public pronouncements of the superiority of English learning can probably be treated

---

29. Hume, *Treatise*, T.I.7, SBN xvi–ii.

30. In the "Abstract," Hume writes that the five authors "tho' they differ in many points among themselves, seem all to agree in founding their accurate disquisitions of human nature entirely upon experience": *Treatise*, T.A.2, SBN 646. This is simply not true of Shaftesbury's neo-Stoic deist teleology, nor of Shaftesbury's great admirers Joseph Butler and Hutcheson, with their extensive appeals to providence and design. Much the same could be said of Locke, who although he does proceed largely by "experience and observation," also makes extensive appeals to the role of God. As for Mandeville, as we shall see below, much of Hume's criticism of this predecessor amounts to his not having paid *enough* proper regard to experience and observation, being overreliant on a lopsided Augustinian view of human nature.

31. Hume to Michael Ramsay, August 31, 1737, in Tadeusz Kozanecki, "Dawida Hume'a nieznane listy w zbiorach muzeum Czartoryskich (polska)," *Archiwum Historii Filozofii i Myśli Społecznej*, 9 (1963), 133–34; cf. John P. Wright, *Hume's "A Treatise of Human Nature": an Introduction* (Cambridge: Cambridge University Press, 2009), 27.

as less than entirely ingenuous. Hume may have listed the five authors simply as an attempt to tie his difficult, dense, and long book to established and well-known English debates on morals and politics—the only areas of philosophy all five authors could be said to have contributed to by 1739—in what he fruitlessly hoped would be a successful commercial, as well as philosophical, publication.

Be that as it may, the reference to the five authors and the attempt to find a new footing for the science of man offers an important clue for bringing into focus central aspects of Hume's enterprise that otherwise remain obscured. Specifically, that there might have been *another* late English author, one with whom each of the five named philosophers was certainly familiar, and in response to whom a new footing was required. In this regard there is indeed an outstanding candidate: a thinker who offered not a science of man, but a science of politics based on a deeply provocative theory of human nature, for whom geometry rather than observation and experience was the scientific archetype. That thinker was Thomas Hobbes.[32]

Chapters 1 and 2 of this book advance the case for understanding Hume's science of man as yielding a science of human sociability, placing Hume's writings in opposition to Hobbes's theory of human nature and his supervening science of politics. This is not an exclusive claim: Hume's attempt to introduce the experimental method of reasoning into moral subjects was a wide-ranging enterprise, with significant application to many areas of philosophy beyond the question of human sociability.[33] Nonetheless, reading Hume this way allows us to place his writings in a long-standing political idiom revolving around the centrality of individual recognition and the possibilities for group cooperation amongst self-interested agents. Even if Hume was less immediately preoccupied by Hobbes's challenge than earlier generations—the intermediate figure

---

32. On Hobbes's self-assessment as the founder of the first political science modeled on the a priori method of geometry, see Thomas Hobbes, *Man and Citizen (De Homine and De Cive)*, ed. B. Gert (Indianapolis: Hackett, 1991) 42–43; *The Clarendon Edition of the Works of Thomas Hobbes: Leviathan*, ed. N. Malcolm (Oxford: Oxford University Press, 2012), vol. 2, 56. For an overview of Hobbes's conception of science and of a science of politics, Noel Malcolm, "Hobbes's Science of Politics and his Theory of Science," in *Aspects of Hobbes* (Oxford, Oxford University Press, 2002). See also Steven Shapin and Simon Schaffer, *Leviathan and the Air Pump: Hobbes, Boyle, and the Experimental Life* (Princeton, NJ: Princeton University Press, 1985), chaps. 3–4.

33. Particularly interesting is the suggestion by Peter Millican that Hume's science of man centers on his theory of causation, which would indicate that the observed regularities of human moral and political practice can be reduced to a science in the same way as any other observed regularities. This would help account both for Hume's insistence that the theory of causation is the "chief argument" of the *Treatise*, and his intention to offer a science of logic, morals, criticism, and politics based on the experience and observation of human nature: Peter Millican, "Hume, Causal Realism, and Causal Science," *Mind* 118 (2009), 647–712, §§ 8–9.

of Bernard Mandeville certainly commanded his attention more directly—he was nonetheless deeply invested in an ongoing debate over human sociability, the parameters of which were set by Hobbes's epochal intervention.[34]

In essence, I argue for a two-step intellectual genealogy in understanding the relationship of Hume to Hobbes. Although there is plentiful evidence that Hume read Hobbes, that evidence also points to his not having read him very closely, or having thought him of particular importance.[35] Hume's characterization of Hobbes's position on sociability frequently bears more resemblance to a (still persistent) popularized caricature than to what Hobbes actually claimed regarding people's capacities for society. Hume does not mention Hobbes in what survives of his correspondence, or in the so-called "Early Memoranda," his reading notes dating from (probably) the late 1730s.[36] Furthermore, the sheer speed with which Hume penned the *Treatise*, and at such an early age, suggests

---

34. My argument is different, however, to the claim of Paul Russell's that Hume's *Treatise* is fundamentally a "Hobbist" work, one modeled specifically on *The Elements of Law*. The general plausibility of Russell's interpretative claim regarding Hume's affinity with Hobbes has already been called into question by James Harris, but in what follows I seek to show that Hume's moral and political thought cannot be accurately construed as Hobbesian when we appreciate his alternative theory of human nature, even though gaining that proper appreciation requires the acknowledgment of Hobbes as a crucial background figure in the debates Hume was entering. See Paul Russell, *The Riddle of Hume's "Treatise": Skepticism, Naturalism and Irreligion* (Oxford, Oxford University Press, 2008); James Harris, "Of Hobbes and Hume," *Philosophical Books* 50 (2009), 38–46. Nonetheless, Russell is right to call attention to Hume's *irreligious* aims more widely, and his suggestion that we tie Hume to a tradition including Hobbes (and also Baruch Spinoza) is valuable insofar as it encourages us to see the unstated conclusions of Hume's work that would have been seen immediately by contemporaries (virtually all of whom would have been sincere believers in some version of Christian faith), but are much less obvious to modern readers. Something similar might be said of sociability, a central category of political analysis in Hume's intellectual context that needs to be excavated for modern eyes, but would have been much more obvious to the original audience.

35. Hume mentions Hobbes explicitly at two points in the *Treatise*: T.1.3.3.4, SBN 80, and T.2.3.1.10, SBN 402—once with regard to causation, the other with regard to human psychology and the capacity to form society. Hobbes's view is alluded to at several points in bk. 3; see especially T.3.2.2.7, SBN 487–88, and T.3.2.8.1, SBN 540–41, although Hume's characterization is rather loose and general. Hobbes is also mentioned in the second *Enquiry*, as an exponent of the "selfish system" of morals: David Hume, *The Clarendon Edition of the Works of Hume: An Enquiry Concerning the Principles of Morals*, ed. T. L. Beauchamp (Oxford: Oxford University Press, 1998), 91. Dugald Stewart thought that Hobbes's psychological theory was known to Hume, and was the only part of the earlier philosopher's corpus that Hume took seriously. See Dugald Stewart, *The Collected Works of Dugald Stewart, Esq., F.R.S.S.*, 11 vols., ed. W. Hamilton, (Edinburgh: Thomas Constable, 1854–60), vol. 1, 63–97; cf. Forbes, *Hume's Philosophical Politics*, 10.

36. Harris, "Hobbes and Hume," 40. More recently it has been suggested that the "Early Memoranda" date from the 1740s and relate to the development of Hume's political economy: Tatsuya Sakamoto, "Hume's 'Early Memoranda' and the Making of his Political Economy," *Hume Studies* 37 (2011), 131–64.

that his predominant mode of engagement in that work was to identify the fundamental structure of other thinkers' arguments, and react to that, rather than spending much time on the details of any particular position. Nonetheless, Hobbes was *the* crucial figure for British thinkers in "the controversy, which of late years has so much excited the curiosity of the public," which Hume presented his own intervention as bearing upon.[37] Hume may not, for the most part, have been responding directly to Hobbes—but the five authors were. Even if Hume named these authors only to indicate the set of problems his work addressed, rather than any close engagement beyond a basic familiarity with the underlying structures of their positions, the point is that he nonetheless *accurately* indicated which problems he was addressing. Specifically, problems generated by the claim that humans are not by nature sociable, wrestled with by all of the five authors, and bequeathed to them by Hobbes.[38]

In emphasizing the centrality of human sociability to understanding eighteenth-century political thought, I am indebted to Hont's path-breaking work in this regard. According to Hont, Hume was a proponent of "commercial sociability," a conceptual middle route between the thoroughgoing natural unsociability account of Hobbes, and alternative (fundamentally Christian) attempts to secure sociability through mutual benevolence.[39] For Hume, sociability is most fundamentally a product of the coordinated seeking of self-interest. Pride—the central item in Hobbes's and Mandeville's accounts of natural unsociability—is relegated to the margins, whilst benevolence is presented

---

37. Hume, *Treatise*, T.2.1.7.2, SBN 295. Hume claims to "reserve" his own intervention until bk. 3, though as we shall see the psychological theory of bk. 2 in fact grounds the moral and political account of the final parts of the *Treatise*.

38. The suggestion that the five authors, and a shared preoccupation with human sociability, could provide the context for understanding Hume's moral and political philosophy was in fact made by James Moore in "The Social Background of Hume's Science of Human Nature," in *McGill Hume Studies*, ed. D. F. Norton, N. Capaldi, and W. L. Robinson (San Diego: Austin Hills, 1979), 23–41. However, Moore has never pursued this possibility, opting instead to place Hume in an "epicurean" framework that exhibits important continuities with Hobbes's (and Mandeville's) approach. My interpretation in what follows seeks to show that the epicurean framework obscures as much as it illuminates, and that we are better off not using it to understand Hume's thought. Moore's principle articulations of the epicurean interpretation can be found in "Hume and Hutcheson," in Stewart and Wright, *Hume and Hume's Connexions*; "The Eclectic Stoic, the Mitigated Skeptic," in *New Essays on David Hume*, ed. E. Mazza and E. Ronchetti (Milan: FrancoAngeli, 2007), 133–70; "Utility and Humanity: The Quest for the *Honestum* in Cicero, Hutcheson and Hume," *Utilitas* 14 (2002), 365–86. Moore's interpretation has been taken up by John Robertson, *The Case for the Enlightenment: Scotland and Naples 1680–1760* (Cambridge: Cambridge University Press, 2005), chap. 6; Luigi Turco, "Hutcheson and Hume in a Recent Polemic," in Mazza and Ronchetti, *New Essays*, 171–98; and Wright, *Hume's "A Treatise,"* chaps. 1 and 9.

39. Hont, "Commercial Society," and "Introduction," 40–41, 101–11, 160–63, 364–68, 476–77.

as inadequate to the task. Nonetheless, Hont's account of Hume's theory of sociability was deployed only highly schematically, and in the form he left it to us too much remains unaccounted for. In particular, there is Hume's apparent insistence in book 2 of the *Treatise* that humans are the most naturally sociable creature in the entire universe thanks to their capacity for sympathy. There is also book 3's suggestion that it is human imagination and the operations of opinion, and not the direct seeking of utility, that fundamentally ensures that modern, large-scale societies are generally cohesive and stable over time. In order to provide proper substantiation for reading Hume as a "commercial sociability" theorist, it is necessary to fully excavate Hume's theory of sociability, which chapter 1 demonstrates to be tripartite in nature: sympathy and imagination must undergird and then supplement utility, even if utility remains the central factor. Chapter 2 extends this account to understand the role of history and the family in debates over human sociability and the foundations of politics, exploring how Hume was able to revolutionize the use of state-of-nature conjectures in order to elucidate the emergence of institutional structures and related moral values. Chapter 3 builds on this to examine Hume's fully fledged political theory as an outgrowth of his commitment to commercial sociability. By basing his analysis on a different understanding of the human capacity to form society, Hume developed a thoroughly anti-Hobbesian theory of politics, culminating in a theory of the state without sovereignty.[40]

Chapters 4 and 5 explore the issues of sociability and the theory of the state with regard to two thinkers who came after Hume, and represent respectively the continuation of a Hobbesian approach and its repudiation in favor of Hume's opinion-of-mankind idiom. Chapter 4 examines the case of Rousseau, and argues that despite his attempting to start from a different place in the theory of sociability, and then offer a purposefully counter-Hobbesian theory of sovereignty, he ultimately could not get past Hobbes, and ended up returning to the latter's positions, and in turn largely considering his own political project a failure. Chapter 5, by contrast, presents Smith as taking up Hume's alternative theoretic idiom. Like Hume, Smith displays a complicated but important intellectual relationship to Hobbes. Employed for much of his working life as a university professor (which Hume never was), Smith inherited a teaching syllabus at Glasgow that emphasized the centrality of Pufendorf, a thinker whom he identified in his lectures as having set out purposefully to

---

40. However, what we will see is that Hume's adoption of a commercial-sociability framework ultimately took him outside of Hont's "modern doctrine of sovereignty" rooted in Hobbes. When fully worked out, therefore, Hont's insistence on recognizing the importance of commercial sociability as a competitor idiom to Hobbesian natural unsociability subverts his own "modern doctrine of sovereignty" thesis, because what emerges from Hume's theory of commercial sociability is a theory of the state entirely outside the Hobbesian mold.

"confute Hobbes."[41] Smith names Hobbes on several occasions, and alludes to his positions on still more, and in the *Theory of Moral Sentiments* shows a working knowledge of Hobbes's arguments and their implications.[42] With regard to the theory of sociability in particular, Hobbes's position—the possibility of constructing society through fear—would have been known to Smith as the unmentioned third alternative in addition to his suggestions of securing society through the ties of benevolence or utility (not least because his teacher, Francis Hutcheson, had earlier assimilated the utility approach of Pufendorf to his bêtes noires, Hobbes and Mandeville).[43] Chapter 5 shows how Smith's development of Hume's alternative theoretic framework of opinion led him to construct a theory of regime forms that was deeply historically inflected, but Smith also ultimately professed the incapacity of philosophy to finally resolve the tensions and predicaments generated by purely secular politics.[44] Chapter 6 considers the implications of this, and assesses the viability of thinking about the state, and political theory more generally, from Hume and Smith's perspective.

Matters of Method

Before finally proceeding to the substance of analysis it may be helpful for me to say something regarding the "method" I have adopted in what follows. Readers who are allergic to this sort of discussion, or who would rather just let the argument do the talking, can simply skip forward. And as in all such cases

---

41. Adam Smith, *The Glasgow Edition of the Works and Correspondence of Adam Smith: Lectures on Jurisprudence*, ed. R. L. Meek, D. D. Raphael, and P. G. Stein (Oxford: Oxford University Press, 1978), LJ(B).3. Hont has suggested that Smith's own theory of commercial sociability, a rejection of Hobbes's natural-unsociability thesis, is itself derived from Pufendorf: see Hont, "Language of Sociability." However, and as the following chapters seek to show, Smith could have—and I believe, probably did—get all of the conceptual materials needed for resisting Hobbes in terms of a utility-based theory of sociability from Hume's *Treatise*, which he read as a student at Oxford long before he was contracted to teach at Glasgow, rather than from Pufendorf's *De Iure Naturae et Gentium*.

42. Adam Smith, *The Glasgow Edition of the Works and Correspondence of Adam Smith: The Theory of Moral Sentiments*, ed. D. D. Raphael and A. L. Macfie (Oxford: Oxford University Press, 1976), VII.iii.1-2 especially.

43. Smith, *Theory of Moral Sentiments*, II.ii.3.1-3; Francis Hutcheson, "On the Natural Sociability of Mankind," in *Logic, Metaphysics, and the Natural Sociability of Mankind*, ed. J. Moore and M. Silverthorne (Indianapolis: Liberty Fund, 2006), 191-216; cf. Hont, "Introduction," 39-40. This point is developed further in chapter 2.

44. Smith thus stands with Hume outside of the Hobbesian "modern doctrine of sovereignty," and it is therefore a mistake to try to present the thought of Sieyès as an amalgam of Rousseau's and Smith's political theories, as Hont suggests: István Hont, *Politics in Commercial Society: Adam Smith and Jean-Jacques Rousseau*, ed. B. Kapossy and M. Sonenscher (Cambridge, MA: Harvard University Press, 2015), 24.

of preemptive apologetics, the proof of the pudding will ultimately be only in the eating: perusal of this author's cookbook will be of real use retrospectively, upon condition that the dish is palatable. Nonetheless, it may perhaps be of some help if I attempt to offer an orientation from the outset as to what I take myself to be doing.

What follows should be understood as an attempt to put into a particular—and, inevitably, idiosyncratic—sort of practice Bernard Williams's underdeveloped, but illuminating, distinction between "the history of philosophy" and "the history of ideas." According to Williams the latter is "history before it is philosophy," whereas the former is the other way around.[45] This distinction is a refined one. It takes as given something like John Dunn's insistence that meaningful examination of past thinkers must be philosophically sensitive, whilst also being attentive to the fact that any philosophy we recover from the past is not a free-floating intellectual phenomenon, but the product of real human agents' attempts to wrestle with complex questions in thick intellectual and practical contexts.[46] Any serious and nonfallacious engagement with past philosophy must involve itself in the practice of both philosophy *and* history. Yet, as Williams remarked, whilst "in any worthwhile work of either sort, both concerns are likely to be represented," nonetheless "there is a genuine distinction" between "the history of philosophy" and "the history of ideas."[47] This, however, requires more explicit working out than Williams supplied.

The "genuine distinction" that I take to be most fruitful consists of the following. When dealing with major philosophical thinkers of the past, in doing "the history of philosophy," what takes priority is the insistence that philosophical arguments be understood primarily *as philosophical arguments*; i.e., as a specific form of intellectual contribution with its own (at least in aspiration, if not always practice) independence, unity, and coherence. By contrast "the history of ideas" concerns itself primarily with tracking, understanding, and explaining the movement and development of ideas and arguments across thinkers, times, and places. It necessarily pays attention to philosophical detail, but with the primary aim not of reconstructing that detail for its own sake so as to understand a philosophical position simply as such, but of understanding

---

45. Bernard Williams, *Descartes: The Project of Pure Enquiry*, rev. ed. (Abingdon: Routledge, 2005), xiii. For an insightful discussion of Williams's distinction, which compellingly urges us to abandon Williams's correlate analogy between reading past philosophy and listening to past music, see Michael Rosen, "The History of Ideas as Philosophy and History," *History of Political Thought* 32, no. 4, 691–720, 693–96 especially.

46. John Dunn, "The Identity of the History of Ideas," in *Political Obligation in Its Historical Context* (Cambridge: Cambridge University Press, 1980), 13–28. Quentin Skinner's insistence that there are no "unit ideas" in the history of philosophy, but only arguments made by living agents in real debates, is also of direct relevance, and likewise correct. See Quentin Skinner, "Meaning and Understanding in the History of Ideas," in *Visions of Politics*, vol. 1, *Regarding Method* (Cambridge: Cambridge University Press, 2002), 60, 62, 83–85.

47. Williams, *Descartes*, xiii.

the transmission, evolution, and success or failure of intellectual projects as primarily historical, not philosophical, phenomena. Clearly, both approaches need to engage philosophy and history if they are to be done well. But one is precisely philosophy "before" it is history, and the other vice versa.

Yet, properly practicing "the history of philosophy" requires that we recover and reconstruct not just particular passages—or even entire works—from past authors, but also the underlying philosophical worldview that both informs, and ultimately promises (if sometimes unsuccessfully) to make coherent and integrated any of the particular arguments offered by individual thinkers. This is because philosophical arguments are embedded not just in an external discursive context constituted by philosophical opponents and allies, but in an internal context determined by the myriad positions and beliefs any given thinker is simultaneously committed to. Whilst it is true that no philosopher argues or thinks in isolation, it is also true that no idea worth bothering to contemplate or recover exists without reference to a great many others, with such ideas being themselves dynamically interrelated: a change in one will frequently generate repercussions for the rest. Any adequate recovery thus demands a serious attempt to grasp the totality of a philosopher's arguments as adding up to something more than the sum of individual positions or points, and this is true even if our aim is only to understand those individual positions or points.

We must, however, proceed carefully. We cannot hope to reconstruct a philosopher's worldview simply by earnestly reading his or her texts very closely; by just looking at their pages over and over again until the "true" meaning emerges. Skinner is right to have insisted that the meaning of an argument depends to a significant extent upon what its author thought he or she was doing in making it, and that in turn depends upon the wider context of communicative intention and reception an agent was embedded in, required for that argument to possess coherent and intelligible content for both its author and its audience.[48] If that context has changed we will misread past authors to varying degrees, ending up with more or less sophisticated forms of anachronism. That may or may not make for good philosophy as conducted purely in the here and now. But it will certainly make for bad readings of Hume,

---

48. As Williams put it elsewhere: "About what a genuine historical understanding of a text is, understanding of what it *meant*, I agree with Quentin Skinner that if it is recoverable at all, it must be in the kind of terms which he has detailed, of those contemporary expectations in terms of which a communicative intention could be realized": Bernard Williams, "Political Philosophy and the Analytical Tradition," in *Philosophy as a Humanistic Discipline*, ed. A. W. Moore (Princeton, NJ: Princeton University Press, 2006), 165. Skinner's point about meaning may need to be supplemented with the observation that sometimes recovery of authorial intention is insufficient, for example in cases of "false consciousness" or misapprehension on the part of the author. But this is a refinement, not a refutation. See, for example, Ian Shapiro, "The Difference that Realism Makes: Social Science and the Politics of Consent," in *The Flight from Reality in the Human Sciences* (Princeton, NJ: Princeton University Press, 2005), 1–18.

Smith, Hobbes, Rousseau, or anybody else not from the here and now, and the poor quality of such readings will be as much philosophical as historical, in the first instance because they won't be readings *of Hume* (or whoever) at all, but of some more or less accurate effigy.[49] Historical sensitivity is essential, and we must always be on guard against exporting what is peculiar to us back into the past. Nonetheless, we will likewise run the risk of getting figures like Hume, Hobbes, Smith, Rousseau, and so on badly wrong, albeit in a different way, if we neglect to make primary the fact that they were, at least when they wrote on politics in the modes I will be examining, *philosophers*, and what is more, philosophers who clearly advanced their arguments in a manner conceived of as contributions to pan-European discourses in which some of the key interlocutors were already dead. Hume's philosophy in particular may well have been (and, as I hope to show, in certain ways was) deeply contextually conditioned. But it must be recovered first and foremost as a philosophy that in many ways aspired to, and often succeeded in, presenting ideas and arguments that could transcend Hume's particular local context, and hold true in many others. The same is the case for Smith.[50] Recovering Hume's and Smith's work in this way means not just viewing their writings as sustained attempts to give an account of how things are in terms of arguments built in the form of premises and conclusions, but also as accounts held together by a wider picture of how the world is, and what makes it that way. This is the case not only with regard to particular details, but also to how all those details fit together to add up to an account that at least aspires to be coherent on the question of how everything is, in light of the fact that if not everything, then certainly a great many things, are connected. We will only properly understand Hume's arguments, and in turn Smith's, if we understand both of them as in the fullest sense philosophers—i.e., *not* simply as depositories of arguments grouped under the same heading because they happened to be proposed by the same historical figures.

We must, however, be alert to a further complicating factor. Philosophers are always committed (implicitly or explicitly, in the best cases consciously, but in many cases revealingly unconsciously) to conceptions about what philosophy itself is, and what it can therefore hope to achieve. Hume and Smith are particularly unusual in this regard, because in many ways their vision of the

---

49. Dunn, "Identity," 21–23.

50. In this regard I am sympathetic to Jeremy Waldron's point that an over insistence on thick contextualization is liable to distort our readings of past political philosophers, in particular by insisting that those thinkers must have been involved in close engagements with immediate political concerns against those thinkers' own manifest insistence that they *are* speaking—and contributing—to an established cross-generational canon of Western thought: Jeremy Waldron, "What Plato Would Allow," in *Theory and Practice: Nomos XXXVII*, ed. I. Shapiro and J. Wagner (New York: New York University Press, 1995) 143–47.

nature and role of philosophy is severely deflationary. As Hume put it in his essay "The Sceptic," "the empire of philosophy extends over a few; and with regards to these too, her authority is very weak and limited."[51] Various aspects of this study—but particularly chapters 3, 5, and 6—examine what it means to recognize that Hume's worldview comprises a revaluation not just of how the world is, but of how philosophy within that world can and should be, and what it can and cannot hope to achieve.

It matters also that both Hume and Smith were *first-rate* philosophers. If they fell into incoherencies or contradictions, these are never obvious, and always require significant effort on our behalf to be sure of and to adequately account for. This is made especially difficult by the fact that Hume in particular sought to reorient many prevalent beliefs and expectations about the nature and role of philosophy, most of which persist today. Hence, when we have found a putative incoherence or mistake in his work we must be alert to the possibility that the fault is at our end; that we are exhibiting pathologies of thought that Hume's approach recommends we get beyond. The same is not true for all past thinkers, especially those whose ability was lower than that of a Hume or a Smith. Nonetheless, I maintain that even in these cases we will likewise get further in understanding what past philosophers were trying to do, as well as understanding why they disagreed as well as what they collectively achieved, if we attempt to consider not just their arguments, but their philosophies in the broader sense. One result of this is that at times I opt to speak of one thinker agreeing or disagreeing (and equivalent locutions) with another, without necessarily intending to make a strict historical claim about the latter theorist consciously and specifically replying to the earlier one (whom indeed they may not even have read, at least on any precise point at issue). The aim rather is to draw out how patterns of argument match up, complement each other, come into conflict, evolve, die, and so on—as we shall see that they do, across both time and different thinkers. When individual authors are consciously responding to the specific points identifiably raised by predecessors, I try to note this, but I do not restrict myself to such cases alone, for we gain a deeper and more textured understanding of the philosophical arguments and positions in play if we compare conceptual alternatives, and not just individuated and discrete historical responses.

---

51. David Hume, "The Skeptic," in *Essays*, 168. There is some debate as to whether "The Skeptic" is an essay *in propria persona*: see especially Robert Fogelin, *Hume's Skepticism in the "Treatise of Human Nature"* (London: Routledge, 1985); M. A. Stewart, "The Stoic Legacy in the Early Scottish Enlightenment," in *Atoms, Pneuma and Tranquility: Epicurean and Stoic Themes in Enlightenment Thought*, ed. M. J. Osler (Cambridge: Cambridge University Press, 1991), 273–96; James Harris, "Hume's Four Essays on Happiness and Their Place in the Move from Morals to Politics," in Mazza and Ronchetti, *New Essays*, 223–35. Yet even if the entire essay is not intended to expound Hume's views exactly, the remark about the empire of philosophy well captures Hume's own attitude.

Here, however, the question of history becomes pertinent once more. For it is not just that historical sensitivity is essential for avoiding anachronism and error when reconstructing philosophical worldviews. The relationship also runs the other way. Once we are in possession not just of appropriately reconstructed arguments, but of wider philosophies and their underpinning worldviews, we can offer a form of history that is driven by the development of such philosophical accounts in their entirety, in particular when they complement or clash with each other, changing, surviving, stagnating, or expiring. The outcome, as well as the method, is thus philosophy before it is history. But the resulting historical story is nonetheless a genuine contribution, albeit one that could only be achieved by taking a particular kind of path through the material.

When we take this approach, we end up with the potential for disagreement with Skinner regarding the point and purpose of the study of past philosophies. Perhaps Skinner's most famous remark on the subject of methodological practice is that there are "no perennial problems in philosophy. There are only individual answers to individual questions, and potentially as many different questions as there are questioners."[52] At a certain level this is doubtless true: questions cannot exist outside the heads of questioners. Yet there are good reasons to be skeptical of Skinner's correlate insistence that "the classic texts are concerned with their own questions and not with ours."[53] This may often turn out to be true—and perhaps especially so the further back one goes—but it is also the case that unsolved questions are typically passed on to subsequent generations, albeit with varying degrees of success and hardiness. It is certainly, as Skinner says, wrongheaded to think that one can straightforwardly turn to the history of ideas for ready-made "lessons" applicable to the here and now. Nonetheless, the questions of past thinkers may turn out to be our questions, for two reasons in particular. First, because we may have inherited them from past thinkers, rather than inventing them ourselves. Second, because we may find that the relevant context separating past thinkers from ourselves has changed only superficially, whilst the more fundamental issues that prompted and shaped the emergence of past questions and answers remain extant today. This does not mean that there are "perennial questions" after all, but rather that

---

52. Skinner, "Meaning and Understanding," 88. It is worth noting that Skinner's own work in practice displays a much more complex and ambiguous relationship to such a statement than might be assumed (and of which he is often accused). John Dunn's review of Skinner's first major monograph, *The Foundations of Modern Political Thought*, captures the point well. As Dunn puts it, the excitement of Skinner's work is generated by the promise of the extreme historicity implied in the "no perennial questions" remark, but the depth and subtlety of Skinner's engagements tend to preclude any straightforward or polemical historicity from being attributable to his arguments: John Dunn, "The Cage of Politics," *Listener*, March 15, 1979, 389–90.

53. Skinner, "Meaning and Understanding," 88.

whether there are or not is largely beside the point. If some questions do endure, and we can identify which ones, then the uses of intellectual history extend beyond the making of comparisons with alien ways of doing things so as to better illuminate our local practices. In particular, they may extend to the possibility that we can legitimately study the answers volunteered in the past to better understand the predicaments of the present, precisely because these predicaments are not new and neither are many of our attempted solutions to them.

Certainly we cannot know this to be the case a priori. Skinner is right about how to proceed in practice: we must check that past philosophers can possibly have meant what we claim they mean, or we will hear simply our own voices echoed back to us, learning only about ourselves, and even then not very much. But if we take appropriate caution, what is frequently revealed is that in many respects the same questions that we struggle to answer in political theory at the start of the twenty-first century were already being wrestled with by the best thinkers of the eighteenth. One thing this book seeks to illuminate is the *persistence* of some philosophical questions. We simply have not succeeded in getting past a great deal of eighteenth-century thought: their questions are in many ways still ours. I therefore put myself closer to the position of Dunn than of Skinner, the former of whom has maintained a view much more like the one I have just outlined than that of the latter, their usual reduction to a unitary "Cambridge school" notwithstanding. As Dunn emphasizes, given that better minds have already attempted to answer many of our questions, we should neither neglect such thinkers, nor turn them into mere mirrors for our own edification. Ultimately, what "lessons" there are to be drawn from the history of political thought depend more upon our own informed and careful judgment, than upon the dictates of any particular "methodology."[54]

I believe, and hope to show in what follows, that one of the most illuminating contexts for understanding Hume's, and then Rousseau's and Smith's, political philosophies is the competing theories their contributions were an alternative to, rather than the material political circumstances of their day, or the structural similarities their thought may exhibit with that of relevant others with regard to particular pieces of argumentation as identified through overarching traditions of thought. As a result, I have steered clear of using the categories of revived Hellenistic philosophies (in particular Epicureanism and Stoicism, and, more vaguely, skepticism) to cross-classify thinkers in order to make historical or conceptual claims, as has been increasingly popular in

---

54. For the earliest and most forthright statements of Dunn's view, see Dunn, "Identity," and "Cage of Politics," but also *The History of Political Theory and Other Essays* (Cambridge: Cambridge University Press, 1996). For Dunn's method as demonstrated in his work, *Political Thought*; "What Is Living"; "Judgment for Mortals."

recent scholarship of the seventeenth and eighteenth centuries.[55] With regard to particular arguments within a philosopher's worldview, labeling an item of thought as "Stoic," or "Epicurean," and so forth may sometimes illuminate, as is the case with, for example, Shaftesbury's and Hutcheson's deployment of specifically and self-consciously Stoic moral and metaphysical ideas. But doing so across and between seventeenth- and eighteenth-century philosophers' positions threatens to obscure as much as it reveals.[56]

Nonetheless, I have no ambitions in the direction of methodological imperialism. It would be foolish and false to claim that "the history of philosophy" is the only valid enterprise, with no room for "the history of ideas" (where the emphasis on Hellenistic traditions of thought has recently enjoyed prominence), or, for that matter, more conventional philosophy and political theory that proceed largely ahistorically. Quite the contrary: we require a division of labor not only to make progress in the detail of historically located philosophical arguments, but in enabling wider conceptualizations of what was going on in any given period. Mine is not the only perspective, and does not aspire to be. The multiple levels of both historical and philosophical analysis required to grapple with topics as large and complex as theories of sociability and of the nature of state, in the eighteenth century and beyond, are so extensive as to make it impossible for one perspective, let alone one person, to achieve all that is required. Be that as it may, by adopting the particular perspective outlined above I hope to offer some new answers, or at least new ways of seeing older problems, whilst recognizing that it is only through an appropriate division of labor—both within and between historical approaches to past philosophies—that we will collectively make meaningful progress.

---

55. See, for example, and in addition to the work of Robertson, Moore, and Turco noted above, Jean Lafond, "Augustinisme et épicurisme au xvii siècle," in *L'homme et son image: morales et littérature de Montaigne à Mandeville* (Paris: H. Champion, 1996), 345–68; Pierre Force, *Self-Interest before Adam Smith: A Genealogy of Economic Science* (Cambridge: Cambridge University Press, 2003); Daniel Carey, *Locke, Shaftesbury, and Hutcheson: Contesting Diversity in the Enlightenment and Beyond* (Cambridge: Cambridge University Press, 2006); Christopher Brooke, *Philosophic Pride: Stoicism and Political Thought from Lipsius to Rousseau* (Princeton, NJ: Princeton University Press, 2012); Catharine Wilson, *Epicureanism at the Origins of Modernity* (Oxford: Oxford University Press, 2008); Michael Sonenscher, *Sans-Culottes: An Eighteenth Century Emblem in the French Revolution* (Princeton: Princeton University Press, 2008), chap. 3; and the essays collected in Osler, *Atoms, Pneuma and Tranquility*.

56. I examine the question of how to think about revived traditions of Hellenistic thought more extensively in Paul Sagar, "Sociability, Luxury and Sympathy: The Case of Archibald Campbell," *History of European Ideas* 39 (2013), 806–14. See also Hont, *Politics in Commercial Society*, 15–16, 31–32.

CHAPTER ONE

Sociability

Hobbes: Pride's Predicament

THOMAS HOBBES OPENED his 1642 *De Cive* with a remarkable declaration:

> The majority of previous writers on public Affairs either assume or seek to prove or simply assert that Man is an animal born fit for Society,— in the Greek phrase, Ζῷον πολιτικὸν. On this foundation they erect a structure of civil doctrine, as if no more were necessary for the preservation of peace and the governance of the whole human race than for men to give their consent to certain agreements and conditions which, without further thought, these writers called laws. This axiom, though widely accepted, is nevertheless false; the error proceeds from a superficial view of human nature.[1]

What might a less "superficial" view of human nature look like? According to Hobbes, when human beings associate "we are not looking for friends but for honour or advantage from them."[2] This compact declaration contained the crux of his view. First, we are not looking for "friends." Neither mutual love nor any natural instinct or appetite for company leads us to associate. Hobbes thus rejected the Aristotelian dictum that human beings are by nature thoroughly sociable.[3] The proof of this was negative: if human beings were looking for

---

1. Thomas Hobbes, *On the Citizen*, ed. R. Tuck and M. Silverthorne (Cambridge: Cambridge University Press, 1998), 21–22.

2. Hobbes, *On the Citizen*, 22. This is an overstatement even by Hobbes's own lights, as demonstrated by the much more expansive range of psychological capacities delineated in *Leviathan*. However, it is useful to focus on Hobbes's explication in *De Cive*, insofar as this most clearly illustrates the fundamentals of his view, which are retained in *Leviathan* even if that work incorporates a more realistic, wider psychological account.

3. In fact, by the time Hobbes issued his political works, late-Renaissance Aristotelianism exhibited a great deal of complexity in analyzing human sociability, and Hobbes's

[27]

friends there would be a cosmopolitan world society, each joining with others out of a general love for mankind, undifferentiated as such.[4] Instead we find humanity divided into hostile groupings—independent political associations that are, as he put it in *Leviathan*, "in continual jealousies, and in the state and posture of Gladiators; having their weapons pointing, and their eyes fixed on one another."[5] The most basic of empirical observations with regard to human associations supplied evidence against the supposition of natural sociability. The proper task was to explain how *any* society was nonetheless possible—as the reality of a divided mankind attested it must in some limited way be— rather than starting from the erroneous supposition that human sociability was natural, innate, or somehow straightforward.

Human associations, Hobbes contended, were founded not on love, instinct, or appetite for company, but in the self-interested seeking of "honour" and "advantage," with friendship at best a "secondary" motive directed at specific individuals. Advantage—i.e., the utilitarian benefit of group cooperation— was a drive to society insofar as naturally indigent man could better satisfy both his basic material, and later his more developed, needs and wants, via association with others in arrangements for reciprocal self-interest. Likewise, honor propelled men to society because human beings craved the good estimation of their peers, something obtainable only in company. Man thus had two drives to society, both of them natural. So why was he nonetheless "not an animal born fit for society"?

Central to Hobbes's account in *De Cive* was the claim that "Every pleasure of the mind is either glory (or a good opinion of oneself), or ultimately relates to glory; the others are sensual or lead to something sensual, and can all be

---

depiction of scholastic teaching was an oversimplistic caricature. Nonetheless, by rejecting *any* natural basis for successful human sociability in large and lasting conditions, Hobbes did put clear water between himself and early modern Aristotelianism. See especially Annabel Brett, *Changes of State: Nature and the Limits of the City in Early Modern Natural Law* (Princeton, NJ: Princeton University Press, 2011), chap. 5; "'The Matter, Forme and Power of a Common-Wealth': Thomas Hobbes and Late Renaissance Commentary on Aristotle's *Politics*," *Hobbes Studies* 23 (2010), 72–102.

4. Hobbes, *On the Citizen*, 22.

5. Hobbes, *The Clarendon Edition of the Works of Thomas Hobbes: Leviathan*, ed. N. Malcolm (Oxford: Oxford University Press, 2012), vol. 2, 196. For discussions of Hobbes's views of natural unsociability, Hont, *Jealousy of Trade: International Competition and the Nation State in Historical Perspective* (Cambridge, MA: Belknap Harvard, 2005), 20–22, 39–45; Kinch Hoekstra, "Hobbes on the Natural Condition of Mankind," in *The Cambridge Companion to Hobbes's "Leviathan*," ed. P. Springborg (Cambridge: Cambridge University Press, 2007), 109–27; Philip Pettit, *Made with Words: Hobbes on Language, Mind and Politics* (Princeton, NJ: Princeton University Press, 2008), chaps. 6–7; Richard Tuck, *The Rights of War and Peace: Political Thought and the International Order from Grotius to Kant* (Oxford: Oxford University Press, 1999), chap. 4.

comprised under the name of advantages."⁶ This division of pleasures—into those of the mind and those of the body—corresponds directly to the two social drives of honor and advantage. Of particular importance is the claim that every pleasure of the mind is glory or a good opinion of oneself. Hobbes here signaled the irreducibly inter-mental and comparative dimension of human self-assessment: agents valued their own worth by the imputed mental estimations of their peers. Human life was comparable to an endless race, defined not by a finish line (which could only be death, man's *summum malum*), but by the constant imperative to be ahead of one's peers: "this race we must suppose to have no other goal, nor no other garland, but being foremost."⁷ Thanks to Rousseau (himself deeply influenced by Hobbes), we principally know the phenomenon of mental self-estimation for agents who evaluate themselves via the imputed judgment of peers as *amour propre*.⁸ The modern, evaluatively neutral term for this is "recognition." For Hobbes, it was captured, albeit somewhat imperfectly, by the label of pride. As he put it in the *Elements of Law*: "GLORY, or internal gloriation or triumph of the mind, is that passion which proceedeth from the imagination or conception of our own power, above the power of him that contendeth with us. The signs whereof, besides those in the countenance, and other gestures of the body which cannot be described, are, ostentation in words, and insolency in actions; and this passion, by them whom it displeaseth, is called pride: by them whom it pleaseth, it is termed a just valuation of himself."⁹ Pride was the name of glory when it offends our peers (reflecting its traditional status as a vice and the deadliest of the seven deadly sins); with the same passion rhetorically redescribed as "just valuation" by agents who believed it appropriate. The crucial problem with glory, however, is that it is by nature positional: "glorying, like honour, is nothing if everybody has it, since it consists in comparison and pre-eminence."¹⁰ Desire for honor pushed men toward society, but successful attempts by some to glory over likewise glory-seeking competitors, and the mental pain felt by those who failed to gain the honor they craved, was liable to cause men to attack: "Since all the heart's joy and pleasure lies in being able to compare oneself favourably with others and

6. Hobbes, *On the Citizen*, 23–24.

7. Thomas Hobbes, *The Elements of Law, Natural and Politic*, ed. F. Tönnies and M. M. Goldsmith (London: Frank Cass, 1969), 47.

8. Jean-Jacques Rousseau, *The Discourses and Other Early Political Writings*, ed. V. Gourevitch (Cambridge: Cambridge University Press, 1997), 152, 171, 218. The term and concept of amour propre was previously used by the French Augustinians at Port Royal in the seventeenth century, especially by Pierre Nicole, in attempts to explain how morally corrupt fallen man could erect a system of utility-promoting substitute morality, thus engendering successful social living. For a discussion of this, and its influence on Mandeville (and in turn Rousseau), see E. J. Hundert, *The Enlightenment's "Fable": Bernard Mandeville and the Discovery of Society* (Cambridge: Cambridge University Press, 1994), 96–115.

9. Hobbes, *Elements of Law*, 36–37.

10. Hobbes, *On the Citizen*, 24.

form a high opinion of oneself, men cannot avoid sometimes showing hatred and contempt for each other, by laughter or words or a gesture or other sign. There is nothing more offensive than this, nothing that triggers a stronger impulse to hurt someone."[11] Whilst competition over material resources would cause flash points of confrontation between individuals, the most consistent and ineliminable source of conflict over men's wanting "the same thing at the same time, without being able to enjoy it in common or to divide it," would be honor, rooted in pride, and the attempt to secure glory as a public display of recognized superiority. "The consequence is that it must go to the stronger. But who is the stronger? Fighting must decide."[12]

Hobbes's central proposition regarding the human capacity to form society was that because "All society . . . exists for the sake either of advantage or of glory, i.e., it is a product of love of self, not love of friends . . . [so] no large or lasting society can be based on the passion for glory."[13] Human beings faced intractable difficulties in the erecting and maintaining of specifically *large and lasting* societies. The twin propulsions of honor and advantage would lead men to associate successfully for a time and in limited groupings: in the "state of nature"—i.e., lacking a common political power—men were dangerous to each other precisely because the weaker could not only lay traps for, but also form in "confederacy" against, the stronger, whilst the more successful would be attacked by those who came with men assembled to dispossess them of their "persons, wives, children, and cattell."[14] The seeking of honor was irreducibly destabilizing in large groups as a minority of individuals craving preeminence would attack others not just for material gain, but for the extraction of imputed superiority and in some cases the bare joy of domination.[15] Knowledge of the existence of even a minority of such individuals generated a permanent incentive for the majority—by disposition moderate and otherwise content with equal standing—to attack first. Indeed, even if the moderate did not attack first, their very moderation would be a provocation to those greedy for comparative recognition: "those men who are moderate, and look for no more but equality of nature, shall be obnoxious to the force of others, that will attempt to subdue them. And from hence shall proceed a general diffidence in mankind, and mutual fear one of another."[16] The destabilizing effects of reiterated attempts at glorying undermined the capacity to form

---

11. Hobbes, *On the Citizen*, 26–27.
12. Ibid., 27.
13. Ibid., 24; cf. Hont, *Jealousy of Trade*, 44.
14. Hobbes, *Leviathan*, vol. 2, 190–92.
15. As Hobbes reminded his readers at the outset of the second part of *Leviathan*, "Of Commonwealth," men "naturally love Liberty, and Dominion over others" (*Leviathan*, vol. 2, 254), recalling his claim in *De Cive* that men are naturally more attracted to domination than to society (*On the Citizen*, 24).
16. Hobbes, *Elements of Law*, 71; cf. *On the Citizen*, 26; *Leviathan*, vol. 2, 190.

stable associations based on mutual advancement of utility and the need to be in company with others to secure recognition. Large and lasting society could not be stably generated out of the materials of honor or advantage alone: "no one should doubt that, in the absence of fear, men would be more avidly attracted to domination than to society. One must therefore lay it down that the origin of large and lasting societies lay not in mutual human benevolence but in men's mutual fear."[17]

In *Leviathan* Hobbes submerged the stark account that was presented in *De Cive*. His depiction of humans' natural unsociability, as put forward in the infamous chapter 13, declared there to be *three*, rather than just one, "principall causes of quarrell." These were competition, diffidence, and glory, where "The first, maketh men invade for Gain; the second, for Safety; and the third, for Reputation."[18] Yet we ought to see that the argument in *Leviathan* in fact employs the same logic that was expanded more starkly in the earlier *De Cive*. After all, the first two causes of quarrel listed by Hobbes are about advancing material interests and security (in reality two sides of the same coin, hence why they are grouped together in *De Cive* under the heading of "advantage"). And the best way to secure these would be through group cooperation, including mutually beneficial agreements to abstain from attacking each other, with defectors who disturbed the peace and threatened commodious living being quickly identified and dealt with by the majority members of the cooperating group. Given the huge risks and poor returns associated with violent conflict, or attempting to cheat the cooperative system and getting caught (and despite the presence of some relatively low level of defectors) if people sought only utility—only the needs of the body, not the mind—then natural sociability ought straightforwardly to be possible, even if imperfectly or messily achieved in practice. Accordingly, however, if humanity's "natural condition" was indeed the one of protracted misery that Hobbes so dramatically insisted upon, then the real problem must lie beyond "competition" and "diffidence," in the third cause of quarrel: "glory." And, indeed, in *Leviathan* it is ultimately the seeking of "reputation," the need to satiate pride through competition for status recognition, that generates humanity's thoroughgoing natural unsociability. Those who would invade—unexpectedly, unpredictably, potentially against their own material interests, and often without being detectable in advance—for "trifles, as a word, a smile, a different opinion, and any other signe of undervalue" are the real destabilizing factor.[19] Against such individuals (and nobody can know for sure who they might turn out to be) one may—indeed ought—to strike preemptively. But this generates a cascade effect of rational preemptive retaliation, as all others carry out the same calculation, thoroughly destabilizing the

---

17. Hobbes, *On the Citizen*, 24.
18. Hobbes, *Leviathan*, vol. 2, 192.
19. Ibid.

possibility for large-scale cooperation over extended periods of time, at least based on natural materials alone.[20]

Hobbes's aggressive rhetorical presentation in *Leviathan* XIII meant that he presented the causes of natural unsociability as thoroughly overdetermined, being simultaneously from interest, security, and glory.[21] This was presumably to convince his readers, via the most forceful and persuasive terms available, of the reasons they had to submit to overawing sovereign power. But beneath Hobbes's rhetoric, the argument for natural unsociability still depended upon the seeking of reputation—of glory, driven by pride—for it to have the validity he claimed.

The result of all this was that (in the words of *De Cive*) "fear" was ultimately necessary to establish "large and lasting" society. According to Hobbes, each human being was possessed of an ineliminable and irreducible drive to self-preserve, in his terminology a "right of nature" constituting a "blameless liberty" to do whatever each individual judged necessary to survive (including killing and using the bodies of others).[22] Human beings' capacity to reason, however, led them to a corresponding set of imperatives, "laws of nature," for how to best secure their own self-preservation.[23] These imperatives indicated that each individual's interest was best secured by a cessation of hostilities. Yet in the absence of guarantees that others would not defect from agreements to conduct themselves peaceably (in Hobbes's language, "covenanting"), it would be irrational (because potentially suicidal) to act unilaterally. This was especially the case given that others might attack not just for material benefit, but for positional superiority, or out of resentment at the relative success of others. Pride interacted disastrously with the irreducible drive to self-preservation.[24] This entailed that humans in their natural subpolitical condition were in a continual state of hostility, a "state of war" characterized not by constant fight-

20. Ibid.
21. On the rhetorical presentation of *Leviathan*, see Quentin Skinner, *Reason and Rhetoric in the Philosophy of Hobbes* (Cambridge: Cambridge University Press, 1996), chaps. 9–10.
22. Hobbes, *Elements of Law*, 71; cf. *On the Citizen*, 34; *Leviathan*, vol. 2, 198.
23. Hobbes, *Elements of Law*, chaps. 15–17; *On the Citizen*, chaps. 2–3; *Leviathan*, vol. 2, chaps. 14–15.
24. We thus cannot agree with Richard Tuck's claim that "Our entire emotional life, according to Hobbes . . . is in fact a complicated set of beliefs about the best way of securing ourselves against our fellow men, with all the familiar complexities of love, pride, and laughter in the end reducible simply to a set of ideas about our own relative safety from other people's power": Richard Tuck, "The Utopianism of *Leviathan*," in *"Leviathan" after 350 Years*, ed. T. Sorell and L. Foisneau (Oxford: Oxford University Press, 2004), 132. If the only problem we faced was other people's power, our relative safety would be secured by forming confederacies for mutual advantage. It is, however, precisely because pride—the need for recognition, expressed via glory seeking—is an irreducible component of human psychological processing that other people's power is dangerous. Pride sets the problem for calculations of self-preservation, rather than being a function of those calculations.

ing, but by the constant inclination to and threat thereof.[25] Propelled by their same ineliminable desire for self-preservation, human beings were rationally compelled to seek ways of escaping their condition of natural misery by entering upon conditions of peace, to which end they would naturally attempt associations based on honor and advantage. Their natural predicament was that from these materials alone no permanent and stable solution was possible. An *artificial* socialization device was therefore required, which Hobbes located in the imposition of fear as a way of altering the structural predicament generated by the interplay of pride and self-preservation.

Hobbes's term for confederacies based on honor and advantage, as well as families based on natural love and the limited bonds of friendship, was "concord."[26] The only viable method for the erection and maintenance of large and lasting societies, however, was "union": an artificial sociability mechanism comprising a system of representative sovereignty wedded to a structure of overarching coercive enforcement that allowed human beings to safely enter into conditions of peace by terrorizing potential defectors into conformity.[27] Hobbes did not think that honor and advantage, or love and friendship, were absent from stable political society, but he insisted that if left uncoordinated, individuals' wills would not come into stable alignment with each other—and this would sooner or later inevitably produce conflict, and ultimately the disintegration of any common peace tentatively reached hitherto.[28] Hobbes's sovereign sought to unify the disparate wills of competing individuals in two parallel ways: employing fear and the threat of overawing force to enable men to converge on the same ends with regard to the preservation of peace, and insisting that insofar as the sovereign was the representative of the will of each, *judgment* about what each person willed was relinquished to a centralized— and in turn, unifying—agency. Union meant the imposition of undivided and absolute political power: the wielding of the "public sword" to keep people in

---

25. Hobbes, *Elements of Law*, 72–73; *On the Citizen*, 29–30; *Leviathan*, vol. 2, 192.

26. Hobbes, *Elements of Law*, 101–2; *On the Citizen*, 72–73; *Leviathan*, vol. 2, 260; cf. vol. 2, 194, on the "government of small Families" of Native Americans, "the concord whereof dependeth on naturall lust."

27. For discussions of the concord-union distinction, Hont, *Jealousy of Trade*, 20–21, 40–44; Richard Tuck, "Hobbes and Democracy," in *Rethinking the Foundations of Modern Political Thought*, ed. A. Brett and J. Tully (Cambridge: Cambridge University Press, 2006), 171–90; Isaac Nakhimovsky, *The Closed Commercial State: Perpetual Peace and Commercial Society from Rousseau to Fichte* (Princeton, NJ: Princeton University Press, 2011), 25–34.

28. This point is perhaps most clearly made by Hobbes in the *Elements of Law* (101–2): "This consent (or concord) amongst so many men, though it may be made by the fear of a present invader, or by the hope of a present conquest, or booty; and endure as long as that action endureth; nevertheless, by the diversity of judgments and passions in so many men contending naturally for honor and advantage one above another: it is impossible, not only that their consent to aid each other against an enemy, but also that the peace should last between themselves, without some mutual and common fear to rule them."

"awe" and thus faithful to peaceable living.[29] The public sword was a *threat* to that minority whose overweening pride and greed for glory demanded more than equal recognition, but a *guarantee* to those whose moderate ambitions meant they merely required protection from the pathologically glory seeking (as well as the vainglorious, who would otherwise be permanent sources of disruption).[30] Ultimately, union involved concord, but not vice versa, and what distinguished the former from the latter was the use of fear to unify the wills of men, enabling an escape from the horrors of man's natural condition and the instantiation of large and lasting society.

In addition to safety secured by fear, however, the bearer of sovereign power must also provide not just a "bare Preservation," but also all other "Contentments of life." Similarly, the rights of sovereignty "cannot be maintained by any Civill Law, or terror of legall punishment" alone, and must instead be "diligently, and truly taught" so that men knew and acknowledged the grounds of their obedience.[31] Fear was the necessary, but not sufficient, condition for large and lasting society. In order to sustain the obedience and allegiance of subjects, sovereigns must provide them with publicly expressed and upheld reasons to obey, both in terms of private material benefit and a good understanding of the grounds of their (ultimately self-interested) political obligation of obedience.[32] This added stipulation reflected both the underlying (if often unappreciated) richness of Hobbes's psychological account, and his consistent position that most human beings are equitable and will faithfully and persistently abide by conditions of peace if given the opportunity, security, and sufficient incentive to do so.[33] Nonetheless, fear was the ineliminable foundation, the "origin," of large and lasting societies owing to the disruptive potential of honor that could not otherwise be kept in check.[34] The artifice of union gave unity to what would otherwise be a formless multitude only temporarily held together by the inadequate bonds of concord. This generated what "is

29. Hobbes, *Leviathan*, vol. 2, 254.
30. Hobbes, *Elements of Law*, 71.
31. Hobbes, *Leviathan*, vol. 2, 520–22.
32. On the publicly affirmed and transparent nature of Hobbes's political principles, see Waldron, "Hobbes and the Principle of Publicity," *Pacific Philosophical Quarterly* 82, no. 3–4 (2001), 447–74.
33. Hobbes's stipulation in chap. 30 of *Leviathan* that terror is insufficient to maintain peace has sometimes been interpreted as yielding incoherence. Quentin Skinner, for example, writes of Hobbes "developing an argument that not only has no parallel in *The Elements* or *De Cive*, but flatly contradicts his earlier line of thought": Quentin Skinner, *Hobbes and Republican Liberty* (Cambridge: Cambridge University Press, 2008), 159. There is, however, no incoherence or contradiction, either within *Leviathan* or between Hobbes's works, if we understand Hobbes as claiming that large and lasting society requires fear as a necessary, but not a sufficient, condition for controlling the disruptions of honor seeking amongst agents craving recognition.
34. Hobbes, *On the Citizen*, 24.

called a COMMON-WEALTH, in latine CIVITAS . . . the Generation of that great LEVIATHAN, or rather (to speake more reverently) of that *Mortall God*, to which we owe under the *Immortal God*, our peace and defence."[35]

The control of pride was thus the heart of Hobbes's account. In discussing the conditions of peace under the headings of the laws of nature, he explicitly stated the ninth to be against pride, and made clear its significance: "If Nature therefore have made men equall; that equalitie is to be acknowledged: or if Nature have made men unequall; yet because men that think themselves equall, will not enter conditions of Peace, but upon Equall termes, such equalities must be admitted. And therefore for the ninth law of Nature, I put this, *That every man acknowledge other for his Equall by Nature*. The breach of this Precept is *Pride*."[36] Pride is here the name given to a refusal to acknowledge others for one's equals, mirroring Hobbes's claim in the *Elements of Law* that pride is what others call the seeking of glory when it offends them. Designated as proud are those who refuse to acknowledge others as equal, seeking instead to extract honor as a publicly signaled positional good. Individuals "who think themselves equal" will not enter terms of peace unless the belief in their own equality is acknowledged. The important point here is thus not whether human beings *are* equal, but that others *acknowledge them as such regardless*.[37] Whilst not everybody seeks glory in terms of absolute positional superiority, nobody wishes to be gloried over: "every man looketh that his companion should value him, at the same rate he sets upon himself."[38] Denial of this valuation by a refusal to recognize equality was a provocation to violence, and thus instability.

The explanation of the fact that all human beings demand to be publicly recognized as equals—that is, not as *un*equals—is precisely that they are proud; i.e., driven by estimations of their own relative standings compared to others. Whilst we *call* violations of the recognition of mutual equality pride, it

---

35. Hobbes, *Leviathan*, vol. 2, 260.

36. Ibid., 234. In *De Cive*, pride is given as violation of the eighth precept of natural law, which likewise commands acknowledgement of equals: Hobbes, *On the Citizen*, 49–50.

37. On this see also Kinch Hoekstra, "Hobbesian Equality," in *Hobbes Today*, ed. S. A. Lloyd (Cambridge: Cambridge University Press, 2012), 76–112.

38. Hobbes, *Leviathan*, vol. 2, 190. Accordingly we must reject Noel Malcolm's claim that there is a "de-psychologizing" of the argument in *Leviathan* as compared to *De Cive*: Noel Malcolm, "General Introduction," in Hobbes, *The Clarendon Edition of the Works of Thomas Hobbes: Leviathan*, ed. N. Malcolm (Oxford: Oxford University Press, 2012), vol. 1, 18. In all of Hobbes's works the subversion of stable, large, and lasting society is generated by the competitive positional nature of honor seeking rooted in pride (in the terminology of *De Cive*, "a good opinion of oneself"), and the instability is engendered by the threat posed by a minority of glory seekers not content with equal standing. In *Leviathan*, chap. 13 especially, Hobbes emphasizes that glory seeking generates structural predicaments even for the moderate, but this remains principally because of the disruptiveness of the desire for recognition. This is continuous with his position in the *Elements* (*Elements of Law*, 70–72), as well as in *De Cive* (*On the Citizen*, 26).

is simultaneously the ubiquity of pride which means that everyone demands, at the very least, recognition as an equal (and in pathological cases of glory and especially vainglory, they disastrously demand even more than that). With good reason, Hobbes claimed that he took the name of his 1651 work from the Book of Job, "where God having set forth the great power of *Leviathan*, calleth him King of the Proud," giving the Biblical quotation of Leviathan as "*King of all the children of pride.*"[39] Hobbes's sovereign is necessarily sovereign of all the people, "the children," the point being not only that Leviathan is king of all the proud children, but that all of the children are proud. The central function of sovereignty was to impose conditions of fear under which individuals would be forced to recognize each other as equals, albeit beneath the decidedly unequal power of the sovereign.[40]

Outside of political society, human beings were consigned to a state of permanent hostility, suspicion, and aggression thanks to the interplay of pride and individual judgments of self-preservation. Despite the temporary relief of confederacies and associations built on concord, men's lives would be "solitary, poore, nasty, brutish and short."[41] The sole means of stable delivery from this predicament was the "artificial man" of the Leviathan commonwealth, whose "soul," its animating principle, was sovereignty.[42] The superstructure of the political theory Hobbes built upon this foundation sought to demonstrate that all members of established political society owed their peace and security, and in turn their obedience, to the sovereign who protected them.[43] Even if all commonwealths in history had been imperfectly built as though on sand, Hobbes's theory was presented as the true science of politics, promising secure and stable foundations, thanks to a clear and definitive understanding of the

---

39. Hobbes, *Leviathan*, vol. 2, 496.

40. Forthrightly: "As in the presence of the Master, the Servants are equall, and without any honour at all; So are the Subjects, in the presence of the Soveraign. And though they shine some more, some less, when they are out of his sight; yet in his presence, they shine no more than the Starres in presence of the Sun." Hobbes, *Leviathan*, vol. 2, 280. This point is rather missed by Philip Pettit, who suggests that Hobbes simply overlooks the possibility that we might all be content with recognizing each other as equals (*Made with Words*, 96). On the contrary, Hobbes explicitly ruled out this possibility through his account of the place of recognition seeking in human nature; cf. Tim Stanton, "Hobbes and Schmitt," *History of European Ideas* 37 (2011), 163–65.

41. Hobbes, *Leviathan*, vol. 2, 192. When Hobbes describes men's lives as "solitary," he does not mean they literally live in isolation, but that the systematic lack of trust and mutual danger engendered by the disruptiveness of honor precludes their forming safe and permanent associations with others.

42. Hobbes, *Leviathan*, vol. 2, 16.

43. Ibid., pt. 2, chap. 18; pt. 3, "A review, and Conclusion," especially. For overviews of Hobbes's account of obedience, see Kinch Hoekstra, "The *De Facto* Turn in Hobbes's Political Philosophy," in Sorell and Foisneau, *"Leviathan" after 350 Years*, 33–74; Skinner, *Hobbes and Republican Liberty*, chap. 6.

requisite mechanisms for successful large-scale society.[44] Predicated on a theory of human nature identifying pride as the central item in the psychologies of thinking and communicating agents, the chief goal of Hobbes's science of politics was to offer a solution to the central problems generated for human sociability by that same pride.

Once natural men had delivered themselves from their natural predicament, however, the artificial men they erected to overawe them were not subject to a parallel security dilemma in the international arena. The "gladiators" of state relations were primarily defensive, their principal endeavor being the security of their domestic peoples, which for the most part they achieved. Although these artificial men lacked a common power, and were thus in a state of nature with regard to each other, "there does not follow from it, that misery, which accompanies the liberty of particular men."[45] Stability could be expected in the international arena in a way not possible for natural men in the state of nature. The natural law requirement of extending considerations of reciprocal self-preservation would still apply between state actors, engendering mutually recognized codes of international conduct.[46] But it would not generate the further imperative to associate under common power. The world would remain stably—if not always peacefully—divided into an arrangement of jealous, but for the most part tolerably accommodated, Leviathans. Once peaceably arranged beneath these "artificial men," the main threat to natural men came not from international conflict, but from internal rebellion propagated by self-aggrandizing glory seekers taking advantage of false doctrines, particularly in religion, and stemming from the lack of a properly known and disseminated science of politics.[47] Human pride forever threatened to plunge human beings back into the miserable natural condition generated by pride. Its control and management was the great achievement of political society; its irreducibility in human psychology the source of the most serious and permanent internal threat.

---

44. Hobbes, *Leviathan*, vol. 2, 320–22.

45. Ibid., 196.

46. Ibid., 236, 246–48. See especially Noel Malcolm, "Hobbes's Theory of International Relations," in *Aspects of Hobbes* (Oxford, Oxford University Press, 2002), 432–56; Tuck, *Rights of War and Peace*, chaps. 4 and 7, and "Utopianism of *Leviathan*," 134–36.

47. Hobbes, *Leviathan*, vol. 2, chap. 29 generally, and especially 282, 516–18; vol. 3, 928–30; *On the Citizen*, 138–39. Pride and glory seeking as the source of internal sedition is a central theme of Hobbes's history of the English Civil War: Thomas Hobbes, *The Clarendon Edition of the Works of Thomas Hobbes: Behemoth*, ed. P. Seaward (Oxford: Oxford University Press, 2010), "Dialogue 1," especially. On Hobbes's use of the imagery of the artificial man (and his sometimes conflicting, or at least alternative, use of the metaphor of the person of the commonwealth), see Paul Sagar, "What is the Leviathan?," *Hobbes Studies* (forthcoming), and David Runciman, *Pluralism and the Personality of the State* (Cambridge University Press, 1997), chap. 2.

Yet, in contrast to this evident pessimism about the inevitable human political predicament, Hobbes's vision of politics also held out a particular kind of promise, a theoretical, and by extension practical, optimism about the human capacity for political self-understanding, and hence the construction of artificial solutions to deep natural problems. This was embodied most clearly in his theory of union as providing the scientific definition of the "commonwealth or civitas." The promise embedded deep in Hobbes's vision was that the state, even if imperfectly realized and problematically generated in practice, was nonetheless a definite and identifiable form of human association that could be revealed by correct method, and which humans could in turn aspire to a more accomplished and complete fulfillment of. In other words, that beneath the chaos of human practical politics lay a final answer regarding the proper form of large-scale human association under organized coercive power, which a proper science of politics could help mankind come closer to perfecting in practice. Hobbes's vision of popular sovereignty as necessarily mediated through representation was purposefully constructed for application to large, heterogeneous political communities (i.e., modern European kingships), making the "res publica" not simply the form of administration of government, but something more intangible, and yet fundamentally prior to that: the permanent entity of the state.[48] This was in large measure a response to the twin threats of terminal internal tumult and external military aggression felt widely across early modern Europe, coupled with the belief that only a unified decision-making power properly equipped to meet these challenges could suffice in order to successfully preserve the political communities in which human beings must live. Yet this promise—of the state as something objectively identifiable and permanent beneath the chaos of human practice, and the theory of sovereignty as the means for both properly identifying and realizing this promise—has exercised enormous appeal and influence in the theoretical imagination of subsequent thinkers, both in the 150 years following Hobbes that this book is concerned with, and in more recent attempts to gain understandings of modern political predicaments through repeated returns to Hobbes's work. What the rest of this chapter, and indeed this book, aims to show is that Hume (and later, Smith) resisted Hobbes's vision at a fundamental level, offering a different way of understanding our political situation. What Hume and Smith supply is a vision of the modern state *without* a theory of sovereignty: the suggestion that modern political entities, at least when existing in sufficiently favorable conditions, are equipped to deal

---

48. As Hont puts it, the state, for Hobbes, "had to remain essentially the totality of the community, impersonal and disembodied; its intended identity being lost as soon as it was mistakenly equated with any of the actual individuals or subordinate corporations that composed the *civitas*." István Hont, "The Permanent Crisis of a Divided Mankind: 'Nation-State' and 'Nationalism' in Historical Perspective," in *Jealousy of Trade*, 466–67.

with the travails of internal and external threats without a totalizing theory of decision-making unity that posits the state as something independent of, and prior to, the actual practice of political rule in the deeply historically conditioned forms in which it actually comes down to any given people. As we shall see in chapter 3, this required a radical reconfiguration of the role and power of political philosophy, one enabling a reconceptualization of the fundamental problem of political obligation. But first, we must understand how Hume opened up that road by reconfiguring the understanding of human sociability. Getting to Hume, however, requires us to appreciate the challenge of a crucial intermediary figure in the British sociability debate of the eighteenth century: Bernard Mandeville.

Mandeville: Pride Redux

Hobbes's vision of human sociability was forcefully rejected by Anthony Ashley Cooper, third Earl of Shaftesbury, in his 1711 *Charactersticks of Men, Manners, Opinions, Times*. Shaftesbury was preoccupied with what he saw as the morally pernicious consequences of Hobbes's philosophy: the reduction of morality to self-interested efforts at cooperation by atomistic biological units attempting to survive whilst competing in a "distracted" universe. If *that* was all morality consisted of, then for Shaftesbury it wasn't worth having at all. To be worthy of the name, morality had to be guaranteed a more fundamental reality and dignity and should not be traceable back to the operations, however well coordinated, of self-interest.[49]

Shaftesbury likewise condemned the philosophy of his former tutor John Locke, alleging that it reduced to nothing better than that of Hobbes.[50] Locke had insisted that the reality of moral distinctions was guaranteed only by God's revelation, though as such it was accessible to all men through the power of reason. Pointing to evidence of vast diversity in human moral practices, however, Locke claimed that in lieu of revelation, human moral practices were outgrowths of local custom and opinion, revealing no underlying uniformity or

---

49. See especially Anthony Ashley Cooper, third Earl of Shaftesbury, "An Inquiry Concerning Virtue, or Merit," in *Charactersticks of Men, Manners, Opinions, Times*, ed. D.J.D. Uyl, (Indianapolis: Liberty Fund, 2001), vol. 2, 1–100. The "Inquiry" was originally published in 1699 (whether with Shaftesbury's permission is unclear), but was redrafted and placed at the center of the *Charactersticks* in vol. 2, expounding Shaftesbury's positive philosophical views after building on the negative critiques advanced in vol. 1. It contains the central statement of his moral philosophy, and was highly influential in eighteenth-century debates, not least via its impact on Joseph Butler and Francis Hutcheson.

50. Anthony Ashley Cooper, third Earl of Shaftesbury, *The Life, Unpublished Letters and Philosophical Regimen of Anthony, Earl of Shaftesbury*, ed. B. Rand (London: Swan Sonnenschein, 1900), 403.

reality.[51] Shaftesbury abhorred what he saw as Locke's theological voluntarism, believing it rendered human beings no better than a "Tiger strongly chain'd" or a "Monkey under the Discipline of the Whip."[52] As for Locke's skepticism about natural human moral practices due to the prevalence of diversity, this opened the door to Hobbes, once one rejected Locke's voluntarist theological solution. If there existed only diversity of custom and opinion, without any more fundamental and immutable standard of vice and virtue, all we could hope for would be Hobbes's coordinating system of self-preserving competitors. Ultimately, Hobbes and Locke were distinguished only by the former's provocative and forthright assertions openly disgracing him, taking the "point" off his philosophy. Locke was altogether more pernicious. By being less candid, he more effectively struck at "all the fundamentals, threw all order and virtue out of the world," making the very ideas of morality "*unnatural*, and without foundation in our minds."[53]

Opposing what he saw as dangerous moral skepticism, Shaftesbury claimed that although extreme diversity could be observed in human ethical practice, this supervened upon an innate dispositional ability to discern and act upon independently valid and universal moral principles.[54] Human beings existed in an ordered teleological system designed by a benevolent deity. Moral distinctions corresponded not to individual opinion or imperatives of self-preservation, but appreciation of the order and beauty of the proper functioning of the harmonious whole, of which each individual was necessarily a part.[55] God's role was not to act as the cosmic dispenser of rewards and punishments (the heeding of which, being self-interested, would anyway negate genuine moral worth), but as the guarantor of an ordered, purposeful system within which man's end was moral living.[56] This allowed Shaftesbury to claim that "*Virtue* and *Interest* may be found at last to agree."[57] In this ordered teleological system, promoting one's own good necessitated the promotion of the good of the wider system; being virtuous (i.e., promoting the good of others) was accordingly the chief means of securing one's own good, in the form of

---

51. See especially Daniel Carey, *Locke, Shaftesbury and Hutcheson: Contesting Diversity in the Enlightenment and Beyond* (Cambridge: Cambridge University Press, 2006), chaps. 1–3.

52. Shaftesbury, *Characteristicks*, vol. 2, 32.

53. Shaftesbury, *Unpublished Letters*, 403.

54. For an overview, see Carey, *Locke, Shaftesbury, and Hutcheson*, chap. 4. For useful discussions of Shaftesbury's moral philosophy see Stephen Darwall, *The British Moralists and the Internal "Ought"* (Cambridge: Cambridge University Press, 1995), chap. 7; J. B. Schneewind, *The Invention of Autonomy* (Cambridge, Cambridge University Press, 1998), 295–309.

55. Shaftesbury, *Characteristicks*, vol. 2, 21–25.

56. Ibid., 43–44.

57. Ibid., 9.

happiness.[58] In this manner Shaftesbury sought to combine a nonvoluntarist Christian theology with a revival of Stoic ethical principles to guarantee the reality of moral distinctions.[59]

Central to Shaftesbury's account was the supposition that human beings were naturally sociable. The entire universe consisted of integrated, overlapping, and harmonious systems, and humanity's natural condition in this ordered teleology was social reciprocity. Shaftesbury thus reversed Hobbes's problematic. What had to be explained was how man born fit for society nonetheless became unsociable, not just divided into rival political associations but each individual degenerating into a pathological individualism degrading his own happiness by disabling him for virtue. Shaftesbury identified an excess of the "self-passions"—i.e., failing to harmoniously integrate with others (and thus producing vice)—as the root cause of pathological individuation, itself an artificial outgrowth of human economic development.[60] Whilst an individual man might act in ways harmful to others, and "he is in this respect justly styl'd *an ill man*," this was nonetheless an aberration from a more fundamental sociable norm that necessarily involved promoting the good of others to promote one's own.[61] Faced with Hobbes's claim that human beings had only two natural drives to society—honor and advantage—Shaftesbury deployed an ontological framework in which neither of these could be of primary conceptual importance. Accordingly, the seeking of recognition was not destabilizing in the way Hobbes had envisaged. Man was born fit for society, and there was no special problem in explaining the existence of specifically large and lasting associations, only in why men moved away from their sociable norm into moral solitude and pathological individualism owing to an excess of artificially induced selfish passion.[62]

Shaftesbury thus did not attempt to go back to the condition *ante-Hobbesius*, to any appeal to natural sociability based on love, appetite, or instinct. Dealing with Hobbes's challenge required new arguments and new materials, which Shaftesbury located in a synthesis of Christian theology and Stoic and Platonic philosophy, as to some degree would his later follower Francis Hutcheson.[63] Yet

---

58. Ibid., 57, 73.

59. On Shaftesbury's stoic commitments, see Carey, *Locke, Shaftesbury, and Hutcheson*, chap. 4; Christopher Brooke, *Philosophic Pride: Stoicism and Political Thought from Lipsius to Rousseau* (Princeton, NJ: Princeton, 2012), 111–24.

60. Shaftesbury, *Characteristicks*, vol. 2, 180–93. On this see especially István Hont, "The Early Enlightenment Debate on Commerce and Luxury," in *The Cambridge History of Eighteenth Century Political Thought*, ed. M. Goldie and R. Wokler (Cambridge: Cambridge University Press, 2005), 395–99.

61. Shaftesbury, *Characteristicks*, vol. 2, 12.

62. Ibid., 178–79.

63. Shaftesbury developed his novel account of natural sociability in "The Moralists: A Philosophical Rhapsody," in *Characteristicks*, vol. 2, especially 174–81. For Hutcheson as following Shaftesbury in a (qualified) revival of stoic ethics combined with a providential

the price of Shaftesbury's innovative attempt to escape the Hobbesian proposition was his ambitious ontological framework: a highly speculative, philosophically taxing, and controversial set of unargued-for metaphysical commitments, which immediately put Shaftesbury at a disadvantage compared with Hobbes's parsimonious account. It also made Shaftesbury vulnerable to attack by anyone who had no interest in following him down this route, but who wished instead to maintain Hobbes's insistence that the control of pride had to be placed at the center of social and political explanation.

Bernard Mandeville, a Dutch émigré, medical doctor, critic, and notorious author of one of the eighteenth century's most infamous, provocative, and influential *succès de scandales*, was precisely such a figure.[64] To the 1723 edition of his hitherto largely unremarked *Fable of the Bees*, Mandeville made two lengthy additions: "An Essay on Charity, and Charity Schools," and "A Search into the Nature of Society." The former, with its satirical indictment of hypocrisy and self-seeking as masquerading beneath the guise of charitable giving, gained Mandeville notoriety as a scandalous libertine. This reputation was undeserved: his was a powerful synthesis of currents in Augustinian and a revived Epicurean philosophy, satirical in presentation but deeply serious in intellectual content.[65] This was evidenced in the less immediately provocative "Search into the Nature of Society," a sustained discussion of the basis of human sociability explicitly attacking "the Lord Shaftesbury... in his Characteristicks." Mandeville identified Shaftesbury as the counterpoint to his own philosophy as it had stood since 1714, when originally issued as a series of extended remarks on his 1705 doggerel verse poem "The Grumbling Hive."[66]

Christian framework, see Brooke, *Philosophic Pride*, 159–66; James Harris, "Religion in Hutcheson's Moral Philosophy," *Journal of the History of Philosophy* 46 (2008), 214–15.

64. On Mandeville's conception of human sociability see especially Hundert, *Enlightenment's "Fable,"* 49–85; John Robertson, *The Case for the Enlightenment: Scotland and Naples 1680–1760* (Cambridge: Cambridge University Press, 2005), 266–80; Hont, *Early Enlightenment Debate*, 387–95. Hundert and, especially, Robertson locate Mandeville as the intellectual successor to Pierre Bayle, taking up the latter's suggestion that a society of atheists is possible if unified by appropriate bonds of reciprocal self-interest (something Robertson contends is transmitted in turn to Hume). I do not wish to deny the influence of Bayle upon Mandeville. Nonetheless, on the question of human sociability Mandeville is more illuminatingly understood as the successor to Hobbes's idiom of politics as centered on the predicament engendered by pride. In turn, the relationship of Hume to Mandeville must come into different focus than that suggested by Robertson.

65. For Mandeville's philosophy as a synthesis of Augustinian and Epicurean ideas, see Robertson, *Case for the Enlightenment*, 124–46, 261–80; Pierre Force, *Self-Interest before Adam Smith: A Genealogy of Economic Science* (Cambridge: Cambridge University Press, 2003), 42–90. Both draw on Jean Lafond, "Augustinisme et épicurisme au xvii siècle," in *L'homme et son image: morales et littérature de Montaigne à Mandeville* (Paris: H. Champion, 1996), 345–68.

66. Bernard Mandeville, *The Fable of the Bees, Volume 1*, ed. F. B. Kaye (Indianapolis: Liberty Fund, 1988), 323.

In 1723, however, Mandeville effectively conceded that any adequate account of human sociability would have to take Hobbes as its starting point. Shaftesbury's mistake was to reject Hobbes's conclusion via a wholesale denial of the starting premise. Mandeville's gambit was to accept the premise, but resist the conclusion.

In the "Search," Mandeville ridiculed Shaftesbury's ontological system as without basis, an arbitrary invention to further a confused philosophical agenda. Due to the great variety of "Modes and Custom," so "the Inferences drawn from their Certainty are insignificant," and "the generous Notions concerning the natural Goodness of Man are hurtful, as they tend to mis-lead, and are meerly Chimerical."[67] Shaftesbury's central supposition that as "Man is made for Society, so he ought to be born with a kind Affection to the whole, of which he is a part" was absurd.[68] Human beings associated only in order to derive pleasure from the esteem they thereby secured. There was no love of company as such, whether rooted in ordered teleology or natural appetite, only the love of carefully tolerated peers who repaid one's self-estimations: "Even the most polite People in the World ... give no pleasure to others that is not repaid to their Self-Love, and does not at last center in themselves."[69] All instances of "friendly Qualities" arise from our "contriving perpetually our own Satisfaction, so on other Occasions they proceed from the natural Timidity of Man, and the sollicitous Care he takes of himself."[70] It was "not the Good and Amiable, but the Bad and Hateful Qualities of Man" which made him "sociable beyond other Animals the Moment after he lost Paradise."[71] As for Shaftesbury's claim that human beings could regulate their tempestuous passions like a well-bridled horse, this was a "vast inlet to hypocrisy," enabling the false belief that "Man, mere fallen Man," could attain virtue without divine assistance, making Shaftesbury's endeavor "not much better than a Wild-Goose-Chase."[72]

Mandeville declared his own work to be a portrait of man as "the Prey and proper Food of a full grown Leviathan."[73] The qualification "full grown" is illuminating. A full-grown Leviathan rules over a full-grown population. If Hobbes's subjects were the children of pride, Mandeville's were cunning adult psychological competitors. (In the immediate context he was invoking, strumpets, duchesses, courtiers, and the sorts of extravagant show-offs who on the one hand needed a litany of poorer manufactures to be employed in the making of luxury goods for the elite's status consumption, and on the other represented the apotheosis of insatiably pride-driven creatures who had

67. Mandeville, *Bees, Volume 1*, 343.
68. Ibid., 323–24.
69. Ibid., 342.
70. Ibid., 342–43.
71. Ibid., 344.
72. Ibid., 323–24, 348, 331.
73. Ibid., 355.

nonetheless been tamed into finding nonviolent outlets for their urges.) Children might be kept in line by fear, but adult humans frequently valued position and standing above even their lives.

In fact, in *Leviathan* Hobbes had indicated two possible ways in which the vagaries of competitive honor seeking might be held in check: "The force of words being (as I have formerly noted) too weak to hold men to the performance of their covenants, there are in man's nature but two imaginable helps to strengthen it. And those are either a fear of the consequence of breaking their word, or a glory or pride in appearing not to need to break it."[74] Hobbes pursued only fear as the necessary (though not sufficient) basis of man's artificial socialization. Mandeville made Hobbes's neglected alternative—pride as a check to the disruptions of pride—the centerpiece of his theory.

Mandeville went even further than Hobbes in claiming that human beings were centrally driven by pride, "the vast esteem we have for ourselves," and that without the correction of artifice the seeking of recognition generated deeply destabilizing consequences.[75] Irreducibly creatures of mental comparison, human beings desired status in terms of superiority and displayed signals of esteem. In their natural, untaught condition, where they were "only solicitous of pleasing themselves," individuals would attempt superiority by acts of immediate physical domination and violence.[76] This made them by nature mutually odious: successful acquisition of status by one was intolerable to the proud agents whose very recognition was being secured, especially if extracted via subjugation and overt displays of glorying. But Hobbes's suggestion that fear be used as a forcible socializing corrective was fundamentally untenable precisely because of the centrality of competitive recognition in human psychology. Some humans valued returns to their pride even more than their lives, as evidenced by the suicide of Lucretia or the contemporary practice of dueling.[77] As an artificial solution to man's natural predicament, the Leviathan was necessarily stillborn: untaught man would rather fight and die in pursuit of immediate status than conform to peaceful conditions out of fear of future retribution.

Mandeville thus forced open a central question suppressed in Hobbes's account: the extent to which the explanation of what *kept* humans in society was or could be coterminous with what *got* them there, historically. Attempting to answer this question by simultaneously offering a working solution to humanity's psychosocial predicament, Mandeville surmised that pride had needed to be redirected, rather than suppressed or controlled directly. This had initially been achieved by the cunning and ambitious, "Skillful Politicians," who

---

74. Hobbes, *Leviathan*, vol. 2, 216.
75. Mandeville, *Bees, Volume 1*, 67.
76. Ibid., 41.
77. Ibid., 209–10, 219–23.

established systems of social virtue promoting behavior that did not affront the pride of others, manipulating the less far-sighted so as to better secure themselves in "Ease and Security."[78] Initially fear was recruited to this end— but it was psychological, rather than coercively physical. People felt shame (a passion supervening on pride) when they fared ill in the gaze of others, something that was deeply psychologically painful.[79] Contravention of the social codes to respect the pride of others brought condemnation and disapproval, a powerful constraining force for creatures whose mental operations centered on judging themselves through the opinions of their peers. On the other hand, adherence to the new social codes was rewarded with praise and esteem. Men rechanneled their desire for superiority into the pleasures gained from restraint and mutual accommodation, each individual regaling himself on "the Pleasure he receives in reflecting on the Applause which he knows is secretly given him."[80] The carrot and stick of pride's redirection encouraged human beings into tolerable and accommodating sociable living. Morality's strictures as constructed by skillful legislators, the "Political Offspring that Flattery begot upon Pride," served as a system of artificial socialization operating in line with what Pierre Bayle had correctly observed, that "man is so unaccountable a creature as to act most commonly against his principle; and this is so far from being injurious, that it is a compliment to human nature."[81] This "was (or at least might have been) the manner after which Savage Man was broke."[82]

Humans had needed to learn to live in society. But once able to satiate their pride by engaging in forms of collectively sanctioned nonviolent status competition, they were well on the path to sociable living. Enjoying the esteem of others, people increasingly sought company not for its own sake but for the returns to their pride that could be gained thereby, in particular via the pursuit of prestige-status goods and fashionable clothing, which in turn promoted economic development and an upward trajectory toward advanced civilization.[83] Governed in flourishing commercial societies by elaborate codes of social conduct evolved from the early systems of social virtue originally broached by skillful politicians, people became unknown even to themselves. In particular, they failed—as Shaftesbury did most spectacularly—to see their desire for social living as a function of their underlying pride, mistaking the instrumental desire after company for a mark of intrinsic sociability.

This genealogy of pride was not, however, vindicatory. For Mandeville, the entire modern edifice of learned sociability was deeply and unavoidably morally

78. Ibid., 47.
79. Ibid., 64–80.
80. Ibid., 78.
81. Ibid., 51, 167.
82. Ibid., 46.
83. Hont, "Early Enlightenment Debate," 387–95, 399.

compromised. Fallen man could attain true virtue only through acts of self-denial assisted by God; the invented morality of skillful politicians, and its modern social descendants, was at best a utility-promoting counterfeit.[84] Modern large and lasting society was entirely predicated upon the redirection, not the suppression, of human passions, in ways that secretly gratified individuals' pride and were thus inescapably morally vicious. It was precisely humans' bad and hateful qualities that rendered them sociable, not Shaftesbury's divinely ordered ontological habitat for well-bridled human horses. Humankind faced an irreducible trade-off between utility and virtue: between the morally compromised comforts of opulent commercial society with its *beau monde* governed by politeness on the one hand, and frugality and self-denial on the other.[85]

In the successor to the first *Fable*, which he entitled simply *The Fable of the Bees, Volume 2*, and presented as a dialogue between "Cleomenes" and "Horatio" (representing roughly his own and Shaftesbury's views respectively), Mandeville accounted for how man transitioned from his savage and imbecilic state of natural indigence and unsociability to his present state of complex, learned sociability. Integrating this with a sometimes-tortuous discussion of the place of revelation in morals and man's natural development, Mandeville offered a conjectural history of humanity's progression through successive stages of development, beginning in the family, developing through tribal groupings, and culminating in the establishment of political government and the administration of law. Insofar as Mandeville historicized (even if only speculatively) sociability, he thus moved considerably beyond Hobbes in the second *Fable*, as will be explored in greater detail in chapter 2.

However, esteem seeking and inter-mental comparison remained entirely central to Mandeville's account, and here he in effect stuck to the terms of psychological analysis Hobbes had employed in *De Cive*. In the second *Fable*, Mandeville introduced a new technical distinction between "self-love" and "self-liking."[86] Self-love referred to the needs of the body, the cares creatures must take to secure their basic material wants and needs. Self-liking, identified as the cause of pride and shame, referred to the needs of the mind and the basis of one's self-evaluations: an instinct "by which every Individual values itself above its real Worth," which "makes us ... fond of the Approbation, Liking and Assent of others; because they strengthen and confirm us in the good Opinion we have of ourselves."[87] Although shared by the higher animals, and placed in creatures as a drive to better preserve and advance their own good, in human beings self-liking was refracted through the prism of other people's

---

84. Mandeville, *Bees, Volume 1*, 72–73.

85. Ibid., 107–23, 124–34, 169–81, 182–98, 225–38.

86. Bernard Mandeville, *The Fable of the Bees, Volume 2*, ed. F. B. Kaye (Indianapolis: Liberty Fund, 1988), 128–36.

87. Mandeville, *Bees, Volume 2*, 129–30.

imputed evaluations. Although individuals had to like themselves before they could like others, they could only like themselves if they secured recognition. Mandeville's conjectural history, presented in dialogues five and six of the second *Fable*, supplied a natural history of how men who craved recognition escaped the natural indigence to which their greedy and direct attempts to secure self-liking initially confined them. By making that transition, human beings eventually arrived at the condition of modern opulence and complex learned sociability described in the first *Fable*. Mandeville's 1732 *An Enquiry into the Origin of Honour, and the Usefulness of Christianity in War* completed the account, tracing the origins of modern politeness to the emergence of medieval honor systems, the final stage in the redirection of self-liking into socially useful and safe forms of expression, before modern conditions were finally established.[88] All this was done, however, largely "without reflection, and Men, by degrees, and great Length of Time, fall as it were into these Things spontaneously."[89]

This conjectural history attempted to reduce and refine the role of cunning politicians. In its original and blunt deployment in the first *Fable*, the device of the legislator was both historically implausible and difficult to render conceptually coherent: if humans were naturally indigent and only solicitous of pleasing themselves, how was it that some nonetheless had the knowledge and foresight to control others through the erection of systems of social virtue that would be incomprehensible to creatures who had no experience of such systems?[90] Attempting to deal with these problems, Mandeville reduced the role of legislators to the initially self-interested establishment of incentives to conform to nonaggressive patterns of competition established by early leaders of tribal groupings, themselves initially formed as confederacies of defense against wild animals. Once men were turned in this direction, learning to disguise their esteem seeking and avoiding affronting the self-liking of others, "the whole Machine may be made to play of itself with as little skill, as is required to wind up a Clock."[91] Of particular importance in achieving this was the final stage of historical development described in the second *Fable*: not only the erection of government out of the most stable tribal bandings and the enforcement of laws, but the introjection of such laws by the governed populace. However much people might try to disguise their irreducible selfishness in their controlled social interactions, they could only ever be induced to behave in specific, reliable, and peaceful ways if they thought their own selfish

---

88. Bernard Mandeville, *An Enquiry into the Origin of Honour and the Usefulness of Christianity in War* (London, 1732), "The first dialogue," especially, 1–52.

89. Mandeville, *Bees, Volume 2*, 139.

90. Hundert, *Enlightenment's "Fable,"* 77.

91. Mandeville, *Bees, Volume 2*, 323. See also Cleomenes's downplaying of the individual qualities and attributes needed of prime ministers: 328–33; Hundert, *Enlightenment's "Fable,"* 67–68.

interests were advanced in the process. Fear of the law's coercive enforcement was insufficient: people had to come to believe that obedience to the law was to their own private advantage. Once they made this psychological leap, they became fully sociable for the first time: a "Creature is then truly governable, when, reconciled to Submission, it has learn'd to construe his Servitude to his own Advantage."[92] Humans became creatures who introjected external commands, internally sanctioning themselves in advance of trespasses they became strongly disinclined to commit—something fear of the public sword alone could never have achieved, but which was indispensable in explaining how and why humans submitted themselves to organized coercive power. Self-love and self-liking combined in a desire for rule-governed society wherein people could safely secure the esteem of others as well as the more developed trappings of comfort and ease. The needs of both the body and the mind were thus harmonized in a learned sociability people forgot that they (or more precisely, their ancestors) had ever needed to learn. Human sociability did not exist "before great Numbers of them are joyn'd together, and artfully manag'd," precisely because "Men become sociable, by living together in Society."[93]

Mandeville did not, however, dispense entirely with the device of the legislator.[94] "Nature," he explained, "had design'd Man for Society, as she has made Grapes for Wine."[95] Individual grapes neither contain wine, nor can be made into wine; what is required is a large number combined together and put through a process of fermentation by the directing intelligence of a wine maker. Although making wine is impossible without the naturally occurring grape, there is nonetheless no wine in nature. The same was true of human sociability. But as Horatio demanded of Cleomenes, "you must shew me, that in Society there is an Equivalent for Fermentation."[96] This was what dialogues five and six supplied: the conjectural working out of the artificial fermentation required for society to be heightened to perfection over many centuries. The complexities of modern society were related to human primitive social beginnings as the mighty seafaring warships of modernity were related to the first rudimentary boats: the former inconceivable to the designers of the latter, who were nonetheless their genealogical ancestors.[97]

Pride's disruptive effects, ran Mandeville's central claim, could only be mitigated by turning pride in new directions. But given that, historically, this must have been achieved *before* men achieved large and lasting society, both the basis and justification for Hobbesian absolutism were removed. Pride did not

---

92. Mandeville, *Bees, Volume 2*, 184.
93. Ibid., 188–89.
94. Hundert, *Enlightenment's "Fable,"* 75–77; Robertson, *Case for the Enlightenment*, 301.
95. Mandeville, *Bees, Volume 2*, 185.
96. Ibid., 189.
97. Ibid., 141, 322.

need to be (and anyway, was not) kept in check by fear of the public sword, whilst established political society was nowhere near as internally precarious as Hobbes supposed. As for the threat of international competition, this was best countered by pursuing luxury-driven economies of opulence as the foundation of national power, a far more effective discouragement to foreign conquest than frugal citizen militias of civic virtue associated with the now-obsolete city-state republics of the Renaissance. Stability and prosperity in Britain, whilst unavoidably morally compromised in Mandeville's Augustinian schema, were best secured by commercial expansion under the constitutional settlement of William III. Mandeville agreed with Hobbes's diagnosis of man's natural predicament, but he was not committed to his solution of the artifice of union yielding sovereign absolutism, not least because Mandeville placed sociability in a historical framework that allowed for the human capacity to form and maintain large and lasting society to evolve over time, which Hobbes did not (as we shall see in more detail in chapter 2). Mandeville's alternative solution to the question of how man born unfit for society nonetheless came to live everywhere in society consistently undergirded his publicly affirmed Whig politics, an outgrowth of a fundamentally Dutch commitment to a modern republicanism of commerce that would in turn play an important contributory role in the evolution of the form of politics that we now call liberalism.[98]

Hume: Sympathy and Sociability

In the *Treatise of Human Nature*, Hume agreed with Hobbes and Mandeville that "there is no such passion in human minds as the love of mankind, merely as such, independent of personal qualities, of services, or of relation to ourself." Like Hobbes, Hume took the proof to be essentially negative. There is a natural appetite for generation between the sexes and "Were there an universal love among all human creatures, it would appear after the same manner"— but this is plainly not the case.[99] There was also no disputing that humans were creatures whose psychological operations were deeply characterized by forming self-estimations based on the evaluations of peers: "Everything in this world is judg'd of by comparison," most especially our self-estimations when "comparing ourselves with others, as we are every moment apt to do."[100]

98. Hans Blom, "The Republican Mirror: The Dutch Idea of Europe," in *The Idea of Europe: From Antiquity to the European Union*, ed. A. Pagden (Cambridge: Cambridge University Press, 2002), 112–15; Rudolf Dekker, "Private Vices, Public Benefits Revisited: The Dutch Background of Bernard Mandeville," *History of European Ideas* 14 (1992), 481–98; Hundert, *Enlightenment's "Fable,"* 6, 11, 204; Hont, *Early Enlightenment Debate*, 388, 392–95.

99. David Hume, *The Clarendon Edition of the Works of David Hume: A Treatise of Human Nature*, ed. D. F. Norton and M. J. Norton (Oxford: Oxford University Press, 2008), T.3.2.1.12, SBN 481.

100. Hume, *Treatise*, T.2.1.11.18, SBN 323; T.2.1.6.5; SBN 292.

There are "few persons, that are satisfy'd with their own character, or genius, or fortune, who are not desirous of shewing themselves to the world, and of acquiring the love and approbation of mankind."[101]

Unlike Hobbes and Mandeville, however, Hume did not locate the propensity to compare and seek recognition in a single principle, such as pride or "self-liking." Instead, pride was one of four central "indirect" passions, alongside humility, love, and hatred. These operated on a "double relation" of "impressions and ideas," compound impressions determined by the manner in which objects (in the broadest sense) generating pleasure or pain were related either to oneself, or to another thinking creature.[102] A beautiful house owned by oneself caused pride; an ugly one, humility. Riches or virtue possessed by another, love; poverty and meanness, humility or hatred. Although these indirect passions—which Hume identified as the basis for human beings' more complex psychological operations such as compassion, envy, and malice—were determined by the operations of pleasure and pain in relation to the self or others, they were fundamentally conditioned by the opinions of peers: "We fancy Ourselves more happy, as well as more virtuous or beautiful, when we appear so to others."[103] Good health was not a source of pride, because shared with too many. Attendance at a fine banquet would bring joy to all, but pride only for the individual who played host.[104] "Men always consider the sentiments of others in their judgment of themselves," and there was no doubt that "Comparison is in every case a sure method of augmenting our esteem of any thing. A rich man feels the felicity of his condition better by opposing it to that of a beggar."[105]

Yet Hume sharply distinguished his account from that of Hobbes and Mandeville. For a start, pride was presented not as a vice, but as a virtue, owing to its being pleasant in both generation and possession. Hume in turn dismissed those "accustomed to the style of the schools and pulpit" who had "never considered human nature in any other light, than that in which they place it," and who insisted on pride's status as a vice.[106] A remark aimed primarily at the rigors of Augustinian, particularly Calvinist, moralities, Hume nonetheless thereby disassociated pride from the vicious and even scandalous connotations it continued to carry in Hobbes and Mandeville.[107] Furthermore, not only was pride only one (albeit arguably the most important) of four

---

101. Ibid., T.2.2.1.9, SBN 331–32.
102. Ibid., T.2.1.1–5, SBN 275–90.
103. Ibid., T.2.1.6.6, SBN 292; cf. T.2.1.11.1, SBN 316.
104. Ibid., T.2.1.6.2–5, SBN 291–92.
105. Ibid., T.2.1.8.9, SBN 303; T.2.1.10.12, SBN 315–16.
106. Ibid., T.2.1.7.8, SBN 297–98.
107. On Hume and the Calvinist tradition in Scotland see James Harris, "Hume's Use of the Rhetoric of Calvinism," in *Impressions of Hume*, ed. M. Frasca-Spada and P.J.E. Kail (Oxford: Oxford University Press, 2005), 141–60.

central passions, it did not need to be irreducibly competitive: a well-placed and moderately exhibited pride could excite *love* in one's companions.[108] Human beings, precisely because they always considered the sentiments of others in their judgments of themselves, were more dynamically interresponsive than Hobbes and Mandeville appreciated.

Most importantly of all, however, human beings were possessed of "sympathy." A technical term, sympathy referred to the transforming of the "idea" of another's emotive state into an "impression," literally entering into their sentiments.[109] The minds of men were "mirrors" to each other, reflecting passions back and forth.[110] The joy of another was sympathized with, something detected by the original agent and in turn augmenting the pleasure attending the original joy. Men were thus not mutually odious in the manner Mandeville supposed: the success of one need not be a provocation in terms of relative failure, because via sympathy human beings could share each other's pleasures. Men sympathized, in Hume's aptly chosen example, with the rich and famous: imagining the pleasures that riches and power brought, the less fortunate transformed this idea into a pleasant sensation of their own, and were led to esteem, rather than resent and attack, superiors.[111]

Certainly, humans were not always entirely amicable. They felt envy when a comparison with the success of another put their own standing in poor light: malice was the passion of provoking misfortune in another so as to draw pleasure by favorable comparison. But these passions not only supervened on the more basic operations of pride, humility, love, and hatred, they accounted for only a small fraction of human psychological processes and interactions. As a result, the picture that emerged of the natural human capacity to form social groupings was very different to that supposed by both Hobbes and Mandeville: "In all creatures, that prey not upon others, and are not agitated with violent passions, there appears a remarkable desire of company, which associates them together, without any advantages they can ever propose to reap from their union. This is still more conspicuous in man, as being the creature of the universe, who has the most ardent desire of society, and is fitted for it by the most advantages. We can form no wish, which has not a reference to society. A perfect solitude is, perhaps, the greatest punishment we can suffer."[112]

Hume notably insists that man has naturally both an ardent desire for society beyond its instrumental utilitarian benefits, *and* that he is fitted for it by the "most advantages." He is here discussing man's endowment with regard to the needs of the mind, the capacity man has in what Mandeville called his "untaught" state, to associate in terms of reciprocal interactions amongst

---

108. Hume, *Treatise*, T.3.3.2.8, SBN 596–97.
109. Ibid., T.2.1.11.8, SBN 319–20.
110. Ibid., T.2.2.6.21, SBN 365.
111. Ibid., T.2.2.5.1–6, SBN 357–65.
112. Ibid., T.2.2.5.15, SBN 363.

agents that judge and compare. And Hume here marks a crucial break with Hobbes and Mandeville: due to the operation of sympathy, men's untaught seeking of esteem via the recognition of peers is not disruptive, but in general the exact opposite. Sympathy assumes the function assigned by Mandeville to the counterfeit virtue of cunning politicians. But rather than regulating their actions because of the sanctions of an externally imposed code, people's inbuilt affective reactions lead them to automatically regulate themselves, insofar as the pain and pleasure of others become their own.

Hume emphasized the point in the *Treatise*'s discussion of free will, where he made people's propensity to form society an example of undeniable necessity founded on experience of uniformity, stating that "we not only observe, that men always seek society, but can also explain the principles, on which this universal propensity is founded." That explanation was the generation of offspring by savage couples, leading to family groupings based on natural affection and a desire for society in turn yielding utilitarian benefits—i.e., securing of the goods of the body, as well as of the mind—which would both be lost if society was dissolved. Such "inconveniences" were purposefully avoided, human beings opting for continued "close union and confederacy" even after arriving at physical maturity.[113] What marked Hume out from Hobbes and Mandeville, therefore, was not the claim that people naturally sought society or reaped utilitarian benefits from its establishment—as we have seen, neither denied this—but his insistence that people's capacity to sympathize tended to the stability of such arrangements by ensuring that the seeking of recognition was socially cohesive rather than disruptive. We can see this point by turning to one of Hume's few explicit references to Hobbes in the *Treatise*:

> Should a traveller, returning from a far country, tell us, that he had seen a climate in the fiftieth degree of northern latitude, where all the fruits ripen and come to perfection in the winter, and decay in the summer, after the same manner as in England they are produced and decay in the contrary seasons, he would find few so credulous as to believe him. I am apt to think a traveller would meet with as little credit, who should inform us of people exactly of the same character with those in *Plato's Republic* on the one hand, or those in *Hobbes's Leviathan* on the other.[114]

It is clear that Hume's characterization of Hobbes (and Plato) is loose, and what this passage provides is only evidence for Hume's general dismissal of Hobbes's position. Nonetheless, we can reconstruct what the more precise point of philosophical disagreement was, even if Hume himself did not make

---

113. Ibid., T.2.3.1.8, SBN 402.
114. Ibid., T.2.3.1.10, SBN 402.

this explicit (something that remains applicable even if Hume did not read Hobbes particularly carefully). In essence, we can understand Hume as indicating that there was no need for a full-blown propriety theory (in Adam Smith's later terminology) such as Plato's—or, Hume might equally have said, Shaftesbury's—requiring human beings to comprehensively regulate their passions through conscious reflection.[115] But, likewise, Hobbes's vision of men engaging in aggressive and destabilizing competition was too extreme. Hume's science of man offered a middle course between Hobbes's position and the metaphysically taxing and excessively hypothetical teleological alternative proposed by Shaftesbury (a speculative system anyway impermissible under a proper science of experience and observation).

And yet, despite Hume's rejection of there being in reality a people of the character described in *Leviathan*, he nonetheless agreed with Hobbes that there existed impassable obstacles to the formation of specifically *large and lasting* human society by *natural* means alone: "Men cannot live without society, and cannot be associated without government. Government makes a distinction of property, and establishes the different ranks of men. This produces industry, traffic, manufactures, law-suits, war, leagues, alliances, voyages, travels, cities, fleets, ports, and all those other actions and objects, which cause such a diversity, and at the same time maintain such an uniformity in human life."[116] Unambiguously an artifice, Hume identified government as necessary to the regulation of ranks and property, and therefore all the complexities of developed large-scale society that supervened upon those innovations. Mandeville had ultimately been correct, albeit for the wrong reasons: explaining modern social conditions of greatness and opulence did require going beyond the capacities generated by men's natural psychological endowments alone. But departing from a different psychological starting point, Hume located both the need for, and mechanism of, artifice in a fundamentally different explanatory matrix. To see this, we must turn to what is now usually known as Hume's "theory of justice," but which in its proper eighteenth-century context

---

115. Adam Smith, *The Glasgow Edition of the Works and Correspondence of Adam Smith: The Theory of Moral Sentiments*, ed. D. D. Raphael and A. L. Macfie (Oxford: Oxford University Press, 1976), 267–93. Smith reprises Hume's analogy of the traveller in his rejection of Mandeville's "licentious system": 314.

116. Hume, *Treatise*, T.2.3.1.9, SBN 402. Accordingly, sympathy alone is not sufficient to explain human sociability in Hume's view, even if we agree with James Harris that the purpose of bk. 2 of the *Treatise* is to outline a new vision of human sociability as "sympathetic sociability": James Harris, "A Compleat Chain of Reasoning: Hume's Project in *A Treatise of Human Nature*, Books One and Two," *Proceedings of the Aristotelian Society* 109 (2009), 129–48. For a relevant discussion see also Christopher J. Finlay, *Hume's Social Philosophy: Human Nature and Commercial Sociability in the "Treatise of Human Nature"* (London/New York: Continuum, 2007), chaps. 6 and 7.

is more properly viewed as a utility-based theory of human sociability for large and lasting conditions.[117]

Hume: Justice and Government

Hume agreed with Hobbes and Mandeville that humans, considered in isolation, were naturally indigent and vulnerable. They lacked the defensive and offensive natural weapons of beasts, whilst possessed of inadequate physical capacity to secure their extensive needs for food, shelter, and raiment: "to consider him only in himself, he is provided neither with arms, nor force, nor other natural abilities, which are in any degree answerable to so many necessities."[118] Man could remedy this situation only by forming associations: "it is by society alone he is able to supply his defects, and raise himself up to an equality with his fellow-creatures, and even acquire a superiority above them."[119] Grouping together in primitive families founded on the sex instinct, savage man learned the advantages of sociable living, which sympathy ensured that psychologically he both desired and was well fitted for. The attendant "mutual succour" generated "additional *force, ability*, and *security*" that made society advantageous, and human beings aware of its advantages.[120]

Problems immediately arose, however, when the utilitarian benefits of society generated the production and increased dissemination of possessions, encouraging people into competition for goods. Against the portrait of psychologically isolated and almost exclusively self-interested individuals painted by Hobbes and Mandeville, Hume was keen to affirm that humans were not by nature excessively selfish:

> I am sensible, that generally speaking, the representations of this quality have been carried much too far; and that the descriptions, which certain philosophers delight so much to form of mankind in this particular, are as wide of nature as any accounts of monsters, which we meet with in fables and romances. So far from thinking, that men have no affection for any thing beyond themselves, I am of opinion, that though it be rare to meet with one, who loves any single person better than himself; yet

---

117. I focus here on Hume's account of justice as it relates to the debate over human sociability. The "theory of justice" is one of the most misread and misunderstood aspects of Hume's philosophy. Useful correctives and overviews can be found in Jason Baldwin, "Hume's Knave and the Interests of Justice," *Journal of the History of Philosophy* 42 (2004), 277–96; Rachel Cohon, *Hume's Morality: Feeling and Fabrication* (Oxford: Oxford University Press, 2008), chaps. 6–9.

118. Hume, *Treatise*, T.3.2.2.2, SBN 485.

119. Ibid., T.3.2.2.3, SBN 485.

120. Ibid., T.3.2.2.4, SBN 486.

it is as rare to meet with one, in whom all the kind affections, taken together, do not overbalance all the selfish.[121]

Nonetheless, man's natural passions were disruptive to the establishment of large and lasting society:

> For it must be confest, however the circumstances of human nature may render an union necessary, and however those passions of lust and natural affection may seem to render it unavoidable; yet there are other particulars in our natural temper, and in our outward circumstances, which are very incommodious, and are even contrary to the requisite conjunction. Among the former, we may justly esteem our selfishness to be the most considerable.[122]

Men's reasonable pursuit of their own self-interest was coupled with a desire to help their families and loved-ones, but indeed so "noble an affection, instead of fitting men for large societies, is almost as contrary to them, as the most narrow selfishness."[123] Acting for either self-interest or the good of one's family, each would seek to acquire the possessions of non-kin. Yet the replication of such behavior across groups was deeply destabilizing: if everyone pursued immediate self-interest, the security of possessions would be lost, and with it the advantages of society humans needed in order to supplement their naturally indigent state. Accordingly, it was the pursuit of utility that principally required regulation in order to explain the emergence of large and lasting societies:

> All the other passions, besides this of interest, are either easily restrained, or are not of such pernicious consequence, when indulged. Vanity is rather to be esteemed a social passion, and a bond of union among men. Pity and love are to be considered in the same light. And as to envy and revenge, though pernicious, they operate only by intervals, and are directed against particular persons, whom we consider as our superiors or enemies. This avidity alone, of acquiring goods and possessions for ourselves and our nearest friends, is insatiable, perpetual, universal, and directly destructive of society.... So that upon the whole, we are to esteem the difficulties in the establishment of society, to be greater or less, according to those we encounter in regulating and restraining this passion.[124]

---

121. Ibid., T.3.2.2.5, SBN 486–87.
122. Ibid., T.3.2.2.5, SBN 486–87.
123. Ibid., T.3.2.2.6, SBN 487.
124. Ibid., T.3.2.2.12, SBN 491–92.

What was needed was agreement amongst individuals to abstain from immediate, unlicensed appropriation of the goods of others in return for mutually accommodating behavior: "This can be done after no other manner, than by a convention entered into by all the members of the society to bestow stability on the possession of those external goods, and leave every one in the peaceable enjoyment of what he may acquire by his fortune and industry."[125] This took the form not of a contract, but of compact: it "may properly enough be called a convention or agreement betwixt us, though without the interposition of a promise; since the actions of each of us have a reference to those of the other, and are performed upon the supposition, that something is to be performed on the other part." Just as "two men, who pull the oars of a boat, do it by an agreement or convention, though they have never given promises to each other," so men came to establish conventions to abstain from each other's possessions, although this was done initially without design and solely for the mutual promotion of self-interest.[126]

This was the origin of the "artificial virtue" of justice: a convention for the regulation of possessions and prerequisite for large and lasting societies composed of agents characterized more by a desire of securing utility than competitive recognition.[127] The path to large and lasting society was blocked not, as Hobbes thought, by the pursuit of honor, but the aggregated pursuit of advantage. The only way around this problem was to redirect the pursuit of advantage into nondestablizing—indeed, actively improving—avenues. The solution Mandeville applied to pride was properly directed at utility: "There is no passion . . . capable of controlling the interested affection, but the very affection itself, by an alteration of its direction." Once that was achieved, humans began their upward progress towards successful large-scale association. "The question, therefore, concerning the wickedness or goodness of human nature, enters not in the least into that other question concerning the origin of society," for whether "the passion of self-interest be esteemed vicious or virtuous, it is all a case; since itself alone restrains it: So that if it be virtuous, men become social by their virtue; if vicious, their vice has the same effect."[128]

Justice first generated what Hume called a "natural" obligation rooted in the self-interested benefits individuals reaped from adhering to the new conventions. But regard for justice rapidly developed beyond immediate regard to self-interest, acquiring a "moral" obligation attended to the belief that upholding the conventions of justice was not merely a matter of individual prudence, but a fully-fledged moral virtue in its own right. This was an effect of sympathy.[129] The advantages of adherence to the social conventions brought

---

125. Ibid., T.3.2.2.9, SBN 489.
126. Ibid., T.3.2.2.10, SBN 490.
127. Ibid., T.3.2.2.10, SBN 490.
128. Ibid., T.3.2.2.13, SBN 492.
129. Ibid., T.3.2.2.23–24, SBN 498–500.

pleasure to those who benefited from them, as did the idea of peaceful, commodious society to which justice was attached. Acts of injustice aroused painful sympathy with victims of violation, whilst disruption of the conditions of social peacefulness aroused uneasiness in men seeking their own secured interests.[130] This sympathetic engagement, and the association of the upholding of justice with pleasure to self or others, generated the belief that justice was a moral virtue (which it indeed thus fully became in Hume's account). This "moral" obligation further motivated people to adhere to justice's strictures, in turn better securing the regulation of possessions and the stability of society. Having established the artifice of justice, they were then able to establish the notion of property, and the idea and practice of its legitimate transference by means of consent.[131] From there humans could practice socially regulated, utility-promoting reciprocal interactions for the exchange of possessions, putting them on a trajectory toward not just large and lasting society, but economically advanced civilization.

Although this entire "progress of the sentiments be *natural*, and even necessary"—humans being an inventive species, it was natural for them to invent artifices—Hume allowed that the process was "forwarded by the artifice of politicians," who in order to "govern men more easily, and preserve peace in human society, have endeavour'd to produce an esteem for justice, and an abhorrence of injustice." But Mandeville had been wrong to make cunning legislators the indispensable condition of the emergence of stable large-scale human association: "nothing can be more evident, than that the matter has been carry'd too far by certain writers on morals, who seem to have employed their utmost efforts to extirpate all sense of virtue from among mankind." The artifice of justice had to supervene on natural materials: "For if nature did not aid us in this particular, it would be in vain for politicians to talk of honourable or dishonourable, praiseworthy or blameable." Hence, "The utmost politicians can perform, is, to extend the natural sentiments beyond their original bounds; but still nature must furnish the materials, and give us some notion of moral distinctions."[132] With the innovation of sympathy, the cunning legislator was explanatorily obsolete, and a wholly naturalistic—and thereby historically and conceptually plausible—story of humanity's progression to large and lasting society could be supplied.[133]

But before men could arrive at fully modern conditions, a further artificial innovation was necessary: government. The initial benefits of adhering to conventions of justice would lead not only to increased material prosperity, but increases in the size of human associations. Still driven primarily by

---

130. Ibid., T.3.2.7.1–8, SBN 534–39.
131. Ibid., T.3.2.3–5, SBN 501–25.
132. Ibid., T.3.2.2.25, SBN 500.
133. Hundert, *Enlightenment's "Fable,"* 84–86; Robertson, *Case for the Enlightenment*, 301.

self-interest, in large-scale conditions people could not easily align their desire for immediate obtainment of possessions promoting their own utility with the conventions demanding abstention from the goods of others. Large-scale association generated anonymity through weight of numbers, and decreased sympathetic engagement with victims of violations of justice one was unlikely to personally encounter. Opportunities were increasingly provided for anonymous defection from the conventions of justice, which on an individual scale would be negligible, but if sufficiently aggregated would topple the entire social arrangement. Humans always preferred contiguous good to remote, and so were powerfully incentivized to violate the rules of justice: self-interest threatened to overpower the (increasingly negligible) "natural" obligation to virtue and the greatly weakened "moral" obligation undermined by anonymity and increased social distance. "You are, therefore, naturally carry'd to commit acts of injustice as well as I." Your example pushes me by imitation, as well as incentivizing me to defect first, "by showing me, that I shou'd be the cully of my integrity, if I alone shou'd impose on myself a severe restraint amidst the licentiousness of others."[134]

The solution was again to make self-interest a check to self-interest, now via the innovation of "magistracy." Specific individuals were charged with and rewarded for the upholding of the conventions of justice, backed by organized public coercive force. The self-interest of the minority of magistrates was aligned with upholding the rules of justice, in turn realigning the majority of humans' contiguous interests (avoiding punishment and securing ease) with their otherwise neglected and remote interest (preventing large-scale defection that would undermine the entire edifice of civilized society erected on the foundation of justice). "By means of these two advantages, in the *execution* and *decision* of justice, men acquire a security against each other's weakness and passion, as well as against their own, and under the shelter of their governors, begin to taste at ease the sweets of society and mutual assistance."[135]

The introduction of magistracy was the origin of government. But again Hume was keen to stress his differences from Hobbes and Mandeville: "so far am I from thinking with some philosophers, that men are utterly incapable of society without government, that I assert the first rudiments of government to arise from quarrels, not among men of the same society, but among those of different societies." As people developed larger and more prosperous associations, the incentive to rapacious conquest by organized outsiders—international war—grew larger. Yet "foreign war to a society without government necessarily produces civil war. Throw any considerable goods amongst men, they instantly fall a quarelling, while each strives to get possession of

---

134. Hume, *Treatise*, T.3.2.7.3, SBN 535.
135. Ibid., T.3.2.7.8, SBN 538.

what pleases him, without regard to the consequences."[136] Governments were originally established in times of crisis, leaders being required to impose internal discipline as well as external security, guaranteeing people's possessions from both within and without. "Camps are the true mothers of cities": humans learned to live under government in times of war, and continued this innovation in times of peace for the advantages rendered by orderly and hierarchical rule in the administration of justice, the stability of property, and the different ranks supervening on both.[137] Although government was originally an innovation of war, human beings became sensible of its advantages and retained it, employing magistrates to facilitate the conventions of justice necessary to secure large and lasting conditions: "And as the failure of any one piece in the execution is connected, though not immediately, with the failure of the whole, they [magistrates] prevent that failure, because they find no interest in it, either immediate or remote. Thus bridges are built; harbours opened; ramparts raised; canals formed; fleets equip'd; and armies disciplined every where, by the care of government, which, though composed of men subject to all human infirmities, becomes, by one of the finest and most subtle inventions imaginable, a composition, which is, in some measure, exempted from all these infirmities."[138] Once government was established, men had an immediate "natural" obligation of obedience derived from its furthering their own interests by the stability it rendered. In other words, because government (at least in general, and in most cases) promoted the good of those it ruled over, those same ruled individuals ipso facto had immediate reasons to obey, albeit reasons rooted in private self-interest. But it was a clearly observable psychological fact, Hume thought, that people were carried beyond the bounds of their interests by "general rules," and came to form a "moral" obligation to government rooted in sympathy: the belief that obedience was owed to established government irrespective of immediate private self-interest, and as a matter of normative principle.[139] This was the origin of political authority, whose undergirding artificial virtue was allegiance.[140] This virtue—i.e., belief that it was morally good to obey rulers, and attendant moral disapproval of those who rebelled against rightful rule—was an artifice, rooted in conventions,

---

136. Ibid., T.3.2.8.1, SBN 540.
137. Ibid., T.3.2.8.2, SBN 540–41.
138. Ibid., T.3.2.7.8, SBN 539.
139. Ibid., T.3.2.9.3, SBN 551.
140. David Hume, "Of the Original Contract," in *Essays Moral, Political and Literary*, ed. E. F. Miller (Indianapolis: Liberty Fund, 1985), 480; Andrew Sabl, *Hume's Politics: Coordination and Crisis in the "History of England"* (Princeton, NJ: Princeton University Press, 2012), 7; cf. István Hont, "Commercial Society and Political Theory in the Eighteenth Century: The Problem of Authority in David Hume and Adam Smith," in *Main Trends in Cultural History: Ten Essays*, ed. W. Melching and W. Velema (Amsterdam: Rodopi, 1994), 54–94.

in just the way that belief in the normative validity of the rules of justice was. But in Hume's picture, that was again simply a genealogical explanation of the phenomenon, with no bearing upon the validity of the practice.

As Hume elaborated in his 1741 essay "Of the First Principles of Government," "Nothing appears more surprising . . . than the easiness with which the many are governed by the few." Force is always on the side of the former, and the latter have "nothing to support them but opinion."[141] "Opinion" was composed of beliefs regarding public interest, the right to power, and the right to property, and upon these "are all governments founded, and all authority of the few over the many."[142] Opinion—that is, human imagination and not just redirected self-interest—was required to explain why people submitted themselves to government beyond immediate regard to, and sometimes in spite of, private advantage, instead obeying the commands of superiors out of a belief in their right to rule.

Yet being at base an invention for the furthering of interest, government could have no continued justification if it became excessively oppressive: "There is evidently no other principle than interest; and if interest first produces obedience to government, the obligation to obedience must cease, whenever the interest ceases, in any great degree, and in a considerable number of instances."[143] Although obedience to tyrannical regimes would not continue indefinitely—it "is both the general practice and principle of mankind . . . that no nation, that cou'd find any remedy, ever yet suffer'd the cruel ravages of a tyrant, or were blam'd for their resistance"—the propensity to allegiance beyond regard to self-interest significantly aided the promotion of social stability. Advanced political society did not fall into rebellion and discord at the first sign of individual interest being violated, because authority in practice depended directly on opinion, and only indirectly upon utility. Likewise, people's propensity to form allegiance—belief that authority could be located in conditions as diverse as "*original contract, long possession, present possession, succession,* and *positive laws*"—allowed them to rapidly reenter political society after times of civil breakdown.[144] Although at points of crisis the designation of rightful rulers was "less capable of solution from the arguments of lawyers and philosophers, than from the swords of the soldiery," human imagination and the propensity to conceive of a "moral" obligation to governmental authority swiftly reconciled people to conditions of political rule, with only minimal regard to the means by which title was acquired.[145] The promotion of utility and the regulation of self-interest remained the decisive function and justification of government. It was simply that "The same interest . . . which causes us to

141. David Hume, "Of the First Principles of Government," in *Essays*, 32.
142. Hume, "First Principles," 34.
143. Hume, *Treatise*, T.3.2.9.4, SBN 553.
144. Ibid., T.3.2.10.15, SBN 562.
145. Ibid., T.3.2.10.15, SBN 562.

submit to magistracy, makes us renounce itself in the choice of our magistrates, and binds us down to a certain form of government, and to particular persons, without allowing us to aspire to the utmost perfection in either."[146]

Hume's account of human sociability is thus ultimately tripartite. Sympathy ensured that human beings had the most ardent desire for society, and when securing the needs of the mind they were psychologically fitted for it naturally by the most advantages. The artifices of justice and government were employed to correct for collective-action problems in the securing of utility when people associated in ever greater numbers to better satisfy the needs of the body, as well as the more developed needs of the mind, which came to depend upon the possession of goods not just of subsistence, but of status and comfort (i.e., luxury as an attendant to, and motor of, economic development). Finally, in advanced conditions human imagination rendered people obedient to forms of government based on authority, without immediate regard to utility, but which best secured that utility even if this underlying fact and origin became obscured by the very experience of living under such conditions. Hobbes and Mandeville, as we have seen, offered accounts which focused primarily on pride and its consequences, but which were finally supplemented by regard to utility. (In Hobbes, providing the contentment and comforts of life and teaching the true grounds of obedience in protection; in Mandeville, rendering subjects "governable" by making them believe political rule was in their own self-interest.) Hume emphasized the inadvertently destabilizing pursuit of utility as the central sociability problem that needed to be accounted for (his "theory of justice"), but supplemented this with an incorporation of the empirically attestable fact that humans in fully developed large and lasting society subscribed to conditions of peace *not* primarily out of regard to self-interest, but out of a belief in the rightfulness of political authority.[147] In a

---

146. Ibid., T.3.2.10.3, SBN 555.

147. With these qualifications, we can identify Hume as ultimately a theorist of what Hont termed "commercial sociability": a middle route, focusing on utility, between the pride-focused natural unsociability of Hobbes, and the more thoroughgoing natural sociability accounts of thinkers such as Shaftesbury and Hutcheson: see István Hont, "The Language of Sociability and Commerce: Samuel Pufendorf and the Theoretical Foundations of the "Four Stages" Theory," in *Jealousy of Trade*, 159–84; "Commercial Society," 54–72; and "Jealousy of Trade: An Introduction," in *Jealousy of Trade*, 40–44. By contrast, it is not accurate to group Hume, as James Moore has done, with Mandeville and Hobbes under the heading of an "Epicurean tradition" in morals, even as opposed to the broadly Stoic philosophy of Hutcheson. Hume's emphasis on the management of utility, not pride, sets him distinctively apart from Mandeville and Hobbes, and likewise means his philosophy cannot accurately or illuminatingly be described as a commitment to straightforward "natural unsociability." See James Moore, "Hume and Hutcheson," in *Hume and Hume's Connexions*, ed. M. A. Stewart and J. P. Wright (Edinburgh: Edinburgh University Press, 1994), 23–57; "The Eclectic Stoic, the Mitigated Skeptic," in *New Essays on David Hume*, ed. E. Mazza and E. Ronchetti (Milan: FrancoAngelli, 2007), 133–70; and "Utility and Humanity: The Quest for the *Honestum* in Cicero, Hutcheson and Hume," *Utilitas* 14 (2002), 365–86.

sense, Mandeville had been right that men thus became, at least partially, unknown to themselves. But Hume's genealogy of justice and government was vindicatory, not debunking.[148] And even if "few persons can carry on this train of reasoning" with regard to the origin of society and government in utility, it was nonetheless true that "all men have an implicit notion of it, and are sensible, that they owe obedience to government merely on account of the public interest."[149]

After government was established, Hume concluded, "Political writers tell us, that in every kind of intercourse, a body politic is to be consider'd as one person."[150] As Hobbes had thought, state persons stood toward each other in a fashion analogous (though, again, not identical) to how natural persons stood towards each other. In both cases the establishment of conventions secured mutual interest: the "laws of nations" were the international equivalent of the rules of justice, which themselves continued to obtain, if somewhat more loosely, between state actors in order to govern transactions of property and commerce. Being founded to promote utility, the laws of nations generated a "natural" obligation, and were likewise attended with a "moral" one too. But because the interest of state actors in obedience to these laws was less rigid and constant than to the domestic implementation of justice, both the natural and moral obligations were in practice much weakened. Although few politicians would openly admit it, the maxim that "there is a system of morals calculated for princes, much more free than that which ought to govern private persons" was "authoriz'd by the practices of all ages."[151]

The existence of the laws of nations, though weaker in force and less rigidly observed than those of domestic justice, attested to the relative stability of

---

Moore's reading has been endorsed by Robertson, *Case for the Enlightenment*, 289-324; Luigi Turco, "Hutcheson and Hume in a recent polemic," in Mazza and Ronchetti, *New Essays*, 171-98; John P. Wright, *Hume's "A Treatise of Human Nature: An Introduction* (Cambridge: Cambridge University Press, 2009), chap. 9. A dissenting voice is James Harris, "The Epicurean in Hume," in *Epicurus in the Enlightenment*, ed. N. Leddy and A. Lifchitz (Oxford: Voltaire Foundation, 2009), 161-81, which questions Hume's being part of an "Epicurean" tradition on different grounds to those advanced here.

148. For a different, but helpfully illustrative, discussion of the possibility of vindicatory genealogy, especially in relation to Hume, see Bernard Williams, *Truth and Truthfulness: An Essay in Genealogy* (Princeton, NJ, Princeton University Press, 2002), chap. 2.

149. Hume, *Treatise*, T.3.2.9.4, SBN 552-53. For a detailed discussion of this matter, see chap. 6.

150. Ibid., T.3.2.11.1, SBN 567. It is noteworthy that Hume does not explicitly endorse this as his own position, but attributes it instead to "political writers." This suggests a certain deliberate distancing from the explicit state-person theory of Hobbes, potentially a function of Hume's jettisoning of the categories of sovereignty and representation (see below, and chapter 3)—although, of course, Hobbes was neither the first nor the last to make such a claim, and Hume's locution indicates that he was aware that the view was not unique to Hobbes.

151. Hume, *Treatise*, T.3.2.11.3, SBN 568.

international relations. In the *Treatise* Hume essentially agreed with Hobbes, but based the conclusion on his alternative theory of artificial conventions: international war would continue to occur, but its destructive potential was limited, and the relations between state persons were broadly stable and tended to the security of domestic populations. Likewise, Hobbes was right that the division of humanity into rival states indicated that the attainment of society at subglobal levels could not be explained by appeal to natural propensities alone.

Hume, however, would later significantly qualify his estimation of the relative stability of the international arena in his 1752 *Political Discourses*, when examining the interaction of modern commercial competition and military-political expansionism. He there identified the innovation of national finance as threatening to turn states into mutually devastating fiscal-military war machines, meaning "either the nation must destroy public credit, or public credit will destroy the nation."[152] The possibilities opened by national debt rendered Mandeville's suggestion that commercial expansion was a safeguard against external conquest dangerously mistaken, whilst the modern international sphere, where war met commerce, was liable to be far more unstable and destructive than Hobbes had supposed.[153] But that is a story for another time.

Conclusion

Hume's science of man, by displacing Hobbes's theory of human nature and establishing an alternative vision of how humans interacted, helped clear the ground for an alternative science of politics, as Hume proposed was possible in his 1741 *Essays, Moral and Political*. The constancy and consistency of human nature meant that institutions, laws, and forms of government were the crucial materials upon which to work, as "consequences almost as general and certain may sometimes be deduced from them, as any which the mathematical sciences afford us."[154] With a proper science of human nature in place, "politics admit of general truths, which are invariable by the humour or education either of subject or sovereign."[155] Of particular importance was "a just *political* maxim, *that every man must be supposed a knave*: Though at the same time, it appears somewhat strange, that a maxim should be true in politics, which is false in fact."[156] The successful ordering of large-scale society turned on institutional design: the pitting of rival interests against each other as mutual

---

152. David Hume, "Of Public Credit," in *Essays*, 360–61. On this see especially István Hont, "The Rhapsody of Public Debt: David Hume and Voluntary State Bankruptcy," in *Jealousy of Trade*, 325–53. See also Nakhimovsky, *Closed Commercial State*, 120–22, 125.
153. Mandeville, *Bees, Volume 1*, 115–23.
154. David Hume, "That Politics May Be Reduced to a Science," *Essays*, 16.
155. Hume, "Reduced to a Science," 18.
156. David Hume, "Of the Independency of Parliament," in *Essays*, 42–43.

checks, so as to secure stability and prosperity via the implementation of good laws. "Legislators . . . ought not to trust the future government of a state entirely to chance, but ought to provide a system of laws to regulate the administration of public affairs to the latest posterity. Effects will always correspond to causes; and wise regulations in any commonwealth are the most valuable legacy that can be left to future ages."[157] Although it was not strictly necessary for Hume to reject Hobbes's theory of human nature in order to reject his theory of government—one could advocate (as others had, and did afterwards) something like Hume's vision of institutional checks, against a vision of sovereign absolutism, based solely on the projected consequences of such an arrangement—it *was* necessary, from Hume's point of view, to get human nature right in order to delineate a proper science of politics. But getting human nature right told decisively against Hobbes, and in turn helped to support the case for Hume's alternative vision of government. For it was in advocating a vision of utility-based, or commercial, sociability that Hume could deny the irreducible need for politics to be structured around a sovereign agent whose job was to unify the disparate wills of competing individuals who would otherwise inevitably fall into devastating conflict. No such unifying power was necessary—in other words, one did not need a *representative* to take over the act of judging on behalf of individuals, so as to pacify their aggregated consequences—and as a result, politics could be conceived of without making sovereignty on Hobbes's understanding a necessary component of large and lasting political arrangements (this matter is explored in detail in chapter 3).

Hume in turn also distanced himself from the "civic humanist," or "republican," tradition that had emphasized the importance of individual citizen virtue and public-spirited participation in the healthy functioning and security of free polities.[158] But he also reconfigured an emphasis on good political institutions as the central building blocks of order, security, and stability in a crucially counter-Hobbesian manner. Not only must authority always be balanced with liberty, but one of the truths revealed by the science of politics was the "universal axiom . . . *That an hereditary prince, a nobility without vassals, and a people voting by their representatives, form the best* MONARCHY, ARISTOCRACY, *and* DEMOCRACY."[159] In other words, the English constitutional structure of the eighteenth century, which did not exemplify unified sovereign absolute power but rather a delicate balance of mixed ele-

---

157. Hume, "Reduced to a Science," 24.

158. See James Moore, "Hume's Political Science and the Classical Republican Tradition," *Canadian Journal of Political Science* 10 (1977), 809–40.

159. Hume, "Reduced to a Science," 18. On the balancing of liberty and authority, see David Hume, "Of the Origin of Government," in *Essays*, 40–41. This essay was Hume's final addition, first published with the posthumous version of his *Essays* in 1777. It is a streamlined and compact summary of Hume's view of the origin, historical progression, and perfection of government, meaning it is in turn a succinct statement of his political thought.

ments, could generate stable and lasting government for advanced societies. This was thus more than a cosmetic modification of Hobbes's emphasis on the importance of state institutions in more auspicious times yielding a mixed government model in support of a cautious mid-eighteenth-century Whiggism.[160] More fundamentally, Hume's science of man displaced the need for a theory of union (which in Hobbes's framework generated, indeed entailed, political absolutism) in accounting for the conceptual origin and continued functioning of the state. Hume accordingly dispensed with the central Hobbesian devices of sovereignty and representation, insisting instead that the authority structures needed to sustain large and lasting society could be generated by the mechanisms of human opinion.

It is of course true that in *Behemoth* Hobbes himself stipulated that "the power of the mighty hath no foundation but in the opinion and belief of the people."[161] That is, in order for sovereign power to be stable and successful, a sufficient majority of subjects must cooperate in its being preserved and upheld—i.e., by adhering to the laws on a daily basis and accepting the inconveniences that living under common power would necessarily impose.[162] To this end, *Leviathan* insisted that sovereigns provide not just a "bare Preservation" but also all other "Contentments of life, which every man by lawfull Industry, without danger, or hurt to the Common-wealth, shall acquire to himself."[163] Yet these sociological considerations were of supplementary and secondary importance in Hobbes's conceptual edifice: they related to how already-instantiated sovereigns were to succeed in ruling continuously, and hopefully ruling well. Mere opinion, however, did not constitute the ultimate grounds for rightful authority: this required consent, authorization, and the erection of union, which constituted the state as an objectively identifiable and specific entity, itself enabling man's definitive exit from the savagery of his natural condition, and into civilization. By contrast, Hume sought to build his

---

160. On Hume's relationship to Whig politics see Duncan Forbes, *Hume's Philosophical Politics* (Cambridge: Cambridge University Press, 1975), chap. 5.

161. Hobbes, *Behemoth*, 128.

162. Certainly imagination is irreducibly important in Hobbes's account, as the Leviathan is in effect an imagined entity, and is only able to sustain its power over men—providing their protection in exchange for their obedience—if enough individuals continue to believe in its right to rule. This point is made in Robin Douglass, "The Body Politic 'Is a Fictitious Body': Hobbes on Imagination and Fiction," *Hobbes Studies* 27, no. 2 (2014), 126–47, and also Stanton, "Hobbes and Schmitt," 165–66. Yet, for Hobbes, the role of imagination is limited to the sociological conditions of success for political structures, and is not extended to apply to the true underlying nature of political society and the constitution of sovereignty itself, which is revealed by a science independent of what people may happen to (correctly or mistakenly) think at any given point. As we shall see in chapter 3, this marks a crucial distinction from Hume, even if the role of imagination in Hobbes at times brings him closer to Hume than he would seem were this ignored.

163. Hobbes, *Leviathan*, vol. 2, 520–22.

political theory of organized coercive power, and the behavior it could rightfully extract from those subjected to it, solely on the foundation of opinion. As we shall see in chapter 3, this required the deployment of a theory of the state without sovereignty, and thus a major departure from Hobbes.

Before that case is presented, however, chapter 2 seeks to recover an important aspect of the sociability debate that has been left relatively marginalized in recent studies: the role of history, and the place of the family, in explaining the emergence of large and lasting human society as put forward first by Hobbes, and then by his eighteenth-century British critics. Appreciation of these neglected themes will allow us to gain a better grip in trying to understand eighteenth-century political thought, Hume's contribution to that wider milieu, and the way in which an alternative counter-Hobbesian conception of political theory could be more fully opened up and exploited, first by Hume, and then by Smith.

CHAPTER TWO

History and the Family

IN CHAPTER 1 we saw how Hume used the innovation of sympathy to recast the question of sociability. Rather than being primarily a problem about pride, it became one about utility. As Hume put it in his discussion of property in the *Treatise*, "The possession of all external goods is changeable and uncertain; which is one of the most considerable impediments to the establishment of society, and is the reason why, by universal agreement, express or tacit, men restrain themselves by what we now call the rules of justice and equity."[1] Yet getting to the point where the analysis of property and its regulation was possible had first necessitated Hume's making substantial changes to underlying conceptions of human psychology as compared with Hobbes's picture.

According to Hobbes, human psychology was fundamentally characterized by the balancing of appetites and aversions: all motivation was explainable in terms of the seeking of private pleasure and the avoidance of private pain. This "whole summe of Desires, Aversions, Hopes and Fears, continued till the thing be either done, or thought impossible, is what we call DELIBERATION." The last act of deliberation "immediately adhering to the action, or to the omission thereof, is that wee call the WILL; the Act, (not the faculty,) of *Willing*."[2] Central to Hobbes's account was that people were motivated precisely by *private* appetites and aversions. Human beings were sentimentally closed off from each other: although positional glory seeking required the imputed estimation of peers, individuals did not share in each other's affections beyond competing for honor and esteem. In the *Elements of Law*, Hobbes claimed that there "can be no greater argument to a man of his own power, than to find himself able, not only to accomplish his own desires, but also to assist other men in theirs,"

---

1. David Hume, *The Clarendon Edition of the Works of David Hume: A Treatise of Human Nature*, ed. D. F. Norton and M. J. Norton (Oxford, Oxford University Press, 2007), T.3.2.3.6, SBN 505.

2. Thomas Hobbes, *The Clarendon Edition of the Works of Thomas Hobbes: Leviathan*, ed. N. Malcolm (Oxford: Oxford University Press, 2012), vol. 2, 90.

and from this phenomenon "is that conception wherein consisteth charity."[3] In other words, men helped others only for the pleasure it brought by reminding them of their own power, with power itself "a general inclination of all mankind, a perpetuall and restless desire . . . that ceaseth onely in Death."[4] Similarly, Hobbes opened the possibility of a capacity for sharing in the sentiments of others only to strip it of any meaningful other-regarding content. Thus was his infamous definition of pity: "*Griefe*, for the Calamity of another is PITTY; and ariseth from the imagination that the like calamity may befall himselfe; and therefore is called also COMPASSION, and in the phrase of this present time a FELLOW FEELING: And therefore for Calamity arriving from great wickedness, the best men have the least Pitty; and for the same Calamity, those have least Pitty, that think themselves least obnoxious to the same."[5] Pity was a secretly self-referential passion which operated by imagining ourselves as subject to the fates we witnessed others suffering. This was necessarily so in Hobbes's psychology: only private pain or pleasure could figure in one's appetites or aversions, forming part of a deliberation whose last act was the will. Pity *had* to be explained in terms of imaginative processes relating the experiences of others to private sentiment: to avoid being motivationally inert, fellow feeling and compassion must ultimately relate to private interest—meaning they were not properly examples of other-regarding sentiment after all. Hobbes's reductionist accounts of charity and pity—of what would otherwise be considered archetypal examples of doing or feeling good to others out of non-self-referential motives—went hand in glove with his position on human sociability. Precisely because human beings were sentimentally closed off and driven by private appetites and aversions, once one jettisoned Aristotelian notions of an appetite or instinct for company, the only natural materials left from which to construct society were honor and advantage.

Here Mandeville essentially followed Hobbes, refusing to give any role to fellow feeling in explaining human sociability. He certainly agreed that men were irreducibly self-regarding: "be we Savages or Politicians, it is impossible that Man, mere fallen Man, should act with any other View but to please himself while he has the Use of his Organs, and the greatest Extravagancy either of Love or Despair can have no other Centre."[6] Unlike Hobbes, however, Mandeville did not offer a formal reduction of pity to secretly self-referential psychological processes (although such a position is at least implied by his frequent insistence on the necessarily egoistic nature of human psychology). In a striking example, Mandeville in fact claimed that if one saw a baby fall into a fire this would be

3. Thomas Hobbes, *The Elements of Law, Natural and Politic*, ed. F. Tönnies and M. M. Goldsmith (London: Frank Cass, 1969), 44.
4. Hobbes, *Leviathan*, vol. 2, 150.
5. Ibid., 90; cf. Hobbes, *Elements of Law*, 40.
6. Bernard Mandeville, *The Fable of the Bees, Volume 1*, ed. F. B. Kaye (Indianapolis: Liberty Fund, 1988), 348.

psychologically painful, even if one was not personally in like danger, and accordingly one would typically act to save the infant from the flames.[7] But rather than exploring the possibility that sharing in each other's sentiments could ameliorate the competitive nature of positional esteem seeking, Mandeville concentrated on exposing pity as a secretly vicious moral motivation. Insofar as one saved the baby from the fire to avoid the pain one would feel in watching it perish, one did not—contrary to appearances and common opinion—act virtuously, but indulged a private passion, and thus forfeited any claim to true moral action.[8] "There would be no need of Virtue or Self-Denial to be moved by such a Scene; and not only a Man of Humanity, of good Morals and Commiseration, but likewise an Highwayman, an House-Breaker, or a Murderer could feel Anxieties on such an Occasion."[9] Pity was not a source of virtue, but vice, insofar as it led to the indulgence of passion instead of self-denial.[10]

Hume was by no means the first to resist Hobbes's and Mandeville's reductive accounts of human psychology, which both precluded the capacity to form large and lasting society from materials other than honor and advantage, and, in Mandeville's case, was presented as entailing that all moral action was inherently fraudulent owing to the ultimately self-interested nature of all human motivation. Most famously, Bishop Joseph Butler offered an extended refutation

---

7. Hobbes, it should be noted, need not have disagreed: in his account one could *imagine* the suffering one would feel if one were to fall into flames, and be motivated to save the baby to relieve the discomfort one would feel. Indeed, this was the explanation Hobbes supposedly gave John Aubrey regarding why he was moved to give alms to a beggar on the streets of London: John Aubrey, *Brief Lives, Chiefly of Contemporaries, Set Down by John Aubrey between the Years 1669 and 1696* (Oxford: Clarendon, 1898), 352.

8. Mandeville, *Bees, Volume 1*, 254–60. For a discussion of Mandeville's conception of pity and his failure to consider where this capacity came from, or what it might enable, see Christian Maurer, "Self-Love in Early Eighteenth Century British Moral Philosophy: Shaftesbury, Mandeville, Hutcheson, Butler and Campbell" (unpublished PhD thesis, Université de Neuchâtel, 2009), 150. Maurer also provides a brief overview of theories of pity in the seventeenth and eighteenth centuries in "Facing the Misery of Others: Pity, Pleasure and Tragedy in Scottish Enlightenment Moral Philosophy," in *The Poetic Enlightenment: Poetry and Human Science 1650–1820*, ed. T. Jones and R. Boyson (London: Pickering and Chatto, 2013), 75–87.

9. Mandeville, *Bees, Volume 1*, 256.

10. Mandeville offered a similar treatment of love in the first volume of the *Fable*. Although this "consists in a Liking and Well-wishing to the Person beloved," even going so far as to say that "his Interest we make on all Accounts our own, even to our Prejudice, and receive an inward Satisfaction for sympathizing with him in his sorrows, as well as Joys," this was nonetheless rooted in self-love, which "makes us believe, that the Sufferings we feel must alleviate and lessen those of our Friend." As with pity, Mandeville did not explore the capacity for love as a resource for explaining sociability, but focused on the morally vicious implications arising from a foundation in self-love: "this fond Reflexion is soothing our Pain, a secret Pleasure arises from our grieving for the Person we love," thus disabling love as a candidate category for genuine virtue which required self-denial: Mandeville, *Bees, Volume 1*, 142.

of Hobbes's psychological egoism, clearing the way for an account of morals that resisted the skeptical debunking implications of Hobbesian psychology.[11] Although Butler did not prioritize the capacity for fellow feeling in his affirmation of human natural sociability—choosing instead to adopt Shaftesbury's idea of an ordered teleology, but now applied solely to the level of individuals and not entire systems—he nonetheless affirmed, against Hobbes and Mandeville, that such a capacity existed and constituted a distinct "cement" to society.[12] Francis Hutcheson adopted the other main aspect of Shaftesbury's anti-Hobbesian edifice, the appreciation of ordered harmony on a model of aesthetic approval, positing the possession of a distinct "moral sense" that both detected purely disinterested actions performed by others, and also motivated such action in individual agents. The moral sense allowed Hutcheson to resist Mandeville's insistence that all action was necessarily selfish, and opened the possibility for genuine moral virtue.[13] Taking his lead from Butler, Hutcheson went on to posit a further "publick sense," which allowed men to share each other's feelings, and told against Hobbes's and Mandeville's claim that human beings were sentimentally isolated positional competitors.[14] In 1733, just six years before Hume published the *Treatise*, the now largely forgotten Scottish philosopher and theologian Archibald Campbell developed a sophisticated version of Hobbes's pity, which Campbell denoted "sympathy" and deployed *against* Hobbes, in order to claim that humans were both naturally sociable and capable of genuine moral action.[15]

Yet even if Hobbes's and Mandeville's psychological accounts had already been subjected to serious attack by the time Hume published the *Treatise*, it remains the case that Hume was the first writer to combine the capacity for sharing the feelings of others with an account that got adequately to grips with explaining how human beings came to form, and then sustain, large and lasting society. This is in large part because lurking alongside, and intertwined with, these issues of psychology lay another set of difficult conceptual problems. These related to humanity's status as a creature engaging in group living *before* achieving large and lasting society, most especially the prepolitical existence of

---

11. Joseph Butler, *Butler's Fifteen Sermons*, ed. T. A. Roberts (London: SPCK, 1970); see especially "Preface" and Sermons 1–3, and pp. 99–110.

12. Butler, *Fifteen Sermons*, 23.

13. Francis Hutcheson, *An Inquiry into the Original of Our Ideas of Beauty and Virtue*, ed. W. Leidhold (Indianapolis: Liberty Fund, 2004), 85–147.

14. Francis Hutcheson, *An Essay on the Nature and Conduct of the Passions and Affections, with Illustrations on the Moral Sense*, ed. A. Garret (Indianapolis: Liberty Fund, 2002), 23.

15. Archibald Campbell, *An Enquiry into the Original of Moral Virtue; wherein It Is Shewn, (against the Author of the "Fable of the Bees," &c.) that Virtue Is Founded in the Nature of Things, Is Unalterable, and Eternal, and the Great Means of Private and Publick Happiness. With Some Reflections on a Late Book, Intitled, "An Enquiry into the Original of Our Ideas of Beauty and Virtue"* (Edinburgh, 1733), 30–48.

the primitive family in the distant historical past. For different kinds of theorist this raised different problems. In the case of those denying natural sociability, the fact that primitive humans must have lived in family groupings in order to survive generated an obvious problem: if humans naturally lived in families, how could they be said to be naturally unsociable? For those affirming natural sociability, the existence of the prepolitical family initially appeared a welcome piece of evidence—but immediately raised the question of why mankind had not stayed content in primitive small-scale arrangements. What explained the development to *large and lasting* society—and ultimately modern advanced civilization—if not the pursuit of nonnatural goods such as utilitarian comforts and positional status, the very materials Hobbes said were the only source of all associations of significant size?

This chapter retraces the debate over the nature and role of history and the family in explaining human sociability from Hobbes to Hume, building on the account given in chapter 1. What we shall see is that Hume again made a revolutionary intervention, in particular by seeing that one must abandon the idea of a state of nature as anything other than a thought experiment for revealing the conventional nature of justice, and thus the utility-oriented nature of sociability for large and lasting conditions. We must begin again with Hobbes, however, for it was he who set the early parameters of the debate. I here only outline the fundamentals of my interpretation, which I have argued for in more detail elsewhere.[16] Readers should refer to that for the fuller case with regard to Hobbes; my aim in the present chapter is to bring out the post-Hobbesian trajectory of debate. But one thing must be stressed at the outset. It is now standard to read Hobbes as a theorist of contract, indeed as the first major social contract theorist, initiating a tradition that some see as running all the way to Rawls, typically via Locke and Rousseau.[17] My interpretation is different in its emphasis. I

16. Paul Sagar, "Of Mushrooms and Method: History and the Family in Hobbes's Science of Politics," *European Journal of Political Theory* 14 (2015), 98–117.

17. Deborah Baumgold in particular has argued that Hobbes's political theory is an attempt to combine the absolutist commitments of Jean Bodin with the contract approach of Hugo Grotius, inaugurating a contractualist tradition in political thought that runs all the way to Rawls: see especially Deborah Baumgold, "Pacifying Politics: Resistance, Violence, and Accountability in Seventeenth-Century Contract Theory," *Political Theory* 21 (1993), 6–27; "When Hobbes Needed History," in *Hobbes and History*, ed. G.A.J. Rogers and T. Sorell (London and New York: Routledge, 2000), 25–43; "Hobbes and Locke's Contract Theories: Political not Metaphysical," *Critical Review of International Social and Political Theory* 8 (2005), 289–308; "Hobbesian Absolutism and the Paradox of Modern Contractarianism," *European Journal of Political Theory* 8 (2009), 207–28. Works as diverse as the following have all endorsed in some form the claim that Hobbes is a contract theorist: Jean Hampton, *Hobbes and the Social Contract Tradition* (Cambridge: Cambridge University Press, 1986); David Gauthier, *The Logic of "Leviathan": The Moral and Political Theory of Thomas Hobbes* (Oxford: Clarendon, 1969); Ross Harrison, *Hobbes, Locke and Confusion's Masterpiece: An Examination of Seventeenth Century Political Philosophy* (Cambridge: Cambridge University Press, 2003); Richard Tuck, *Hobbes* (Oxford: Oxford University Press,

suggest that Hobbes may be illuminatingly interpreted by paying less attention to what have been taken to be the contractualist elements of his political theory, focusing instead on the ways he thinks that commonwealths actually come into being as a matter of real history—and where contract turns out *not* to be the mechanism of generation.[18] This reading is both motivated and bolstered by the fact that some of Hobbes's most interesting philosophical respondents in the next century read him in this way, and engaged with Hobbes not primarily on issues of contract, but regarding the role of history and the family in explaining the capacity for sociability, and the attendant possibilities for normative assessments of political arrangements that thereby arose. What this chapter therefore attempts is an alternative history of political thought that moves away from an emphasis on contract, and toward the debates that some of the most interesting eighteenth-century British theorists were actually having.

Doing so, furthermore, has particular implications for our appreciation of Hume as a political thinker. One of Hume's leading contributions to political theory is typically taken to be his refutation of contract theory, as found especially in the essay "Of the Original Contract," and book 3 of the *Treatise*.[19] But this stands as an equivocal achievement on the traditional terms of analysis. To those who consider contract theory a naïve or misguided phase of the development of Western political thought, Hume's contribution risks amounting to simply pointing out the mistaken nature of the approach, but without offering anything in its place. To those who view Hume's attack on a vulgarized Lockean version of contract theory as fundamentally failing to see what Locke himself was attempting to achieve, or who more generally find Hume's sociologically orientated objections as missing the normative purpose of contractualism as a device in philosophical thought, his contribution appears yet more limited. But this ought to change if we come to believe that some of the most insightful theorists after Hobbes were not predominantly interested in

---

1989); Howard Warrender, *The Political Philosophy of Hobbes: His Theory of Obligation* (Oxford: Oxford University Press, 1957); Patrick Riley, *Will and Political Legitimacy: A Critical Exposition of Social Contract Theory in Hobbes, Locke, Rousseau, Kant and Hegel* (Cambridge, MA: Harvard University Press, 1982); Jody S. Kraus, *The Limits of Hobbesian Contractarianism* (Cambridge: Cambridge University Press, 1994); Mark E. Button, *Contract, Culture and Citizenship: Transformative Liberalism from Hobbes to Rawls* (University Park, PA: Pennsylvania State University Press, 2008). There are of course many more.

18. For a not dissimilar reading to that put forward below, see Robin Douglass, "The Body Politic 'Is a Fictitious Body': Hobbes on Imagination and Fiction," *Hobbes Studies* 27, no. 2 (2014), 126–47, although Douglass is less concerned with the question of whether Hobbes is best thought of as a contract thinker than I am.

19. For example, of the two lectures Rawls dedicated to Hume in his student teaching, the first is on the essay "Of the Original Contract," the second is on the theory of justice: John Rawls, *Lectures on the History of Political Philosophy* (Cambridge, MA: Harvard University Press, 2007), 159–87.

contractualist ways of thinking, and it was in reference and response to these thinkers that Hume was shaping his arguments. If so, gaining a proper appreciation of Hume's intervention in the early modern debate over the foundations of political theory will require us to properly reconstruct the terms of the debate that he was actually entering into.

Hobbes's History: Mushrooms, Families, and Conquerors

Throughout his works Hobbes was clear that there were three ways in which "someone can have *Dominion* over the *person* of another."[20] The first was sovereignty "by institution": disparate individuals coming together and out of mutual fear of each other agreeing to institute some overarching power to hold them in awe.[21] Receiving the most detailed and sustained treatment in Hobbes's works, this model has also commanded the attention of the majority of Hobbes's more recent readers. Although Hobbes is clear that individuals only covenant with each other as "natural" individuals, and neither covenant nor contract with their sovereign (properly understood as a representative "artificial" person), it is the vision of individuals of equal power agreeing to enter political society on equal terms that gives primary inspiration to the view that Hobbes is fundamentally a theorist of contract. Yet Hobbes was always clear that there existed another way political power could be erected, which in *Leviathan* he denoted "commonwealth by acquisition."[22] With regard to sovereignty by acquisition, men erected sovereign power not out of fear of each other indiscriminately, but out of fear of the superior force of a specific other who demanded submission. Yet in all other respects sovereignty was the same, whether instituted or acquired. Despite the influence and prominence of Hobbes's account of sovereignty by institution in both his presentation and more recent commentary, if we look carefully we see that Hobbes's underlying position was that all sovereignty was in reality founded in acquisition. The model of sovereignty by institution, by contrast, is a device for elucidating the mechanics of a properly constituted sovereign power, and is emphasized by Hobbes as part of his wider attempt to reconcile people to the inevitability of political subjugation. Yet, if acquisition is indeed how sovereignty comes about in practice, then the impetus for seeing Hobbes as primarily a theorist of contract—at least when understood as an idealized agreement between individuals of equal power—is weakened, in favor of examining his historical account. In turn, we can see his work and its legacy in a light that has thus far tended not to be cast upon it, but which is nonetheless illuminating.

20. Thomas Hobbes, *On the Citizen*, ed. R. Tuck and M. Silverthorne (Cambridge: Cambridge University Press, 1998), 102.

21. Hobbes, *Leviathan*, vol. 2, 262; cf. *On the Citizen*, 74.

22. Hobbes, *Leviathan*, vol. 2, 308. In *De Cive* these were labeled as "*natural commonwealths*," as oppose to designed, "political" ones: *On the Citizen*, 74.

In *De Cive* Hobbes revealingly insisted that his procedure would be "To return once again to the natural state and to look at men as if they had just emerged from the earth like mushrooms and grown up without any obligation to each other."[23] This was no arbitrary stipulation or minor expository device, nor an idle allusion to the Lucretian postulate that humanity sprang from the earth fully formed, offered in lieu of a working explanation of human primordial origins. Rather, it was a product of Hobbes's peculiar insistence that politics be studied as a science of a priori demonstration. History for Hobbes was "the register of knowledge of fact," and specifically "the register we keep in books."[24] But as it was merely the register of facts of experience, history could not provide infallible proofs, could be no source of demonstration, which Hobbes took a proper science of politics to be in the business of providing. Men had to be considered as mushrooms because the rights and obligations they owed to each other, and the possibilities for associating they were thereby capable of, had to be wholly understandable, and fully accounted for, in a purely analytical framework without appeal to contingent historical or genetic factors known only by experience. Although Hobbes had a fully worked-out theory of how humans had in actual historical practice arrived in the condition of political society, this history had to be *supplementary* to scientific demonstration of both why people needed to live in commonwealths to escape their natural condition, and what forms such an artificial association must take.

For Hobbes, human beings without collective power holding them in awe were ipso facto in their "natural condition": it did not matter whether people had always lived in a primitive prepolitical state, having never experienced government, of if they had lost established political society owing to civil war, putting them into a postpolitical state. How humans arrived in such a condition was irrelevant to the science of demonstrating what must be done for them to exit it. Similarly, a proper science based on deduction must take as given human psychology: there was no place in Hobbes's scheme for a *developmental* account of human cognitive capacities that might make the conditions and methods for achieving peace contingent upon stages of mental change, as Mandeville and Rousseau would later posit. Hobbes's a priori method excluded any possibility of a developmental—even less, a *conjectural* developmental—account of how human beings came to learn to live in society. Man was properly considered, in scientific terms, as like a mushroom having popped into existence.

Nonetheless, Hobbes readily admitted that such human mushrooms both came into existence and were sustained in their earliest years in a very different manner to their fungal analogues. Human beings were everywhere born into, and raised in, families. If children were not cared for and nurtured throughout

23. Ibid., 102.
24. Hobbes, *Elements of Law*, 25.

their long human infancy outside political society, humanity would not have survived long enough to exit its *natural* condition. Yet if human beings lived in families, forming bonds of natural affection and reaping utilitarian benefits from such associations, how could they properly be said to be animals not born fit for society?

Hobbes's solution was to render the family an expressly political institution, based on the consent children gave to ruling patriarchs, who in return provided protection.[25] Parental dominion "is not so derived from the Generation, as if therefore the Parent had Dominion over his Child because he begat him; but from the Childs Consent, either expresse or by other sufficient signs declared."[26] As always, for Hobbes, the consent of the ruled was the ultimate foundation of political authority rendered in exchange of reciprocal condition of obedience. Yet Hobbes's gambit of making the family an expressly political institution generated a host of internal problems for his theory. These relate especially to how children could properly be said to consent to the rule of their parents (even on Hobbes's extremely expansive understanding of that term), and more fundamentally regarding Hobbes's insistence that all properly political power was an instance of union, not mere concord, and provided protection for members who in turn owed obedience.[27] Hobbes was always clear that man's natural condition contained families, tribes, and confederacies: the supposition of natural sociability was one that pertained to *large and lasting* society, not to the existence of any human grouping whatsoever. The problem was that if the family were indeed to be considered an instance of union, and not mere concord (as would seem to be implied by Hobbes's insistence that the family was a political grouping, although he never says this explicitly), then the sovereign patriarch must also provide security to subjects, who thereby consented to be ruled *as* subjects. Yet if exposed to the ravages of aggressor families and tribes in the state of nature, the family fell short of fulfilling this criterion. Either the family was union without protection, thus falling short of the conditions of sovereignty, and hence was not really a properly political association, or it was merely concord—i.e., a defensive formation based on natural appetites for preservation and mutual affection—that fell short of union, and hence of sovereignty proper. Such problems were endemic to Hobbes's position.[28]

---

25. For a discussion of this, and a useful overview of Hobbes's conception of the nature and role of the family both with and without sovereign power, see Richard Allen Chapman, "Leviathan Writ Small: Thomas Hobbes on the Family," *American Political Science Review* 69 (1975), 76–90. See also Philip Abbott, "The Three Families of Thomas Hobbes," *Review of Politics* 43 (1981), 242–58.

26. Hobbes, *Leviathan*, vol. 2, 308.

27. See Sagar, "Of Mushrooms and Method," 101–2, for details.

28. As Kinch Hoekstra observes, "Hobbes does not take a consistent position on this issue: sometimes he talks of families in the natural condition, sometimes he says that where there is familial authority there is no natural condition, and sometimes he says that a

Lurking alongside the question of the family is another complicated set of issues regarding how Hobbes conceived of the state of nature. It is clear that Hobbes thought that humanity's natural condition was a real historical fact that had obtained in (for example) primitive Europe, and still obtained in seventeenth-century North America, where "the savage people in many places" were said to live "with no government at all" excepting "the government of small Families, the concord whereof dependeth on natural lust" (an instance, it is worth noting, of Hobbes revealing the inconsistencies between his accounts of family and of political government).[29] In the European case, Hobbes possessed a clear enough historical story of how the natural condition had been transcended and modern large and lasting society had emerged. When discussing the origins and functions of heraldry in *Leviathan*, he stated that "Germany, being anciently, as all other countries in their beginnings, divided amongst an infinite number of little lords, or masters of families, that continually had wars one with another," nonetheless eventually made the transition through cycles of conquest to modern kingship, "when many such families, joined together, made a greater monarchy."[30] In *A Dialogue between a Philosopher and a Student of the Common Law*, Hobbes claimed that "great monarchies have proceeded from small families" following war, "wherein the victor not only enlarged his territory, but also the number and riches of his subjects." In this "manner, *which is by war, grew up all the great kingdoms of the world*, viz. the Egyptian, Assyrian, Persian, and Macedonian monarchy, and so did the great kingdoms of England, France and Spain."[31] Similarly, Hobbes claimed in *Behemoth* that "the Greeks had for a while their petty kings, and then by sedition came to be petty commonwealths; and then growing to be greater commonwealths, by sedition again

---

family is a commonwealth if and only if it is sufficiently large": Kinch Hoekstra, "Hobbes on the Natural Condition of Mankind," in *The Cambridge Companion to Hobbes's "Leviathan,"* ed. P. Springborg (Cambridge: Cambridge University Press, 2007), 109–27, 118.

29. Hobbes, *Leviathan*, vol. 2, 194. For a discussion of how Hobbes's views of "savage" peoples as outside of sovereign power, and thus exempt from the international law of nations, influenced subsequent European colonial attitudes; see Pat Moloney, "Hobbes, Savagery and International Anarchy," *American Political Science Review* 105 (2011), 189–204; on Hobbes's attitudes to slavery as conditioned by contemporary experiences of Barbary piracy and the intellectual inheritance of a Roman legal tradition, see Deborah Baumgold, "Slavery Discourse before the Restoration: The Barbary Coast, Justinian's *Digest*, and Hobbes's Political Theory," *History of European Ideas* 36 (2010), 412–18.

30. Hobbes, *Leviathan*, vol. 2, 144.

31. Thomas Hobbes, *The Clarendon Edition of the Works of Thomas Hobbes: A Dialogue between a Philosopher and a Student of the Common Laws of England*, ed. A. Cromartie (Oxford: Oxford University Press, 2005), 138. See also R. P. Kraynak, "Hobbes on Barbarism and Civilization," *Journal of Politics* 45 (1983), 92, which also provides a valuable summary of Hobbes's view of the progress of historical commonwealths from antiquity to the present.

became monarchies."[32] This demonstrates that Hobbes believed humanity to have originally existed in a prepolitical state of nature, the exit from which was achieved by a historical process of conquest driven by the most successful warring patriarchal families. More recently, England had been in the state of nature when Charles I lost the ability to protect his subjects owing to the actions of the parliamentary rebels. There can be no doubt that Hobbes believed humans had frequently lived in the state of nature, even if such a condition "was never generally so, over the world," and were dangerously apt to fall back into it owing to the ravages of civil war.

Because Hobbes's deductive method postulated that man without sovereign power was ipso facto in the state of nature, regardless of whether this was a *pre-* or *post*political state of affairs, his most famous stylizations of man's natural condition—in *Leviathan*, chapter 13, and *Elements*, chapter 14—are constructed as idealized descriptions designed to cover both sorts of cases simultaneously. They are not, that is, descriptions of specific times or places, or any actual condition that simultaneously exhibited all the features Hobbes lists as characteristic of the state of nature in, e.g., *Leviathan*, chapter 13: lack of industry, culture, navigation, trade, "commodious Building," cartography, measuring of the passing of time, art, letters, or "society" *tout court*.[33] Instead, Hobbes's descriptions of the state of nature outline the general contours of humanity's situation absent sovereign power, even if no actual time and place has ever exactly corresponded to the descriptions he provides. This, however, is unimportant from Hobbes's perspective, because insofar as there existed an absence of sovereign power there would be "a continuall feare, and danger of violent death."[34] The state of nature would obtain, and enough of the characteristics Hobbes elucidated as part of the natural condition of mankind would feature, thus ensuring that humanity's condition was one of misery, with the necessary solution being the erection of common overawing power.

But how did such overawing power actually come into being? Did Hobbes believe that human beings exited their natural condition via "institution," or via "acquisition"? Despite its apparently paradigmatic status regarding how to form a commonwealth in his theory, Hobbes's account of sovereignty by institution is best thought of not as a literal proposition for how commonwealths ever have, or ever could, come into existence, but as an irenic device for reconciling people to the necessary conditions of political authority. There are several cumulatively compelling reasons for adopting this view. Firstly, sovereignty by institution is deeply implausible if understood as a proposition

---

32. Thomas Hobbes, *The Clarendon Edition of the Works of Thomas Hobbes: Behemoth*, ed. P. Seaward (Oxford: Oxford University Press, 2010), 198.
33. Hobbes, *Leviathan*, vol. 2, 192.
34. Ibid.

about how humans in practice might erect common power. If individuals are as mutually suspicious and disposed to the seeking of positional superiority as Hobbes suggests, it is difficult to see how they will come to trust others sufficiently to assemble in one place long enough to make agreements, and why they would ever be content, or sufficiently trusting, to invest one individual—even when understood as a representative of their own wills, itself a complex idea it took Hobbes three substantial works of political philosophy to adequately elucidate—with unlimited power and superiority. More fundamentally, in order for the natural person (or persons) chosen to bear the artificial person of sovereignty to in fact truly be sovereign, he (or she, or they) must immediately exercise overwhelming coercive force over all others, so as to be able to offer the protection that is a necessary condition of sovereign power. How could any such public force be suddenly and immediately brought into existence, and brought to bear with sufficient efficacy to terrorize all potential defectors into conformity? It will be no solution to say that in the founding moment all sovereigns are democratic. Not only must we note that Hobbes appears to abandon, or at least massively downplay, this claim in *Leviathan* compared with his earlier works,[35] we must also ask: what would guarantee that members of the new democratic sovereign—those, for example, who are in the minority after a majority vote (which Hobbes in *De Cive* stipulates as the necessary basis of democratic decision making)[36]—would not immediately defect from their previous agreement and attack others, exposing the nonexistence of the public sword required to keep them in awe, punishing them for their covenant breaking? And if the above objections apply only to a prepolitical state of nature, the situation is no better with a postpolitical one. In situations of civil war, new sovereigns are erected not by institution amongst equal parties mutually afraid of each other, but by the victory of the strongest, whom losing parties submit to in order to avoid death. The end of civil war, on any plausible view of human conflict, is sovereignty by acquisition, not institution.

Furthermore, and as we have seen, Hobbes gives clear indication that he thinks that historically all commonwealths emerged from family-based arrangements and conquest. As well as the quotations supplied above, there is also Hobbes's suggestion that prior to his own science of politics all commonwealths have had their foundations laid as though "on the sand," something which his "Rules" for the "skill of making, and maintaining Common-wealths" are intended to correct. Given the complexity of sovereignty by institution, it

---

35. On whether the abandonment of a necessary founding democratic moment in sovereignty by institution in *Leviathan* is indeed only apparent (with the earlier account of *Elements* and *De Cive* still present, but now suppressed in the presentation), see Arash Abizadeh, "Sovereign Jurisdiction, Territorial Rights, and Membership in Hobbes," in *The Oxford Handbook of Hobbes*, ed. K. Hoekstra and A. P. Martinich (Oxford: Oxford University Press, 2016), 413–15.

36. Hobbes, *On the Citizen*, 94.

is doubtful Hobbes considered anybody—for want of "leisure ... the curiosity, or the method"—had been capable of achieving it prior to his political works being published.[37] When coupled with the implausibility of understanding sovereignty by institution as something that could ever actually have obtained in practice, this strongly suggests that of the two ways in which a commonwealth may be formed, sovereignty by acquisition is how Hobbes believes it occurs in actuality, with sovereignty by institution an analytic device used to examine the internal mechanisms of political authority, illustrating the manner in which it is necessarily founded upon the consent of the ruled.[38]

This raises the question of why Hobbes emphasizes sovereignty by institution, according it greater space for discussion in his works than sovereignty by acquisition. Several complementary answers are forthcoming. First, Hobbes is consistently clear that the *rights* of sovereigns do not change according to genesis: "the Rights, and Consequences of Soveraignty, are the same in both."[39] All sovereignty is founded upon consent and out of fear, be it fear of each other indiscriminately or of a specific other, at the point of a sword or in the absence of imminent mortal danger.[40] By first examining in detail the mechanism of sovereignty by institution, Hobbes can demonstrate that sovereignty by acquisition has the exact same basis in fear and consent. Furthermore, not only does sovereignty by institution usefully illustrate the workings of sovereignty *tout court*, it can help reconcile people to what they would otherwise be disposed to claim was compromised or illegitimate—i.e., giving consent at the point of a conqueror's sword—by showing them that their objections regarding the influence of fear are confused. By emphasizing the legitimate basis of all sovereignty via the model of institution, Hobbes presents the most pleasing face of his theory, encouraging readers to accept what they might otherwise not be well disposed to, gutting the language of consent and covenant of its previous association with democratic or monarchomach theory, and putting it to the service of his unique version of sovereign absolutism.[41] Furthermore, in sovereignty by institution it is made clear that no covenant takes place between subjects and the sovereign—something Hobbes was at pains to insist upon—which is much less obvious in the case of sovereignty by acquisition, and may also have encouraged Hobbes to emphasize the former over the latter.

None of which need marginalize the conceptual importance of institution in Hobbes's account: one major conclusion of Hobbes's thought experiment is that by imagining sovereign power coming into being "as if every man should say to every man" that he will suspend immediate exercise of the right of nature

37. Hobbes, *Leviathan*, vol. 2, 322.
38. Ibid., 312.
39. Ibid., 306.
40. Hobbes, *On the Citizen*, 74.
41. Quentin Skinner, *Hobbes and Republican Liberty* (Cambridge: Cambridge University Press, 2008), chap. 6.

by erecting common power, this procedure simultaneously vindicates the *authoritative* character of that power—an authority, Hobbes's expansive understanding of consent is designed to show, equally conferred upon sovereigns by acquisition.[42] Hobbes's central aim of demonstrating that all legitimate political power must take the form of his version of sovereign absolutism is advanced by presenting the reader with an extended examination of the mechanics of sovereignty in the model of institution, with the conclusion generated there applicable to instantiations of political power in the real world—with the correlate obligation that humans submit to established political power, wherever they find it and however it actually arose, recognizing it as founded ultimately in their own consent. As Kinch Hoekstra has demonstrated, Hobbes's philosophy is fundamentally conditioned by the guiding aim not of stating what he necessarily thinks is *true*, but of what he thinks will best promote *peace*, should the two diverge.[43] Insofar as this was better served by concentrating on sovereignty by institution over acquisition, this was what Hobbes supplied.

Hobbes possessed a functioning and coherent account of how men not born fit for society had nonetheless come historically to form commonwealths and achieve large and lasting society: sovereignty by acquisition, initially by generation and later by conquest. Yet being historical (and in part necessarily conjectural) this account could form no part of Hobbes's science of politics, and thus was not appealed to in establishing the basis of his theory of sovereign authority. The "condition of meer Nature" was to be understood as a real historical proposition (in both pre- and postpolitical senses), despite being analyzed predominantly in ideal terms, whilst sovereignty by institution was an illustrative, irenic device for explaining the grounds of legitimate political authority. Yet subsequent critics, who rejected both Hobbes's conception of natural unsociability and the theory of sovereign absolutism that supervened upon it, were not committed to Hobbes's rigid understanding of political theory as a science founded on demonstration. This freed them to explore ways in which history could be used to draw alternative conclusions. Yet because, from this perspective, the fundamental item to be contested was not contract, but sociability, this was the matter around which the subsequent debate was oriented, at least amongst those of Hobbes's eighteenth-century British successors who responded to his political vision by tackling his theory of human nature. All of which may make what follows in this chapter seem irrelevant if one remains wedded to a more orthodox view of the history of early modern political thought as fundamentally shaped by theories of contract, running from Hobbes through Locke and Rousseau especially. But as following

42. Hobbes, *Leviathan*, vol. 2, 260.
43. See especially Kinch Hoekstra, "The End of Philosophy (the Case of Hobbes)," *Proceedings of the Aristotelian Society* 106 (2006), 25–62; "Hobbes and the Foole," *Political Theory* 25 (1997), 620–54.

chapters will show, Locke may also be usefully understood in terms other than that privileging the role of contract, whilst Rousseau is a very special case, who can only be properly understood by putting him into close dialogue with Hobbes over the question of human sociability, which in turn reshapes our view of what is actually being argued in his *The Social Contract*. Before getting to such points, however, we must first appreciate the debate that Hobbes's British successors down to Hume were having.

Confronting Hobbes's Challenge: Shaftesbury, Mandeville, and Hutcheson

As we saw in chapter 1, Shaftesbury's central strategy for rejecting Hobbes's vision of man as not born fit for society was the construction of an ordered teleology that entailed human natural sociability, and thereby reversed Hobbes's problematic. Yet Shaftesbury was agitated by Hobbes's specific arguments for natural unsociability, and throughout the *Characteristicks* repeatedly attempted to discredit Hobbes's position.[44]

According to Shaftesbury, despite acting in the "Spirit of Massacre," Hobbes communicated his ideas to others, thus revealing putative truths that would be better kept quiet if humans really were as unsociably competitive as he claimed. Accordingly, natural unsociability in Hobbes's hands was better thought of as a theoretical postulate for refuting inadequate Aristotelian accounts rather than a serious proposition in its own right.[45] Similarly, Hobbes's theory of covenanting could only be made coherent by tacitly assuming the prepolitical possibility of promise keeping, making the supposition of a state of natural unsociability incompatible with Hobbes's professed political solution to that natural predicament.[46] Furthermore, whereas Hobbes took histories of faction and cabal as evidence that humans were naturally unsociable owing to the disruptiveness of glory seeking and honor, Shaftesbury countered that when spread in large modern territories, people craved closer association with their peers and rebelled against central power to restore intimate society. Revolt was an outgrowth of the *"herding* Principle . . . so *natural* and strong in men."

---

44. Indeed, and as Lawrence E. Klein has shown, Shaftesbury was deeply concerned by the possibility of a morally compromised pseudosociability founded on the seeking of private esteem in the midst of polite interactions—precisely the concerns Mandeville would later make central to his own polemic against Shaftesbury's positions. In the published works, however, Shaftesbury left these doubts about his own personal moral integrity aside, focusing on the wider system he wished to propound. See Lawrence E. Klein, *Shaftesbury and the Culture of Politeness: Moral Discourse and Cultural Politics in Early Eighteenth-Century England* (Cambridge: Cambridge University Press, 1994), 70–90.

45. Anthony Ashley Cooper, third Earl of Shaftesbury, *Characteristicks of Men, Manners, Opinions, Times*, ed. Douglas Den Uyl (Indianapolis: Liberty Fund, 2001), vol. 1, 56.

46. Shaftesbury, *Characteristicks*, vol. 1, 69.

It was paradoxically from the "Violence of this Passion that so much Disorder arose in the general Society of Mankind."[47] Finally, if human beings always pursued their own self-interest, as Hobbes alleged, this pointed toward natural sociability: dogged and narrow pursuit of self-interest led to isolation and misery, whereas true self-interest was achieved by communing with others and engaging in the "natural affections," themselves equated with real virtue.

Yet such considerations were piecemeal, Shaftesbury circling Hobbes's position rather than engaging it directly. By contrast, in the essay "The Moralists: A Philosophical Rhapsody," Shaftesbury identified the crucial weakness in Hobbes's account with regard to the family, combining this with his rival ontology to offer a sustained rejection of Hobbes's position.[48] In the course of the dialogue that forms the center of "The Moralists," conversation between the two main characters—Philocles and Theocles—is interrupted by an elderly gentleman who seeks to supplement Theocles's positions with "many Particulars from the common Topicks of the *School-men* and *Civilians*." The old gentleman demands that Philocles, who is at this point playing devil's advocate in the style of academic skeptic, admit whether he has "strongly imbib'd that Principle, that *the State of Nature* was a *State of War*."[49] Yet Philocles knows his Hobbesian principles well, and makes serious mischief. The elderly gentleman is forced to admit that prior to entering civil society via "*Compact*," men exist in a state of nature. But "If Man therefore could *endure* to live without

---

47. Ibid., 70. At this point Shaftesbury's account threatens to undermine itself. If a teleological framework was put in place to defeat Hobbes's claim that *large and lasting* societies could not be attained by natural means, Shaftesbury's suggestion that the natural sociability provided by that framework leads to faction and rebellion in large societies was not a particularly effective strategy for resisting Hobbes.

48. "The Moralists: A Philosophical Rhapsody" (in *Characteristicks*, vol. 2, 101–247) is centrally a dialogue between Philocles and Theocles, although the action is in fact reported retrospectively by Philocles to a young gentleman, Palemon, who is seeking philosophical guidance. The essay is effectively Shaftesbury's advice book to young gentlemen seeking to avoid moral corruption. Philocles represents philosophy as unaided by religion, which issues in an academic skepticism questioning everything, frequently threatening to tip over into a thoroughgoing and dangerous Pyrrhonism that issues in the denial of real moral distinctions and an embracing of licentious practical principles. This Pyrrhonian skepticism is frequently equated with, or likened to, Shaftesbury's other chief target in the dialogue: a neo-Epicureanism advancing materialistic atheism and a conspicuously Hobbist moral skepticism. Ultimately, Philocles is aided by Theocles to see the error of academic skepticism in favor of a broadly Stoic-cum-Platonic outlook, and to decisively reject both Pyrrhonism and the specter of atheistic Epicureanism. The moral of the story is not hard to discern. Philosophy taken alone will lead to intellectual error and practical vice, and free-thinking religion provides the necessary corrective. Palemon represents the young Shaftesbury, or a youth following in his footsteps, Theocles voices Shaftesbury's final settled philosophical outlook, whilst Philocles shows the transitional stage, and the errors one might fall into if—like Locke and Hobbes—one is insufficiently attentive to the complementary roles of philosophy and religion.

49. Shaftesbury, "Moralists," 175.

Society; and if it be true that he *actually* liv'd so, when in *the State of Nature*; how can it be said, That he is *by Nature sociable?*" The old man replies that although man may perhaps not have had a *"natural Inclination"* to associate (as the possibility of a presocietal existence appears to entail), he might nonetheless have been moved to associate "by some particular *Circumstances*."50 Yet having extracted this much, Philocles springs the trap:

> His *Nature* then . . . was not so very good, it seems; since having no *natural Affection*, or *friendly Inclination* belonging to him, he was forc'd into a social State, *against his will*: And this, not from any necessity in respect of outward Things, (for you have allow'd him a tolerable Subsistence) but in probability from such Inconveniences as arose chiefly from himself, and his own malignant Temper and Principles. And indeed 'twas no wonder if Creatures who were *naturally* thus unsociable, shou'd be as naturally mischievous and troublesom. If *according to their Nature*, they cou'd live out of Society, with so little Affection for one another's Company, 'tis not likely that upon occasion they wou'd spare one another's Persons. If they were so sullen as not to meet *for Love*, 'tis more than probable they wou'd fight *for Interest*. And thus from your own Reasoning it appears, "That the *State of Nature* must in all likelihood have been little different from *a State of* War."51

Shaftesbury understood Hobbes's proposition thoroughly when he put it into Philocles's mouth: humans do not succeed in forming large and lasting society out of natural appetite for company, or because of the successful pursuit of the utility gains on offer, but "against their will" (i.e., out of fear) in order to secure themselves from the state of war precipitated by their own "malignant temper and principles." Shaftesbury here signaled that Hobbes's argument *succeeded* against its intended target: the Aristotelian version of natural sociability rooted in appetite or instinct for association, as represented by the elderly gentleman drawing on the "school-men and civilians." To refute Hobbes a new approach was required, one that did not appeal to scholastic Aristotelianism but drew on a synthesis of Stoic and Platonic ideas.52

Taking over the argument from the flummoxed elderly gentleman, Theocles claims that a state of war cannot be considered a state at all: "For what if speaking of an Infant just coming into the World, and in the moment of the Birth, I shou'd fansy to call this *a State*; wou'd it be proper?" Philocles

---

50. Ibid., 175.
51. Ibid., 175–76.
52. On scholastic theories of sociality prior to Hobbes, see Annabel Brett, *Changes of State: Nature and the Limits of the City in Early Modern Natural Law* (Princeton, Princeton University Press, 2011). Regarding Shaftesbury's use of Stoic and Platonic philosophy, see Daniel Carey, *Locke, Shaftesbury and Hutcheson: Contesting Diversity in the Enlightenment and Beyond* (Cambridge: Cambridge University Press, 2006), chap. 4.

concedes that it would not: a human creature was only properly considered in a state when it had "attain'd natural Perfection."[53] If Hobbes's putative "natural" condition ever did actually obtain, it was ipso facto a condition of violence and insufficiency. But creatures in such a condition—unable to take part in the ordered teleology that was constitutive of their essential natures—were at best "the *rough Draught* of Man, the *Essay* or *first Effort* of *Nature* . . . unform'd; not in its *natural* state."[54] Theocles pressed the point by implicitly drawing on the ontology of Shaftesbury's *Inquiry*. Creatures in Hobbes's state of nature might look and act like fully fledged humans, but these presocial hominoids could be human only in appearance: isolated and asocial, they did not partake in the nature of human beings as necessarily constituted by integration within the ordered teleology of harmonious systems. They were no more fully men than "the human Egg, or Embrio," but at best a forerunner or precursor to true man: "The Bug which breeds the Butterfly is more properly *a Fly*, tho without Wings, than this imaginary Creature is a *Man*."[55] Shaftesbury thus pressed a dilemma against Hobbes: either "*Man* must have been from Eternity, or not." If man had always been as he is now, there could have been no "*primitive* or *original State*, no *State of Nature*" in which he was naturally unsociable.[56] But if man had not always been as he is now, he must have *developed* into his present condition—meaning that the genealogical ancestors populating a putative state of nature were not true humans, and could not be used to infer anything about true humans' status as sociable creatures.

Shaftesbury's argument could only proceed by granting the supposition that humanity's natural condition was one of amicable sociability guaranteed by the ordered harmony of wider systems, meaning he begged the question against Hobbes. But having taken this position (which, from his own perspective at least, was simply a statement of the conditions of ordered reality), Shaftesbury was able to deploy a straightforward argument for humans' historical progress to large and lasting society as developing out of the basic family unit, conceptualized along intuitively plausible lines of natural affection and the furthering of mutual need. Philocles was right to point out that man's natural indigence and weakness make him "more fitted to be Prey himself, than live by Prey on others," whilst his natural needs meant he required more extensive nutrition and shelter than hardier herding animals.[57] But the way humans had historically secured such needs and conveniences, and something also essential for the raising of highly vulnerable offspring, was via the "Union and strict Society . . . requir'd between the *Sexes*." Nobody could deny, Shaftesbury

---

53. Shaftesbury, "Moralists," 176.
54. Ibid., 176.
55. Ibid., 177.
56. Ibid., 176.
57. Ibid., 179.

pointedly noted, that this "kind of *Society*" between man and woman is "*natural*."[58] Yet admitting this opened the floodgates:

> And can we allow this social Part to Man, and go no further? Is it possible he shou'd pair, and live in Love and Fellowship with his Partner and Offspring, and remain still wholly wild, and speechless, and without those Arts of Storing, Building, and other Œconomy, as natural to him surely as to the Beaver, or to the Ant, or Bee? Where, therefore, shou'd He break off from this Society, if once begun? For that it began thus, as early as Generation, and grew into a Houshold and Œconomy, is plain. Must not this have grown soon into a Tribe? and this Tribe into a Nation? Or tho it remain'd a Tribe only; was not this still a Society for mutual Defense and common Interest? In short, if Generation be natural, if natural Affection and the Care and Nurture of the Offspring be natural, Things standing as they do with Man, and the Creature being of that Form and Constitution he now is; it follows, "That Society must be also natural to him"; And "That out of Society and Community he never did, nor ever can subsist."[59]

This compact statement constituted a decisive refutation of Hobbes from Shaftesbury's perspective. With competitive esteem seeking ruled out via the ontological account of the *Inquiry*, and with the family restored to the status of a natural association based on the twin foundations of affection and the promotion of mutual need, a straightforward historical story could be supplied to account for how humans achieved large and lasting society. In fact, this historical story would be *the same as Hobbes's*: tribal expansion leading to wars of aggression, with nations eventually emerging according to the most successful patriarchal conquests in pre-recorded history. This fact was acknowledged by Shaftesbury, albeit obliquely. He granted that despite its intellectual defects, the avowed merit of Hobbes's system was that it taught people that obedience to established authority was deeply preferable to the condition of anarchy and violence they would otherwise be exposed to: "To speak well of [the state of nature], is to render it inviting, and tempt Men to turn Hermites. Let it, at least, be look'd on as many degrees worse than the worst Government in being. The greater Dread we have of *Anarchy*, the better *Country-men* we shall prove, and value more the *Laws* and *Constitution* under which we live, and by which we are protected from the outrageous Violences of such an unnatural State."[60] The twin benefits of society were that it enabled men to attain their essential moral nature through group interaction rather than "turning Hermites" and withdrawing into pathological isolation, whilst protecting

58. Ibid., 179.
59. Ibid., 179.
60. Ibid., 180.

them from the violence that necessarily accompanied lack of established and authoritative civil power amongst human beings who had acquired a taste for material aggrandizement.

Nonetheless, the foundations of Shaftesbury's account were decisively unlike Hobbes's. Whereas Hobbes had dismissed the possibility that bees and ants could be considered sociable in a manner akin to human beings owing to their not engaging in positional competition and the harmony of their collective ends, Shaftesbury's eliminating of Hobbes's "honour" as a source of disruption by appealing to an undergirding ontological system allowed "advantage" to operate as a natural source of society, enabling large and lasting conditions as a historical outgrowth of basic family relations. Such utility seeking supervened on the more fundamental teleological order that guaranteed human natural sociability. Shaftesbury remained an essentially teleological thinker, therefore, with utility only a supplement for explaining the historical progress of large-scale human associations. In turn, Shaftesbury's main philosophical concern came to the fore: when properly diagnosed, human unsociability related not to a prepolitical condition of violence and scarcity, but to a post- or intrapolitical condition of pathological moral withdrawal that humans were prone to fall into when the large and lasting societies they erected became so materially abundant that people were corrupted by the pleasure they sought from the acquisition of goods and the securing of positional status. Not only was luxury the gateway to moral degradation by creating the pathological condition of insatiability, but humanity's entire history could be interpreted as a story of declension from a simple sociable ideal into a pathological state of luxury-induced atomized corruption.[61] The appropriate political solution to this predicament was not an overawing absolutism founded on fear, but a well-governed classical republic carefully managing its commercial affairs to ensure the interests of citizens were directed toward moral virtue rather than luxury, providing the safe space in which refined members could practice the rigors of rational self-direction and moral cultivation.[62]

All of which was a compounded anathema to Mandeville, as we have already seen. But Mandeville was faced with his own problem in accounting for how human beings not born fit for society nonetheless subsisted in great metropolises of commercial opulence. Mandeville's explanation in the first *Fable* suffered from two obvious weaknesses. First, the account of savage man being "broke" by cunning politicians was deeply implausible as a historical

---

61. Cf. István Hont,"The Early Enlightenment Debate on Commerce and Luxury," in *The Cambridge History of Eighteenth Century Political Thought*, ed. M. Goldie and R. Wokler (Cambridge: Cambridge University Press, 2005), 377–418, 395–99 especially.

62. On the political conclusions of Shaftesbury's moral philosophy, see J. B. Schneewind, *The Invention of Autonomy* (Cambridge: Cambridge University Press, 1998), 295–306; cf. Christopher Brooke, *Philosophic Pride: Stoicism and Political Thought from Lipsius to Rousseau* (Princeton, NJ: Princeton University Press, 2012), 119–20.

conjecture of how complex social relations might have emerged. Secondly, and more fundamentally, the internal coherence of Mandeville's position could not easily be sustained. If humans really were irreducibly selfish and only solicitous of pleasing themselves, how could some individuals in the state of nature acquire the foresight and self-restraint—even for selfish ends—needed to erect the social codes of counterfeit virtue required to redirect other people's pride?[63] Mandeville thus faced two central challenges in writing *The Fable of the Bees, Volume 2*, published in 1728: rectifying the latent implausibility in his 1714 position, and properly meeting the challenge issued by Shaftesbury according to which the family as founded upon natural affection could provide the starting point for a straightforward historical story of humans' steady progress to large and lasting society. Mandeville addressed these problems, however, by setting himself in explicit opposition not to Shaftesbury or Hobbes, but to the account given in William Temple's 1673 "Essay on the Original and Nature of Government."[64] This was because whilst Temple was Mandeville's official target, the former's "Essay" functioned as an ideal stalking-horse for Mandeville's attempt to articulate a vision between the conceptual spaces occupied by Hobbes and Shaftesbury.

Temple was a theorist of authority and opinion: all political power was necessarily founded on the continued indulgence of the ruled, who always outweighed rulers in both numbers and force, and thus the authority of rulers was necessarily a function of, and dependent upon, the opinion of the ruled.[65] This proto-Humean position encouraged Temple to bypass the sociability question altogether, principally by overtly rejecting any theory of contract as the origin of government. According to Temple, the first political contracts would be made by heads of families who already ruled subordinate groupings by authority derived from opinion. From this "may perhaps be deduced a truer original of all governments among men, than from any contracts: though these be given us by the great writers concerning politics and laws."[66] Humans would already be capable of social living, as learned in the family, by

---

63. E. J. Hundert, *The Enlightenment's "Fable": Bernard Mandeville and the Discovery of Society* (Cambridge: Cambridge University Press, 1994), 77.

64. The bulk of Mandeville's discussion takes place in dialogues five and six, and is significantly complicated by his desire to make his speculative conjectural history compatible with sacred history, whilst defending the necessity of revelation and postulating the importance of divine providence. I here concentrate exclusively on Mandeville's arguments in "profane" (conjectural) history, for reasons of space and focus. Much remains to be written, however, on the significant religious dimensions of this work, which have thus far received sustained attention only in John Robertson, *The Case for the Enlightenment: Scotland and Naples 1680-1760* (Cambridge: Cambridge University Press, 2005), 270-77.

65. William Temple, "Essay on the Original and Nature of Government," in *The Works of Sir William Temple, Bart. Complete. In Four Volumes*, ed. S. Hamilton (London, 1814), vol. 1, 6.

66. Temple, "Nature of Government," 9.

the time they erected governments based on agreement, with commonwealths being outgrowths of early walled cities established by the largest and most successful families. Authority, not contract, was the origin and foundation of government, with the family being the engine of early historical progress. The question of whether humans were naturally sociable animals was simply irrelevant if one admitted the obvious truth that they subsisted in families in prepolitical conditions.

Temple denied that *any* animals could be meaningfully and uniformly grouped as either sociable or unsociable, rejecting the usefulness of the distinction *tout court*. But even if, *per impossibile*, humans could be consistently understood as being uniformly one or the other, Temple professed a corresponding incomprehension: "if men are like sheep, why [do] they need government; or, if they are like wolves, how ... can [they] suffer it"?[67] The sociability question was best ignored: all one needed to know was that humans necessarily grew up in families founded first on natural affection, and later on the authority of the patriarch who inspired reverence. Over time these families expanded in size, warred with each other, settled in walled cities, and became monarchies, and later aristocracies and democracies. This was the true origin of government. Contract came, if ever, only much later.

Temple's reading of Hobbes's position on contract, a principal target of the "Essay," was based on a technical misunderstanding (albeit an extremely common one that persists to this day). As we have seen, Hobbes's position on how government in practice came to emerge was *the same* as that put forward by Temple. But by collapsing the sociability question as irrelevant once the fact of historically prepolitical families was admitted, Temple in turn collapsed (albeit preemptively) the debate between Hobbes and Shaftesbury. As a result, his account served as the perfect foil for Mandeville, who was keen to preserve the distinction between Hobbes and Shaftesbury in order to articulate a reworked version of the former's foundational claim against the latter.[68]

Temple had chastised contract theory for being suited only to the Epicurean maxim, expounded most famously by Lucretius, that men sprung from the earth fully formed: "this principle of contract ... seems calculated for the account given by some of the old poets, of the original of man, whom they raise out of the ground by great numbers at a time, in perfect stature and strength."[69] Again, this remark was off target if aimed at Hobbes. In any case, Mandeville promptly turned the tables on Temple. By positing that men met as heads of families in order to establish government, Temple committed

67. Ibid., 10.

68. This is not an exclusive claim: Mandeville may have had other reasons for focusing on Temple's essay. Somewhat surprisingly given the prominence with which Mandeville cites it in order to set up his own conjectural account, this is a topic which, as far as I am aware, has so far received no scholarly attention.

69. Ibid., 11.

exactly the error he accused the poets of. The hypothetical head of family Temple described was "no Savage, or untaught Creature; he is fit to be a Justice of Peace." Temple's bypassing of sociability served only to beg the question, as Mandeville joked: "Did this Man spring out of the Earth, I wonder, or did he drop from the Sky?"[70] Temple was of course right about the historical progress from families to modern commonwealths through cycles of conquest. But that was all quite beside the point: *nobody* denied *that* story. What needed to be explained was how families could possibly serve as the basis for human sociability: how humanity ever reached the point of family-organized social living from which modern systems of government for large and lasting conditions evolved.

Mandeville flatly denied that the family, considered alone, could account for advanced human social living. In their savage untaught condition, human beings would propagate quickly as soon as each generation reached puberty, with many offspring rapidly appearing. An innate desire for "sovereignty" over all thinking others, and the untaught belief that anything one desired should be one's personal possession, led savage parents to claim dominion over their offspring.[71] Limited natural affection, and the joy derived from glorying over dependents, would ensure vulnerable children were initially cared for, whilst anger and violent retaliation for untoward behavior kept wayward offspring in check. The superior power of parents, and the desire to emulate them, was the origin of parental reverence, the true spring of authority (a sideswipe at Temple).[72] But this was not enough to account for the origin of society. Whilst grandfathers would possess the greatest degree of reverence, being themselves untaught savages it was impossible that such family patriarchs could possess the foresight to curb their own passions and begin the process of psychological evolution required to explain how men's pride became redirected over time into nonviolent forms of status competition and peaceful modes of emulation. On the contrary, "a Man who never had been taught to curb any of his Passions, would be very unfit for such a Task."[73]

An external causal influence thus had to be posited. Mandeville located this in the ravages of wild beasts that forced human beings to form alliances for defense: the danger of being eaten pushed people into group living, the first step to society.[74] After forming alliances for defense from animals, however, humans were increasingly in danger not from beasts, but from other humans. As the utilitarian benefits of group living resulted in increased prosperity, intergroup competition for material advantage accelerated. The second

70. Bernard Mandeville, *The Fable of the Bees, Volume 2*, ed. F. B. Kaye (Indianapolis: Liberty Fund, 1988), 192–93.
71. Mandeville, *Bees, Volume 2*, 204–5.
72. Ibid., 201–2.
73. Ibid., 203.
74. Ibid., 230.

step to society was learning to live in groups for defense against not animals, but humans.[75] At this stage early tribal leaders, attempting to secure their own safety whilst augmenting their material comforts, began the process of seeking to make others useful by encouraging socially beneficial behavior—in short, the invention of moral virtue, as originally (albeit imperfectly) sketched in the 1714 "Enquiry into the Origin of Moral Virtue."[76] The third and final step to society was the invention of letters: "No Multitudes can live peaceably without Government; no Government can subsist without Laws; and no Laws can be effectual long, unless they are wrote down."[77] With this third step came the transformation by which humans became fully governable, construing servitude to leaders of tribal society as to their own private advantage, introspecting law, internalizing social restraints, and finally becoming predisposed to not transgress social conventions and established laws, thus enabling peaceful living en masse without conscious reflection.[78]

This three-stage account explained how naturally unsociable, proud man had eventually become sociable. At the outset of the *Enquiry into the Origin of Honour and the Usefulness of Christianity in War*, Mandeville surveyed his two previous works, claiming to have set down the origin of "Virtue" in the first *Fable*, "Politeness" in the second.[79] The *Enquiry* explored the origin of honor, a "Gothick" invention.[80] Although socialized people in all times and places possessed basic concepts of martial conduct and cultivated bravery, developed in conjunction with the status acquired from military engagement and the need to discipline and control troops, European honor was a culturally specific artifice Mandeville now identified as more interesting and powerful than the invention of virtue in explaining humanity's advanced socialization under commercial conditions. European honor systems had emerged in the culture of the late- and postmedieval periods, an outgrowth of feudal loyalty systems and mechanisms for securing status: honor was the parent of politeness, a phenomenon unique to European modernity.

Mandeville's self-assessment of his two previous works in the *Enquiry* is instructive, even if he made the transition between his earlier works look cleaner than it in reality had been. (One problem, we might note, was that the original 1714 formulation of Mandeville's account of sociability simply wasn't very convincing; he knew then the position he wanted to defend, but not how best to defend it.) Nonetheless, we can reconstruct the trajectory of

75. Ibid., 266–67.
76. Ibid., 268.
77. Ibid., 269.
78. For a detailed overview of Mandeville's three steps to society, see Hundert, *Enlightenment's "Fable,"* 62–75.
79. Bernard Mandeville, *An Enquiry into the Origin of Honour and the Usefulness of Christianity in War* (London, 1732), 1.
80. Mandeville, *Origin of Honour*, 15.

Mandeville's evolving thought as follows. The sociability story of the first *Fable* concentrated on the needs of the body: the way competitive humans made each other safe, and thereby useful, through redirecting pride such that private vices became not just public benefits, but resulted in luxury and opulence. The second *Fable* provided the undergirding account not just of human prehistory, but of how people had satisfied the needs of the mind in coming to live under the artifice of society: self-liking's evolution, via disguised pursuit of pride satiation, with the emergence of early forms of politeness as a method for avoiding physical fighting.[81] Owing to the centrality of recognition in Mandeville's accounts these were, however, two sides of the same coin: pride underpinned the advantage-oriented vision of the first *Fable* as much as the honor-focused story of the second. The *Enquiry* attempted to supply the connecting explanation, historical and conceptual, between the two earlier works. Mandeville always agreed with Hobbes—indeed, was at pains to show—that the prepolitical existence of the family did not constitute evidence for natural sociability. But not being committed to Hobbes's rigid categorization of the state of nature in both pre- and postpolitical terms, he could appeal explicitly to both conjectural (the second volume of the *Fable*) and real (the *Enquiry*) history in explaining how man came to live in society, despite being an animal not born fit for it. Shaftesbury, as much as Temple, was answered accordingly.

When Francis Hutcheson took the chair of moral philosophy at the University of Glasgow in 1730, the delivery of an inaugural lecture provided the opportunity to offer an account of what had up until that point been conspicuously outstanding in his work: in what sense humans could properly be said to be sociable. Hutcheson objected to the term "state of nature" on theological grounds, preferring the term "state of liberty from human government."[82] Although the best writers had affirmed humans' natural sociability as the foundation of morality, lack of care in explaining what exactly was meant by this had opened the door to "a whole battery of cavils and absurdities" by "certain writers, who seem to vaunt and pride themselves on depicting human nature in the worst and most disgraceful light."[83] However, Hutcheson's main attention in the lecture was focused not on the accounts of natural unsociability rooted in pride as put forward by Hobbes and Mandeville, but on a sub-Hobbesian account he filed as likewise "Epicurean": that of Samuel von Pufendorf.[84]

---

81. Mandeville, *Bees*, Volume 2, 295.

82. Francis Hutcheson, "On the Natural Sociability of Mankind," in *Logic, Metaphysics and the Natural Sociability of Mankind*, ed. J. Moore and M. Silverthorne (Indianapolis: Liberty Fund, 2006), 201; cf. István Hont, *Jealousy of Trade: International Competition and the Nation State in Historical Perspective* (Cambridge, MA: Belknap Harvard, 2005), 36.

83. Hutcheson, "Natural Sociability," 194–95.

84. Ibid., 202; cf. Hont, *Jealousy of Trade*, 36; Brooke, *Philosophic Pride*, 159–61.

Hutcheson's two works of moral philosophy down to 1730 constituted a sustained rejection of the view that positional competition for recognition characterized humans' central psychological processes.[85] He thus felt entitled to largely ignore the view of Hobbes and Mandeville that man was not born fit for society because of his competitive pride. Hutcheson also denied—as was by now standard—any role for a natural appetite or instinct for company: "in no philosopher does our natural sociability signify that 'men desire the company of other men for its own sake, or that it is agreeable in itself for a man to pass his time in a crowd.'"[86] Furthermore, everybody likewise admitted that utility was a drive to society: "perhaps this has not been denied, and could not be denied, by anyone, even by Hobbes himself, who, of course, teaches that one may see by a very easy reasoning that peace and harmless life are to every man's advantage."[87] The real debate concerned the question of whether human sociability was primarily a function of the seeking of utility, or whether the pursuit of advantage supervened on some more fundamental sociable characteristic.

On Hutcheson's reading, Pufendorf claimed that humans are ultimately driven by self-interest, but social life is nonetheless still natural because "such is the nature of external things, and such the nature of men, that we need the help of others to avoid almost all the human evils and to obtain almost all the external pleasures or advantages which human life affords."[88] This was a utility-first view: people formed society because it was to their mutual material advantage. But although what "Pufendorf taught is indeed true . . . he omitted many of the most important observations that may be made on this subject," having at best explicated a derivative conception of sociability, inadequate when taken alone. "For human nature is not sociable only in this secondary sense for the sake merely of our own advantage or pleasure, whatever it may be, but is in itself immediately and primarily kind, unselfish, and sociable without regard to its advantage or pleasure."[89]

To resist Pufendorf, Hutcheson reached back to the strategy Shaftesbury had employed in "The Moralists," but did away with the earl's speculative and metaphysically taxing ontology. In place of this Hutcheson substituted

85. Namely the 1725 *Beauty and Virtue*, and the 1728 *Passions and Affections*.

86. Hutcheson, "Natural Sociability," 201. The reference to the crowd is likely a rejection of the depiction of natural sociability theory presented in Mandeville's "A Search into the Nature of Society" (cf. Moore's footnote 28 in Hutcheson, "Natural Sociability," 201). As Moore points out, the final sections of the inaugural lecture are dedicated to rebutting criticisms of Hutcheson's theory put forward by Archibald Campbell and Mandeville (James Moore, "Introduction," in Moore and Silverthorne, *Logic, Metaphysics*, 20–22).

87. Hutcheson, "Natural Sociability," 202.

88. Ibid., 202.

89. Ibid., 205. Also: "Of course we have desires which seek satisfaction in private pleasure and advantage; we have equally, as I hope I have sufficiently shown, more creditable desires which make us sociable": ibid., 209.

a principle of "sympathy" (*contagio* in the Latin original), according to which "there are few or no pleasures, even physical pleasures, which are not augmented by association with others." There is nothing "more cheering for a man than to share his happiness with others. And therefore, though they claim that it is his own pleasure or advantage that each man seeks, yet such is the nature of certain pleasures, including the greatest of them, and of most of our desires, that they prompt us to seek social life by themselves almost without any reasoning; and by themselves they make the duties of social life agreeable and delightful."[90] The ability to share in each other's sentiments constituted a preutility drive to social living, with the pursuit of material advantage supervening upon this. From here, however, Hutcheson recapitulated Shaftesbury's basic account. Humans were always born in families and equipped with a capacity for sympathy, hence even in the "state of liberty from human government" they could not be considered unsociable in the ways that Hobbes, Mandeville, or even Pufendorf supposed. Sympathy, not self-interest, was the foundation of sociable living, although material gain was undeniably a benefit of association, and hence a supplement to natural sociability. Historically, the family was the origin of government, as families grew into tribes, expanded into the earliest monarchies, and so on, through the upward trajectory that nobody denied. Sympathy and the family were accordingly made the basis of a natural human sociability, the affirmation of which allowed Hutcheson to simply bypass the conjectural edifice of *The Fable of the Bees, Volume 2*.

Hume: Family and a "Mere Idle Fiction"

Were Mandeville and Hobbes adequately refuted by Hutcheson's adoption of sympathy as a basis for human sociability, with utility seeking simply a supervening trait that could straightforwardly account for human progress from primitive conditions to advanced civilized living via the expansion of primitive families into tribal groupings and eventually nations and states? Hume was emphatic that it could not be so. As we saw in chapter 1, Hume agreed with Hutcheson that humans were equipped with the capacity for sympathy, enabling him to likewise reject the pride-centered accounts of Hobbes and Mandeville.[91] But Hume denied that sympathy could be the foundation of

90. Ibid., 204.
91. However, Hume had almost certainly not read Hutcheson's inaugural for himself: he was not in the audience, and is unlikely to have read a print copy given that circulation was largely limited to Glasgow: Thomas Mautner, "Inaugural Lecture on the Social Nature of Man: An Overview," in *Francis Hutcheson on Human Nature* (Cambridge: Cambridge University Press, 1993), 107–8; cf. Moore, "Introduction," 17–18. When I say that Hume "agreed" with Hutcheson, I mean this at the level of congruence of ideas, not literal approval and endorsement. Indeed, that Hume did not realize how stridently opposed

large and lasting society. Precisely because it was not a general goodwill to all humanity, but only a particular capacity to share the sentiments of specific others, sympathy could not explain the origin of justice. Yet it was justice—i.e., the ordering of utility—that needed to be explained if sociability in large and lasting conditions was to be accounted for. As a result, sympathy could not be treated as the conceptual equivalent of a natural appetite for society, plugged in to one's preferred explanatory framework as a like-for-like surrogate for displaced pre-Hobbesian suppositions—as Hutcheson, building on Shaftesbury, essentially attempted to do. Instead, an entirely new framework was required, but one which in turn took a novel stance on the importance of the family and of history. To see this, and to appreciate the nature and depth of Hume's own intervention, we must return to the conceptual foundations of his theory of justice as an artificial virtue, as explicated in book 2, part 2, of the *Treatise*.

According to Hume, no action could be considered morally good unless there was a motive to produce it antecedent to the sense of its morality. With "natural" virtues like parental care of children this was straightforward: emotive approval of natural affection preceded the notion of a duty of care to children, with the latter grounded in the former. But with acts of justice things were not so straightforward. Taking man in his "civiliz'd state" and asking why one should return a sum of money to a creditor or some equivalent archetypically just act, a "regard to justice, and abhorrence to villainy and knavery" was sufficient answer. But "in his rude and more *natural* condition, if you are pleas'd to call such a condition natural," such an answer would be wholly unintelligible.[92] Without the prior establishment of a convention for governing possessions, individuals would lack the appropriate motive of honesty required as an antecedent ground that would qualify the act as virtuous. Regard to "public interest" was no answer: what if the loan was secret, its repayment likewise, so that the public could never know and thus not have its interest affected? In any case, experience proved that "men, in the ordinary conduct

---

Hutcheson was to even a sub-Hobbesian utility-first view like Pufendorf's (precisely because Hume had not read the inaugural) may go a long way to explaining why he was apparently so surprised by Hutcheson's hostile reception of bk. 3 of the *Treatise*. On this matter more generally, see David Fate Norton, "Hume and Hutcheson: The Question of Influence," in *Oxford Studies in Early Modern Philosophy*, vol. 2, ed. D. Garber and S. Nadler (Oxford: Oxford University Press, 2005), 211–260; "The Foundations of Morality in Hume's *Treatise*," in *The Cambridge Companion to Hume*, 2nd ed., ed. D. F. Norton and J. Taylor (Cambridge: Cambridge University Press, 2009), 270–310; James Moore, "Hume and Hutcheson," in *Hume and Hume's Connexions*, ed. M. A. Stewart and J. P. Wright (Edinburgh: Edinburgh University Press, 1994), 23–57, and "The Eclectic Stoic, the Mitigated Skeptic," in *New Essays on David Hume*, ed. E. Mazza and E. Ronchetti (Milan: FrancoAngelli, 2007), 133–70; Luigi Turco, "Hutcheson and Hume in a Recent Polemic," in Mazza and Ronchetti, *New Essays*, 171–98.

92. Hume, *Treatise*, T.3.2.1.9, SBN 479.

of life, look not so far as the public interest, when they pay their creditors, perform their promises, and abstain from theft, and robbery, and injustice of every kind. That is a motive too remote and too sublime to affect the generality of mankind."[93] More fundamentally, once one admitted—as both Hutcheson and Shaftesbury did—that "there is no such passion in human minds, as the love of mankind, merely as such, independent of personal qualities, of services, or of relation to ourselves," then explaining the origin of justice was seriously problematic.[94] Men were equipped with sympathy, but this was "no proof of such an universal affection to mankind, since this concern extends itself beyond our own species." There were "no phenomena that point out any such kind affection to men, independent of their merit, and every other circumstance. We love company in general; but 'tis as we love any other amusement. An *Englishman* in *Italy* is a friend; a *European* in *China*; and perhaps a man wou'd be belov'd as such, were we to meet him in the moon. But this proceeds only from a relation to ourselves; which in these cases gathers force by being confin'd to a few persons."[95] It was impossible to account for justice through some general public benevolence, or regard to the interest of humanity. Still less could *private* benevolence directed at specific individuals account for justice. What if the person owed money was an enemy, or a miser, or a vicious individual deserving of people's hatred? In all such cases, the "original motive" to justice would fail. There was therefore "no real or universal motive for observing the laws of equity, but the very equity and merit of that observance"—an unacceptably circular piece of reasoning.[96] Unless we wished to conclude that nature had established a sophistry, Hume insisted, we should conclude that justice was artificial and not natural, and hence account for it by other means.

But what means? There was no doubting that society was advantageous. Yet "in order to form society, 'tis requisite not only that it be advantageous, but also that men be sensible of its advantages, and 'tis impossible, in their wild, uncultivated state, that by study and reflection alone, they shou'd ever be able to attain this knowledge."[97] Furthermore, the artifice of justice was a prerequisite of *all* social living: "tho' it be possible for men to maintain a small uncultivated society without government, 'tis impossible they shou'd maintain a society of any kind without justice."[98] How could the origin of society—coterminous, Hume made clear, with the origin of justice—be explained, given that humans could not know the benefits of justice antecedent to having experienced them, and thus could not have willfully designed the

93. Ibid., T.3.2.1.11, SBN 481.
94. Ibid., T.3.2.1.12, SBN 481.
95. Ibid., T.3.2.1.12, SBN 482.
96. Ibid., T.3.2.1.117, SBN 483.
97. Ibid., T.3.2.2.4, SBN 486.
98. Ibid., T.3.2.8.3, SBN 541.

solution to their predicament? The beginning of the answer was to emphasize, as Hutcheson and Shaftesbury had done, that humans were always born into families. Alongside the necessities of food and shelter, nature had annexed the satisfaction of the sex instinct. This inevitably brought savages together, who copulated and associated first through lust, later forming a new and more enduring tie of affection as they raised offspring together. Superior strength and wisdom allowed parents to rule their children, whilst natural affection for offspring restrained the exercise of excessively severe discipline. In turn, "a little time, custom and habit operating on the tender minds of the children, makes them more sensible of the advantages, which they may reap from society, as well as fashions them by degrees for it, by rubbing off those rough corners and untoward affections, which prevent their coalition."[99]

Yet this insistence on natural affection, plus the heuristically learned utility benefits of cooperation, was not a replay of either Shaftesbury's or Hutcheson's account. Sympathy plus group cooperation as exhibited amongst primitive savages did not explain the rise of *large and lasting* society via any straightforward historical trajectory out of the natural family. Yet the natural family nonetheless did provide the source of an adequate explanation. For it was in the primitive family that humans had first learned the benefits of respecting possessions, and in turn came to establish the conventions of justice at the very earliest stage of human group living.

Yet in order to conclusively demonstrate the artificial nature of justice—and hence its original role as a facilitator of utilitarian gains enabling large-scale group living—Hume suspended this conjectural historical account of how human societies had actually developed and invoked the idea of man in a prepolitical state of nature where he lived isolated and alone. In such a condition humans would have needed to invent the artifice of justice to secure group living. This state of nature was not, however, a literal proposition, but a pure thought experiment for advancing understanding of difficult conceptual truths. Precisely because human beings were always born in families, "'tis utterly impossible for men to remain any considerable time in that savage condition, which precedes society; but that his very first state and situation may justly be esteem'd social." Nonetheless, "philosophers may, if they please, extend their reasoning to the suppos'd *state of nature*, provided they allow it to be a mere philosophical fiction, which never had, and never cou'd have, any reality."[100] Making this move enabled Hume to get beyond the limitations that Shaftesbury and Hutcheson ran into when they failed to see that it was the organization of utility seeking that needed to be explained in a fully functional theory of sociability. The state-of-nature paradigm enabled Hume to

---

99. Ibid., T.3.2.2.4, SBN 486.
100. Ibid., T.3.2.2.14, SBN 493.

demonstrate that justice was inherently a piece of artifice, one required to supplement the prepolitical existence of the family if large and lasting society was to be achieved. Yet, equally, because not burdened by Hobbes's complex theoretical commitments or his stipulation that politics be understood as a demonstrative a priori science, Hume could make the move that Hobbes was forced to partially employ, but could never fully commit to: making the state of nature a purely hypothetical postulate for illustrating the nature of human sociability, without needing it to simultaneously apply to a condition humans ever, or ever could have, actually found themselves subsisting in. Hume's decisive innovation was thus to operate in two complementary, but separate, registers. On the one hand, real (albeit conjectural) history, was appealed to in order to claim that humans never lived in a state of nature, because even the most primitive of peoples had lived in family-based tribes exercising the basic conventions of justice, thus accounting for the actual historical origin of this innovation amongst primitive peoples who needed to regulate their material interactions insofar as groups were larger than the nuclear family. On the other, the hypothetical state of nature, although only "to be regarded as an idle fiction," nonetheless "deserves our attention because nothing [could] more evidently show the origin" of the virtue of justice in artificial conventions for the promotion of utility.[101] Hume hypothesized people as living in a solitary condition to disentangle the complicating fact that it was natural for humans to invent artifices. The thought experiment of the state of nature allowed Hume to bring out the artificiality of justice by suspending considerations of how it had actually originated—not to deny the truth of the fact that humans had spontaneously invented justice without calculated direction, but simply to show that what had been invented was, indeed and nonetheless, artifice.

When imagining humans in an isolated and diffident prepolitical state of nature, it was evident that the combination of their limited generosity, and the scarcity of natural resources, would render them unable to subsist in groups larger than the nuclear family founded on natural affection alone, as competition over possessions would quickly drive them apart. The only remedy to this was the artifice of justice—i.e., a set of initially self-interested conventions for regulating the pursuit of utility—whose artificial status as a response to real-world human neediness was further confirmed by the fact that justice would be redundant if humans' benevolence to all others equaled their own self-interest, or if the materials of the earth were unlimited, like manna from heaven. Yet from within the state-of-nature perspective—i.e., imagining human beings as essentially solitary and competitive—accounting for *how* justice could ever have been invented would be extremely problematic. It would require either a legislator figure immediately imposing the institution upon

---

101. Ibid., T.3.2.2.16, SBN 494.

others, or a complex conjectural account of the gradual evolution of such a solution over great spans of time (exactly, we might note, what Mandeville had alternatively attempted in the successive volumes of the *Fable of the Bees*).[102] Hume, however, did not need to attempt a solution to the immensely difficult problem of explaining how justice could have arisen within the state of nature, because no such attempt was necessary, and would anyway be redundant. The state of nature was simply a thought experiment for illustrating the artificial nature of justice—i.e., its reliance upon established background conventions, upbraided in time by various forms of sympathy, but which would never have existed had external pressures not forced humans into mutually self-interested patterns of behavior for securing material security. In real history, where there never was a state of nature, justice had been invented in early tribes structured around small groups of families, and evolved out of that primitive arrangement as small tribes gradually grouped together to form larger associations, developing from a "natural" to a "moral" virtue (changing its normative shape, and the obligations for obedience experienced by its practitioners, accordingly) as human society increased in size, with sympathy reinforcing the beneficial effects of justice insofar as these were useful and agreeable to oneself and others.[103]

For ease of illustration Hume broke the account of justice's content into time-consecutive stages in the expository sections of book 3, part 2, section 2 (which we examined in chapter 1), imagining justice as evolving through successive stages of development as presented via the state-of-nature paradigm. But this was, precisely, illustration. In real history early tribal families practiced the conventions of justice as a piece, and the only time-dependent change was the upgrading of justice from a "natural" virtue based on calculations of

---

102. As we saw in chapter 1, Hume was certainly aware of the central tenets of *The Fable of the Bees, Volume 1*, as indicated by the accuracy with which he rehearsed Mandeville's arguments. As John P. Wright has established, Hume also knew Mandeville's *Enquiry into the Origin of Honour*, to which his early piece "An Historical Essay on Chivalry and Modern Honour" was a partial response: John P. Wright, "Hume on the Origin of 'Modern Honour': A Study in Hume's Philosophical Development," in *Philosophy and Religion in Enlightenment Britain*, ed. R. Savage (Oxford: Oxford University Press, 2012), 187–209. Although we lack any direct evidence that Hume read vol. 2 of the *Fable*, it seems likely, in respect to the above, that he did. But even if he did not, I suggest that he did not need to have read it to know where he differed from Mandeville. Hume's alternative answer to the puzzle of human sociability moved him away from the sort of conjectural history Mandeville attempted, not least through the privileging of sympathy over pride in the explanatory account—of which knowledge only of the first *Fable* was essentially required.

103. As discussed in chapter 1, and again in chapter 3, for Hume a "natural" virtue obliges insofar as one's self-interest is promoted thereby, whereas a "moral" virtue carries independent normative weight *without* regard to one's personal situation or prospects of improvement.

self-interest to a "moral" virtue based on a sense of normative obligation. But even this time-dependent change would, historically speaking, have been completed early on: small-scale societies operating justice prior to the invention of government were entirely possible, as proved by the American Indian experience of several thousand years prior to contact with the West.[104]

Hume's analysis of justice, however, retained an important affinity with Hobbes's earlier account of the necessary preconditions of political society. For Hobbes, although the actual historical path to legitimate political power—i.e., sovereignty proper—would take a locally contingent route through variations on the themes of violence and conquest, all sovereignty was at base the same. For Hume, different forms of society would emerge in different ways in different places, reflecting local pressures, but nonetheless all societies would have to adopt the basic aspects of the artifice of justice as a means for regulating possessions in order to go on subsisting successfully, before growing into more opulent and advanced conditions if circumstances allowed.[105] Hence, again, the importance of Hume's remark that "tho' it be possible for men to maintain a small uncultivated society without government, 'tis impossible they shou'd maintain a society of any kind without justice."[106] Where Hume differed from Hobbes was in construing the state of nature solely as a thought experiment for illustrating the necessity of justice to sociable living, not a proposition about how human beings necessarily lived in the absence of governmental power, either in their primordial condition or during civil war. In turn, Hume reversed Hobbes's proposition about the relationship of justice to the state. It was not the Leviathan that created justice via sovereign decree, as Hobbes supposed, but justice that eventually created the Leviathan, after the ability to regulate possessions via convention over time engendered the innovation of magistracy and government. Where this left the matter of sovereignty is the question examined in chapter 3.

With the artificial nature of justice established, Hume inflected the well-established story of historical progress from the small tribal family to large-scale society through his utility-centered explanation that we examined in chapter 1. International war between early tribal patriarchies, sparked by

---

104. In this way we can see that Hume's account is free of incoherence, and we do not need to claim that the synthesis of his historical and analytical accounts is rushed or inadequately thought out, as Haakonssen suggests. See Knud Haakonssen, *The Science of a Legislator: The Natural Jurisprudence of David Hume and Adam Smith* (Cambridge: Cambridge University Press, 1981), chap. 1.

105. In particular it was not historically necessary or guaranteed that all human societies would develop the artifice of government. See chapter 6 for a discussion of this point, in relation to Hume's counter-Lockean theory of the origin of government and its attendant authority.

106. Hume, *Treatise*, T.3.2.8.3, SBN 541.

competition for goods as material abundance accompanied larger-scale sociable living, drove the innovation of government, with camps being the true mothers of cities, and the progress to advanced civilization proceeding from there. This was in essence a return to Temple's story, but powered by a much more sophisticated conceptual engine, and which properly accounted for the foundational item in the debate: in what sense man was an animal born fit for society. Hume's position was complex, but when placed in its proper intellectual context, clear. Humans were an inventive species, originally born into and raised in the family, where they had first learned the rudiments of justice as part of small groups, naturally retained and developed this utility-regulating artifice, out of which they had eventually evolved the further artifice of government, which at last became undergirded by the artificial virtue of allegiance. The role of history and the family were thus accounted for in a utility-centered explanation that moved decisively beyond Hobbes's problematic employment of the state of nature as a genuine historical proposition (something Mandeville, by the *Fable of the Bees, Volume 2*, had arguably also started to do, albeit in an importantly different way to Hume), whilst progressing beyond Shaftesbury's and Hutcheson's inadequate attempts to explain sociability via teleological question begging, or simplistic theories of sympathy, which could not adequately explain the emergence of large and lasting society. Hume's marriage of commercial sociability—the halfway house between pride-centered denials of natural sociability on the one hand, and claims that humans were straightforwardly naturally sociable on the other—with a functioning account of history and the family ought in turn to be recognized as a major achievement in the history of political thought.

Conclusion

Hume's position amounted to an almost paradoxical one. Immanuel Kant, surveying the sociability debate in his 1784 "Idea for a Universal History with a Cosmopolitan Purpose," would take a more Hobbesian view than Hume (as influenced in no small measure by Rousseau), in describing humanity's central political characteristic as "unsocial sociability," a nod to man's being by nature psychologically ill-fitted for large-scale sociable living.[107] By contrast, but in similar vein, Hume's strategy of making sympathy the natural corrective to pride, whilst requiring the natural invention of artifice to regulate the pursuit of utility, can be rendered as a theory of "naturally artificial sociability." Whilst Hume's use of conjectural history in developing this account was ultimately (and purposefully) limited, his theory of justice as a theory of human sociability, as well as the enduring challenge represented by both volumes of

---

107. Immanuel Kant, "Idea for a Universal History with a Cosmopolitan Purpose," in *Political Writings*, ed. H. S. Reiss (Cambridge: Cambridge University Press, 1970), 44.

Mandeville's *Fable*, transmitted a set of concerns and intellectual methods to the next generation of Scottish philosophers. In particular, Adam Smith, in his *Lectures on Jurisprudence* and the third book of the *Wealth of Nations*, and Adam Ferguson, in the *Essay on the History of Civil Society*, were indebted to Hume and Mandeville, albeit in quite different ways, when advancing their political and philosophical positions via conjectural explorations of humanity's historical progress.[108] As a result, Hobbes's theory of the family and history, alongside his general account of the state of nature and humanity's natural unsociability, emerges as an important genealogical ancestor for what has come to be known as Scottish Enlightenment conjectural history, with Hume featuring as a major innovator, and source of transmission, for these ideas.

This finding lacks the glamour of a Whiggish history tracing the emergence of popular democratic rule back through a series of canonical texts in a contract tradition, one increasingly emphasizing the sovereignty of the people and the accountability of their contractually bound rulers. But we should remember that Whig histories are usually wrong, and in any case moving away from an emphasis on contract, and toward the debates over history and the family that British thinkers in the eighteenth century were having when wrestling with Hobbes's legacy, may in the end prove more enlightening. After all, the Scottish thinkers of the eighteenth century were centrally concerned with the nature of, and prospects for, liberty under the auspices of the state, itself the central fact of political modernity.[109] As such, their concerns may turn out to be much the same as ours. Of course, these Scottish thinkers were not alone in this regard: I have not here considered continental European currents of thought in response to Hobbes, most especially those inaugurated or influenced by Pufendorf, whose innovation of a double contract was used to resist Hobbes, and who may in turn be more responsible than any other thinker for transmitting an emphasis on contract in Hobbes's thought into the eighteenth

---

108. As we shall see in greater detail in chapter 5, Smith endorsed Hume's theory of justice as the sociological basis of human sociability, whilst questioning the plausibility of Hume's utility-orientated account of justice as a moral virtue. Adam Ferguson drew upon Shaftesbury's and Hutcheson's Stoic theories of sociability, but supplemented these with the new method of conjectural history to advance an anti-Epicurean account intended to defeat Hobbes and Mandeville, without making recourse to Hume's or Smith's sympathy-plus-interest explications of sociability: Adam Ferguson, *An Essay on the History of Civil Society*, ed. F. Oz-Salzberger (Cambridge: Cambridge University Press, 1995), 7–105. For an overview and discussion see Iain McDaniel, *Adam Ferguson in the Scottish Enlightenment: The Roman Past and Europe's Future* (Cambridge, MA: Harvard University Press, 2013), chap. 3.

109. For discussions see Duncan Forbes, *Hume's Philosophical Politics* (Cambridge: Cambridge University Press, 1975); István Hont, "Adam Smith's History of Law and Government as Political Theory," in *Political Judgment: Essays for John Dunn*, ed. R. Bourke and R. Geuss (Cambridge: Cambridge University Press, 2009), 131–71; McDaniel, *Ferguson in the Scottish Enlightenment*.

century and beyond.[110] Nonetheless, I hope to have shown that much might be learned by turning toward what Hobbes—and some of his most astute subsequent British opponents—had to say about the role of history in the generation of political arrangements. If so, knowing the true origins of their ideas, and appreciating the complexity of their responses, may in turn help us to make better sense of our own.

---

110. As Adam Smith is recorded as saying, "the sole intention of the first part" of Pufendorf's "large treatise" (i.e., *De iure naturae et gentium*) was to "confute Hobbes" (Adam Smith, *The Glasgow Edition of the Works and Correspondence of Adam Smith: Lectures on Jurisprudence*, ed. R. L. Meek, D. D. Raphael, and P. G. Stein (Oxford: Oxford University Press, 1978), 398. In Smith's case, there is the added complication that he inherited, and then taught, a syllabus at Glasgow that was organized around teaching Pufendorf's thought. Attempts to place Pufendorf in a genealogy of the origins of Scottish Enlightenment thinking, in particular via the influence of Gershom Carmichael (Hutcheson's and Smith's predecessor in the chair of moral philosophy at Glasgow), have been offered in James Moore and Michael Silverthorne, "Natural Sociability and Natural Rights in the Moral Philosophy of Gershom Carmichael," in *Philosophers of the Scottish Enlightenment*, ed. V. Hope (Edinburgh: Edinburgh University Press, 1984), 1–12, and "Gershom Carmichael and the Natural Jurisprudence Tradition in Eighteenth-Century Scotland," in *Wealth and Virtue: The Shaping of Political Economy in the Scottish Enlightenment*, ed. I. Hont and M. Ignatieff (Cambridge: Cambridge University Press, 1983), 73–87, as well as more generally in Knud Haakonssen, *Natural Law and Moral Philosophy: From Grotius to the Scottish Enlightenment* (Cambridge: Cambridge University Press, 1996), and *The Science of a Legislator*. Hont has specifically argued that Smith's theory of commercial sociability, and in turn his famous four-stages account of societal development, is directly indebted to Pufendorf's attempted refutation of Hobbes: István Hont, "The Language of Sociability and Commerce: Samuel Pufendorf and the Theoretical Foundations of the 'Four Stages' Theory," in *Jealousy of Trade*, 159–84. I am partially skeptical of this reading: Smith more likely learned commercial-sociability theory from Hume, even if his four-stages theory does owe important debts to the Pufendorfian wrestling with the questions of how property and political power interrelated to explain human sociopolitical development. In other words, the four-stages theory and sociability are connected, but not necessarily in the way Hont suggests by locating the genesis of both for Smith in Pufendorf: Hume, after all, had no stages theory and may never even have read Pufendorf—but he developed a sophisticated utility-based theory of sociability nonetheless.

CHAPTER THREE

The State without Sovereignty

The Problem of Political Obligation

HUME HAS NO theory of sovereignty. By extension, he offers no attempt to explain political obligation in terms of what rulers are justified in expecting (and if necessary, extracting) from the ruled, by virtue of the particular kind of relationship they stand in toward them *as* rulers. Instead, Hume's analysis focuses upon the ruled themselves—the bearers of the "opinion of mankind"—and the psychological processes by which they believe themselves bound by the authority of their superiors, whom they always outnumber but nonetheless typically obey.[1] Because of this it may appear that Hume fails to offer a political theory proper, providing only a political sociology that is incapable of adequately addressing, let alone answering, the problem of political obligation: why obedience is owed to established power, and why such power may legitimately coerce those who disobey by virtue of its possession of supreme rightful authority—that is, sovereignty.[2]

Political obligation is a, if not the, central problem of Western political theory. If it cannot be adequately accounted for, the legitimacy of all other activities undertaken by the state, as the locus of organized coercive power, is jeopardized.[3] The earliest investigation in the Western tradition (far in

---

1. David Hume, "Of the First Principles of Government," in *Essays Moral, Political and Literary*, ed. E. F. Miller (Indianapolis: Liberty Fund, 1985), 32–33.

2. For the view that Hume lacks a proper political theory see in particular John Dunn, "From Applied Theology to Social Analysis: The Break between John Locke and the Scottish Enlightenment," in *Wealth and Virtue: The Shaping of Political Economy in the Scottish Enlightenment*, ed. I. Hont and M. Ignatieff (Cambridge: Cambridge University Press, 1983), 119–35. See also P. F. Brownsey, "Hume and the Social Contract," *Philosophical Quarterly* 28 (1978), 132–48.

3. Recent treatments that have emphasized the centrality of political obligation to political theory include Robert Nozick, *Anarchy, State, and Utopia* (Oxford: Blackwell, 1974);

advance of the emergence of the modern state, but addressing the same fundamental issue) is Plato's *Crito*. In this dialogue, Socrates famously refuses to flee Athens after being condemned to execution, citing a duty of gratitude and obligation to the city as like a parent that has nurtured him, to which he has previously consented, and which must therefore be obeyed even when putting him to death.[4] Few have been convinced by that answer in the two and a half millennia since, whilst the problem takes on new forms with the rise of the modern state: its scale, anonymity, territorial ubiquity, and capacity for coercive power and control pushing a Platonic city-parent analogy even further beyond breaking point.[5]

In the modern context, Hobbes remains a particularly illuminating author—even if only because his parsimonious attempt to settle matters could not evade the complexity of the problem. For Hobbes, that individual or assembly possessing sovereignty had not just supreme power, but legitimate authority to use coercive power to enforce obedience. Hobbes's claim was never that might made right. Sovereignty was generated by the consent of the ruled, even if extracted at the point of a sword.[6] Being the basis of all sovereignty, consent was thus also the foundation of political obligation: one was obliged to that power one had consented to be sovereign, and could be legitimately coerced by that power to ensure obedience (that of oneself, and others). Everyone within an established commonwealth consented, everyone was obliged, and hence everyone could be legitimately coerced, even if a residual right to resist wounds and death remained. Yet this parsimonious account of the

---

Carole Pateman, *The Problem of Political Obligation: A Critical Analysis of Liberal Theory* (Chichester: Wiley, 1979); A. John Simmons, *Moral Principles and Political Obligation* (Princeton, NJ: Princeton University Press, 1979); the essays collected in John Dunn, *Political Obligation in its Historical Context* (Cambridge: Cambridge University Press, 1980); John Horton, *Political Obligation* (Basingstoke: Palgrave Macmillan, 2010).

4. Plato, *Euthyphro; Apology; Crito; Phaedo; Phaedrus*, trans. H. North Fowler (Cambridge, MA: Harvard University Press, 1982), 175–91. Hume describes the *Crito* as building a Tory doctrine of passive obedience on a Whig principle of original contract, and emphasizes that because eighteenth-century doctrines of authority as founded in consent have no historical precedent, this is a strong argument against their being true: "Of the Original Contract," in *Essays*, 487.

5. Adam Smith adapted Plato's "divine maxim" that one was made for the state and not the reverse, and should no more harm the state than one's parent, but this presupposed a post-Humean innovation regarding the nature and content of political authority. See István Hont, "Commercial Society and Political Theory in the Eighteenth Century: The Problem of Authority in David Hume and Adam Smith," in *Main Trends in Cultural History: Ten Essays*, ed. W. Melching and W. Velema (Amsterdam: Rodopi, 1994), 89.

6. Hence Hobbes's dictum that "it is not therefore the victory that giveth the right of dominion over the vanquished, but his own covenant": Thomas Hobbes, *The Clarendon Edition of the Works of Thomas Hobbes: Leviathan*, ed. N. Malcolm (Oxford: Oxford University Press, 2012), vol. 2, 312 [NB: all citations of *Leviathan* in this chapter are from this edition, unless otherwise stated].

grounds of sovereignty and obligation ran into difficulty when consent and power came apart. What if a sovereign, previously consented to, lost power to unlawful, but successful, rebels? If unable to protect, because no longer wielding the public sword keeping subjects in awe, such a sovereign could no longer *be* sovereign. To whom, then, was obedience owed, and why? Individual judgment, which Hobbes saw as a primary source of interminable strife and quarrel, and which he therefore sought to entirely exclude, reappeared at precisely the point where political obligation was an issue with more than just theoretical import.[7]

Hobbes's ambiguity in addressing political obligation at its limit has rightly attracted much scholarly attention.[8] I do not address that vexed matter here, but wish merely to note that if political obligation is indeed a central item in Western political theory, umbilically connected to the notion of sovereignty, and by extension the theory of the modern state (as exemplified by Hobbes), then the suggestion that Hume disabled himself from addressing this issue owing to the mode of his political enquiry should be, at the very least, deeply surprising. Hume was a political thinker of the utmost genius and seriousness, whilst his status as a philosopher of epistemological, metaphysical, and moral

---

7. For a discussion, see Kinch Hoekstra, "Tyrannus Rex *vs.* Leviathan," *Pacific Philosophical Quarterly* 82 (2001), 420–46. As Hoekstra concludes (438): "Though he strives to minimize its role, Hobbes must recognize that private judgment is ineliminable. The very feet of his great Leviathan are of mortal clay."

8. This focuses not just on the contents of his theory and whether he was a royalist, a "de facto" theorist, or a theorist of consent, and in particular the addition of "A Review, and Conclusion" to *Leviathan* with its "twentieth" law of nature that humans are to defend in times of war that power which protected them in times of peace. There is also Hobbes's returning to England in 1650 and submitting himself to the new regime, which had overthrown a monarchy Hobbes was unequivocal in maintaining had held rightful "sovereignty from a descent of six hundred years was alone called sovereign, had the title of Majesty from every one of his subjects, and was unquestionably taken by them for their king": Hobbes, *Leviathan*, vol. 2, 286. For discussions of Hobbes's theory of political obligation, see Quentin Skinner, "The Context of Hobbes's Theory of Political Obligation," and "Conquest and Consent: Hobbes and the Engagement Controversy," in *Visions of Politics*, vol. 3, *Hobbes* (Cambridge: Cambridge University Press, 2002), 264–86; 287–307; "Historical Introduction," in Thomas Hobbes, *The Clarendon Edition of the Works of Thomas Hobbes: Writings on the Common Law and Hereditary Right*, ed. A. Cromartie and Q. Skinner (Oxford: Oxford University Press, 2005), 159–76; Kinch Hoekstra, "The *De Facto* Turn in Hobbes's Political Philosophy," in *"Leviathan" after 350 Years*, ed. T. Sorell and L. Foisneau (Oxford: Oxford University Press, 2004), 33–74; Jeffrey R. Collins, *The Allegiance of Thomas Hobbes* (Oxford: Oxford University Press, 2005); Mary G. Dietz, "Hobbes's Subject as Citizen," in *Thomas Hobbes and Political Theory*, ed. M. G. Dietz (Lawrence: University Press of Kansas, 1990), 91–119; Howard Warrender, *The Political Philosophy of Hobbes: His Theory of Obligation* (Oxford: Oxford University Press, 1957); Annabel Brett, *Liberty, Right and Nature: Individual Rights in Later Scholastic Thought* (Cambridge: Cambridge University Press, 1997), chap. 6, and *Changes of State: Nature and the Limits of the City in Early Modern Natural Law* (Princeton, NJ: Princeton University Press, 2011), 108–14.

matters is in doubt by nobody. Is it plausible to suppose that he nonetheless failed to grapple with the outstanding item of concern in Western political thought? I suggest not. We must instead come to see Hume's project as attempting a fundamental recasting of how to think about both the status of philosophy as an enterprise with practical political import, and what we can coherently hope and expect from any notion of political obligation appropriate to a secular world. Hume understood very well the centrality of political obligation to our thinking about politics. His aim was to change our thinking.

The central and most instructive comparison to be drawn in this matter is between Hume's political thought and that of John Locke. This is for two reasons. Firstly, Locke (or at least, a secularized and vulgarized version of Locke's ideas) is Hume's primary confrontation point in the *Treatise*, which remains the site of Hume's most fundamental engagement with the issue of political obligation.[9] Secondly, lying beneath Hume's direct arguments against contract theory is an attempted reconfiguration of what political philosophy can hope to achieve, and of how the issue of political obligation can and should be conceptualized. Hont has previously identified that Hume, like his friend and philosophical successor Adam Smith, objected to Locke not on the principle (to employ Smith's later terminology) of "utility," but of "authority."[10] Utility related to the well-being of a governed populace: "*Salus Populi Suprema Lex* is certainly so just and fundamental a Rule, that he, who sincerely follows it, cannot

---

9. The later essay "Of the Original Contract" restates much of Hume's position in the *Treatise*, but largely assumes, without explicit statement, Hume's reconfiguration of the nature and role of philosophy for its coherence. To properly appreciate that reconfiguration, and hence Hume's thought as a whole, we must concentrate our attention on the *Treatise*, where Hume delineates the foundations of his philosophical approach. For the context of Hume's attack on contract theory, see Duncan Forbes, *Hume's Philosophical Politics* (Cambridge: Cambridge University Press, 1975), chaps. 3, 5, and 6; Stephen Buckle and Dario Castiglione, "Hume's Critique of the Contract Theory," *History of Political Thought* 12 (1991), 457–80. For discussions of Hume's theory of allegiance and his attack on contract theory, see Rachel Cohon, "The Shackles of Virtue: Hume on Allegiance to Government," *History of Philosophy Quarterly* 18 (2001), 393–414; Frederick G. Whelan, "Hume and Contractarianism," *Polity* 27 (1994), 201–24; Thomas W. Merrill, "The Rhetoric of Rebellion in Hume's Constitutional Thought," *Review of Politics* 67 (2005), 257–82; David Gauthier, "David Hume, Contractarian," *Philosophical Review* 88 (1979), 3–38. On Hume's shift from the *Treatise* to his self-presentation and self-identity as an essayist, see James Harris, *Hume: An Intellectual Biography* (Cambridge: Cambridge University Press, 2015), chap. 3.

10. Adam Smith, *The Glasgow Edition of the Works and Correspondence of Adam Smith: Lectures on Jurisprudence*, ed. R. L. Meek, D. D. Raphael, and P. G. Stein (Oxford: Oxford University Press, 1978), 318–21, 401–3; István Hont, "Adam Smith's History of Law and Government as Political Theory," in *Political Judgment: Essays for John Dunn*, ed. R. Bourke and R. Geuss (Cambridge: Cambridge University Press, 2009), 139.

dangerously err," wrote Locke.¹¹ Hume and Smith did not disagree. Government was legitimate only so long as the safety of the people was in practice, and not just in theory, the supreme law.¹² But Hume and Smith could not accept Locke's insistence that the "authority" of present government—by which it could rightfully claim, and if necessary, coercively extract, obedience—was founded upon the consent of the ruled.

Hont writes that Hume "doggedly tried to develop a rounded theory of political allegiance with a proper emphasis on the importance of authority" in the *Treatise*, political *Essays*, and *The History of England*. Still, he does not identify Hume as fully engaging with the Lockean challenge regarding the basis of political authority. Instead it is Smith, in his history of law and government, who "went even further than Hume in this direction and made the task of developing a new principle of authority the central task of post-Lockean political theory."¹³ Yet this assessment faces a serious difficulty. How can a *history* of law and government provide an answer to the *normative* problem of why some agent or agents hold authority, thus obligating others and generating a condition of political obedience that can be coercively enforced? Despite Hont's insistence that "Secular political theorists can lose nothing and stand to gain a great deal both by taking Smith seriously as a political thinker and by abandoning the attempt to try to pigeon-hole his work as mere historical sociology," the reader is left wanting.¹⁴ Hont's claim that Smith offered the resources for a theory of natural authority enabling us to progress beyond the theistic basis of Locke's thought on the one hand, and an inadequate Hobbesian prudentialism on the other, is left at the level of a promise not made good on, his magisterial reconstruction of

11. John Locke, *Two Treatises of Government*, ed. P. Laslett (Cambridge: Cambridge University Press, 1960), 373, § 158. As Hume later put it, "The maxim, *fiat Justitia & ruat Cœlum*, let justice be performed, though the universe be destroyed, is apparently false, and by sacrificing the end to the means, shews a preposterous idea of the subordination of duties," whereas "*Salus populi, suprema Lex*, the safety of the people is the supreme law" is a "maxim . . . agreeable to the sentiments of mankind in all ages": Hume, "Of Passive Obedience," in *Essays*, 489; cf. David Hume, *The Clarendon Edition of the Works of David Hume: An Enquiry Concerning the Principles of Morals*, ed. T. L. Beauchamp (Oxford: Oxford University Press, 1998), 22.

12. For a detailed discussion of how Hume and (especially) Smith positioned themselves on the conflict between the principles of *salus populi* and *fiat justitia* in political practice, and in the context of an intellectual inheritance from an earlier natural-law tradition, see István Hont and Michael Ignatieff, "Needs and Justice in the *Wealth of Nations*," in István Hont, *Jealousy of Trade: International Competition and the Nation State in Historical Perspective* (Cambridge, MA: Belknap Harvard, 2005), 389–443, especially 412–19.

13. Hont, "Smith's History of Law," 141. Hont outlines Smith's "sociological" account of authority, and the practical political consequences of understanding it in those terms (especially in opposition to both French physiocracy and the enthusiasm of systematizing zeal), in "Commercial Society," 86–91.

14. Hont, "Smith's History of Law," 168.

Smith's account of the emergence of modern liberty notwithstanding.[15] And it is difficult to see how that promise could be made good on, at least in the terms Hont presents. For a history of law and government to become a political theory capable of explaining the normative content of authority, some normative account must ultimately be offered. History alone cannot supply that: political theory needs philosophy. Without it, Smith's history of law and government can offer only an interesting dead end.

Yet what if Smith's history of law and government is not best taken as a freestanding intervention, but presupposes a prior reconfiguration of our philosophical thinking on the question of authority? That is the suggestion I wish to advance. That Smith did not, as Hont suggests, go "even further" than Hume, but rather was expanding the analysis within a new philosophical idiom forged *by* Hume, supplied most clearly in the *Treatise*, and which Smith presupposed as the normative philosophical background for his history of law and government as political theory. To see this, however, we must first turn to Locke in some detail. For it is only after properly examining the foundations of Locke's theory of authority that we can examine Hume's engagement with the problem from a vantage point that allows us to appreciate its considerable philosophical profundity and ambition.

Locke's Two Frameworks: Juridical and Historical

As is now well recognized, Locke's political thought is irreducibly theistic.[16] His central premise was that all human beings are created equal by God, with their natural condition being one wherein "all the Power and Jurisdiction is reciprocal, no one having more than another," meaning all are "equal one amongst another without Subordination or Subjection."[17] Some could obtain political authority over others only if those who became subordinate agreed to

---

15. On the effort to progress beyond Hobbes without resort to theistic foundations, see John Dunn, "The Politics of Imponderable and Potentially Lethal Judgment for Mortals: Hobbes's Legacy for the Understanding of Modern Politics," in Thomas Hobbes, *Leviathan*, ed. I. Shapiro (New Haven: Yale University Press, 2010), 433–52. Dunn himself attempted to provide a secular alternative to Locke and Hobbes in "Political Obligations and Political Possibilities," in *Political Obligation*, 243–300, though by his own admission the attempt is unsuccessful.

16. The classic statement remains John Dunn, *The Political Thought of John Locke: An Historical Account of the "Two Treatises of Government"* (Cambridge: Cambridge University Press, 1969). See also John Dunn, "What Is Living and What Is Dead in the Political Theory of John Locke?" in *Interpreting Political Responsibility: Essays 1981–89* (Padstow, UK: Polity, 1990), 9–25; David Gauthier, "Why Ought One Obey God? Reflections on Hobbes and Locke," *Canadian Journal of Philosophy* 7 (1997), 425–46, especially 432.

17. Locke, *Two Treatises*, 269, § 4. For a sustained investigation both of the importance of this premise to Locke's thought and of its relevance to contemporary political theory, see Jeremy Waldron, *God, Locke, and Equality: Christian Foundations in Locke's Political Thought* (Cambridge: Cambridge University Press, 2002).

this change of affairs. Just as each individual's own body was only on loan from its maker—meaning suicide, as much as harm to others, was naturally outlawed—so no person could come to have legitimate temporal political authority without this ultimately being divinely sanctioned.[18] Such sanction came not through any act of intervention by God, but by the specific mechanism He had approved for the establishment of earthly political power: the consent of the ruled.[19] As John Dunn noted some time ago, "There is no such category in Locke's political theory as authority which is both intrinsically human and legitimate."[20]

Locke rejected Hobbes's thoroughgoing conception of natural unsociability, but he did not counter this with a statement of, man's being thoroughly sociable, either.[21] Instead he claimed that "God having made Man such a Creature, that, in his own Judgment, it was not good for him to be alone, put him under strong Obligations of Necessity, Convenience and Inclination to drive him into *Society*, as well as fitted him with Understanding and Language to continue to enjoy it."[22] Human beings lack any specific appetite for society. But in their natural condition the human predilection for (to revert to Hobbes's term) "honour" was not sufficient to disrupt pursuit of the clear utility gains of grouping together for "advantage." Hence whilst humans were "driven" to society rather than seeking it for its own sake, this was essentially unproblematic. Locke here postulated man as he was in his specifically *natural* condition, understood as obtaining prior to the establishment of political society and before a subsequent process of moral corruption rendered the desire for recognition much more

---

18. Locke, *Two Treatises*, 270–71, § 6.

19. "Men being . . . by Nature, all free, equal and independent, no one can be put out of his Estate, and subjected to the Political Power of another, without his own *Consent*": ibid., 330, § 95.

20. Dunn, *Political Thought*, 127.

21. Thanks to Peter Laslett (see his introduction to John Locke, *Two Treatises of Government*, ed. P. Laslett [Cambridge: Cambridge University Press, 1960], 3–122) it is now widely recognized that Locke's primary intellectual target in writing the *Two Treatises* was not Hobbes, but the patriarchal theory of Sir Robert Filmer. I here broadly agree with the reading offered in Dunn, *Political Thought*, chap. 7, that Locke did not undertake serious intellectual engagement with Hobbes in the *Two Treatises*, but mostly made polemical remarks intended to implicate that position without troubling to tackle it directly. That said, Locke was clearly familiar with Hobbes's views, and in asserting that humanity was driven to society in efforts to secure utility would have known that he was writing in opposition to Hobbes. Indeed, it is precisely by asserting an attenuated utility-oriented view of human sociability that Locke is able to largely bypass Hobbes's arguments. His alternative conception of sociability contributes to the state of nature being a state of inconvenience rather than full-blown war, meaning the departure point for Locke's intellectual endeavor is crucially different from Hobbes's, enabling the marginalization of Hobbes's political theory that Dunn describes.

22. Locke, *Two Treatises*, 318–19, § 77.

problematic.[23] It is essential, however, to appreciate that this natural condition was analyzed by Locke in two complementary, but distinct, frameworks: juridical and historical.[24] We must carefully distinguish, and then interrelate, both these frameworks if we are to properly appreciate the foundations and force of Locke's political theory.

Locke's juridical account of man's natural condition was styled under the heading of the "state of nature," and has attracted by far the greatest attention (although its status as a normative framework, rather than a real historical proposition, is often misunderstood).[25] Considered from the juridical viewpoint, men in the state of nature are not only natural equals, but also in a state of liberty to do as they please within the bounds set by natural law, itself accessible to anybody with the basic capacities of reason (thus Locke's famous dictum that a state of liberty was not a state of license).[26] Property could be acquired in the state of nature by mixing one's labor with the materials of the earth, following God's imperative that mankind must not only use but also improve His bounty, being permitted to keep the increased fruit of their labors so long as their appropriation of what was previously held in common left "enough, and as good . . . for others."[27] Property rights were hence entirely

---

23. In this sense, Locke embryonically foreshadows Rousseau's response to Hobbes. On the relationship between Rousseau and Locke, see Christopher Brooke, "'Locke en particulier les a traitées exactement dans les mêmes principes que moi': Revisiting the Relationship between Locke and Rousseau," in *Locke's Political Liberty: Readings and Misreadings*, ed. C. Miqueu and M. Chamie (Oxford: Voltaire Foundation, 2009), 69–82.

24. This stylization is necessarily somewhat oversimplified. What I call Locke's juridical framework was not *ahistorical*; in particular, it contained an important *sacred* historical aspect. For a detailed discussion of this complex matter, see Tom Pye, "Property, Space, and Sacred History in John Locke's *Two Treatises of Government*," *Modern Intellectual History* (forthcoming).

25. cf. Dunn, *Political Thought*, 97, 103, and in general chap. 9; Hont, "Smith's History of Law," 142. For detailed discussions of Locke's juridical political theory see Ross Harrison, *Hobbes, Locke and Confusion's Masterpiece: An Examination of Seventeenth Century Political Philosophy* (Cambridge: Cambridge University Press, 2003); A. John Simmons, *On the Edge of Anarchy: Locke, Consent, and the Limits of Society* (Princeton, NJ: Princeton University Press, 1993); "'Denisons' and 'Aliens': Locke's Problem of Political Consent," in *Justification and Legitimacy: Essays on Rights and Obligations* (Cambridge: Cambridge University Press, 2001); John Marshall, *John Locke: Resistance, Religion and Responsibility* (Cambridge: Cambridge University Press, 1994), chap. 6; James Tully, *An Approach to Political Theory: Locke in Contexts* (Cambridge: Cambridge University Press,1993), chap. 1. For the historical context of Locke's political intervention, see especially Richard Ashcraft, *Revolutionary Politics and Locke's "Two Treatises of Government"* (Princeton, NJ: Princeton University Press, 1986), and Mark Goldie, "John Locke and Anglican Royalism," *Political Studies* 31 (1983), 61–85.

26. Locke, *Two Treatises*, 269–72, §§ 4–9.

27. Ibid., 288, § 27. For an overview of Locke's theory of property and its fundamentally theistic basis, see Alan Ryan, *Property and Political Theory* (Oxford: Blackwell, 1984), chap. 1; Karl Olivecrona, "Appropriation in the State of Nature: Locke on the Origin of

compatible with prepolitical circumstances. Yet their enforcement in such conditions was deeply problematic. Locke put forward the "strange doctrine," earlier suggested by Grotius, that all individuals were equipped with a natural right to punish those who violated their rights.[28] But as a consequence, the state of nature was characterized by "inconvenience" of dual foundation. On the one hand, without settled laws and enforcement mechanisms one's property was forever at risk from the illegitimate acquisitive advances of others. On the other, one was tasked with the enforcing of one's rights—both defensively and retributively—oneself, a considerable and dangerous burden. Given that men are naturally partial and tend to be poor judges of equity in matters that regard themselves, individual exercise of the right to punish led to exacerbated conflict.[29] The solution was for people to relinquish their natural right to punish to a centralized system of arbitration, undertaken by an impartial power enforcing judgments.[30] This was the foundation of political power proper: the erection of a common arbiter for the defense and regulation of property, thus better promoting the mutual advancement of utility.[31] Men consented to be ruled by others so as to escape the inconvenience of the state of nature, on condition that such rule continued to advance their utility. Locke's juridical framework thus supplied a tandem account of both the utility and authority of government. The end of political society was the advancement of utility as furthered by the institution of property, overseen and protected by government, whilst the authority of that government came from the consent of those natural equals who freely agreed to submit themselves to it for the utility benefits it yielded.

Being a juridical stylization, Locke's state of nature was not temporally bounded, but defined by the absence of a common arbiter to settle disputes, entailing that people had to resort to individual exercise of the natural right to punish. As a consequence, the state of nature could potentially obtain at *any* historical moment. A highwayman demanding one's purse when there was no hope of rescue by the established authorities of the land put himself into a state of nature with his victim, who in turn had the right to fight off, and if necessary kill, the assailant.[32] Locke turned this notion to his specific polemical purposes in the *Two Treatises*, arguing that because political society was the imposition

---

Property," *Journal of the History of Ideas* 35 (1974), 211–30; Waldron, *God, Locke and Equality*, chap. 6.

28. Locke, *Two Treatises*, 272; Hugo Grotius, *De iure praedae commentarius*, ed. G. L. Williams (Oxford: Clarendon Press, 1950), 92, and *The Rights of War and Peace*, ed. R. Tuck (Indianapolis: Liberty Fund, 2005), 953–68.

29. Locke, *Two Treatises*, 274–76, §§ 12–13.

30. Ibid.

31. Ibid., 350–53, §§ 123–31.

32. Ibid., 279–80, § 18, though natural law forbade the seizing of the assailant's property.

of a common arbiter, it was incompatible with absolute power (which was by definition arbitrary power) and thus an extension of the state of nature into even more incommodious and dangerous conditions.[33] The result that Locke left for readers to infer was that alongside his frontal assault on Robert Filmer's patriarchalist theory of monarchical power, he was sanctioning the legitimacy of individuals attacking and killing any ruler who claimed absolute power over subjects, as being on a par with the "wild Savage Beasts with whom Men can have no Society or Security," to be destroyed in legitimate self-defense.[34]

Locke's juridical theory was not, however, intended as an account of how human beings had in historical practice come to form modern societies ruled by government as found everywhere in Western Europe.[35] Human beings initially formed family groupings to satisfy the sex instinct, continued them in order to better rear the resulting offspring, experienced the utility benefits of ongoing association that they therefore sustained, and gradually expanded these to include master-and-servant relationships.[36] Historically these groupings remained within the juridical state of nature insofar as obedience was delivered to the patriarch not because subservient family members consented to his rule as a political relationship, but out of gratitude, filial piety, and informal convenience.[37] Yet, over time, patriarchal families organically transitioned to the status of political society proper as facilitated by the consent of the ruled. Being accustomed to the rule of a patriarch before nonage, when children reached maturity they would look to this established source of leadership to become the neutral arbiter for settling disputes, as well as the most effective governmental structure for organizing defense against incursions by aggressive rival groupings attracted by increased material prosperity.[38] In this way humans historically consented to be ruled by a common arbiter, and to give up exercise of their natural right to punish, with succession typically granted to the sons of successful patriarchs. "Thus the natural *Fathers of Families*, by an insensible change, became the *politick Monarchs* of them too." This explained why the earliest political societies were always kingdoms. As the

---

33. Ibid., 284–85, 326–27, §§ 23–24, 90–92.
34. Ibid., 274, § 11.
35. As Hont puts it, "Locke was obviously not a theorist of original contract when thinking about the historical emergence of government": "Smith's History of Law," 143. Likewise, Peter Laslett long ago pointed out that the term "contract" appears only about ten times in the entire second "Treatise," and that it is "compact" and "agreement" that create a society in historical practice: Peter Laslett, "Introduction," in Locke, *Two Treatises*, 113–44.
36. Locke, *Two Treatises*, 316–18, 321–23, §§ 74, 81–83.
37. Ibid., 303–15, 336–44, §§ 52–72, 105–12.
38. Ibid., 338–40, §§ 107–8; "As Locke pointed out, communities were threatened existentially much more from the outside, by other communities, than by the domestic criminality of individuals. Hence the idea of leadership, the rule of man over man, first originated from attempts to deal with issues of external security which necessitated the creation of military command": Hont, "Smith's History of Law," 143.

first patriarchs "chanced to live long, and leave able, and worthy Heirs, for several Successions, or otherwise; So they laid the Foundations of Hereditary, or Elective Kingdoms, under several Constitutions, and Manners, according to Chance, Contrivance, or Occasions happen'd to mould them."[39] The juridical state of nature as a prevailing condition over large areas of territory was historically exited by an "insensible" transition from patriarchal authority (which was *ex hypothesi* nonpolitical) to political power proper as founded in the consent of the God-created free equals who benefited from its establishment and enlargement, and who thus agreed to its erection and continuation.

Yet to this historical story—which in its basic dimensions was the same as that posited by the theorists we surveyed in chapter 2—Locke added a further postulation. This was that after entering political society, humans had undergone a process of corruption that caused them to lose the "Golden Age" of the earliest political societies.[40] The cause of this corruption was economic. The invention of money had allowed men, whilst remaining within the bounds of natural law, to accumulate vast quantities of nonperishable material wealth, thus avoiding violation of the "enough, and as good" proviso but drastically increasing inequality and in turn comparative envy.[41] This led to the rise of economies of luxury and the pursuit of material superfluities, which produced "vain Ambition, and *amor sceleratus habendi*, evil Concupiscence" and "corrupted Mens minds into a Mistake of true Power and Honour."[42]

The political consequences of this economic revolution were profound. Whereas in the golden age men had "more Virtue, and consequently better Governours, as well as less vicious Subjects," the advent of "Ambition and Luxury" caused "Princes to have distinct and separate Interests from their People." As a result "Men found it necessary to examine more carefully *the original and Rights of Government*; and to find out ways to *restrain the Exorbitances*, and *prevent the Abuses* of that Power which they having intrusted in another's hands only for their own good, they found was used to hurt them."[43] Checks to judicial and executive power had to be introduced to guarantee the *salus populi*, as rulers increasingly abused the trust put in them. This was achieved by the innovation of legislative power, a mechanism for better arbitrating the dramatic increase in the incidence of social conflict following the advent of economic prosperity and the proliferation of property rights, whilst protecting people from the ravages of rulers who could not be trusted outside the relatively idyllic simplicity of premodernity.[44] Furthermore, and of particular importance for the question of political authority, the corruption of people's

39. Locke, *Two Treatises*, 318, § 76.
40. Ibid., 338–43, §§ 107–11.
41. Ibid., 341–43, §§ 110–11; cf. Hont, "Smith's History of Law," 143–44.
42. Locke, *Two Treatises*, 342, § 111.
43. Ibid., 342–43, § 111.
44. Hont, "Smith's History of Law," 144.

sentiments by ambition and luxury meant that present governments could not claim legitimacy by direct descent from the earliest kings, who had directly received their authority by the consent of the ruled. The economic sea change that introduced and enabled advanced civilization meant that governmental legitimacy in juridical terms had to be *refounded* in the consent of the people, in line with full acknowledgement that humanity's situation was now characterized by potentially severe misalignment of the interests of princes and subjects.

Providing for such consent, however, threatened to constitute a serious stumbling block for Locke. Manifestly there had never been any act of political refounding for modern conditions in recorded—or even plausible conjectural—history, no moment at which modern peoples' had expressly given their consent to forms of government on the basis of *salus populi* with especial regard to the defense of property, which Locke identified as the justificatory basis of all government.[45] Locke's solution to this predicament—much more powerful and conceptually adept than is typically realized—was his notorious invocation of tacit consent.[46] Men were said to have given "*sufficient Declaration*" of consent to be "*subject*" to the Laws of any Government" when they "hath any Possession, or Enjoyment, of any part of the Dominions of Government," extending not just to the possession of land under the protection of law, but "barely travelling freely on the Highway."[47] Whilst naturalized foreigners needed to engage in an act of explicit consent to join a political society, those born into it gave their sufficient consent tacitly by enjoying the benefits of organized power and choosing not to decamp to the wilderness of America to start political society afresh upon reaching maturity.

Lying behind Locke's supposition of tacit consent was his juridical framework with its stipulation that government was founded on the twin principles of utility and authority. Tacit consent was a bilateral phenomenon. Subjects indicated that they gave such consent by staying within a government's territory and taking advantage of the improved living it made possible. But, equally, such consent was always given on condition that the rulers of political society continuously promoted the interests of the ruled to a sufficient degree. If a government failed with regard to the *salus populi*, it violated the grounds of utility, and hence forfeited the basis of authority. Due to Locke's polemical purposes in writing the *Two Treatises* as an intellectual justification for armed revolution, it is the insurrectionist side of his conceptual coin that tends to be emphasized: that if government sufficiently harms the interests of the people, then the people may rightfully rebel and overthrow it—even if there is no intrinsically secular justification for such action, human judgment being fallible,

---

45. Locke, *Two Treatises*, 350–51, §§ 123–24.

46. Compare, for example, A. John Simmons's criticisms of Locke on tacit consent, which if I am correct in my reading, miss their mark: A. John Simmons, "Justification and Legitimacy," in *Justification and Legitimacy*, 137–38, and "'Denisons' and 'Aliens'", 158–78.

47. Locke, *Two Treatises*, 347–48, § 119.

and with the situation ultimately devolving to "an appeal to heaven."[48] But Locke was clear that such a situation was highly unusual, with the interests of the people needing to be pushed a very long way before rebellion was actually likely to be triggered.[49]

The more normal state of affairs, which Locke's juridical framework also covered, related not to the right of revolution but to the right of legitimate governmental coercion. The government of a political society that successfully upheld *salus populi* and was tacitly consented to by its subjects possessed rightful authority over its populace. As a consequence, such a government could legitimately deploy coercive force—the necessary means of political rule—with regard to that populace. Utility and authority were thus deeply intertwined for Locke, and the innovation of tacit consent was much more than an ad hoc innovation to get around the evident lack of a historical ur-revolution at the foundation of modern politics. Tacit consent tied subjects to established government whilst generating the legitimacy of such government's authority in the ordering of political society. Accordingly, whilst governmental authority certainly depended upon the delivery of utility, the point also cut the other way. Insofar as citizens were the recipients of sufficient levels of utility, they granted authority to the government that provided it—tacitly, but no less conclusively.[50]

This was Locke's account of political obligation. It was irredeemably theistic insofar as its linchpin—consent—could only have the normative force Locke ascribed to it by granting Locke's foundational premise that God made us all equal and free in juridical terms, even if in real history the central fact that had to be negotiated was that humans were everywhere and always unequal in their physical, economic, and rational capacities. But it was nonetheless a powerful, and within its own terms, coherent, account of why legitimate government could coerce, and why by the very same lights illegitimate government could be removed. Smith's later history of law and government was an ambitious attempt to "fill the enormous gap that Locke left between his history of early governments and the emergence of the English constitutional crisis of the seventeenth century."[51] Smith displaced Locke's historical story,

---

48. Ibid., 282, 426–27, §§ 20, 240–42.
49. Ibid., 416–18, § 228.
50. Hont's claim that Locke believed "that the corruption of early governments could be reversed only through active resistance and revolution" is therefore an overstatement ("Smith's History of Law," 143). The advent of tacit consent meant that resistance and revolution were the exception, not the norm, resorted to only in cases of extreme necessity. As Locke rhetorically put it when making a different but connected point: "how came so many lawful Monarchies into the World?"—the point being that the world *was* populated with lawful (i.e., legitimate) monarchies, for the most part, and despite the general lack of ur-acts of resistance and revolution (Locke, *Two Treatises*, 344, § 113).
51. Hont, "Smith's History of Law," 149.

replacing the account of liberty gained and lost owing to a luxury-engendered corruption with a complex historical triad of liberty gained, lost, and regained thanks to the motor of economic luxury, which could ultimately be politically vindicated as the basis of modern liberty.[52] But the central political theoretical action in Locke's account is ultimately not in his historical story of man's natural condition (and his subsequent exit from that condition in real historical practice), but in his underpinning normative juridical framework. Smith's history of law and government by itself cannot touch Locke's underlying explanation of how and why legitimate political authority is generated: it can only propose a different, more optimistic, view of mankind's past and progress. For an alternative theory of political obligation, one that presents a direct alternative to Locke's theism, we must ultimately locate the primary point of disagreement as being with regard to the juridical, not the historical, account. Although in the cases of both Hume and Smith we shall see that reorganizing the historical story still matters—hence why it is worth having Locke's alternative before us in detail as I have tried to set it out above. But understanding the proper role of history in both Hume's and Smith's political theories depends upon our appreciating the normative reconfiguration that was first achieved by Hume.

Hume's Alternative

Hume agreed with Locke that property could exist prior to the erection of governmental power, although he accounted for this through the workings of human imagination rather than a labor-mixing theory of acquisition. Property was a species of causation: the mind attributed a "necessary connexion" to external relations (in this case, human individuals and physical objects), which in fact had its basis in the mind itself owing to repeated exposure to regularities of convention, not any relations detected between external objects.[53] Establishing conventions for the stability of possessions was a crucial prerequisite for sociable living, and in human beings' most primitive conditions the obvious innovation accordingly settled upon would be for each individual to

---

52. Ibid., 165. Whether luxury could be morally vindicated is a separate question. Smith's late skepticism on this matter, expressed in a revision to the final edition of the *Theory of Moral Sentiments*, is well-known: "The disposition to admire, and almost to worship, the rich and the powerful, and to despise, or, at least, to neglect persons of poor and mean condition, though necessary both to establish and to maintain the distinction of ranks and the order of society, is, at the same time, the great and most universal cause of the corruption of our moral sentiments": Adam Smith, *The Glasgow Edition of the Works and Correspondence of Adam Smith: The Theory of Moral Sentiments*, ed. D. D. Raphael and A. L. Macfie (Oxford: Oxford University Press, 1976), 61.

53. David Hume, *The Clarendon Edition of the Works of David Hume: A Treatise of Human Nature*, ed. D. F. Norton and M. J. Norton (Oxford: Oxford University Press, 2007), T.2.1.10.1, SBN 310; T.3.2.3.6–8; SBN 505–7.

have sanctity over whatever they presently possessed. Hume here drew upon his innovative use of state-of-nature theory, now recast as thought experiment, to make the point:

> I first consider men in their savage and solitary condition; and suppose, that being sensible of the misery of that state, and foreseeing the advantages that would result from society, they seek each other's company, and make an offer of mutual protection and assistance. I also suppose, that they are endowed with such sagacity as immediately to perceive, that the chief impediment to this project of society and partnership lies in the avidity and selfishness of their natural temper; to remedy which, they enter into a convention for the stability of possession, and for mutual restraint and forbearance. I am sensible, that this method of proceeding is not altogether natural; but besides that I here only suppose those reflections to be formed at once, which in fact arise insensibly and by degrees.[54]

More complex relations, however, required the emergence of new conventions, and property relations evolved to encompass the grounds of occupation, prescription, accession, and succession, as well as specified ways in which property could be legitimately transferred, principally by consent, thus allowing dynamic exchanges between utility-seeking individuals.[55] Yet, after human societies grew to such a size that anonymity and the possibility for self-interested defection overcame the bonds of sympathy and mutual affection, the innovation of magistracy was required to settle disputes over property in a satisfactory way, impartial arbitration in such conditions being much preferable to the partial and self-interested judgments of individual plaintiffs.[56] The innovation of magistracy, initially introduced to regulate the possession and transfer of property by redirecting the short-term pursuit of contiguous self-interest to socially cohesive ends, led to the erection of government. In time, government developed to take on the role not just of protecting possessions, but of compelling subjects to partake in "concurrence in some common end or purpose." This enabled large-scale collective action, and thus "bridges are built; harbours open'd; ramparts rais'd; canals form'd; fleets equip'd; and armies disciplin'd."[57]

But there was no guarantee that human beings would, as a matter of actual historical development, create the artifice of government. The tribes of North America demonstrated that humans could live in "concord and amity" for thousands of years without formalizing mechanisms for resolving disputes

---

54. Hume, *Treatise*, T.3.2.3.3, SBN 502–3.
55. Ibid., T.3.2.3–4, SBN 501–16.
56. Ibid., T.3.2.7.7, SBN 538.
57. Ibid., T.3.2.7.8, SBN 538–39.

over property. Instead, the bonds of tribal affection and the "natural" and "moral" obligations to justice were sufficient to maintain successful small-scale societies able to meet the needs and wants of their members.[58] "The state of society without government is one of the most natural states of men, and may subsist with the conjunction of many families, and long after first generation."[59] Government in its modern form was a specific and geographically peculiar invention, carried to particular perfection in Europe (although other locales had also achieved this innovation, China being the oldest remaining non-European example). Its origin thus required special explanation.

Hume broadly agreed with Locke that the decisive change from pregovernmental society to political organization proper came about owing to the growth of competition between groups following economic development: "Nothing but an increase of riches and possessions cou'd oblige men to quit" their natural condition of concord and amity.[60] Men could maintain small-scale primitive society, operating the artifice of justice even without government, only in conditions of external security. If threatened by aggressive outsiders attracted by the material prosperity generated by group living, things were different:

> Men fear nothing from public war and violence but the resistance they meet with, which, because they share it in common, seems less terrible; and because it comes from strangers, seems less pernicious in its consequences, than when they are expos'd singly against one whose commerce is advantageous to them, and without whose society 'tis impossible they can subsist. Now foreign war to a society without government necessarily produces civil war. Throw any considerable goods among men, they instantly fall a quarrelling, while each strives to get possession of what pleases him, without regard to the consequences. In a foreign war the most considerable of all goods, life and limbs, are at stake; and as every one shuns dangerous ports, seizes the best arms, seeks excuse for the slightest wounds, the laws, which may be well enough observed while men were calm, can now no longer take place, when they are in such commotion.[61]

Military organization for defense taught people the benefits of submitting to the rule of an individual who provided the decisive leadership required for security. Learning the advantages of this mode of organization, humans later imported it back into civil arrangements. Magistrates were appointed for the regulation of possessions, thus improving the workings of the artifice of justice in large and lasting conditions, and eventually enabling large-scale

---

58. Ibid., T.3.2.8.2, SBN 540.
59. Ibid., T.3.2.8.2, SBN 541.
60. Ibid., T.3.2.8.2, SBN 541.
61. Ibid., T.3.2.8.1, SBN 540.

coordination to enhance public utility to the benefit of all. This was the birth of government. Again, the American Indian tribes provided the proof, albeit via implicit comparison with their alternative historical experience. Only during times of war did individual Indians "pay any submission to any of their fellows," when "their captain enjoys a shadow of authority, which he loses after return from the field, and the establishment of peace with neighbouring tribes."[62] When hostilities ceased, the abundance of the North American geographic bounty meant the Indian tribes could revert to small-scale societies operating justice without government.[63] The origin of European government lay in the geographic pressures of a smaller territory where resource scarcity and the proximity of rivals necessitated the retention of authoritative leadership in civil, as well as military, matters, not least because future conflicts with neighbors were correctly expected to recur. Paradoxically, the less resource-rich environment of Europe had required more intensive cultivation of the land, which owing to the benefits of organized industry led to more rapid and considerable economic development than in North America, greed for which eventually triggered the wars of acquisition that gave birth to leadership, magistracy, and eventually government.

Smith's attempt to fill the gap Locke left between his history of early governments and the English constitutional crisis thus had precedent. Hume had already suggested the outlines of a historical story predicating economic development as the motor of history, even if in the *Treatise* we have to infer this from the logic of his position rather than it being stated outright.[64] Hume later supplied at least part of the story directly in *The History of England*, the medieval volumes of which argued that the English barons had dissolved their own power by pursuing luxury status goods at the expense of military power, allowing in turn for the emergence of modern liberty as feudalism was replaced with modern constitutional government.[65] That is, Hume offered the same basic account of the historical relationship between luxury and modern liberty that Adam Smith later placed at the heart of book 3 of *The Wealth of Nations*.

In the *Treatise* Hume disparaged the Lockean suggestion that political leadership first emerged as the patriarchs of families were bequeathed political power by offspring already accustomed to their rule, taking his economic-military hypothesis about the origin of government to "be more natural, than

62. Ibid., T.3.2.8.2, SBN 540.
63. Ibid., T.3.2.8.2-3, SBN 540-41.
64. Hont, "Smith's History of Law," 149.
65. David Hume, *The History of England from the Invasion of Julius Caesar to the Revolution in 1688*, foreword by William B. Todd (Indianapolis: Liberty Fund, 1983), vol. 1, 463-64; vol. 2, 523-24; cf. Andrew Sabl, *Hume's Politics: Coordination and Crisis in the "History of England"* (Princeton, NJ: Princeton University Press, 2012), 63-68.

the common one deriv'd from patriarchal government, or the authority of the father, which is said first to take place in one family, and to accustom the members of it to the government of a single person."[66] Furthermore, early leadership conceived of as an outgrowth of economically triggered military competition straightforwardly accounted for why all political societies started as monarchies, and why "republics arise only from the abuses of monarchy and despotic power." Military leadership had to be strictly hierarchical, a single decision-making power vested with final say, which in turn became the essence of kingship as a form of civil rule.[67]

As a consequence, historically speaking Hume was more thoroughly a theorist of the original contract than Locke. Members of tribal groupings living in "amity and concord," and operating the artifice of justice but not yet government, would, recognizing the threat from external aggressors, initially meet together to expressly pledge obedience to the individual perceived as most capable in organizing defense: "When men have once perceiv'd the necessity of government to maintain peace, and execute justice, they wou'd naturally assemble together, wou'd choose magistrates, determine their power, and *promise* them obedience." Learning the benefits of leadership in times of war, and seeing that the administration of justice would be better maintained in times of peace if the innovation were retained, people initially promised obedience and erected government through a foundational act of consent. At the very beginning of political societies, therefore, obedience to government *was* founded in the obligation arising from an act of promising, and the authority of the earliest governments was straightforwardly a function of the consent of the ruled: "a promise" being "suppos'd to be a bond or security already in use, and attended with a moral obligation, 'tis to be consider'd as the original sanction of government, and as the source of the first obligation to obedience."[68]

Yet Hume denied that promising could be the foundation of authority or the basis of obligation with regard to government in conditions of European modernity. To demonstrate this he attacked not Locke's specific account in the second "Treatise," but the popularized Lockean position advanced by the Whig party of his day. The "foundation of our fashionable system of politics" and the "creed of a party amongst us" transplanted the historical plausibility of an original promise directly into contemporary conditions: "*All men*, say they, *are born free and equal: Government and superiority can only be established by consent: The consent of men, in establishing government, imposes on them a new obligation, unknown to the laws of nature. Men, therefore, are bound to obey their magistrates, only because they promise it; and if they had not*

---

66. Hume, *Treatise*, T.3.2.8.2, SBN 541; cf. "Original Contract," 468–69.
67. Hume, *Treatise*, T.3.2.8.2, SBN 540.
68. Ibid., T.3.2.8.3, SBN 541; cf. Hume, "Original Contract," 468, 474.

given their word, either expressly or tacitly, to preserve allegiance, it would never have become a part of their moral duty."[69] This was a vulgarized and secularized version of Locke's account.[70] (Indeed without appeal to consent as the divinely sanctioned mechanism by which authority could be generated, Locke himself would have repudiated it as conceptually incoherent and normatively inert.) Hume was scornful of this popularized Whig view: "when carry'd so far as to comprehend government in all its ages and situations, [it] is entirely erroneous."[71] Such vulgar Lockeanism proceeded as though there were no difference between primitives establishing the first systems of hierarchical social organization and European moderns who had inherited hundreds of years of constitutional history and institutional political practice. Such an equation was an absurdity, refuted by any common observation of the facts not corrupted by excessive party philosophy. By contrast, Hume maintained that although "the duty of allegiance be at first grafted on the obligation of promises, and be for some time supported by that obligation, yet as soon as advantages of government are fully known and acknowledg'd, it immediately takes root of itself, and has an original obligation and authority, independent of all contracts."[72]

Dispatching the vulgarized version of Locke's account was child's play. Drawing on his own theory of artificial virtues, Hume demonstrated that the "natural" and "moral" obligations to promise keeping and obedience to authority were entirely distinct, as were the ends for which human beings first invented, and then engaged in, such practices. One might as well resolve the convention of promise keeping into allegiance, as the other way around.[73] As

---

69. Hume, *Treatise*, T.3.2.8.3, SBN 542. There is a historical puzzle here, however, insofar as by the late 1730s popularized Lockeanism was unlikely to have been altogether fashionable, being instead something of an embarrassment to establishment Court Whigs, and evidently of no appeal to opposition Tories. It is also arguable that the territory of political argument by this point had shifted from philosophical and jurisdiction notions of contract to historical narrative about an ancient constitution. Why, then, did Hume claim Lockeanism as the foundational philosophical theory of contemporary Whiggism? We may never possess a definitive answer, but it is surely relevant that Hume composed the *Treatise* in France, away from the day-to-day party controversies of England. Furthermore, his interests were arguably of a deep philosophical kind, even if he took himself to be also capable of addressing relevant contemporary issues. That is, here is an example where attempting to tie Hume closely to the live practical political context of his time is liable to confuse, rather than illuminate, the nature of his political thought.

70. For Hume as criticizing "vulgar" Whig doctrines in the mode of fundamentally friendly, if severe, critic, who sought instead to supply a "scientific" basis for Whig politics, see Forbes, *Hume's Philosophical Politics*, 126, 139, 150–53. The division between "vulgar" and "scientific" Whiggism is something of a joke on Forbes's part: Hont, "Commercial Society," 59.

71. Hume, *Treatise*, T.3.2.8.3, SBN 542.

72. Ibid., T.3.2.8.3, SBN 542.

73. Ibid., T.3.2.8.4–8, SBN 543–47; Hume, "Original Contract," 481–82.

for tacit consent, Hume lambasted this as simply a further absurdity. On the one hand, "what is given tacitly and insensibly can never have such influence on mankind, as what is perform'd expressly and openly," thus drastically reducing the plausibility that tacit consent could provide sufficient basis for the erection of political authority. On the other, tacit consent presumed—at least if it was to have any meaningful content—the willed intention of the individual that signs other than explicit speech be taken as the giving of consent: "a will there must certainly be in the case, and can never escape the person's notice, who exerted it, however silent or tacit." Yet, manifestly, "were you to ask the greatest part of the nation, whether they had ever consented to the authority of their rulers, or promis'd to obey them" they would think "very strangely of you" and reply that "the affair depended not on their consent, but that they were born to such obedience."[74] Trying to get around this by saying that a person's continued residency in a territory constituted consent to political authority was only a further absurdity. Could it be reasonable to claim that a poor peasant without the means to emigrate nonetheless freely gave willed and meaningful consent via continued residency?[75] Nobody not led astray by party frenzy could seriously maintain so, evidenced by the fact that nobody had ever suggested the doctrine of tacit consent before the constitutional crises of the late seventeenth century, a sure sign that it was not the basis of authority in modern (or indeed any) conditions.[76]

Hume's task was made easy by his total disregarding of Locke's juridical motivations in making tacit consent the *normative* linchpin of his account of authority. Hume bypassed this central aspect of Locke's theory—a casualty of his insistence on an entirely secular account of politics, as we shall see below, which from Hume's perspective simply ruled out Locke's peculiar theistic grounding of the normativity of consent as an admissible option—whilst torpedoing the vulgarized version of Locke's ideas that drew upon tacit consent not as a normative justification for authority in the absence of a political ur-revolution, but as an *empirical* claim about the foundations of authority in present circumstances. This has led some of Locke's more recent admirers to bemoan Hume's arguments as a failure to engage with Locke's most serious underlying position, supplying only a straw-man version of his ideas easily put up for burning.[77] Yet whilst Hume's presentation of his arguments is liable to give the impression of sloppy misrepresentation, further fuelling the

74. Hume, *Treatise*, T.3.2.8.9, SBN 547–48.
75. Hume, "Original Contract," 475.
76. Hume, *Treatise*, T.3.2.8.9, SBN 547–48; "Original Contract," 475–77.
77. Dunn, "Applied Theology," 129; Brownsey, "Hume and the Social Contract," 145; Martyn P. Thompson, "Hume's Critique of Locke and the 'Original Contract'," *Il pensiero politico* 10, no. 10 (1977), 189–201. Buckle and Castiglione, "Hume's Critique," defends Hume from the complaints Thompson advances, in a spirit similar to the argument advanced here.

suspicion that he lacks a theory of politics proper and offers only a political sociology, it is nonetheless a serious mistake to conclude that this is all he in fact supplies. Hume fully engaged the fundamental challenge bequeathed by Locke: the need to supply an alternative theory of authority that did away entirely with consent as the normative linchpin within a theistic framework. Yet his response to Locke, unlike his direct reply to the popularized Lockeanism of his day, is offered by implication rather than direct engagement. It is revealed—and must ultimately be judged—by the coherence and conclusion of his own rival positive account of authority, which if successful would entirely displace not just Locke's conceptual edifice, but the fundamental worldview upon which it was predicated. It is that positive account of political authority we must therefore examine.

Utility and Authority

Hume agreed with Locke that identifying the proper basis of authority required understanding its relation to utility. The appropriate point of analysis was the one Locke had identified: under what circumstances government was owed obedience, and when it forfeited a rightful claim of allegiance by prejudicing utility. Hume summarized the Lockean position concisely. Because government was an invention for the furthering of "protection and security," people would only reasonably consent to the authority of such government so long as these things were provided. If instead they were met with "tyranny and oppression," they were "freed from their promises (as happens in all conditional contracts) and return to that state of liberty, which preceded the institution of government."[78] Authority was conditional on utility: if government did not supply the latter, it forfeited the former. In times of crisis rebellion was therefore licensed, but in times of stability obedience was owed. Hume did not question that the *outcome* of this argument was "perfectly just and reasonable."[79] The problem was that "the conclusion is just, tho' the principles be erroneous." The most erroneous principle of all was making the connection between utility and authority dependent upon a conditional promise given by the ruled—something which had never actually taken place, and which nobody other than party philosophers had ever thought to be the basis of political authority in modern conditions.[80] By contrast, Hume believed that he could "establish the same conclusion on more reasonable principles."[81]

78. Hume, *Treatise*, T.3.2.9.1, SBN 549–50. In the "Original Contract," Hume added the insistence on natural equality to the secularized version of Locke's argument, which maintained that "all men are . . . born equal and owe allegiance to no prince or government unless bound by the obligation and sanction of a promise": "Original Contract," 469.
79. Hume, *Treatise*, T.3.2.9.1, SBN 549.
80. Ibid., T.3.2.8.8, SBN 547.
81. Ibid., T.3.2.9.2, SBN 550.

To do so he turned to his own theory of artificial virtues, coupled with observation of the actual psychological processes undergone by agents living under modern political rule. Allegiance, like justice, was attended with both a "natural" and a "moral" obligation. The natural obligation was straightforward and obvious. Being an artifice for the promotion of utility, the natural obligation to obey government extended only so far as utility was indeed promoted: "This interest I find to consist in the security and protection, which we enjoy in political society, and which we can never attain, when perfectly free and independent. As interest, therefore, is the immediate sanction of government, the one can have no longer being than the other; and whenever the civil magistrate carries his oppression so far as to render his authority perfectly intolerable, we are no longer bound to submit to it."[82] As well as making appeals to promising as a method of securing utility being insufficiently parsimonious and explanatorily redundant, the natural obligation to allegiance explained why the Lockean conclusion that abusive governmental power may legitimately be resisted was correct: "The cause ceases; the effect must cease also."[83]

But with regard to the "moral" obligation to obedience, "the maxim wou'd here be false, that *when the cause ceases, the effect must cease also*." It was readily observable that human beings are "mightily addicted to *general rules*, and that we often carry our maxims beyond those reasons, which first induc'd us to establish them."[84] The moral obligation to allegiance outran the natural. On the one hand, allegiance (like justice) took on the quality of a moral virtue in its own right, the agreeableness and utility of which did not make direct recourse to calculations of individual interest, and were strengthened by sympathy with the public weal. The prospect of rebellion made one uneasy for the interests of oneself and one's neighbors, and the typically vain and selfish ambitions of rebels were manifest to others, who accordingly found their actions disagreeable, likely to be contrary to utility, and thus vicious—further strengthening the virtue of allegiance by comparison.[85] Established power received enhanced sanction from the very fact that it was established, and people were apt to tolerate infractions of their immediate interest (undermining their "natural" obligation to virtue) without this translating into a forfeiture of the "moral" obligation.[86] The basis of modern authority was thus a function of complex psychological processes supervening on the securing of interest,

82. Ibid., T.3.2.9.2, SBN 550–51.
83. Ibid., T.3.2.9.2, SBN 550–51.
84. Ibid., T.3.2.9.3, SBN 551.
85. Ibid., T.3.2.10.3, SBN 555.
86. Ibid., T.3.2.10.19, SBN 566: "that power, which at first was founded only on injustice and violence, becomes in time legal and obligatory. Nor does the mind rest there; but returning back upon its footsteps, transfers to their predecessors and ancestors that right, which it naturally ascribes to the posterity, as being related together, and united in the imagination."

rather than being straightforwardly utilitarian—dependent upon the workings of human imagination in line with general rules and sympathy with public utility, not the direct calculation of individual advantage.

Humans only gave up the "moral" obligation to obedience when the "general rule" of allegiance was confronted with an exception that itself had the qualities of a "general rule, and be founded on very numerous and common instances." Although people fundamentally submit to the "authority of others" in order "to procure themselves some security against the wickedness and injustice of men," nobody was naïve enough to believe that those appointed to rule thereby automatically transcended the partiality and rapaciousness that ordinary individuals were prone to. What was expected from rulers "depends not on a change of their nature but of their situation, when they acquire a more immediate interest in the preservation of order and the execution of justice." Nonetheless, separated from their subjects by wealth and power, rulers were apt to neglect even their immediate interest in providing the *salus populi*, instead being "transported by their passions into all the excesses of cruelty and ambition." Awareness of these facts provided the "general rule" that could, in extreme enough circumstances, outweigh the general rules underpinning our "moral" obligation to obedience. "Our general knowledge of human nature, our observation of the past history of mankind, our experience of present times" all combined to yield the conclusion "that we may resist the more violent effects of supreme power, without any crime or injustice."[87]

Hume's account received added credibility by being "both the general practice and principle of mankind." Likewise, "no nation, that cou'd find any remedy, ever yet suffer'd the cruel ravages of a tyrant, or were blam'd for their resistance."[88] The Tory doctrine of passive obedience was an "absurdity," decisively revealed as such by reconfiguring the Lockean conclusion of a right of resistance on an empirically credible and intellectually coherent foundation.[89] When one got down to the fundamentals of what government was an invention for, "There evidently is no other principle than interest." Accordingly, "if interest first produces obedience to government, the obligation to obedience must cease, whenever the interest ceases, in any great degree, and in a considerable number of instances."[90]

Yet rebellion was sociologically a highly unusual phenomenon: people's interests had to be pushed a very long way before they took up arms en masse, whilst the vain ambitions of rebels seeking self-aggrandizement rather than the *salus populi* met with the disapproval and rejection of the populace. Furthermore it was "certain, that in the ordinary course of human affairs nothing

---

87. Ibid., T.3.2.93, SBN 551–52.
88. Ibid., T.3.2.9.4, SBN 552.
89. Ibid., T.3.2.9.4, SBN 552; cf. Hume, "Passive Obedience," 489–91.
90. Hume, *Treatise*, T.3.2.9.4, SBN 553; cf. Hume, *Principles of Morals*, 28.

can be more pernicious and criminal" than rebellion. Whilst "numerous and civiliz'd societies cannot subsist without government," it was equally the case that "government is entirely useless without an exact obedience." The means and end of government would be debilitated were individuals to withdraw obedience whenever they personally judged that it was in their interest to do so: "We ought always to weigh the advantages, which we reap from authority, against the disadvantages; and by this means we shall become more scrupulous of putting in practice the doctrine of resistance. The common rule requires submission; and 'tis only in cases of grievous tyranny and oppression, that the exception can take place."[91] A "blind submission" was due to magistracy in all cases other than the extreme one of resistance to tyranny.[92] Implicit in Hume's sociological analysis of allegiance and obligation is therefore a utilitarian justification for the necessity of obedience in normal conditions, couched in terms of the likely disastrous effects of aggregated individual judgment. If the decision whether to obey was left to each individual on a case-by-case basis, this would jeopardize the continued functioning of government, which required "blind submission" in the aggregate.[93] Hobbes's conclusion had therefore been just, though his principles erroneous: individual judgment was not a primary source of destructive confrontation, but its elimination was nonetheless a requirement for political obligation and the securing of obedience in modern conditions. Fortunately, the moral obligation to allegiance ensured that human beings spontaneously reconciled themselves to obedience, refraining from case-by-case judgment in favor of a "blind submission" in ordinary circumstances. Government power thus did not need to explicitly take over the function of individual judgment as a necessary condition of continued political stability.

Nonetheless, the right of revolution was not something that could be clearly determined in advance by disgruntled individuals, or prescribed a priori by the

---

91. Hume, *Treatise*, T.3.2.10.1, SBN 553–54; cf. "Original Contract," 480.

92. Hume, *Treatise*, T.3.2.10.2, SBN 554.

93. Ibid., T.3.2.10.1, SBN 553–54. Of course, this justification could only work with regard *to the aggregate*, and could gain little traction with the solitary individual who pointed out that *his* or *her* particular act of self-interested defection, if undetected and unpunished, would benefit him- or herself without bringing down the social edifice. Regarding the problem of this "free rider," as the concept came to be known to the chagrin of twentieth-century political and economic scientists, see Richard Tuck, *Free Riding* (Cambridge, MA: Harvard University Press, 2008), chap. 4 of which explicitly examines Hume's theory of artificial virtues. I do not, however, agree with Tuck's reading, and suggest that Hume's answer to the political free rider is better understood as paralleling that of his answer to the free-riding "sensible knave" of the second *Enquiry*: the self-approval flowing from adherence to the moral obligation to allegiance is the reason individuals should "blindly submit" to government. Regarding Hume and the "sensible knave," see Paul Sagar, "Minding the Gap: Bernard Williams and David Hume on Living an Ethical Life," *Journal of Moral Philosophy* 11, no. 5 (2014), 615–38.

theorist. Although no reasonable person blamed subjects for overthrowing a Nero or a Philip II, this judgment was only admissible when made retrospectively.[94] Hume acknowledged that a right of revolution existed, but this was distinct from a right to openly promote revolution. Such action threatened to destabilize government by undermining the authority upon which it irreducibly depended.[95] If authority became genuinely forfeit owing to assaults upon utility, revolution would (eventually) spontaneously occur. Political theory could not validate such spontaneity beyond its sociological manifestation as a consequence of the degradation of the *salus populi* eventually eroding the imaginative basis of authority. Whilst revolutions could be legitimate, Hume's philosophy told strongly against the possibility of a *justificatory theory of a right of revolution*, one that could be appealed to over and above the interplay of utility and authority in the imagination of the citizenry. The practice of politics in any given time and place, not the dictates of philosophy, should (and would) determine the conduct of a people with regard to tyrants. Indeed, Hume felt that sometimes the sentiments of the people tended *too far* toward authority and paradoxically threatened to undermine utility, as had occurred when the general citizenry of England had almost prevented the Glorious Revolution through a dogmatic loyalty to the dangerously reactionary James II.[96] By the mid-eighteenth century, however, Hume saw the pendulum as swinging too far the other way: an overemphasis on liberty by the victorious descendants of 1688, coupled with the vulgar Lockean justification of a right of revolution, jeopardized the simultaneous maintenance of authority upon which all viable government depended. Hume's "skeptical Whiggism" was a perspective urging a corrective to both excesses.[97]

With the basis of authority accordingly delineated, the question arose as to whom obedience was due. Hume identified five bases upon which modern authority was granted, none of them founded upon an act of promising: long possession, present possession, conquest, succession, and positive law.[98] Again, these were all determined more by human imagination—with a peculiar predilection for members of established ruling families—than by direct appeal to interest.[99] "The same interest . . . which causes us to submit to magistracy, makes us renounce itself in the choice of our magistrates, and binds us down to a certain form of government, and to particular persons, without allowing us to aspire to the utmost perfection in either." Determining the "objects of allegiance" paralleled the conventions established for the

94. Hume, *Treatise*, T.3.2.9.4, SBN 552.
95. Hume, "Of the Origin of Government," in *Essays*, 40.
96. Hume, *Treatise*, T.3.2.10.16-19, SBN 360-62; Hont, "Smith's History of Law," 151-52; Forbes, *Hume's Philosophical Politics*, 96-98, 139.
97. Ibid., chap. 5.
98. Hume, *Treatise*, T.3.2.10.4-14, SBN 556-62.
99. Ibid., T.3.2.10.11-13, SBN 559-61.

government of possessions. It is "highly advantageous, and even absolutely necessary to society, that possession shou'd be stable; and this leads us to such a rule." But were we to pursue that same advantage "in assigning particular possessions to particular persons, we shou'd disappoint our end, and perpetuate the confusion, which that end is intended to prevent." Likewise, we come "to choose our magistrates without having in view any particular advantage from the choice."[100] Deciding on the "objects" of allegiance in practice, as with analysis of the phenomenon of authority more generally, was only indirectly a function of utility, being more primarily dependent upon the "general rules" that influenced human imagination. In the terminology Hume would adopt after the *Treatise*, authority was therefore ultimately a function of "opinion." It is "on opinion only that government is founded," even in the most despotic and military governments, analytically decomposing into that of "interest" and that of "right" (itself subdivided between that of "power" and that of "property"), corresponding to what the *Treatise* had labeled the "natural" and "moral" obligations to allegiance.[101]

Explicated in this manner, Hume's account may indeed appear to offer only a sociology of politics. "Opinion" resembles the contemporary category of "public opinion," and an empirically plausible sociological account of how and why people do or do not obey particular forms of rule is duly forthcoming. Yet the question of why obedience and authority are owed not just as a matter of psychological observation of how people are, but as a *normative obligation over and above contingent local practices*—one which is binding upon citizens in all times outside of tyranny, and can be legitimately coercively extracted by rightful rulers—remains conspicuously outstanding. In short, despite the astuteness of his psychological account and his allowing for the justice of rebellion in times of tyrannical oppression, Hume apparently fails to address the outstanding philosophical issue: how the phenomenon of political obligation, a permanent feature of social organization under modern government, can be *normatively justified*, rather than merely *sociologically explained*. Yet what we need to recognize is that Hume's "sociology" is predicated upon an underlying philosophical worldview that rejects the possibility of external normative justification as granted by the pronouncements of philosophy, and seeks to reconfigure our thinking about how even to pose, and then answer, the question of what political obligation can coherently consist of. Until that is realized we will radically underappreciate and misunderstand the nature and scale of Hume's ambition, as well as his "sociology." To do better we must pay close

100. Ibid., T.3.2.10.3, SBN 555–56.
101. Hume, "First Principles," 31–34; cf. Dunn, "Applied Theology," 121: "Property, justice, allegiance, loyalty, duty, fidelity, all human rights and all human duties, are in the last instances functions of opinion."

attention to Hume's conception of what philosophy is, and the little it can hope to achieve in practical matters.

Opinion and the Role of Philosophy

By Locke's account, God's having creating men free and equal, and able to generate legitimate political authority only via the mechanism of consent, ensured that there was always an evaluative philosophical position external to particular human practices from which those practices could be judged, with specific arrangements impugned or justified accordingly. Hume entirely rejected this.[102] His wholly secular political theory contended that human political practice could only be judged from the inside, by its own standards and values. As he put it when concluding his case against the popular secularized version of Locke's position:

> Lest those arguments shou'd not appear entirely conclusive (as I think they are) I shall have recourse to authority, and shall prove, from the universal consent of mankind, that the obligation of submission to government is not deriv'd from any promise of the subjects. Nor need any one wonder, that tho' I have all along endeavour'd to establish my system on pure reason, and have scarce ever cited the judgment even of philosophers or historians on any article, I shou'd now appeal to popular authority, and oppose the sentiments of the rabble to any philosophical reasoning. For it must be observ'd, that the opinions of men, in this case, carry with them a peculiar authority, and are, in a great measure, infallible.[103]

Morality—which for Hume includes assessments of political legitimacy, authority, and obligation—"is founded on the pleasure or pain, which results from the view of any sentiment, or character." Yet such pleasure or pain "cannot be unknown to the person who feels it," hence there is only so much virtue or vice in any character or circumstance as one actually places in it.[104] Morality is a purely human construction, built out of the materials of natural sentiment (though it is no less real for being that). There is therefore *only* the internal perspective of sentiment from which to make moral and political judgments. But, moreover, the pronouncements of that perspective are ipso facto "infallible," because there just is no external perspective (such as God's) from which to judge them otherwise. Likewise, it is impossible that

---

102. Duncan Forbes, "Hume's Science of Politics," in *David Hume: Bicentenary Papers*, ed. G. P. Morice (Edinburgh: Edinburgh University Press,1977), 48–49; cf. Buckle and Castiglione, "Hume's Critique," 465–69.
103. Hume, *Treatise*, T.3.2.8.8, SBN 546.
104. Ibid.

with regard to what our sentiments find pleasure or pain in, we, as the sources and bearers of those sentiments, "can ever be mistaken."[105] Errors can be made about the "origin" of vices or virtues, but not about whether things *are* vices or virtues to us. With specific regard to authority and obligation, and the attendant artificial virtue of allegiance, the question of importance is not about "origin," but about "degree"—about whether we believe ourselves obliged to authority, thus owing obedience in given circumstances. Hume's conclusion, entailed by his underlying ethical sentimentalism, is that insofar as the opinion of mankind judges that some power possesses authority and is owed obedience, *it therefore does and is*.[106]

Locke would have entirely rejected Hume's position. But the action of disagreement would have taken place on the grounds of whether an external position is possible with regard to normative assessment of our present practices, and hence ultimately over the question of the existence of God and what we can know He wills and commands.[107] The same could not be said for the vulgarized Lockean position Hume deliberately put up as his target in the *Treatise*. This was deliberate, because Hume's science of man proceeded in entirely secular terms and hence he engaged not Locke's argument proper, but only that version of it that could be admitted under the principles of experience

---

105. Ibid. For a discussion (that is much more hostile to Hume) see Brownsey, "Hume and the Social Contract," 137–40, 147; for a counterview see Buckle and Castiglione, "Hume's Critique," 463–69.

106. Hume's approach, however, invites a serious worry about the mechanisms by which belief in political legitimacy is generated. Even if legitimacy can only ultimately be judged internally, we nonetheless need some way of identifying illegitimate methods, and in turn outcomes, when it comes to the securing the psychological assent of citizens, both when judging the conditions of historical and geographic others, and in assessing our own practices to decide whether they generate belief in legitimacy in the right sort of way. Hume does not address himself to this important concern, but after the twentieth century and following the growth in the modern state's capacity to manufacture consent via manipulation and intimidation, it cannot now be ignored. On precisely this point, however, see the importance that Bernard Williams assigns to what he calls the "Critical Theory Test" in his own Humean internalist political theory—i.e., the requirement that belief in a regime's legitimacy is not itself a function of the very power being putatively legitimated. Bernard Williams, *Truth and Truthfulness: An Essay in Genealogy* (Princeton, NJ: Princeton University Press, 2002), chap. 9, and also his essays collected in *In the Beginning Was the Deed: Realism and Moralism in Political Argument*, ed. G. Hawthorn (Princeton, NJ: Princeton University Press, 2005). See also Edward Hall, "Bernard Williams and the Basic Legitimation Demand: A Defence," *Political Studies*, 63 (2015), 466–80, and Paul Sagar, "From Scepticism to Liberalism: Bernard Williams, the Foundations of Liberalism, and Political Realism," *Political Studies* 64 (2016), 368–84. I return to this matter in chapter 6 below.

107. Hume would likely have had the better of that argument, as indicated by his posthumously published *Dialogues Concerning Natural Religion*. For a summary of the power of Hume's position in this work, see Simon Blackburn, *How to Read Hume* (London: Granta, 2008), chap. 8.

and observation—excluding any underlying theism, however essential for the coherence of a supervening account.[108] Hume demonstrated that the secularized version of Locke's view collapsed into incoherence when attempting to retain the external justificatory philosophical perspective whilst lacking the theocentric *weltanschauung* required to make it coherent. The most telling sign of this was the generation of absurd conclusions:

> Any one, who finding the impossibility of accounting for the right of the present possessor, by any receiv'd system of ethics, shou'd resolve to deny absolutely that right, and assert, that it is not authoriz'd by morality, wou'd be justly thought to maintain a very extravagant paradox, and to shock the common sense and judgment of mankind. No maxim is more conformable, both to prudence and morals, than to submit quietly to the government, which we find establish'd in the country where we happen to live, without enquiring too curiously into its origin and first establishment. Few governments will bear being examin'd so rigorously. How many kingdoms are there at present in the world, and how many more do we find in history, whose governors have no better foundation for their authority than that of present possession?[109]

Taking the example of the Grecian and Roman empires, it was evident that all titles in these periods were founded upon, and maintained by, violence: it "was by the sword ... that every emperor acquir'd, as well as defended his right." Accordingly, we must "either say, that all the known world, for so many ages, had no government, and ow'd no allegiance to any one or must allow, that the right of the stronger, in public affairs, is to be receiv'd as legitimate, and authoriz'd by morality, when not oppos'd by any other title."[110] It was absurd to insist that government founded upon the sword rather than the consent of the ruled was no government at all (and hence owed no obedience), simply because such a form of government did not conform to one's preferred philosophical tenets. Any philosophy that maintained that there had been no government owed obedience in the Graeco-Roman world did not offer a credible account of

---

108. We thus need to qualify Dunn's statement that Hume was not "at all a careful critic of Locke's text" and does not "appear to have grasped even the essentials of its argument," though he "certainly mounts an intellectual and polemically effective enough critique of vulgar Whig shibboleths": Dunn, "Applied Theology," 129; cf. Thompson, "Hume's Critique of Locke." Whether Hume was a careful reader of Locke becomes beside the point when we realize that his entire intellectual project in the *Treatise* was to conduct an investigation only in terms of "experience and observation," meaning theocentric political theory was excluded from the outset, to be entirely replaced by Hume's alternative secular philosophical worldview.

109. Hume, *Treatise*, T.3.2.10.7, SBN 558.

110. Ibid. Hume extended his list of examples in "Original Contract," 483–85.

authority and obligation. The correct response was to find a better philosophy, one able to account for the evident realities of the world.[111]

Indeed, Hume urged more than just the finding of a better philosophy: he aimed to call into question, and then realign, our underlying conception of what political philosophy is and can do. If one viewed the role of political philosophy as being the issuing of pronouncements as to the legitimacy of human social practices, predicated upon an external and ultimately superior standard of justification, whilst specifically making consent the condition by which the legitimacy of political authority was achieved, then one must claim that any government not actually consented to by its population was ipso facto illegitimate. As Hume demonstrated, the consequence of this was to end up committed to the apparently absurd conclusion that all government everywhere is, and has always been (at least after the first age of primitive founding), illegitimate.[112] Locke avoided such an embarrassing conclusion by appealing to tacit consent not as an empirical claim about how authority was actually generated in practice, but as a normative mechanism for securing the sanction of external justificatory legitimacy in the absence of a historic refoundation of political legitimacy, otherwise required to validate present arrangements.[113] But the secularized version of Locke's argument—which treated tacit consent not as a normative justification within a theistic juridical framework, but as a descriptive empirical claim about the actual basis of present authority in modern conditions—collapsed into absurdity. Because tacit consent was itself a manifest absurdity as an empirical proposition, secular Lockeans were confronted with a dilemma. Either maintain their system upon the absurdity of tacit consent, or claim that because no modern government ever in fact received authority by express consent, then all modern government was illegitimate and thus not owed obedience.[114] This latter conclusion was also itself

---

111. "The necessities of human society, neither in private nor public life, will allow of such an accurate enquiry: And as there is no virtue or moral duty, but what may, with facility, be refined away, if we indulge a false philosophy, in sifting and scrutinizing it, by every captious rule of logic, in every light or position, in which it may be placed": ibid., 482. For a view resistant to Hume's urging that we adopt a new philosophy, because it rejects Hume's underlying attempted reconfiguration of what political philosophy is and can hope to be, see Brownsey, "Hume and the Social Contract."

112. Hume explicitly refers to such a conclusion as the advancing of "absurdities": "Original Contract," 470.

113. By asking rhetorically of his opponents "how came so many lawful Monarchies into the World?" Locke indicated that he believed legitimate government was the norm, not the exception: Locke, *Two Treatises*, 344, § 113.

114. This dilemma remains for those who wish to maintain a secular Lockeanism in present political theory. A. John Simmons, for example, takes the second horn and concludes that because no present government has in fact been consented to by anything like a sufficient number of its citizens, no government in the world can presently be considered legitimate: Simmons, "Justification and Legitimacy," 155–56. A similar view is taken by P. F. Brownsey, who claims that "if history discloses no social contracts in the histories of

absurd, however, because the legitimacy of governmental authority was not something determined by the theories of philosophers, but by the opinion of mankind rooted in moral sentiment. Though "an appeal to general opinion may justly, in the speculative sciences of metaphysics, natural philosophy, or astronomy, be deemed unfair and inconclusive," by contrast "in all questions with regard to morals, as well as criticism, there is really no other standard by which any controversy can ever be decided."[115]

Hume illustrated this with the example of absolute government. By furthering utility and receiving the allegiance of the subjects who judged it to have authority, absolute rule was "as *natural* and *common* a government as any," and hence "must certainly occasion some obligation; and 'tis plain from experience, that men, who are subjected to it, do always think so."[116] The fact that such subjects "do always think so" means that obligation *was* therefore owed by subjects under such conditions, there being no other coherent standard from which to judge. If secular Lockeans continued to decry absolute government as no government at all, insisting that their philosophy was *right*, and that it was the world that needed to change in line with the dictates of their speculations, this only confirmed and enhanced their absurdity. Nothing "is a clearer proof, that a theory of this kind is erroneous, than to find, that it leads to paradoxes, repugnant to the common sentiments of mankind, and to the practice and opinion of all nations and ages."[117]

Hume's outlook, unlike that of a secularized Lockeanism, fully recognized, indeed embraced, the fact that "if we remount to the first origin of every nation, we shall find, that there scarce is any race of kings, or form of a commonwealth, that is not primarily founded on usurpation and rebellion, and whose title is not far worse than doubtful and uncertain."[118] The lesson to draw was not that all government was therefore illegitimate, but that we must "learn to treat very lightly all disputes concerning the rights of princes," becoming "convinc'd that a strict adherence to any general rules . . . hold less of reason, than of bigotry and superstition."[119] In real political practice, philosophy had almost no power to determine serious controversies over authority, which were themselves not usually amenable to purely intellectual resolution anyway: the

---

actual governments, the contract theorist can simply conclude 'so much the worse for the governments of this world; none of them is legitimate'": Brownsey, "Hume and the Social Contract," 133. This conclusion may be met by Hume's heirs today with the same response Hume urged: that it is to put the cart of theory before the horse of political practice, and to render one's philosophical position, and indeed one's entire philosophical outlook, absurd as a consequence. For an illustration, see Hall, "A Defence."

115. Hume, "Original Contract," 486.
116. Hume, *Treatise*, T.3.2.8.9, SBN 549; cf. "Original Contract," 486–87.
117. Ibid., 486.
118. Hume, *Treatise*, T.3.2.10.4, SBN 556; cf. "Original Contract," 474–75.
119. Hume, *Treatise*, T.3.2.10.15, SBN 562.

"study of history confirms the reasonings of true philosophy; which, showing us the original qualities of human nature, teaches us to regard the controversies in politics as incapable of any decision in most cases, and as entirely subordinate to the interests of peace and liberty." Indeed, "when these titles are mingled and oppos'd in different degrees, they often occasion perplexity; and are less capable of solution from the arguments of lawyers and philosophers, than from the swords of the soldiery."[120]

Hume's point was double-edged: not only was philosophy ill equipped to resolve real disputes over authority, which usually revealed no single correct answer but only a plethora of competing claims, it would never be the decisive factor even if it could, *per impossibile*, reveal a final unitary answer.[121] In turn, rather than bemoaning the inadequacy of the real world for its failure to live up to one's preferred philosophy, one would be better off rethinking one's philosophy so that it better fitted the real world, and the actually existing conclusions of common sentiment, which gave the only genuine conditions of meaning and coherence one was ever going to get. Philosophy's role was to help us better understand our state of affairs, in particular to better appreciate the nature of our values, whilst being aware that such values must, and could only ever be, our own creations.[122] As regards practical politics, "I am afraid we shall never be able to satisfy any impartial enquirer, who adopts no party in political controversies, and will be satisfy'd with nothing but sound reason and philosophy."[123]

Yet whilst Hume's philosophical outlook repudiated the possibility of any external justificatory perspective, it was nonetheless firmly vindicatory of established human political practice in propitious circumstances, whilst by the same lights accounting for the legitimacy of altering those circumstances through violent means if necessary for the maintenance of the *salus populi*. Government was an invention for the promotion of utility, garnering authority insofar as the human agents living under its arrangements came to believe that it did indeed possess such authority. As a result, the question of political

---

120. Ibid.

121. As Hume later put it, "the Empire of philosophy extends over a few; and with regard to these too, her authority is very weak and limited": Hume, "The Sceptic," in *Essays*, 169.

122. Indeed, excessive philosophical thinking in matters of real political dispute was liable to do more harm than good, exacerbating rather than resolving conflicts as sound reasoning was twisted to the ends of party prejudice. In *The History of England* Hume warned against appeal to a mythical ancient constitution in attempts to vindicate present political change. The "only rule of government, which is intelligible or carries any authority with it, is the established practice of the age," whereas those "who, from a pretended respect to antiquity, appeal at every turn to an original plan of the constitution, only cover their turbulent spirit and their private ambition under the appearance of venerable forms": Hume, *History of England*, vol. 2, 525.

123. Hume, *Treatise*, T.3.2.10.15, SBN 563.

obligation—the need to obey government outside conditions of tyranny, and nontyrannical government's legitimate right to extract obedience by coercion if necessary—could be given a positive and clear answer, which vindicated rather than condemned the general practice of mankind. Obedience was owed when a people thought that it was, and could (and eventually would) be withdrawn when a people believed that it ceased to be owed—i.e., when their interests were sufficiently damaged by governmental oppression such that the "moral" obligation to allegiance ceased to outrun the "natural."

Hume's account was sociological in its surface manifestation only, an effect of the philosophical reconfiguration he simultaneously sought to bring about. Rather than avoiding the crucial normative issues surrounding political obligation, he presented these as coherently intelligible only from within the internal perspective generated by human political practice. This yielded the possibility of natural authority: possessing no external justification, but built upon a science of man that denied the coherence or need for any such justification. Natural authority stood apart from its two obvious alternatives: the supernatural authority that derived ultimately from God (in either its theistic Lockean form, or the cryptotheism of the natural lawyers), and the artificial authority generated by Hobbes's sovereignty theory rooted in prudential self-interested calculation. It was this reconfiguration of the nature and scope of political philosophy that Adam Smith followed Hume in adopting as the underlying normative framework for conceiving of authority in entirely secular terms.[124] What Hume had left outstanding was a detailed explanation of how natural authority had been generated in the specific historical experience of ancient and then modern Europe. This was the contribution made by Smith's history of law and government, aspects of which we shall explore in chapter 5.

Conclusion

We may conclude by reconnecting this evaluation of Hume's underlying philosophical ambitions with the question of sovereignty and Hume's wholesale omission of any such category. Sovereignty theory is fundamentally *justification* theory: it seeks to explain not only who has (or should have) ultimate political decision-making power, but more fundamentally who has (or should have) the legitimate authority to exercise that power. The sovereign, by virtue

---

124. Although it is unclear whether Smith shared Hume's optimism at the final prospects for such a secular normative theory. As he put it in the final revisions to his *Theory of Moral Sentiments*, "the very suspicion of a fatherless world, must be the most melancholy of all reflections; from the thought that all the unknown regions of infinite and incomprehensible space may be filled with nothing but endless misery and wretchedness. All the splendour of the highest prosperity can never enlighten the gloom with which so dreadful an idea must necessarily over-shadow the imagination." Smith, *Theory of Moral Sentiments*, 235; cf. Dunn, "Applied Theology," 128.

of being sovereign, is justified in using coercive force against those who do not obey his or her or its rightful authority, whilst those subject to sovereign power are not justified in resisting that sovereign's directions or impositions, insofar as these fall within the remit of that rightful authority.

Since at least Hobbes, we have been accustomed to seeing sovereignty as a necessary feature of a theory of politics, and of the theory of the state in particular. Hobbes represents a particularly interesting case, because he seeks to provide a theory of sovereignty with recourse only to materials available from within a secular political theoretical framework.[125] His is justification theory, but it does not posit any *external* justificatory ground by which human political practice is to be assessed. Hobbes attempted this by making consent the linchpin of his theory: the sovereign was such because all had consented to be held in awe by common power, even if such consent happened to be given in the utmost extremes of duress.[126] Yet the expansive understanding of consent Hobbes relied upon to generate a purely internal standard of justification for sovereignty was predicated for its coherence upon his radically reductive view of freedom as the absence of physical impediments to movement.[127] Insofar as one is unconvinced of the coherence or plausibility of that view, one will be doubtful that consent can in fact play the crucial role Hobbes assigns to it in the generation of sovereignty, or in the justificatory ambitions his theory of sovereignty embodies.[128]

---

125. Although Hobbes certainly recognized that his secular theory of politics must be squared with the realities of religion as a historical and sociological fact of the seventeenth century, hence the third part of *De Cive*, "Of Religion," and the third book of *Leviathan*, "Of Christian Commonwealth." But this was a matter of the specific application of political science to contingent circumstances.

126. Hobbes, *Leviathan*, vol. 2, 306–8, 312, 326. The effect was heightened in *Leviathan* by adding the conception of "authorization," whereby subjects individually came to own all the actions of the sovereign as their representative: Hobbes, *Leviathan*, vol. 2, 244–52. Yet the theory of authorization is imposed by Hobbes via conceptual fiat: highly useful as it may be for his purposes within his deeply impressive conceptual edifice, there is in fact no reason whatsoever, other than Hobbes's insistence, to accept the legalistic analogy by which consent equates to authorization and renders a representative an extension of one's own causal actions, and particularly when it generates the absolutist conclusions Hobbes aspired to. On the wider background to Hobbes's theory of representation, and its place in the modern political theory of representation, see Mónica Brito Vieira and David Runciman, *Representation* (Cambridge: Polity, 2008), chaps. 1–2.

127. For a helpful and clear discussion, see Quentin Skinner, *Hobbes and Republican Liberty* (Cambridge: Cambridge University Press, 2008), chap. 6.

128. Hume was clearly skeptical of anything like Hobbes's minimalist negative view of freedom, as revealed by his discussion of how we conceive of liberty in relation to the power of others insofar as they are restrained by law: Hume, *Treatise*, T.2.1.10.1–12, SBN 309–16. Recent commentators have illustrated the implausibility of Hobbes's purely negative view of liberty. See, for example, Philip Pettit, *Republicanism: A Theory of Freedom and Government* (Oxford, Clarendon, 1997), chaps. 1–4; Quentin Skinner, "The Idea of Negative Liberty," in *Philosophy of History: Essays on the Historiography of Philosophy*,

Furthermore, Hobbes's absolutist vision failed—as both Locke and Hume recognized—to properly configure the balance between utility and authority. Hobbes correctly identified that the primary task of the state was the provision of order and security, but he radically overestimated the threat posed by internal dissention whilst underestimating that posed by the rapacity of rulers. His system granted too much to authority, dangerously imperiling utility. As Locke famously remarked, to agree with Hobbes would be to think that "Men are so foolish that they take care to avoid what Mischiefs may be done them by *Pole-Cats*, or *Foxes*, but are content, nay think it Safety, to be devoured by *Lions*," a sentiment shared by Hume, and facilitated in both cases by less bellicose conceptions of human sociability.[129]

Locke's alternative to Hobbes was to retain the justificatory ambitions of sovereignty theory (his preference was to speak of "supreme power"), locating the basis of that justification in consent, but now understood as the only mechanism that could generate legitimate relations of political authority between creatures created free and equal, and which took the place of Hobbes's theory of freedom embedded in a metaphysic of matter in motion, in order to provide the normative centrality of consent.[130] Hume by contrast embraced secular political theory whilst abandoning the aspiration to provide any external justificatory grounding for our moral and political practices, settling instead for their internal vindication by the lights of the opinion of mankind, purposefully downscaled from the ambitions of Hobbes's vision of a theory of sovereignty able to delineate the proper functioning of politics understood, and then administered, as an a priori science. For Hume, a proper science of politics could precisely not be a priori, and the crucial mistake to avoid was the putting of the cart of theory before the horse of practice, appreciating instead that it was always the latter that gave any worth or validity to the former. Accordingly, the category of sovereignty was redundant for Hume's purposes. In political *practice* it may well remain that talk of sovereignty is not only highly useful, but a real and permanent part of the constitutional and institutional makeup that must be taken account of, in particular with regard to identifying

---

ed. R. Rorty and J. B. Schneewind (Cambridge: Cambridge University Press, 1984), 193–221; *Liberty before Liberalism* (Cambridge: Cambridge University Press, 1998); "Freedom as the Absence of Arbitrary Power," in *Republicanism and Political Theory*, ed. C. Laborde and J. Maynor (Oxford: Blackwell, 2008), 83–101—although, as is well known, the positive "republican" theories Pettit and Skinner advance are not without their own problems. For a sketch of what an adequate theory of liberty must be able to achieve, see Bernard Williams, "From Freedom to Liberty: The Construction of a Political Value," in *In the Beginning*, 75–96.

129. Locke, *Two Treatises*, 328, § 93.

130. For Locke, supreme power must be vested in the legislature, the necessary check to judicial and executive power liable to be abused by rulers following the loss of the golden age: *Two Treatises*, 355–63, §§ 134–42.

who holds (and by the lights of opinion, should hold) decision-making power at any given point. Insofar as theory aims to have something to say to, as well as about, practice, then sovereignty will remain a noneliminable and central category of modern politics, and must to that extent be taken into account.[131] Yet in political theory prior to the engagement of practical politics as it happens to be given by the practice of the age, sovereignty is not a primary or useful category of political analysis from Hume's perspective. Who is or is not thought to hold sovereignty in any given time and place is determined by opinion, and hence it is the mechanisms of opinion that ought properly to occupy our philosophical attention, being sensitive to the fact that these can and do change as human circumstances alter. The result of this is that Hume ultimately offered a theory of the state without sovereignty: what looks like political sociology transpires to be an attempted reconfiguration of our fundamental thinking about what organized power consists of for human beings in what Smith called a "fatherless" world.[132] This can only be properly appreciated if we simultaneously recognize the seriousness of Hume's engagement with political obligation. In turn we are invited to reconsider whether a theory of sovereignty is in fact a necessary part of an adequate theory of politics, or whether post-Hobbesian political theory can get by, and perhaps even flourish, without it.[133]

---

131. I am grateful to both Richard Tuck and Richard Bourke for this point, though both will likely disagree with the ends to which I put it. On the complexity of sovereignty theory and its messy interface with political practice, in particular as refracted through the French Revolution as a central event in the emergence of the modern representative republic, see István Hont, "The Permanent Crisis of a Divided Mankind: 'Nation-State' and 'Nationalism' in Historical Perspective," in *Jealousy of Trade*, 447–528—although it should be observed that Hont notes (487) that the new modern theory of sovereignty forged by Sieyès and offered to the French revolutionaries was no better understood by the principle political actors than the earlier accounts of Hobbes and Rousseau had been in previous generations.

132. Smith, *Theory of Moral Sentiments*, 235.

133. On the enormous historical, as well as theoretical, legacy of sovereignty theory that an opinion-of-mankind idiom must nonetheless reckon with, see Hont, "Permanent Crisis."

CHAPTER FOUR

Rousseau's Return to Hobbes

Rousseau, through a Scottish Lens

In his 1756 "A Letter to the Authors of the Edinburgh Review," Adam Smith called the attention of Scottish readers to a recent work by Jean-Jacques Rousseau. This was *The Discourse on Inequality*—and Smith's most famous claim was that: "Whoever reads this last work with attention, will observe, that the second volume of the Fable of the Bees has given occasion to the system of Mr. Rousseau, in whom however the principles of the English author are softened, improved, and embellished, and stript of all that tendency to corruption and licentiousness which has disgraced them in their original author."[1] Smith went on to list several points of similarity between the *Discourse* and *The Fable of the Bees, Volume 2*. These included a denial of natural sociability determining human beings "to seek society for its own sake"; the use of conjectural accounts to explain how humans had left their primitive state of natural indigence to achieve modern civilized living; and the fact that although Rousseau attributed to humans the "amiable principle" of pity—meaning they were capable of possessing all the virtues the reality of which Mandeville denied—owing to pity's being possessed "in greater degree of perfection" by savages and the vulgar than those of polished manners, in Smith's final estimation Rousseau "perfectly agrees with the English

---

1. Adam Smith, "A Letter to the Authors of the Edinburgh Review," in *The Glasgow Edition of the Works and Correspondence of Adam Smith: Essays on Philosophical Subjects*, ed. W.P.D. Wightman, J. C. Bryce, and I. S. Ross (Oxford: Oxford University Press, 1980), 250. The claim that Rousseau's system was strictly "given occasion" by Mandeville's work is at least open to question. Although there is direct evidence that Rousseau read *The Fable of the Bees, Volume 1*, which Rousseau refers to in the *Second Discourse*, there is none that he made a careful study of *Volume 2*, although a French translation of both had been available since 1740.

author."[2] These claims of congruence between Mandeville and Rousseau are certainly open to question, even if only because of the latent ambiguity generated by Smith's highly condensed renderings. What is particularly significant, however, is a further claim Smith made: "According to both, those laws of justice, which maintain the present inequality amongst mankind, were originally inventions of the cunning and the powerful, in order to maintain or to acquire an unnatural and unjust superiority over the rest of their fellow-creatures."[3] What is noteworthy here is that, at least at face value, Smith's equation of Mandeville and Rousseau seems to be based on an oversimplification so severe that it makes the claim at best misleading, and at worst flatly false. Did Smith oversimplify to the point of getting it wrong?

There is no doubt that the "English" and "French" authors in fact maintained quite different technical accounts of how the laws of justice were used to acquire domination over the bulk of humanity. For Mandeville (as we saw in chapters 1 and 2) the key processes of deception that people were subjected to took place in the early stages of human psychosocial development, albeit requiring large stretches of time to be completed. This centered upon the way the more intelligent manipulated the less intelligent into modes of behavior that were not just "submissive," but "governable"; i.e., the emergence of a creature which "when, reconcil'd to Submission ... has learn'd to construe his Servitude to his own Advantage; and rests satisfy'd with the Account it finds for itself, in the Labor it performs for others."[4] The "inventions" of the "cunning and the powerful" envisaged by Mandeville related to the manipulation and redirection of a basic and immutable human psychology, such that the inherent desire for status and esteem eventually became consistently expressed in nonviolent and socially beneficial modes of engagement. Rousseau's account of the human sociability predicament was different, as was his account of how "the cunning and the powerful" introduced "laws of justice" to acquire superiority. The crucial innovation that had to be understood was the introduction of property rights. The subordinated came, at the behest of their subordinators, to accept this institution because they mistakenly believed that it operated to their advantage, when in truth it led to their exploitation and socioeconomic enslavement. Why, then, did Smith equate Rousseau and Mandeville on the question of socially sanctioned and coercively enforced inequality? Not because he was sloppy as either a reader or reviewer. Rather it was because he had, by 1756, already encountered and absorbed Hume's argument for natural

---

2. Smith, "Letter to the Authors," 250–51. Smith assimilated the Genevan Rousseau to the recent French intellectual advancement, just as Mandeville and Hutcheson were claimed as earlier English authors, despite being Dutch and Irish respectively.

3. Smith, "Letter to the Authors," 251.

4. Bernard Mandeville, *The Fable of the Bees, Volume 2*, ed. F. B. Kaye (Indianapolis: Liberty Fund, 1988), 184.

authority.[5] With that in hand, Smith knew that the capacity to form large and lasting societies in modern conditions of material inequality and hierarchical stratification could be explained without the need to appeal to *any* process of systematic manipulation or deception by the cunning and powerful, themselves selfishly seeking to achieve "unjust and unnatural superiority." Thus, although Mandeville and Rousseau differed in their technical accounts of how the few gained superiority over the many, from Smith's post-Humean perspective, theirs was a distinction without a difference. The proper explanation lay elsewhere, as Hume had shown.

In chapter 5 I examine in detail Smith's taking up of Hume's opinion idiom, and thus the possibility of natural authority without the need for manipulated deception on behalf of the ruled. In this chapter, I examine Rousseau's intervention in the debate over human sociability, principally in the *Second Discourse*, and show how it ultimately led in the opposite direction to that pointed out by Hume: back to Hobbes. However, it is important to note—as, to my knowledge, has not previously been done—that Rousseau's and Hume's analyses of the human capacity to form society are in important respects, and up to a crucial point, structurally identical. Revealingly, where the two authors part company is not on the question of humans' basic sociability in primitive conditions—where they in fact agree—but afterwards, in the trajectory that leads to large and lasting society marked by extensive and institutionalized status hierarchy and material inequality. Whereas Hume makes recourse to natural authority to explain the relative stability of large-scale human associations, Rousseau reaches for the explanatory mechanism of deception, and suggests that as a consequence large-scale stability is not destined to last. Smith, having already sided with Hume, saw that Rousseau thus achieved only an advanced form of Mandevillean explanation, even if the Genevan rejected the Dutchman's belief in the stability of politics founded upon systematic deceit.

The Prehistory of Sociability

When Smith claimed that *The Fable of the Bees, Volume 2*, had "given occasion" to Rousseau's *Discourse*, this is best understood not as positing a strict identity between the two works, but rather as presenting Rousseau's intervention as a form of advanced Mandevilleanism: an attempt to take a particular style of explanation further, whilst improving on the shortcomings of earlier efforts. The *Discourse* was evolution, not restatement.

---

5. We know that Smith spent a great deal of time reading and absorbing the arguments of Hume's *Treatise* during his unhappy years as a visiting undergraduate at Balliol College, Oxford, from 1740 to 1746. The impact Hume's ideas had on him at such a formative point of his intellectual development was particularly profound. See Nicholas Phillipson, *Adam Smith: An Enlightened Life* (London: Allen Lane, 2010), chap. 3, especially 64–66.

Rousseau agreed with Mandeville that Hobbes's mistake was to project needy, civilized man back onto the sturdy and rugged savage individuals of the original state of nature. And as is well known, Rousseau went even further back than Mandeville: "Philosophers who have examined the foundations of society have all felt the necessity of going back as far as the state of Nature, but none of them has reached it."[6] Yet we must be careful in handling Rousseau's claim that he was the first thinker to have truly reached the state of nature, thus freeing himself from imposing the distorting artifices of civilized man. By going so far back, Rousseau risked taking himself out of the sociability debate altogether.

Whereas Mandeville's savages were fully formed humans equipped with needs of both the body and the mind, in "Part 1" of the *Discourse* Rousseau made the bold step of positing man in the state of nature as equipped with only *amour de soi-même* ("a natural sentiment which inclines every animal to attend to its self-preservation"), and not amour propre ("a relative sentiment, factitious, and born in society"): needs only of the body, not of the mind.[7] This of course raised problems regarding theological orthodoxy that were even more severe than those that Mandeville had encountered, and which Rousseau was distinctly aware of. Not only, he insisted, had Adam received "some light and Precepts immediately from God," but scripture made it clear that even before the Flood men were never in the "pure state of Nature."[8] And it was most awkward to suggest that men had since lapsed into such a condition, only to emerge once again. Rousseau sidestepped these problems, however, by

---

6. Jean-Jacques Rousseau, "Second Discourse." in *The Discourses and Other Early Political Writings* ed. V. Gourevitch (Cambridge: Cambridge University Press, 1997), 132. On Rousseau's debts to the older French "noble savage" literature, and his use of travellers' reports in conjecturing the condition of "savage" humans, see Sankar Muthu, *Enlightenment against Empire* (Princeton, NJ: Princeton University Press, 2003), 31–46. On the French reception of Hobbes's ideas, and thus Rousseau's intellectual context in coming to engage with Hobbes, see Robin Douglass, *Rousseau and Hobbes: Nature, Free Will, and the Passions* (Oxford: Oxford University Press, 2015), chap. 1.

7. Rousseau, "Second Discourse," 218. For detailed discussion see Frederick Neuhouser, *Rousseau's Critique of Inequality: Reconstructing the Second Discourse* (Cambridge: Cambridge University Press, 2014), 63–78. On the intellectual origins of Rousseau's conceptions of amour de soi-même and amour propre, see Christopher Brooke, "Rousseau's Political Philosophy: Stoic and Augustinian Origins," in *The Cambridge Companion to Rousseau*, ed. P. Riley (Cambridge: Cambridge University Press, 2001), 111–6, but also Brooke's autocorrective in "Rousseau's *Second Discourse*: Between Epicureanism and Stoicism," in *Rousseau and Freedom* (Cambridge: Cambridge University Press, 2010), 44–58. For a discussion of, and overview of the literature on, Rousseau's development of his ideas in the later *Émile*, see Christopher Brooke, *Philosophic Pride: Stoicism and Political Thought from Lipsius to Rousseau* (Princeton, NJ: Princeton University Press, 2012), chap. 8. See also Michael Sonenscher, *Sans-culottes: An Eighteenth Century Emblem In the French Revolution* (Princeton, NJ: Princeton University Press, 2008), chap. 3, on Rousseau as a Cynic philosopher.

8. Rousseau, "Second Discourse," 132.

claiming that he was "setting aside all the facts, for they do not affect the question," presenting his account as a pure conjecture, one used simply to elucidate present truths. Whether Rousseau really believed this is a complex question, although it seems rather doubtful that we can take him at face value.[9] Fortunately, what is more important for present purposes is to ask what, if anything, was achieved by Rousseau beginning his analysis with creatures equipped only with needs of the body, and not of the mind. After all, if bracketing the question of scriptural orthodoxy (as Rousseau himself proposed be done), there was no inherent reason why the philosophers he was chastising—in particular Hobbes, but also Grotius, Locke, Pufendorf, and Mandeville—need deny that fully developed humans had a prehistory, one in which they lacked their present needs of the mind. "Part 1" of the *Discourse* risked being simply irrelevant by starting the story at a point at which previous contributors to the pan-European debate on human sociability and the foundations of politics just weren't interested, because their target was unambiguously a creature equipped with needs of both body and mind, the interplay of which made human sociability such a difficult phenomenon to explain.

In fact, I believe that this is a fair statement regarding much—though, crucially, not all—of "Part 1" of the *Discourse*, and that Rousseau's flamboyant chastisement of the inadequacies of his forerunners should be treated with considerable skepticism. The savage, isolated, and solitary men that Rousseau describes in "Part 1," as becomes clear in the appended notes, are in effect not really humans at all, but much more like the "Pongos" and "Orang-Outans"—i.e., large primates and great apes—known to Europeans from travellers' reports from the East Indies and Africa.[10] Rousseau may have been quite right

9. For a defense of Rousseau's state of nature as a purely analytic device not making any historical truth claims, see Neuhouser, *Rousseau's Critique*, 33-37; Victor Gourevitch, "Rousseau's Pure State of Nature," *Interpretation* 16 (1988), 23-59; John T. Scott, "Rousseau's Unease with Locke's Uneasiness," in *The Challenge of Rousseau*, ed. C. Kelly and E. Grace (Cambridge: Cambridge University Press, 2012), 295-311. For the state of nature as a depiction of (to some degree) a historical condition, see Roger D. Masters, *The Political Philosophy of Rousseau* (Princeton, NJ: Princeton University Press, 1979), 115-8; Marc F. Plattner, *Rousseau's State of Nature: An Interpretation of the Discourse on Inequality* (DeKalb, IL: Northern Illinois University Press, 1979), 17-25.

10. On this see especially Robert Wokler, "Perfectible Apes in Decadent Cultures: Rousseau's Anthropology Revisited," in *Rousseau, the Age of Enlightenment, and Their Legacies*, ed. B. Garsten (Princeton, NJ: Princeton University Press, 2012), 6-13; also Muthu, *Enlightenment against Empire*, 42-43; Neuhouser, *Rousseau's Critique*, 37-55, 85-86 (although I am skeptical of Neuhouser's claim that Rousseau's savage man is a purely analytic thought experiment, and suggest that this draws a far clearer set of distinctions in Rousseau's text than accurately reflects the wide array of aims and arguments being deployed there). On the proximity of Rousseau's discussion of the orangutan to racist discourses and the legitimation of black African slavery, see Silvia Sebastiani, "L'orang-outang, l'esclave et l'humain: une querelle des corps en régime colonial," *L'Atelier du Centre de Recherches Historiques* 11 (2013), doi:10.4000/acrh.5265.

that this savage "man" was both individually sturdy and, owing to his independent and solitary existence, subsisting in a condition that could not reasonably be described, as Hobbes had notoriously done, as in any way miserable or bellicose.[11] Yet, thus stated, this risked being nothing more substantial than a semantic difference. What Rousseau insisted in "Part 1" on calling the state of nature, in turn chastising Hobbes for "improperly includ[ing] in Savage man's care for his preservation the need to satisfy a multitude of passions that are the product of Society,"[12] was an epoch of human development in which Hobbes, and indeed all the other major thinkers in the sociability debate, were uninterested. Hobbes's story, and his use of the idea of a state of nature, began when humans had needs both of the body and of the mind, when the need to satiate pride caused them to compete for eminence and react preemptively against the anticipated aggression of peers whose intentions were opaque. If Rousseau refused to call this latter stage the "state of nature" on account of the later, artificially induced emergence of amour propre, that was his prerogative. But Hobbes's underlying account was untouched as things stood. Simply conjecturing that human beings had a prehistory in which they weren't (really) human could not touch the question of (genuinely) human sociability.

What prevented Rousseau's disagreement with his forerunners from being in the end merely semantic was not his long conjectural account of humanity's prehistory as a solitary apelike creature, but his insistence that alongside amour de soi-même, savage man shared with the other animals a natural instinct of pity (we will, however, have to wait a little to see exactly why this matters). This was a "Principle which Hobbes did not notice and which . . . tempers [man's] ardor for well-being with an innate repugnance to see his kind suffer."[13] Antecedent to the emergence of amour propre, pity was a crucial reason why savage man in the state of nature was largely peaceful: his fellow feeling for other sentient creatures made him disinclined to harm them, and given the natural abundance of the original state of nature this drastically reduced the incidence of flash points for violent confrontation. Savage humans would engage in aggression only in the way a dog bites a stone thrown at it. Although, as Smith noted, Rousseau turned the fact of pity against Mandeville's attempt to present all natural morality as self-serving artifice and hypocrisy; Rousseau also made clear that it was the existence of natural pity that gave the lie to Hobbes's claim that the state of nature would be one of misery and violence. Pity "in the state of Nature, takes the place of Laws, morals, and virtue, with the advantage that no one is tempted to disobey its gentle voice; pity that will

---

11. Rousseau, "Second Discourse," 149–51.
12. Ibid., 151.
13. Ibid., 152. On Rousseau's use of pity as a principle with which to resist Hobbes, see Douglass, *Rousseau and Hobbes*, 68–69, 90–93.

keep any sturdy Savage from robbing a weak child or an infirm old man of his hard-won subsistence if he can hope to find his own elsewhere."[14]

We will see the significance of this below. But what I am claiming at this stage is that as a contribution to the debate on human sociability, with the crucial exception of the discussion of pity, "Part 1" of the *Discourse* could have been entirely omitted and there would have been no significant loss in Rousseau's theoretical matrix. Indeed, it is telling that all three of Smith's lengthy translations from the *Discourse* supplied in his 1756 review are taken from "Part 2," where Rousseau offers his discussion of man as a creature equipped with needs of not just the body, but also the mind. Yet there is a striking lacuna between "Part 1" and "Part 2" of the *Discourse*. "Part 1" discusses savage humans in their primitive condition, solitary and peaceful, but largely without language, the emergence of which Rousseau famously despaired of being able to explain. "Part 2," however, begins with a discussion of humans *talking* to each other in order to establish relations of property, itself the outcome of a significant process of transformation that had taken many generations to effect, but which must have occurred long after the "fortuitous concatenation of foreign causes," postulated at the end of "Part 1," which pushed humans out of their state of natural indigence and in the direction enabled by their "perfectibility"—i.e., toward the social virtues and mental faculties that human beings could not have developed if they had remained forever in their original state.[15]

To understand what is going on we must turn to a text not available to Smith, but composed at around the same time as the *Discourse*, and which can usefully be thought of as a missing "middle part" of that work: the "Essay on the Origin of Languages."[16] Rousseau there attempted to get beyond the impossibilities of explaining how language had emerged amongst the solitary, dispersed creatures of the original state of nature as described in the *Discourse*. His insight was that the "great failing of Europeans is always to philosophize about the origin of things in the light of what happens right around them"—i.e., to assume that all history was European history, situated in a climate of relative hardship

14. Rousseau, "Second Discourse," 154. For a more detailed discussion, Béla Kapossy, *Iselin contra Rousseau* (Basel: Schwabe AG, 2006), 218–22.

15. Rousseau, "Second Discourse," 159; Kapossy, *Iselin contra Rousseau*, 215. On the context of Rousseau's arguments for perfectibility in eighteenth-century debates over "optimism" with regard to humans' existential and practical condition, see Christopher Kelly and Roger D. Masters, "Human Nature, Liberty, and Progress: Rousseau's Dialogue with the Critics of the *Discours sur l'inégalité*," in *Rousseau and Liberty*, ed. R. Wokler (Manchester: Manchester University Press, 1995) 53–69.

16. István Hont, *Politics in Commercial Society: Jean-Jacques Rousseau and Adam Smith* (Cambridge, MA: Harvard University Press, 2015), 58–61; Muthu, *Enlightenment against Empire*, 43.

where mutual cooperation was required to survive.[17] This was a mistake. Humans had originated in warm and fertile areas where they could easily survive independently, the most likely candidate being sub-Saharan Africa where the "pongos" described in the *Discourse*'s notes were found. What had brought them together was not mutual cooperation, but mutual meeting points: watering holes scattered throughout hot lands. Experiencing interactions with each other in these places, humans recognized their similar outward appearances and inferred similar inward states. Here came the first stirrings of amour propre: savages around the watering hole wanted to be admired and looked at—thus their first words were "love me!"[18] Language developed as a way of gaining attention, stirred by nascent amour propre, then inflating it in turn. The origin of languages was a southern phenomenon. What happened in due course was that the communicating humans of southern climates were displaced by natural disasters such as erupting volcanoes, earthquakes, and tidal waves, and moved north. In their new harsh and cold climates, humans had to cooperate to secure amour de soi-même, not just amour propre. But, fortunately, the new inhabitants of the north already had language. Their first words were not "love me!", but "help me!"[19] The increased utility gains of linguistic cooperation produced an ironic outcome: the comparatively less bountiful lands of the north could be subjected to greater intensification, and thus were made by artifice more plentiful than the south had been by nature. The peoples of the north flourished, and began expanding. The subsequent history of humanity was the migration of millions of people across the globe, transporting the rudiments of group living back to Africa and causing the displacement and loss of the original communities organized solely around the primitive interactions of the watering hole. This process took tens of thousands of years, but explained how the primitive apelike creatures of "Part 1" of the *Discourse* could come to be in the position Rousseau would analyze in "Part 2," finally making his intervention in what might be termed the real sociability debate: how a creature equipped with needs both of the mind and of the body managed to form large and lasting society.

Amour Propre and the State(s) of Nature

The outset of "Part 2" is best remembered for Rousseau's declaration that the first man to have enclosed a piece of ground and declared ownership of it "was the true founder of civil society." Yet what is most arresting here is not Rousseau's sudden postulation of advanced language, nor his immediate qualification of his

---

17. Jean-Jacques Rousseau, "Essay on the Origin of Languages," in *The Discourses and Other Early Political Writings* ed. V. Gourevitch (Cambridge: Cambridge University Press, 1997), 266.

18. Rousseau, "Origin of Languages," 279.

19. Ibid.

own dramatic claim by admitting that by the point at which complex ideas of property had emerged things were actually too far gone for anybody to be in a position to reject the specious claims of the first "imposter."[20] More important is Rousseau's subtle extension of his own idea of the state of nature from that of a state of primitive primordial indolence into that of a continuum with many different stages, but all brought to an end by the formal instantiation of property relations backed by collective sanction. Rousseau was clear that the moment at which an individual successfully claimed to be the sole owner of property in land, and had this claim accepted by others, was explicitly the "last stage of the state of Nature."[21] When that claim became not just accepted by others, but enforced coercively by a centralizing agency, humans decisively left the state of nature once and for all. This is of the utmost importance in properly understanding Rousseau's account.

As will be recalled from chapter 1, according to Hobbes what separated the state of nature from civil society was that in the former men were capable only of the imperfect bonds of "concord" (mutual agreements for cooperation that could not unite people in large and lasting associations owing to the inevitable disruptions caused by pride), whereas civil society was founded upon "union" (the erection of centralized power via an act of representation, able to conform people's wills and thus stabilize the otherwise disruptive effects of glory seeking). By making the instantiation and enforcement of property relations the point at which humanity chronologically exited the state of nature and entered society, Rousseau adopted a different criterion to Hobbes, but sought to preserve something of the clear demarcation that Hobbes's concord-union distinction provided. Rousseau's move was ingenious: in a single stroke he eliminated the problems that we saw in chapter 2 that Hobbes's account ran into when trying to hold together the analytic purity of the concord-union distinction against the background fact that, historically speaking, modern states had emerged only gradually from chaotic processes of war and conquest. Rousseau, by contrast, was able to preserve a working distinction between the state of nature and civil society—one of the most powerful analytic devices of the sociability debate—but without the need to make recourse to an implausible condition of brutish indigence in the period immediately before the erection of large and lasting society. Instead, the state of nature was conceived of as a continuous progression of many consecutive stages of development, from humans' primordial origins up until the point where formal instantiation of property relations changed everything—i.e., when claims of property became not just individually asserted, and respected by others, but coercively enforced by third-party structures. In other words, when property rights became formally instituted by collective power, men exited the state of

20. Rousseau, "Second Discourse," 161.
21. Ibid.

nature because this was the advent of the state, understood specifically as the enforcer of property rights—a point at which the "wise" Locke's influence can probably be discerned in Rousseau's thought.[22]

The central task Rousseau faced was thus to account for how property had, indeed, changed everything. He therefore backed up his account after the famous dramatic opening statements of "Part 2." Not all the way to "Part 1," but to where the "Essay on the Origin of Languages" left off—i.e., with primitive language users in northern climates cooperating for utility gains. Such cooperation had stimulated reflection, which happened alongside the initial domestication of animals. These two developments gave rise to the first stirrings of full-blown amour propre: "while as yet scarcely able to discriminate ranks, and considering himself in the first rank as a species, he was from afar preparing to claim first rank as an individual."[23] Primitive languages developed as humans increasingly became aware of their likeness to each other and continued to cooperate imperfectly for utility gains, although they were still beset by serious collective-action problems—illustrated by the famous stag hunt, liable to be ruined because every individual was prone to chasing passing hares.

Rousseau made clear that he here covered "multitudes of Centuries in a flash"—as Mandeville had done in *The Fable of the Bees, Volume 2*—because "the more slowly events succeed one another, the more quickly they can be described."[24] Eventually, however, crude notions of property began to emerge. These were not formal instantiations of rules governing possessions, but simple acts of accumulation by naturally indigent creatures seeking to augment utility. These early divisions did not cause confrontation, however: the strongest were the first to make permanent dwellings that they were confident they could defend from others, and the weaker judged it safer to imitate than to attempt to dispossess those who had begun to settle. Such settled habitations gave rise to true family-based living for the first time, already a significant progression from the savages who copulated and then immediately separated in the first, primordial, stage of the state of nature. "Each family became a small Society," and in turn the ferocity and ruggedness of early humans began to wear off, not least thanks to the emergence of different gender roles as women stayed in the home to raise children, and men became softer as cooperation reduced the need to be individually self-sufficient.[25] This new mode of living was an advanced stage of what was still the state of nature. It was filled with leisure, which men now used to acquire "several sorts of conveniences

---

22. On Rousseau and Locke, see Hont, *Politics in Commercial Society*, chaps. 3 and 4, and Christopher Brooke, "Locke and Rousseau," in *Locke's Political Liberty: Readings and Misreadings*, ed. C. Miqueu and M. Chamie (Oxford: Voltaire Foundation, 2009), 69–82.
23. Rousseau, "Second Discourse," 162.
24. Ibid., 164.
25. Ibid., 164.

unknown to their Fathers." Without realizing it, however, they had donned "the first yoke . . . the first source of evils they prepared for their Descendants," by beginning the process by which human *wants* were transformed successively into *needs*, putting men onto a perpetual hedonistic treadmill of endless dissatisfaction with their present lot. This was the original inception of the scourge of luxury: greed for external ornaments resolved itself into the phenomenon by which "it became much more cruel to be deprived of them than to possess them was sweet, and men were unhappy to lose them without being happy to possess them."[26]

Human beings were now well on the path to becoming fully socialized for large and lasting conditions. Repeat iterations of social interaction caused great psychological change as amour propre became ever more necessary to satisfy: "The more they see one another, the less they can do without seeing one another more."[27] As amour propre matured, humans' subsequent decline threatened to begin: "jealousy awakens with love; Discord triumphs, and the gentlest of all passions receives sacrifices of human blood."[28] However, all was by no means lost at this stage. Ever-increasing social bonds drew people together, and they frequently gathered around their huts or a large tree, where singing and dancing emerged as the first and principle means for satisfying amour propre. The most eloquent were the most highly regarded—but this in turn gave birth to vanity and contempt on the one hand, envy and shame on the other. Humans now had fully developed needs of the mind, not just of the body. Rousseau was finally dealing with fully formed humans, and indeed affirmed that this was the stage of development most "savage" peoples known in the eighteenth century had reached.[29] Crucially, it could be seen "how far these People already

26. Ibid., 164–65. As Hont notes, however, Rousseau confines discussion of luxury to the notes of the *Second Discourse*, and does not discuss this in the main text. This is surprising, and still needs explaining, given that as Hont rightly states a core strand of the argument of the *Discourse* is "essentially a conjectural history of luxury": Hont, *Politics in Commercial Society*, 71.

27. Rousseau, "Second Discourse," 165.

28. Ibid.

29. That humans required both amour de soi-même and amour propre to be fully operational in order to be truly human, and that the latter is not simply a bad, or deformed, psychological trait, but in fact the basis of reason itself, the capacity to make interpersonal judgments, and ultimately the ability to engage in normative assessments, is brought out especially clearly in Fredrick Neuhouser, "Rousseau on the Relation between Reason and Self-Love (*Amour Propre*)," *Internationales Jahrbuch des Deutschen Idealismus* 1/2003 (2003), 221–39. Neuhouser shows that amour propre for Rousseau is an essential component of human psychological existence, and thus not necessarily bad, although it is undoubtedly the source of many evils. On this see also Frederick Neuhouser, *Rousseau's Theodicy of Self Love: Evil, Rationality and the Drive for Recognition* (Oxford: Oxford University Press, 2008); John Rawls, *Lectures on the History of Political Philosophy*, ed. S. Freeman (Cambridge, MA: Harvard University Press, 2007), 191–248.

were from the first state of Nature"—the first being precisely only one staging post on a long road to fully civilized living.[30]

However, Rousseau emphasized, this condition was anything but one of misery and war. This is important because it is at *this* stage of human development that Hobbes wished to apply the term state of nature (or, in *Leviathan*, "man's natural condition") as a historical epithet—i.e., when pertaining to small tribal groupings based on concord, not union, probably structured around the primitive family under the guidance of a patriarch. Rousseau and Hobbes were here finally on the same page regarding the analysis of fully fledged humans. But what Rousseau resisted was Hobbes's contention that in this (as Rousseau saw it) very advanced stage of the state of nature, the human condition was one of hardship and bellicosity. Rousseau did so by invoking the principle of pity: "[M]any hastened to conclude that man is naturally cruel and that he needs political order in order to be made gentle, whereas nothing is as gentle as he in his primitive state, when placed by Nature at equal distance from the stupidity of the brutes and the fatal enlightenment of civil man, and restricted by instinct and by reason alike to protecting himself against the harm that threatens him, he is restrained by Natural pity from doing anyone harm, without being moved to it by anything, even after it has been done to him."[31] Pity was a natural restraint upon direct and violent ways of satisfying amour propre. This was instead secured by singing and dancing, and even savages employed "the first duties of civility" to avoid piquing the pride of others.[32] Humans in this advanced stage of the state of nature had needs of both the body and the mind, but they were not subject to a crippling interplay of pride and utility whereby attempts to secure the latter were constantly destabilized by greed for the former, as Hobbes contended. In a sense, therefore, despite lacking (as Smith put it) any principle to "seek society for its own sake," humans in the last stage of the state of nature were in a sense minimally *naturally sociable*, or at least *not dramatically unsociable* in the thoroughgoing sense Hobbes implied by emphasizing the disruptiveness of competitive pride.[33] As human beings continued to experience the utility gains of group living, society increased in size and thus the relations that people experienced between each other changed. "Morality was beginning to enter into human Actions," whilst because individuals enforced primitive claims of possession themselves, as "the sole judge and avenger of the offenses [they] had received,"

30. Rousseau, "Second Discourse," 166.
31. Ibid.
32. Ibid.; Douglass, *Rousseau and Hobbes*, 90–93.
33. Although, as Hobbes had always made clear, the real problem was to explain sociability in *large and lasting* conditions (as we saw in chapter 1). In this regard, although Rousseau rejected Hobbes's diagnosis of the state of nature as one of misery, he agreed that by itself such a state could provide no model or explanation for large-scale sociable living.

this meant that the goodness of the "pure state of Nature was no longer the goodness suited to nascent Society." Terrors and punishments for violations of the persons and property of others were introduced to compensate for waning attachment to the innate restraint of respect for nascent laws, and society began to move in the direction of collective organization for the securing of property relations.[34]

Thus, although men by this point were in a "just mean" between pure savage indolence and modern civility, with their amour propre awakened and their pity already weakened, nonetheless Rousseau insisted that this must have been "the happiest and most lasting epoch" of human existence. As he famously put it—and in the first of the three passages Smith translated for Scottish readers—so long as men were happy to adorn themselves in feathers and dance before their rustic huts, existing with only minimal dependence upon others, they lived "free, healthy, good, and happy as far as they could by their Nature be." It was only when they became mutually dependent upon each other for subsistence, and some got the idea that they could appropriate for one the provisions for two, that "property appeared, work became necessary, and the vast forests changed into smiling Fields that had to be watered with the sweat of men."[35] All of which would have immediately caught Smith's attention, because with the important exception of Rousseau's declamation of what he saw as the seeds of the later misery of modern society—i.e., the corrupt descendent of humanity's primitive halcyon condition—Smith had seen exactly this account of human sociability before. Not in *The Fable of the Bees, Volume 2*, but in Hume's *Treatise of Human Nature*.

PITY AND JUSTICE, PROPERTY AND DECEPTION

In its critical mechanics, if not its fine detail, Rousseau's account of fully formed humans' primitive sociability up to the point so far described is structurally identical to that of Hume. Certainly, Hume's concept of sympathy was a much more complex and extensively worked-out notion than Rousseau's fairly simplistic idea of pity. But with regard to the question of human sociability, Hume's sympathy checked the disruptive potential of pride in exactly the way that Rousseau's pity did. For both thinkers, in men's primitive state, prior to the rise of large and lasting society, natural sentiment ensured that the pursuit of amour propre was tempered, and violent outbursts of vanity were a sporadic nuisance, not a deep and perpetual source of social breakdown. In terms of sociability theory, in explaining the human ability to live in small-scale primitive groupings, Hume's sympathy and Rousseau's pity were functionally identical, as were their corresponding views on men's capacity to associate.

34. Rousseau, "Second Discourse," 167.
35. Ibid.

Even the most primitive tribal groupings, however, needed some system of regulating possessions. Here, Hume's and Rousseau's ideas were again aligned. For Hume, primitive property was not a major source of disruption because even the most savage societies based around the basic family unit deployed the rudiments of the artificial convention of justice. For Hume, at this stage justice could be the barest of conventions: a tacit understanding that one's own self-interest was augmented by desisting from appropriating the possessions of others on the assumption of reciprocal behavior.[36] Yet the primitive convention Hume described was, again, functionally identical to the unwritten and voluntarily adhered-to "laws" that Rousseau imagined governed the first savage societies, violation of which was punished by either the wronged individual or the outraged collective, and which only later became formalized with the institution of judges.[37] This point is easily missed or misunderstood because Rousseau appears to offer a diametrically opposed theoretical sequence to that offered by Hume, and later Smith.[38] Rousseau declares that "to say that the Chiefs were chosen before the confederation was established, and that the Ministers of the Laws existed before the Laws themselves, is an assumption not worthy of serious refutation."[39] Hume and Smith, however, are clear that first there arise conventions of compact for the governing of possessions, then judges are instituted to better uphold these conventions, and only finally in the sequence are conventions formalized into written and publicly promulgated legal codes—i.e., laws proper. Yet what needs to be appreciated here is that whereas Hume and Smith have a well-worked-out distinction between

36. David Hume, *The Clarendon Edition of the Works of David Hume: A Treatise of Human Nature*, ed. D. F. Norton and M. J. Norton (Oxford: Oxford University Press, 2007), T.3.2.2.9–22, SBN 489–98; T.3.2.7.1–8, SBN 534–39.

37. On a not-unconnected issue, Céline Spector has noted that with regard to the notion of promise keeping, Rousseau's account in *Émile* bears some important affinities with Hume's convention-based explanation in the *Treatise*—although the two are ultimately separated by the question of God's role in the foundations of key moral concepts. See Céline Spector, "Y a-t-il un gardien des promesses? L'hétéronomie de la conscience dans L'*Émile*," in *Penser l'homme: treize études sur Jean-Jacques Rousseau*, ed. C. Habib and P. Manent (Paris: Classiques Garnier, 2013), 172–76, 179–82.

38. Hont has made a great deal of stressing the difference between Rousseau and Smith on this matter, going so far as to claim that their different sequencing regarding the emergence of law and judges explains all of Smith and Rousseau's subsequent differences in politics. This is a mistake: the question of "which comes first, judges or the law?" is a red herring. What matters is that Hume operates (as does Smith) with a theory of natural authority, whereas Rousseau employs the explanatory mechanism of deception, and all of their political differences flow from this, not a technical question in conjectural history (which they all agree on, against Hobbes). See Hont, *Politics in Commercial Society*, chap. 3, and also "Adam Smith's History of Law and Government as Political Theory," in *Political Judgment: Essays for John Dunn*, ed. R. Bourke and R. Geuss (Cambridge: Cambridge University Press, 2009), 147–50.

39. Rousseau, "Second Discourse," 176.

prelegal conventions tacitly governing human associations prior to codification, and written laws that exist after codification, Rousseau speaks much more loosely and talks of "laws" prior to judges to refer to what Hume and Smith more specifically termed conventions. What Rousseau was really rejecting was not the Hume-Smith sequencing—which he in fact also affirmed, despite not drawing a sharp technical distinction between conventions and laws—but *Hobbes's* idea that prior to the erection of civil society there was no justice, because there was no judge or arbiter, and hence no meaningful content to the notions of possession or property.[40] Far from disagreeing with Hume on this point, Rousseau in effect sided with him to claim that it is justice—i.e., the collective regulation of property relations—that eventually creates the Leviathan, not the other way around. (This agreement was, however, probably an unknowing one: there is no compelling evidence of Rousseau having read Hume before composing the *Second Discourse*.)

Yet despite this identity in the fundamental structure, if not the fine details, of their arguments, Hume's account of the changes subsequently wrought by the innovation of conventions, and later laws, to uphold property, took him in a completely different direction to that pursued by Rousseau. What separates these thinkers is not their theories of sociability with regard to humans' basic psychology and attendant primitive capacities, but how they explained the transition from primitive conditions to large and lasting society, given that both agreed that bare affective sentiment could not do the explanatory work required. Sympathy, taken on its own, could no more explain large and lasting society than pity, Hume's more elaborate and complex theoretical articulation of the notion of fellow feeling notwithstanding.

Rousseau located man's exit from the final stage of the state of nature, and the beginning of the process of individual psychological corruption and the advent of enormous material inequality, in the artificially induced pathological inflammation of amour propre. This inflammation had a very specific cause. "Metallurgy and agriculture were the two arts the invention of which brought about this great revolution" in human affairs: it was "iron and wheat that civilized men, and ruined Mankind."[41] Rousseau postulated the emergence of a two-sector economy, where wheat growers traded with ironmongers. The problem (one must here infer from the text, as Rousseau's reasoning is left ambiguous) was that ironmongers needed to eat every day, whereas farmers only needed new tools a few times a year.[42] Farmers thus began to acquire wealth

---

40. Thomas Hobbes, *The Clarendon Edition of the Works of Thomas Hobbes: Leviathan*, ed. N. Malcolm (Oxford: Oxford University Press, 2012), vol. 2, 196, 274.

41. Rousseau, "Second Discourse," 168.

42. As Rousseau puts it, "As soon as men were needed to melt and forge iron, others were needed to feed them. The more the number of workers increased, the fewer hands were engaged in providing for the common subsistence, without there being any fewer mouths to consume it; and as some had to have foods in exchange for their iron, the others

faster than their economic trading partners, creating the threat of imbalance between the emergent productive classes. When combined with natural inequalities of talents, effort, and intelligence, the concentration of material inequalities increased apace. Class divisions emerged, and things "having reached this point, it is easy to imagine the rest"; namely, the emergence of the arts and sciences and human progress towards advanced civilized living.[43]

Human beings were now fully developed, on the cusp of leaving the state of nature once and for all: "our faculties developed, memory and imagination brought into play, *amour propre* interested, reason become active, and the mind almost at the limit of the perfection of which it is capable," and when "to be and to appear become two entirely different things."[44] The final step, however, was taken through an act of deception. The new and growing inequalities of material assets were concentrated in the hands of a minority of property holders who were forever in danger of being attacked and dispossessed by the envious poor, themselves just as animated by pathologically inflated amour propre as their superiors. To alleviate this situation the rich hit upon the idea of instituting formal rules of property ownership enforced by collective sanction—i.e., codified laws proper for the enforcement of property rights. They sold this idea to the poor by presenting it as to the poor's own advantage, claiming that their meager possessions were in danger of being taken from them by their near-standing social competitors, and hence all should unite to uphold the sanctity of property as a way of securing each his own. Although the poor were the true losers of this arrangement by accepting a system of social control in which they would forever be subjugated and held in relations of oppression and dependency, they were easily seduced via the appeal to the short-term calculations of their amour propre, and in any case "had too much business to sort out amongst themselves to be able to do without arbiters, and too much greed and ambition to be able to do for long without Masters."[45] All ran headlong into their chains, believing that they were securing their freedom.

---

finally discovered the secret of using iron to increase foods" (ibid., 169). However, it is possible, as Hont does, to read Rousseau as here positing the early emergence of an imbalance between town and country, and thus the origins of rural depopulation that would come to preoccupy him and many others in mid-eighteenth-century France. This is because industry would likely be far more dynamic than agriculture, and can produce new products for which there is infinite demand, and if food is cheap but metallurgic products are expensive, then the agriculturalists would rapidly come to lose their initially advantaged position. For alternative readings of the logic of the two-sector economy in Rousseau's argument, see Hont, *Politics in Commercial Society*, 99, and Neuhouser, *Rousseau's Critique*, 94–95.

43. Rousseau, "Second Discourse," 170.
44. Ibid., 170.
45. Ibid., 173.

This was the true origin of civil society, the final exit from the state of nature. Once one fully fledged political society was operational, others quickly followed: centralized organization was a necessary defensive measure to protect one's own group from the ravages of outside attackers, the most organized of all being those who had instituted formalized rules of property and collective sanction. (A claim, it is worth remembering, also made by Hume.[46]) Formal instantiation of property rules thus created the state, which served as the source of arbitration for disputes, collective sanction for those who disrupted social arrangements, continued enforcer of the division of assets, and coordinator of military defense and attack. It was founded upon a deception, but not the one that Mandeville had supposed. Humans' psychological change had not been artificially orchestrated by cunning legislators, but had developed organically over millennia. The true act of purposeful deception was much more recent: the rich rigging the game of property in their own favor and erecting institutional structures to preserve their advantage throughout successive generations.[47] In other words, the invention of the state as the enforcer of property rights was the end point of political manipulation by the powerful cunning to gain advantage and domination over the weak. Yet having reconfigured the account of human sociability in large and lasting conditions in this way, the conclusions Rousseau drew regarding the stability of such arrangements were diametrically opposed to the Dutchman's.

Rousseau's prognosis for the future of the European state form was bleak. As well as the massive wars of destruction that large modern states were sure to constantly wage against each other, human societies erected on a foundational act of deception centered on the manipulation of amour propre were faced with inevitable cycles of corruption and revolution, ultimately tending to despotism. The first epoch of civilized society was the division of rich and poor, which gave way to that of strong and weak, and then finally to that of "Master and Slave, the last degree of inequality, and the state to which all the others finally lead, until new revolutions either dissolve the Government entirely, or bring it closer to legitimate institution."[48] Rousseau's dramatic prediction was that across the great states of Europe "despotism" would rear its "hideous head," finally succeeding "in trampling Laws and People underfoot . . . establishing itself on the ruins of the Republic."[49] To properly understand Rousseau's warning that Europe's future would inevitably be marked by cycles of revolution and despotism, however, it is necessary to recall two things.

46. Hume, *Treatise*, T.3.2.7.5–7, SBN 536–38.
47. For a discussion of Rousseau's account of deception, tying it closely to his notion of pathologically inflamed amour propre, see Michael Rosen, *On Voluntary Servitude: False Consciousness and the Theory of Ideology* (Cambridge: Polity, 1996), 80–95.
48. Rousseau, "Second Discourse," 182.
49. Ibid., 185.

First, that although Rousseau rejected Hobbes's picture of savage humans as a back projection of modern humans, he entirely accepted Hobbes's depiction of humanity in its current civilized state—i.e., after the ameliorating effects of pity had been firmly repressed by the ravages of pathologically inflamed amour propre. What Hobbes had gotten wrong was the explanation of how humans had achieved sociability given their present psychological incapacity for large and lasting society, not the seriousness of their present predicament. On the contrary, Rousseau ended up with *exactly* Hobbes's problem when considering modern humans, although as we have seen he arrived at it for different reasons, by the route of a conjectural history not a deductive "science" of politics. Rousseau agreed entirely that considering humans as they are found in modern society, they had only two "drives" to society: honor and advantage. His point against Hobbes was that it could not always have been this way, or else people would never have been able to achieve large and lasting society (this was Hobbes's true mistake of back projection). What Hobbes was not wrong about was how humanity was *now*.[50] As a result, Rousseau and Hume certainly did not agree about humanity's modern predicament, despite their shared rejection of Hobbes's account of primitive human sociability. This is because whereas Rousseau could only explain the advent of large and lasting society via a process of deception, and ended up coming to adopt the picture of psychologically deformed, pity-suppressed, bellicose humans that Hobbes had always posited, Hume's more sophisticated concept of sympathy allowed him to develop the theory of natural authority we considered in chapter 3, and which took him wholly outside of the Hobbesian framework. Smith would follow Hume in this regard, whereas Rousseau (as we shall see below) fell back to Hobbes's theory of union, whilst simultaneously resisting the built-in argument for representative sovereign absolutism that Hobbes had made central to his theoretical edifice.[51]

The second thing to bear in mind when considering Rousseau's prediction of instability and revolution is that the closing passages of the *Discourse* may be read as a rejection of Montesquieu's new political theory, as propounded in *The Spirit of the Laws* of 1748.[52] Montesquieu posited that large European states should be organized not along the lines of a classical republic demanding patriotic self-sacrifice in egalitarian conditions, but through carefully structured

50. Douglass, *Rousseau and Hobbes*, 100–101.
51. That Rousseau ultimately ended up being much closer to Hobbes than he presented himself as being was noticed by some of his immediate critics: see Sonenscher, *Sans-Culottes*, 173–75.
52. On this see especially Hont, *Politics in Commercial Society*, 45–47; Sonenscher, *San-Culottes*, 206–7. For Rousseau's earlier engagement with Montesquieu in the *First Discourse* on the arts and sciences, Christopher Kelly, "Rousseau and the Illustrious Montesquieu," in Kelly and Grace, *The Challenge of Rousseau*, 19–33.

systems of ranks and hierarchy. The "spring" of Montesquieu's monarchy was "honor"—i.e., the manipulation of the desire for status and esteem, which could easily be made to work with "false-honor" if necessary.[53] This was in effect a direct adoption of Mandeville's central insight that pride could be made socially useful if it was coaxed into mimicking virtue, although Montesquieu probably learnt it from Mandeville's French predecessors, the seventeenth-century Augustinian thinkers centered in Port Royal, especially Blaise Pascal and Pierre Nicole.[54] Montesquieu posited that the human need for the satiation of amour propre could in modern conditions be safely channeled into collectively beneficial directions. An honor-based state could be combined with a careful separation of powers and the rule of law to produce a large-scale political entity governed by a legally controlled form of monarchy. This avoided Hobbesian absolutism on the one hand, whilst also leaving behind antiquated civic humanist theories of frugality and patriotic self-sacrifice on the other, seeking to both supply and guarantee the liberty of citizens through the constancy of law. Montesquieu's vision was of a hierarchically stratified but stable state, one in which competitive amour propre was suitably channeled so as to work for the cohesion, not the collapse, of large-scale politics, which in practice meant modern, postfeudal European monarchy.[55]

Rousseau's *Discourse* was a reaffirmation of the Hobbesian challenge against Mandeville's, and more recently Montesquieu's, attempts to defuse the Hobbesian problem of pride's threat to social and political stability. For Rousseau, civilized people, fundamentally driven by pathologically inflamed amour propre, had only ever been deceived, not fundamentally tamed or changed, when coming to accept the system of private property and supervening hierarchies of wealth and status that characterized modern states. It was therefore hopeless to believe that systems of rank and honor could indefinitely contain the pathologically inflated pride of modern subjects, especially as commercial societies tended toward ever more extreme levels of luxury and inequality. As

---

53. Montesquieu, *The Spirit of the Laws*, ed. A. M. Cohler, B. C. Miller, and H. S. Stone (Cambridge: Cambridge University Press, 1989), xli, 27.

54. On Montesquieu and French Augustinianism, see Michael Sonenscher, *Before the Deluge: Public Debt, Inequality, and the Intellectual Origins of the French Revolution* (Princeton, NJ: Princeton University Press, 2007), 153–59. On Augustinianism in the development of French political philosophy more generally, Nannerl O. Keohane, *Philosophy and the State in France: The Renaissance to the Enlightenment* (Princeton, NJ: Princeton University Press, 1980), chaps. 6, 9, and 10.

55. I discuss Montesquieu's thought in this regard in more detail in chapter 5. Following Hont and Sonenscher, we can see Montesquieu's vision of the modern monarchy as a *Rechtsstaat* as the original eighteenth-century articulation of what would become the modern—i.e., liberal—republic, roughly the state form of the democratic West at present. Whether this is compatible with Hobbesian sovereignty doctrine, however, can be called into question (as I do in chapters 5 and 6).

inequalities naturally increased thanks to wealth first protecting, and then reproducing, itself, the mass of losers in society would eventually see through the deception embedded in the system of private property. Greedy for their "fair" share, the dispossessed would attack their economic (and, by extension, political) superiors. Pride would destabilize utility—as Hobbes had said that it would—unless people were overawed by common power, which was what Rousseau meant when he predicted the rise of despotism as the outcome of the trajectory of the politics based on inequality described in the *Second Discourse*. The end of that work carried a grim prognosis of the cataclysmic fate that awaited Europe thanks to the upcoming ravages of despotism, military competition, and societal collapse. Montesquieu's hope that pride could be tamed and controlled was a mirage. Modern Europeans would be fools, Rousseau was insisting, to believe in it.

Counter-Hobbesian Hobbism: The Social Contract

Rousseau thus found himself with exactly Hobbes's political problem, although he arrived at it by a different theoretical route: how could pride-driven competitors be stably arranged in large groupings without the entire enterprise collapsing owing to the very pride that needed to be controlled? Yet Rousseau was implacably opposed to Hobbes's absolutist monarchical solution based on representative sovereignty, seeing it as a form of despotism reducing subjects to brute political subjugation. The immensely ambitious task Rousseau set himself was to find a counter-Hobbesian answer, whilst starting from Hobbes's basic principles. The sheer difficulty of this task—and the attendant need to incorporate the international, not just the national, dimension of politics—probably explains why Rousseau ultimately abandoned his masterwork, the *Political Institutions*, only fragments of which now survive.[56] Yet the largest surviving part of this project Rousseau did publish as a separate treatise, although he eventually intimated that it was also a failure. This turned out to be his most famous work of all.

The Social Contract was an exercise in full-blooded Hobbesian sovereignty theory, even if it centrally rejected Hobbes's insistence that sovereign power must be conceived of as a form of representation. Rousseau agreed entirely that sovereign power must be absolute: that fact was both built into the logic of the concept, and was required in order to affect the change in human relationships that could institute legitimate political arrangements. The problem, as Rousseau saw it, was that by making sovereignty representative its legitimacy was automatically compromised: sovereignty became a manifestation

---

56. See especially the so-called "Geneva Manuscript" of *The Social Contract*, and Jean-Jacques Rousseau, "The State of War," in *The Social Contract and Other Later Political Writings*, ed. V. Gourevitch (Cambridge: Cambridge University Press, 1997), 153–61, 162–76.

of the problem it was supposed to solve. Attempting to avoid this conundrum may in part have constituted the motivation behind Rousseau's opening proclamation that he would "try always to combine what right permits with what interest prescribes, so that justice and utility may not be disjoined"—in other words, to find a form of politics that could combine justice and utility in a way Rousseau took Hobbes to have conspicuously failed to do.[57]

The core problem addressed by *The Social Contract* was that humanity in its present condition was an animal that needed politics to associate safely and stably, and thus live well (Hobbes was right about that). But politics was simultaneously an inherently dangerous activity, because it was always liable to slip into either the tyranny of the rulers, or the corruption of the ruled, or (most likely) both. Humans needed politics, but also needed to be saved from politics. Rousseau made a response to this predicament his central task, which he encapsulated thus: "To find a form of association that will defend and protect the person and goods of each associate with the full common force, and by means of which each, uniting with all, nevertheless obey only himself and remain as free as before." In Rousseau's own words, "This is the fundamental problem to which the social contract provides the solution."[58] The subsequent argument was an attempt to articulate a complete theoretical account of both the "problem" and its "solution."

Rousseau's social contract was explicitly a theory of union in Hobbesian vein. Individuals were envisioned as coming together and unanimously agreeing to erect common power and to live under it: "in place of the private person of each contracting party, this act of association produces a moral and collective body made up of as many members as the assembly has voices, and which receives by the same acts its unity, its common *self*, its life and its will." This act of union created the "*Republic*" or "*body politic*," which should be known as the "state when it is passive, *Sovereign* when active, *Power* when comparing it to similar bodies."[59] Thus Rousseau here followed Hobbes: the unanimous act of consenting to live under common power created a "moral person," which was the state. Where Rousseau disagreed with Hobbes was on the question of sovereignty, which for the Genevan could only ever be wielded directly by the assembled individuals who freely put themselves under common power. These individuals self-legislated by a process of disinterested voting, which

---

57. Rousseau, *Social Contract*, 41; Keohane, *Philosophy and the State*, 444–45.

58. Rousseau, *Social Contract*, 49; see also Frederick Neuhouser, "Freedom, Dependence, and the General Will," *Philosophical Review* 102, no. 3 (1993), especially 366–73. On Rousseau's rejection of Hobbes's political solution as centering on the Genevan's particular conception of freedom, which he saw as in need of preservation for any political arrangement to be legitimate, but which was entirely compromised by Hobbes's solution, see Douglass, *Rousseau and Hobbes*, chap. 3.

59. Rousseau, *Social Contract*, 50–51; see also Neuhouser, "Reason and Self-Love," 226–28.

sought to secure the freedom and equality that all aimed at when engaging in the essentially paradoxical task of both living under politics—i.e., the rule of others—whilst nonetheless obeying "only themselves," and thus remaining "as free as before." This was what Rousseau hoped to achieve by invoking the idea of the "general will." Established by disinterested voting in the creation of laws by the assembled sovereign body, the general will was not an attempt to reveal some objective metaphysical good that existed independently of citizens' actual wills or beliefs, nor a way of forcing citizens to obey their "true" selves, but was Rousseau's effort to make good on the explication of how a form of truly legitimate politics could be instantiated.[60] In order to preserve the integrity and thus legitimacy of the general will, however, sovereignty could never be represented. The general will must be revealed directly by those who wielded sovereignty, or else it would not *be* the general will, but merely the particular will of some portion(s) of the citizenry. The moment that sovereignty became represented—i.e., when the general will ceased to legislate—the collective power of the state became exercised by an alien agency, and individuals ceased to obey only themselves, and thus lost the freedom that the social contract as the only legitimate form of politics was there to secure and guarantee: "the sovereign, which is nothing but a collective being, can only be represented by itself; power can well be transferred, but not will."[61] So whereas Hobbes used a principle of radical popular sovereignty via the consent of the ruled to generate an argument for absolute power in the hands of a representative (ideally a monarch), Rousseau insisted on the necessarily direct democratic basis of sovereignty, itself coterminous with the state properly conceived.

Diverging from Hobbes in this manner, Rousseau nonetheless exploited a resource that was derivable from Hobbes's *De Cive*, the version of the Englishman's political thought that the Genevan was most familiar with.[62] This was the introduction of a sharp distinction between sovereignty and government.[63]

---

60. On this see especially Neuhouser, "Reason and Self-Love," 228–33; John Hope Mason, " 'Forced to Be free'," in Wokler, *Rousseau and Liberty*, 121–24.

61. Rousseau, *Social Contract*, 57; Keohane, *Philosophy and the State*, 444–45.

62. Richard Tuck, "Hobbes and Democracy," in *Rethinking the Foundations of Modern Political Thought*, ed. A. Brett and J. Tully (Cambridge: Cambridge University Press, 2006), 172, 183–90; Isaac Nakhimovsky, *The Closed Commercial State: Perpetual Peace and Commercial Society from Rousseau to Fichte* (Princeton, NJ: Princeton University Press, 2011), 26–32; Douglass, *Rousseau and Hobbes*, 16–20.

63. This has been most extensively analyzed by Richard Tuck in *The Sleeping Sovereign: The Invention of Modern Democracy* (Cambridge: Cambridge University Press, 2015). See also Sonenscher, *San-Culottes*, 154–55; Nakhimovsky, *Closed Commercial State*, 29–32. However, Hobbes may not have been the *only* source for the sovereignty-government distinction: as Robin Douglass points out, Locke may have influenced Rousseau here, the latter apparently mapping his distinction between sovereignty and government onto Locke's distinction between legislative and executive power, as oppose to Hobbes's distinction (taken over from Bodin) between *imperium* and *administratio* (Robin Douglass, "Tuck, Rousseau

Whereas sovereignty (which Rousseau made clear consisted of legislative activity) must always be direct and democratic, by contrast government—i.e., the execution of the practical running of the affairs of the body politic—could be safely delegated to magistrates. Rousseau, like Hobbes, differentiated government in the familiar way—i.e., according to the number who partook in it: if one, a monarchy; if several, an aristocracy; if the many, a democracy. But he also took from Montesquieu an emphasis on fitting the type of government to the size of the territory being administered, with monarchies best for large nations, aristocracies for smaller ones, and democracies (insofar as they were possible at all, which Rousseau famously doubted) extremely small associations. Yet the sharp differentiation between sovereignty and government allowed Rousseau to claim that because all legitimate instantiations of sovereignty were democratic, whatever the form of government a state adopted, if it was itself legitimate—i.e., if its laws emanated from the general will—then it must necessarily be a republic: "I therefore call Republic any State ruled by laws, whatever may be the form of administration: for then the public interest alone governs, and the public thing counts for something. Every legitimate government is republican." As Rousseau clarified in a footnote, government was only ever the "minister" of the sovereign, chosen by it to administer affairs on a daily basis in line with the laws laid down by the general will. A monarch could thus be appointed by the sovereign to do this work, in which case "monarchy itself is republican."[64]

However, Rousseau provided a raft of reasons for thinking that a monarchy was likely to prove ill-fated if chosen as the form of government for a legitimate state, with his own preferred option being a merit-based aristocracy (a rejoinder to Hobbes's preference for kingship). The deep theoretical point being made was that sovereignty was the same in all times and places, even if government took on many different forms. By extension, the legitimate state, when properly conceived, was also the same thing in all times and places, because the state was simply the "moral person" that existed when sovereignty was exercised by citizens collectively, and this could take only one legitimate form, even if the supervening institutional structure for administering government varied widely in practice. Rousseau thus ended up espousing a counter-Hobbesian Hobbism: proper method could reveal the true essence of the state as resting in direct popular sovereignty, but now understood as something incompatible with representation, meaning that Hobbes's absolutist representative solution was automatically ruled out as being necessarily illegitimate.

This, however, left Rousseau with insurmountable practical problems. Whereas Hobbes's (illegitimate) solution sought to constrain proud

---

and the Sovereignty of the People," *History of European Ideas* 42 (2016), 1111–14). On Rousseau's admiration for and proximity to Locke, see also Brooke, "Locke and Rousseau."

64. Rousseau, *Social Contract*, 67.

competitors via the overawing power of the representative sovereign, Rousseau's sovereign—necessarily composed of those very same proud competitors who needed to be held in check—had to control itself. *The Social Contract* proffered numerous institutional measures designed to assist the suppression of the self, so that those same citizens who composed the sovereign could control their inherent desire for status and competition, in turn preventing them from voting partially and thereby allowing the general will to become "subordinated to others that prevail over it."[65] To this end luxury must be tightly controlled, meaning an austere repression of free commercial activities. A relatively severe egalitarianism would need to be instantiated, and forcibly maintained, to keep citizens' interests sufficiently aligned such that the general will could be reliably revealed, meaning in turn that society must be classless: "no citizen be so very rich that he can buy another, and none so poor that he is compelled to sell himself."[66] A slave population, however, would be necessary in order to generate the time and independence for citizens to participate directly in politics without recourse to general-will-destroying representatives, something Rousseau believed would vitiate the entire legitimacy of the society being posited, insofar as slavery was itself unjustifiable.[67] Meetings of the sovereign would have to take place face to face at regular intervals (but not so regularly as to generate factions and competition), long enough to pass good laws (but not too long so as to expose people to the ravages of political competition), and without parties or interest groups that would inevitably disrupt the homogeneity of the population necessary to make the general will easily discernable. A civil religion and a censor would be needed, invested with draconian powers (including the right of execution) to keep people's interests and patriotic devotion in harmony. Most fancifully of all, a quasi-mythical lawgiver had to be posited in order for a legitimate state to ever get off the ground. This visionary figure must know the *mores* of the people well enough to give them the constitution best suited to their specific territorial size and climate, but who had no part in the continued running of the state after the

---

65. Ibid., 122.
66. Ibid., 78; Neuhouser, "The General Will," 387; but also John P. McCormick, "Rousseau's Rome and the Repudiation of Populist Republicanism," *Critical Review of International Social and Political Theory* 10, no. 1 (2007), 3–27.
67. Rousseau, *Social Contract*, 115. Rousseau well recognized that the ancient political arrangements he admired were all predicated upon slavery, but he never proposed slavery as a modern possibility—an important point against readings of Rousseau that paint him as nostalgic for, and desiring to return to, a lost ancient past. However, even if slavery were outlawed, Rousseau is clear that not all inhabitants of the state would be citizens, but more something along the lines of Geneva's qualified republican constitution at the time. On these themes see Helena Rosenblatt, *Rousseau and Geneva: From the "First Discourse" to the "Social Contract," 1749–1762* (Cambridge: Cambridge University Press, 1997), chap. 6, and Richard Whatmore, *Against War and Empire: Geneva, Britain and France in the Eighteenth Century* (New Haven: Yale University Press, 2012), chap. 3.

constitution's adoption. Even more challengingly, the proposals of the original legislator must be accepted by a people via a noncoercive method based not on the force of reason, but "an authority of a different order" that must "persuade without convincing"—all with reference to a people that was itself (somehow) not already too corrupt to be unable to live under the arrangements gifted to them.[68] And in addition to all of this there was the dramatic problem of the international dimension: how could such a state establish itself and survive in a world of aggressive competitor states that would impinge both commercially and economically upon the affairs of the legitimate republic? This last issue was so severe that Rousseau closed *The Social Contract* by confessing his inability to deal with an "object too vast for my short sight."[69]

Rousseau was no fantasist. He understood perfectly well that his remedies could not be adopted anywhere in the mid-eighteenth century (although it is conceivable that he was sketching a guide for how political societies might one day be legitimately founded, albeit after the devastation of Europe predicted at the end of the *Second Discourse*).[70] The central purpose of *The Social Contract* was not to offer a blueprint for a working political society, but to supply a theoretical rejoinder to Hobbes: to show the impossibility of achieving a legitimate political society for humans in their current condition, via a simultaneous working out of what genuine political legitimacy would actually require. In *practical* terms, Rousseau endorsed Hobbes's solution as being the only realistic prospect of keeping competitive amour propre in check. But

---

68. Rousseau, *Social Contract*, 71. That the legislator figure is essentially incompatible with the conditions of legitimacy set down in the *Social Contract* itself, see John Hope Mason, "Individuals in Society: Rousseau's Republican Vision," *History of Political Thought* 10, no. 1 (1989), 107–10. For helpful further discussions, see Mason, "Forced to Be Free," 130–32; Christopher Kelly, "'To Persuade without Convincing': The Language of Rousseau's Legislator," *American Journal of Political Science* 31, no. 2 (1987), especially 322–24.

69. Rousseau, *Social Contract*, 152. On the international dimensions of Rousseau's thought, see especially Richard Tuck, *The Rights of War and Peace: Political Thought and the International Order from Grotius to Kant* (Oxford: Oxford University Press, 1999), chap. 7.

70. The famous allusion to Corsica is confirmation of Rousseau's belief that his proposals simply could not be adopted by any modern state. Corsica is described as the "one country left in Europe capable of receiving legislation"—but it was still in need of "some wise man to teach it to preserve" its "valor and steadfastness" (Rousseau, *Social Contract*, 78). In other words, of all European states, the only one that might be reconstituted on a legitimate foundation was Corsica, but even it would require a lawgiver in order to achieve this—and Rousseau was under no illusion as to the prospects of that actually happening. Although in Rousseau's earlier writings—such as the "Epistle Dedicatory" to the *Second Discourse*, and his "Letter to D'Alembert"—he seemed to hold out that Geneva might still be capable of a legitimate constitution, by the time of the *Social Contract* this hope was clearly abandoned: Mason, "Rousseau's Republican Vision," 97–98; Douglass, *Rousseau and Hobbes*, 198–202.

whereas Hobbes celebrated this conclusion, Rousseau openly lamented it.[71] As he wrote to Mirabeau, trying to get beyond Hobbes by finding "a form of Government that might place the law above man" was a task equivalent to "squaring the Circle in geometry." Accepting that his own solution could not be implemented, "I am of the opinion that one has to go to the other extreme and all at once place man as much above the law as he can be, consequently to establish a despotism that is arbitrary and indeed the most arbitrary possible." As a consequence, "I see no tolerable mean between the most austere Democracy" (his own solution in *The Social Contract*) and "the most perfect Hobbesism."[72]

We should appreciate the full import of this. Rousseau, his best efforts notwithstanding, failed to get past Hobbes—and admitted as much. Despite attempting to start from a different place in the theory of sociability, and explicitly attempting a theory of sovereignty cast in the Hobbesian mold, he ultimately concluded that the task could not be practically achieved. Even if in theory a legitimate state form could be imagined, such a condition was beyond the grasp of men, and they had to settle for Hobbes's repressive absolutism if they were to avoid societal collapse.

In considering the theory of the state, therefore, we are presented with a choice when it comes to Rousseau. On the one hand we might conclude that although Rousseau himself failed, he developed theoretical resources that would enable future theorists to take matters further, and achieve a developed form of Hobbesian sovereignty theory that could come to terms with the conditions of commercial modernity. In this regard, the leading candidate for the thinker who squared Hobbes's circle for conditions of commercial modernity is Emmanuel Sieyès.[73] But that depends upon seeing Rousseau and Sieyès as essentially on the right track in attempting to follow Hobbes in the construction of a theory of the state centered on the concept of sovereignty. By contrast, once we appreciate—as Adam Smith did—the resources that Hume had opened up by reconfiguring the theory of the state in terms of the opinion of mankind, then Rousseau's efforts in *The Social Contract* may look far more

---

71. In typically colorful rhetoric, Rousseau embellished his reluctant endorsement of Hobbes in practical matters thus: "But the Caligulas, the Neros, the Tiberiuses! . . . My God! . . . I writhe on the ground, and bewail being a human being": Jean-Jacques Rousseau, "Letter to Mirabeau," in *Social Contract*, 270.

72. Rousseau, "Letter to Mirabeau," 270; Hont, "The Permanent Crisis of a Divided Mankind: 'Nation-State' and 'Nationalism' in Historical Perspective," in *Jealousy of Trade: International Competition and the Nation-State in Historical Perspective* (Cambridge, MA: Belknap Harvard, 2005), 470–72; Keohane, *Philosophy and the State*, 443–44; Sonenscher, *Sans-Culottes*, 200–201.

73. See especially Hont, "Permanent Crisis," 474–92, and also *Politics in Commercial Society* 24, 101; Sonenscher, *Before the Deluge*, 67–94; Tuck, *Sleeping Sovereign* (although Tuck takes a much more ambivalent view of Sieyès's role in the development of the idea of modern democracy).

futile and misguided. From Smith's Scottish perspective, the most promising way forward was not to attempt to square Hobbes's circle, but to step outside of it. That is, to construct an alternative form of political theory undergirding a different kind of theory of the state. Smith's attempt to do precisely this is the subject of the next chapter.

CHAPTER FIVE

Adam Smith's Political Theory of Opinion

THIS CHAPTER EXAMINES Adam Smith as political philosopher, in the particular light of what has been said so far about the contributions of Hume and, to a lesser extent, Rousseau, regarding sociability and the state. Hume and Smith were correspondents and friends, as well as theorists of sympathy in morals and "skeptical Whigs" in politics.[1] Hence, they have often been taken, not unreasonably, to be speaking with something of a shared voice. This, however, is not always an accurate portrayal of their intellectual relationship, and with regard to some matters it is potentially misleading. Smith may frequently be read as working in the medium of what would now be called "internal critique" with regard to Hume's work: sharing many of the same fundamental aims and objectives, and departing from many of the same points, but prepared to subject Hume's arguments to forceful criticism when they failed to yield the results claimed for them. On the other hand, Smith is now widely regarded as having either been influenced by, or shared fundamental concerns with, Rousseau.[2] What I suggest, however, is that whilst Smith

---

1. The classic statements of Hume and Smith as "sceptical" (as oppose to "vulgar") Whigs come from Duncan Forbes, *Hume's Philosophical Politics* (Cambridge: Cambridge University Press, 1975), and "Sceptical Whiggism, Commerce, and Liberty," in *Essays on Adam Smith*, ed. A. Skinner and T. Wilson (Oxford: Oxford University Press, 1976), 179–202.

2. For example, Michael Ignatieff, "Smith, Rousseau and the Republic of Needs," in *Scotland and Europe 1200–1850*, ed. T. C. Smouth (Edinburgh: Edinburgh University Press, 1986), 187–206, and *The Needs of Strangers* (London: Hogarth, 1990); Dennis C. Rasmussen, *The Problems and Promise of Commercial Society: Adam Smith's Response to Rousseau* (University Park, PA: Pennsylvania State University Press, 2008); Ryan Patrick Hanley, "Commerce and Corruption: Rousseau's Diagnosis and Adam Smith's Cure," *European Journal of Political Theory* 7 (2008) 137–58; "From Geneva to Glasgow: Rousseau and Adam Smith on the Theatre of Commercial Society," *Studies in Eighteenth Century Culture* 35 (2006),

certainly worked over the same or similar terrain to Rousseau, and that reading them in the light of each other can be extremely illuminating, nonetheless as a *biographical* contention, Smith's work indicates that he was relatively uninterested in Rousseau's political philosophy (as found especially in the *Second Discourse*), and found his arguments straightforward enough to answer, a case I have previously made at length elsewhere.[3] For Smith, Rousseau was not a primary target, but featured more like collateral damage—a provocative but mistaken thinker, easily dealt with in passing whilst undertaking the main task of correcting and improving Hume's positions, whilst also dealing with the challenge still issuing from Mandeville.[4]

Whatever the precise nature of Smith's relationship to Rousseau, however, what I contend to be of most significance and interest in Smith's political thinking is his acceptance of Hume's prioritization of opinion as the primary item in political-theoretical analysis, alongside his attendant insistence on the centrality of natural authority in explaining and vindicating such arrangements. In doing so, Smith went on to develop what remains a still underappreciated political theory of his own. This is most helpfully brought out by contrasting it with that of Montesquieu, which in turn helps us to see the

---

177–202; *Adam Smith and the Character of Virtue* (Cambridge: Cambridge University Press, 2009), chap. 1; "Enlightened Nation Building: The Science of the Legislator in Adam Smith and Rousseau," *American Journal of Political Science* 52 (2008), 219–34; Pierre Force, *Self-Interest before Adam Smith: A Genealogy of Economic Science* (Cambridge: Cambridge University Press, 2003); Christopher J. Berry, "Adam Smith and the Virtues of Commerce," in *Virtue: Nomos XXXIV*, ed. J. W. Chapman and W. A. Galston (New York: New York University Press, 1992), 69–88, and "Smith under Strain," *European Journal of Political Theory* 3 (2004), 455–63; Charles L. Griswold, "Smith and Rousseau in Dialogue: Sympathy, Pitié, Spectatorship and Narrative," in *Adam Smith Review*, vol. 5, *The Philosophy of Adam Smith: Essays Commemorating the 250th Anniversary of the "Theory of Moral Sentiments,"* ed. V. Brown and S. Fleischacker (Abingdon: Routledge, 2010), 59–84; E. J. Hundert, *The Enlightenment's "Fable": Bernard Mandeville and the Discovery of Society* (Cambridge: Cambridge University Press, 1994), 105–15, 219–36; John Robertson, *The Case for the Enlightenment: Scotland and Naples 1680–1760* (Cambridge: Cambridge University Press, 2005), 392–403.

3. Paul Sagar, "Smith and Rousseau, after Hume and Mandeville," *Political Theory* (forthcoming).

4. That Smith and Rousseau be read alongside each other, as tackling the same basic questions, with a comparative juxtaposition yielding valuable interpretative insights into problems in both the history of political thought and contemporary politics, was the approach urged by Hont at the end of his life: István Hont, *Politics in Commercial Society* (Cambridge, MA: Harvard University Press, 2015). My claim here is intended to be precise: that even if it is illuminating to read Smith and Rousseau in a comparative frame, Smith himself was largely unmoved by Rousseau's earlier challenge, and we would do best to be aware of this or else we risk attributing Rousseau's views to Smith, when a careful reading in fact shows that they are subtly but importantly different *precisely because* Smith thought Rousseau could be easily answered. Again, see Sagar, "Smith and Rousseau," for detailed substantiation.

profound differences between Smith's vision of politics and Rousseau's—giving us further reason to doubt that the Scot could have been much moved by the Genevan's writings. Smith examined the nature of political authority and the fundamental basis of regime classification with regard to the distribution of power, and suggested how forms of rule were necessarily adapted to historical and material situations, which in turn opened and closed political possibilities for different peoples in different times. Ultimately, this put him firmly outside the Hobbesian legacy of thinking about the modern state, allowing him to entirely avoid the entanglements in which Rousseau became enmeshed.

Unfortunately, Smith's political theory can be recovered only piecemeal from sections of *The Wealth of Nations*, and more extensively from the two sets of student notes of Smith's Glasgow lectures on jurisprudence dating from the 1760s. We simply do not have Smith's political theory in any complete or final form, something he ensured by having his unpublished treatise on law and government destroyed shortly before his death.[5] Nonetheless, by making the necessary efforts at reconstruction we can come to appreciate Smith as a political theorist of the highest caliber, whilst also seeing the intellectual range and power afforded by adopting the opinion of mankind as an analytic heuristic.

Smith's Sociability

Like Hume, Smith made utility—rather than pride or benevolence—the central factor in explaining human sociability. This was stated clearly in part 2, section 2, of his 1759 *Theory of Moral Sentiments*, entitled "Of Justice and Beneficence." "All members of human society," Smith wrote, "stand in need of each other's assistance, and are likewise exposed to mutual injuries." Such a predicament might conceivably be resolved by extensive mutual beneficence: "Where the necessary assistance is reciprocally afforded from love, from gratitude, from friendship, from esteem, the society flourishes and is happy."[6] This, however, was only one possibility for explaining the existence of enduring social relations—and not a particularly likely one. By contrast, "though the necessary assistance should not be afforded from such generous and disinterested motives . . . the society, though less happy and agreeable, will not

---

5. See Nicholas Phillipson, *Adam Smith: An Enlightened Life* (London: Allen Lane, 2010), 3–4, for details. See also the account by Smith's earliest biographer: Dugald Stewart, "Account of the Life and Writings of Adam Smith, LL.D.," in Adam Smith, *The Glasgow Edition of the Works and Correspondence of Adam Smith: Essays on Philosophical Subjects*, ed. W.P.D. Wightman, J. C. Bryce, and I. S. Ross (Oxford, Oxford University Press, 1980), 327.

6. Adam Smith, *The Glasgow Edition of the Works and Correspondence of Adam Smith: The Theory of Moral Sentiments*, ed. D. D. Raphael and A. L. Macfie (Oxford: Oxford University Press, 1976), II.ii.3.1.

necessarily be dissolved." This was because "Society may subsist among different men, as among different merchants, from a sense of its utility, without any mutual love or affection."[7] For Smith, as for Hume, utility was organized and promoted in large-scale human groupings via the imposition of strict rules of justice that regulated people's material interactions, in turn guaranteeing stability in possessions over time, and facilitating an upward trajectory to advanced civilized living. Beneficence was less essential than justice to the existence of society, because large-scale human sociability could be achieved without the former, but never without the latter. Justice was "the main pillar that upholds the whole edifice," which if removed would see "the great, the immense fabric of human society . . . crumble into atoms." Beneficence was merely "the ornament which embellishes, not the foundation which supports the building."[8]

Whilst Smith agreed with Hume that large-scale sociability was primarily enabled by the coordination of utility seeking, rather than spontaneous natural benevolence or the control of competitive pride, he insisted that the technical foundations of Hume's case needed substantial correction.[9] Most fundamentally, Hume failed to see that prior to the adoption of conventions to regulate possessions, humans were *already* equipped with a natural propensity toward the upholding of justice. This emanated not from any regard to the utility of conventions, but from natural resentment: an innate, prereflective sentiment, easily forwarded to third-party observers via sympathy (a principle Smith shared, albeit in substantially modified form, with Hume).[10]

---

7. Smith, *Theory of Moral Sentiments*, II.ii.3.2.

8. Ibid., II.ii.3.4. For further elaboration on this point, see István Hont, "Commercial Society and Political Theory in the Eighteenth Century: The Problem of Authority in David Hume and Adam Smith," in *Main Trends in Cultural History: Ten Essays* ed. W. Melching and W. Velema (Amsterdam: Rodopi: 1994), 54–94, and also "Jealousy of Trade: An Introduction," in *Jealousy of Trade: International Competition and the Nation State in Historical Perspective* (Cambridge, MA: Belknap Harvard, 2005), 39–45, 101–11.

9. It is important, however, to remain sensitive to the fact that Smith was making a corrective from broadly *within* a philosophical outlook shared by Hume. Failure to see this has led some commentators to dramatically overstate Smith's differences from Hume on the question of justice, and thus to mischaracterize the nature of Smith's political theory more generally. See, for example, Robert Shaver, "Virtues, Utility, and Rules," in *The Cambridge Companion to Adam Smith*, ed. K. Haakonssen (Cambridge: Cambridge University Press, 2006), 189–213, which mistakenly claims a fundamental opposition between Smith and Hume on the question of justice.

10. Smith, *Theory of Moral Sentiments*, II.ii.2.1–4. On Smith's extensive development of the principle of sympathy, James R. Otteson, *Adam Smith's Marketplace of Life* (Cambridge: Cambridge University Press, 2002), 30–39; Eugene Heath, "The Commerce of Sympathy: Adam Smith and the Emergence of Morals," *Journal of the History of Philosophy* 33 (1995) 447–66. For discussions of Smith's account of sympathy more generally, Charles L. Griswold, *Adam Smith and the Virtues of Enlightenment* (Cambridge: Cambridge University

Yet without acknowledging the priority of natural resentment, Hume could not explain how people ever grouped together long enough to devise rules to regulate conduct for the promotion of utility in the first place:

> Men, though naturally sympathetic, feel so little for another, with whom they have no particular connexion, in comparison of what they feel for themselves; the misery of one, who is merely their fellow-creature, is of so little importance to them in comparison even of a small conveniency of their own; they have it so much in their power to hurt him, and may have so many temptations to do so, that if this principle did not stand up within them in his defence, and overawe them into a respect for his innocence, they would, like wild beasts, be at all times ready to fly upon him; and a man would enter an assembly of men as he enters a den of lions.[11]

Smith's point was that justice, Hume's paradigmatic artificial virtue, must necessarily possess a natural foundation, or else humans could never have achieved the large-scale sociable living Hume endeavored to explain.[12] The innate propensity for resentment originally translated into spontaneous retaliatory punishment by wronged individuals and their sympathetically engaged peers. This ensured that although "every individual, in his own breast, naturally prefers himself to all mankind, yet he dares not look mankind in the face, and avow that he acts according to this principle."[13] In turn, people learned to place themselves in the position that others regarded them as occupying, and thus realized that their own self-preferment could not be shared by disinterested observers, concluding that selfish acts of aggression (including their own) *merited* punishment. They internalized the basic legitimacy of claims for respecting others' persons and possessions, and all came spontaneously to agree (in principle, if not necessarily in practice) that "In the race for wealth, and honours, and preferments, he may run as hard as he can, and strain every

---

Press, 1999), chaps. 2–3; Samuel Fleischacker, *On Adam Smith's "Wealth of Nations": A Philosophical Companion* (Princeton, NJ: Princeton University Press, 2005), chap. 3; Alexander Broadie, "Sympathy and the Impartial Spectator," in Haakonssen, *Cambridge Companion to Adam Smith*, 158–88. I examine the differences between Hume's and Smith's moral theories, emanating from their difference over the nature and role of sympathy, at length in Paul Sagar, "Beyond Sympathy: Smith's Rejection of Hume's Moral Theory," *British Journal for the History of Philosophy* 25 (2017), 681–705.

11. Smith, *Theory of Moral Sentiments*, II.ii.3.4.

12. For a different take, see Fleischacker, *Smith's "Wealth of Nations*," 150–52. For a detailed substantiation of this point, see Sagar, "Beyond Sympathy."

13. Smith, *Theory of Moral Sentiments*, II.ii.2.1.

nerve and every muscle, in order to outstrip all his competitors," but it was strictly forbidden to "justle, or throw down any of them."[14]

Justice had to be widely observed and consistently enforced in order to facilitate the utility gains that Smith agreed with Hume it promoted. In other words, justice required systematic and regular institutionalization—i.e., the public coercive enforcement of known criminal codes, which originally occurred when dominant individuals instituted judges to formally enforce what had previously been only tacit conventions for the regulation of possessions. This innovation eventually enabled men to attain large-scale social living, a historical development that had clearly happened in all developed nations known to the mid-eighteenth century. Nonetheless, justice originated in the innate impulse to avenge harm and punish wrongdoers. Configuring things this way enabled Smith to correct one of Hume's theory's most obvious weaknesses: that it implausibly held that justice originally related solely to the protection of material possessions, with the concept only later (Hume never specifying how) extending to aspects of moral, legal, and political life that had nothing to do with the regulation of external assets. By contrast, in Smith's account the origins (and indeed the proper continued remit) of justice lay not solely in conventions for the regulation of material goods, but pertained also to central aspects of what would later become the publicly enforced criminal law, including especially injuries to the body (paradigmatically murder and assault). More generally, the status of justice as a moral virtue in Smith's picture necessarily preceded its emergence as a successful means for coordinating utility seeking, reversing Hume's claim that justice began as a merely instrumental convention for the promotion of self-interest, only later upgraded to the status of a fully fledged virtue thanks to the effects of sympathy.

This insistence on natural resentment as the foundation of justice enabled Smith to reconfigure Hume's account of the relationship between justice, utility, and sociability. Smith understood Hume's position in exactly the way explicated in chapter 1: "As society cannot subsist unless the laws of justice are tolerably observed, as no social intercourse can take place among men who do not generally abstain from injuring one another," Smith wrote, and

---

14. Ibid., II.ii.2.1. Because justice was a virtue that related only to forbearance, to abstaining from encroaching upon the good of others simply for personal advancement, it was considered a mere "negative virtue," one fulfilled by doing nothing, and meriting little praise or approval for its observance: ibid., II.ii.1.9. For discussions of Smith's views of justice, see Fleischacker, *Smith's "Wealth of Nations,"* chap. 8; Griswold, *Virtues of Enlightenment*, chap. 6; Lisa Herzog, "Adam Smith's Account of Justice between Naturalness and Historicity," *Journal of the History of Philosophy*, 52 (2014), 703–26; Craig Smith, "Adam Smith: Left or Right?" *Political Studies* 61 (2013), 784–98; and István Hont and Michael Ignatieff, "Needs and Justice in the *Wealth of Nations*," in Hont, *Jealousy of Trade*, 394 (but see also Fleischacker, *Smith's "Wealth of Nations*," chap.10, for a dissenting view).

so "the consideration of this necessity, it has been thought, was the ground upon which we approved of the enforcement of the laws of justice by the punishment of those who violated them."[15] Smith went on to summarize Hume's overall position:

> Man, it has been said, has a natural love for society, and desires that the union of mankind should be preserved for its own sake, and though he himself was to derive no benefit from it. The orderly and flourishing state of society is agreeable to him, and he takes delight in contemplating it. Its disorder and confusion, on the contrary, is the object of his aversion, and he is chagrined at whatever tends to produce it. He is sensible too that his own interest is connected with the prosperity of society, and that the happiness, perhaps the preservation of his existence, depends upon its preservation. Upon every account, therefore, he has an abhorrence at whatever can tend to destroy society, and is willing to make use of every means, which can hinder so hated and so dreadful an event. Injustice necessarily tends to destroy it. Every appearance of injustice, therefore, alarms him, and he runs, if I may say so, to stop the progress of what, if allowed to go on, would quickly put an end to every thing that is dear to him.[16]

The problem with Hume's account, however, was that it conflated "efficient" with "final" causes. Whilst it was true that regard to the rules of justice had the aggregate effect of promoting utility, and thus of making large-scale sociable living possible, it did not follow that it was *a regard for that utility itself* that typically motivated people to either institute, or continue to respect, the rules of justice. To believe so was to make a mistake analogous to thinking that because all the components of a watch operate together to indicate the time, that it must be the intention of each of those components themselves to tell the time.[17] What underlay rules of justice in their original manifestations, as well as in their continued typical observance by ordinary people, was resentment at injury caused by self-interested agents who infringed upon the persons or possessions of others. Hume was right that the *overall* effect of the observance and enforcement of justice was the highly effective promotion of utility seeking, and in turn the successful attainment of large-scale sociability. But, nonetheless, "though it commonly requires no great discernment to see the destructive tendency of all licentious practices to the welfare of society, it is seldom this consideration which first animates us against them. All men, even the most stupid and unthinking, abhor fraud, perfidy, and injustice, and delight to seem them punished. But few men have reflected upon the necessity

---

15. Smith, *Theory of Moral Sentiments*, II.ii.3.6.
16. Ibid., II.ii.3.6.
17. Ibid., II.ii.3.5.

of justice to the existence of society, how obvious soever that necessity may appear to be."[18] The truth of this was confirmed by the fact that explicit regard to the utility of justice was the exception rather than the norm in daily life, with Smith supplying examples, such as the reprimanding of licentious and provocative behavior in the young or executing a sleeping sentinel *pour encourages les autres*, to prove the point.[19] Similarly, humans' prereflective desire for justice as the need for retaliation against those whose bad conduct deserved resentment merely as such was confirmed by the fact that all cultures gave themselves "superstitions" of "a Tartarus as well as an Elysium; a place provided for the punishment of the wicked, as well as one for the rewards of the just."[20] This reflected the human desire that wrongdoers be punished *simpliciter*, even when they were dead and could no longer hinder the pursuit of utility. For Smith, the foundations of justice lay in natural resentment, not the artificial promotion of utility—even if the latter was the unanticipated major consequence of the former.

Utility and the Nature of Politics

Smith continued his critical corrective of Hume in part 4 of the *Theory of Moral Sentiments*, which was dedicated to challenging and displacing Hume's insistence on the priority of utility in moral assessment. The details of Smith's engagement with Hume's moral theory are beyond the scope of this chapter, yet part 4 is nonetheless worth our attention.[21] This is because Smith offered what he took to be a crucial and original insight into the correct understanding of the role of utility in human psychology, which carried extensive implications for politics. Appreciating the exact nature of Smith's argument is important, as it clears the way for a proper examination of what we have of Smith's only partially completed political theory.

According to Hume—Smith reminded his readers—the "utility of any object . . . pleases the master by perpetually suggesting to him the pleasure or conveniency which it is fitted to promote," with spectators able to share in this pleasure via sympathy.[22] Despite the initial plausibility of this account, however, Smith insisted that it was subtly and importantly mistaken. In fact, human psychology exhibited a pervasive and wide-ranging quirk, such that

18. Ibid., II.ii.3.9.
19. Ibid., II.ii.3.7–11.
20. Ibid., II.ii.3.12.
21. For wider discussions, see F. Rosen, "The Idea of Utility in Adam Smith's *The Theory of Moral Sentiments*," *History of European Ideas* 26 (2000), 79–103; Marie Martin, "Utility and Morality: Adam Smith's Critique of Hume," *Hume Studies* 16 (1990), 107–20; F. L. van Holthoon, "Adam Smith and David Hume: With Sympathy," *Utilitas* 5 (1993), 35–48; and Sagar, "Beyond Sympathy."
22. Smith, *Theory of Moral Sentiments*, IV.I.2.

the "fitness, this happy contrivance of any production of art, should often be more valued, than the very end for which it was intended." Bizarrely—at least, to a sober philosophical eye—"the exact adjustment of the means for attaining any conveniency or pleasure, should frequently be more regarded, than that very conveniency or pleasure, in the attainment of which their whole merit would seem to consist."[23] Smith took himself to be the first to have noticed this, yet pointed to a multitude of everyday examples to prove its truth: the man who expends much effort arranging the chairs in a room to achieve an order which costs him more in convenience than is gained by having the floor clear; the person who is excessively curious about watches and rejects one model on the grounds that it loses two minutes in a day, replacing it with a much more expensive one that loses only a minute in a fortnight, despite both being perfectly adequate for the basic function of telling the time; the man who adores "trinkets of frivolous utility" and walks about "loaded with a multitude of baubles" which cost him more inconveniency to constantly carry about than can ever be gained from having them to hand.[24]

Taken alone, these examples would constitute little more than a simple refinement of Hume's account. But Smith's next case—that of "The poor man's son, whom heaven in his anger has visited with ambition"—opened up the deeper implications of his corrective. It is vital to note, however, that Smith's ambitious poor man's son is *not* primarily motivated by amour propre. One might well expect Smith to suggest that a desire for esteem and status underlie such "ambition," especially in the context of his having read both Rousseau and Mandeville.[25] Yet it is categorically not status recognition that does the central work in Smith's explication: the "love of distinction so natural to man" is at best only a secondary consideration in this part of the work. Rather, the

23. Ibid., IV.I.3.
24. Ibid., IV.I.4-6.
25. Indeed, commentators often assume this as something like Smith's central message, even if they typically go on to argue that Smith offers a different solution to the predicament identified by Mandeville and Rousseau. See especially Hanley, "Commerce and Corruption"; Jerry Z. Muller, *Adam Smith in His Time and Ours: Designing the Decent Society* (New York: Free Press, 1993), 133; Hont, *Politics in Commercial Society*, 92. See also Fleischacker, *Smith's "Wealth of Nations,"* chap. 6, which is a response to Griswold, *Virtues of Enlightenment*, 222-27. Hanley, for example, writes that Smith was "particularly sympathetic to Rousseau's insistence that commercial society is fundamentally driven by a vanity that threatens to corrupt its participants" ("Commerce and Corruption," 137-38), and that "Smith in his own name advances the claim originally made in his translations of the *Second Discourse*: that markets are driven by solicitude for praise and recognition, and that such dependence on the esteem of others is also the source of the corruption of all our moral sentiments" (ibid., 141). This is a mistake, caused by Hanley equating Smith's emphasis on the need for social recognition when forming our ideas of the virtues with the species of "vanity" Smith delineates as specifically underlying the majority of material progress, which as I explicate here is related not to status competition (amour propre), but to conceptions of the promotion of utility.

poor son feels his own life's inconveniences and compares those to what he *imagines* are the pleasures of the rich afforded to them by their many devices for promoting utility. Whereas he must walk, they ride in carriages; whereas he must labor for all his wants, they have a retinue of servants. The poor son sees these conveniences and imagines that because they are fitted to promote pleasure they make the rich happy—and that if he had them, then he would be happy too. Accordingly, the poor son becomes "enchanted with the distant idea of felicity," and devotes himself to the endless "pursuit of wealth and greatness." But the outcome is a paradox: the poor son spends his life laboring and toiling in efforts to achieve wealth as a means of securing instruments of pleasure, and in the process expends far more effort, and incurs far more inconvenience, than could ever be compensated for by the riches he does manage to amass. "Through the whole of his life he pursues the idea of a certain artificial and elegant repose which he may never arrive at, for which he sacrifices a real tranquility that is at all times in his power." The situation ends in irony: because the poor man's son is enchanted with the idea of utility promotion rather than of utility itself, he will never achieve the levels of wealth that he thinks will make him happy, because such levels are constantly receding from him owing to the very quirk of human psychology that makes him pursue the imagined *means* of pleasure, rather than solidly attainable pleasures themselves. In old age such a man may finally come to see, with regret and bitterness, the error of his ways: that "wealth and greatness are mere trinkets of frivolous utility, no more adapted for procuring ease of body or tranquility of mind than the tweezer-cases of the lover of toys." But by then it will largely be too late, and he will realize that he has wasted most of his life in self-defeating chimerical pursuits.[26]

It is important to recognize, however, that Smith's poor man's son is an *extreme* example. He is not supposed to represent how all people typically think and behave, but merely illustrates, in acute and dramatic form, tendencies that are usually much less pronounced. Smith certainly did not deny that the condition of the rich and the great received widespread admiration from ordinary people, and that this forwarded the desire of ordinary people to themselves become rich and great. However:

> If we examine . . . why the spectator distinguishes with such admiration the condition of the rich and the great, we shall find that it is not so much upon account of the superior ease or pleasure which they are supposed to enjoy as of the numberless artificial and elegant contrivances for promoting this ease or pleasure. He does not even imagine that they are really happier than other people: but he imagines that they possess more means of happiness. And it is the ingenious and

---

26. Smith, *Theory of Moral Sentiments*, IV.I.8.

artful adjustment of those means to the end for which they were intended, that is the principle source of his admiration.

Things are complicated, however, by the fact that Smith appears to take a much more Rousseau-like position in part 1 of the *Theory of Moral Sentiments* with regard to these matters. He there writes that "To be observed, to be attended to, to be taken notice of with sympathy, complacency, and approbation, are all the advantages which we can propose to derive" from "that great purpose of human life which we call bettering our condition." Indeed, Smith even seems to contradict what he says in part 4, declaring that "It is the vanity, not the ease, or the pleasure, which interests us."[27] This passage is what commentators usually have in mind when they claim that Smith concedes Rousseau's claim about amour propre and status competition as the underlying driver of material consumption beyond bare necessity.[28] But we must read carefully. The context of these part 1 passages is Smith's claim that "mankind are disposed to sympathize more entirely with our joy than our sorrow," where he follows Hume's position that we tend to love and esteem, rather than hate and envy, the rich and powerful.[29] And Smith's "vanity" here is not Rousseau's amour propre—i.e., a competitive, zero-sum, psychological characteristic whereby recognition must be secured at the expense of observing others. What Smith claims, by contrast, is that individuals pursue riches because observers sympathize with the pleasure that the rich ought to receive from their wealth, and this in turn augments the pleasures the rich themselves expect to experience from their material affluence.[30] "The rich man glories in his riches, because he feels that they naturally draw upon him the attention of the world, and that mankind are disposed to go along with him in all those agreeable emotions with which the advantages of his situation so readily inspire him."[31] According to Rousseau, we primarily desire riches to rub other people's noses in our superiority: "the ardent desire to raise one's relative fortune less out of genuine need than in order to place oneself above others, instills in all men a black inclination to harm one another . . . and always the hidden desire to profit at another's expense."[32] For Smith, by contrast, we pursue riches to

27. Ibid., I.iii.2.1.
28. For example, Hanley, "Commerce and Corruption," 143; Hont, *Politics in Commercial Society*, 92.
29. David Hume, *The Clarendon Edition of the Works of David Hume: A Treatise of Human Nature*, ed. D. F. Norton and M. J. Norton (Oxford: Oxford University Press, 2007), T.2.1.10–11, SBN 309–24.
30. The contempt the poor receive, through lack of spectator sympathy with their poverty, operates in exactly the reverse manner.
31. Smith, *Theory of Moral Sentiments*, I.iii.2.1.
32. Rousseau, *The Discourses and Other Early Political Writings*, ed. V. Gourevitch (Cambridge: Cambridge University Press, 1997), 171, also 184 on how the rich "value the things they enjoy only to the extent that the others are deprived of them."

augment the pleasures that wealth brings by the added pleasure that arises from having others themselves take pleasure, via sympathy, in our prosperous condition. Hence "that emulation which runs through all the different ranks of men" is not a zero-sum game of brute status competition, but a complex effect of the capacity to share each other's sentiments, in the context of Smith's central claim that having other people agree with our sentiments via sympathy is itself pleasurable.[33]

To summarize: Smith wishes to emphasize two distinct features of our psychology. The first is that we admire the rich and powerful, but not because of any happiness we suppose them to in fact be possessed of, but because of the considerable *means* of happiness that they possess. The idea of possessing these means strikes us, via sympathy, as being pleasurable (even if their possessors are, in actual fact, miserable or indifferent). In this regard, what we desire most highly is *not* the good opinion of others, at least for its own sake. The second feature of our psychology Smith draws attention to is that when we *do* wish to be thought well of by others, this is not primarily to do with the acquisition of status goods, and is crucially not necessarily a zero-sum competitive game—we can (and often do) find ways of securing the esteem of our peers for us, whilst also securing their own self-estimation in turn. This means that the seeking of recognition, and thus mental satisfaction, via the opinion of judging others need not trigger severe and disruptive social consequences likely to be associated with fierce competition over scarce goods that cannot be held simultaneously. The needs of the mind certainly had to be satisfied, Smith thought, but their satisfaction did not typically precipitate psychological warfare of all against all. Quite the opposite.

The contrast with Rousseau is therefore sharp. As we saw in chapter 4, Rousseau's account in the *Second Discourse* postulated not only that the poor man's son was motivated primarily by competitive amour propre, but that following the introduction of private property and the advent of inequality, the poor man's son was not the extreme, but the archetype, of how corrupted human beings behaved after the final exit from the state of nature.[34] Smith

33. Smith, "Of the Pleasure of Mutual Sympathy," in *Theory of Moral Sentiments*, I.i.2, which also lays out Smith's core claim about how "mutual" sympathy brings pleasure, and hence is the foundation of normative approbation and disapprobation.

34. Frederick Neuhouser has suggested that for Rousseau amour propre need not necessarily be zero-sum, if it can be appropriately regulated. We might, for example, read the *Social Contract* as laying out the institutional means of achieving precisely this. Even if this is so, however, the difference between Smith and Rousseau's account in the *Second Discourse* is as I describe it. See Frederick Neuhouser, *Rousseau's Critique of Inequality: Reconstructing the Second Discourse* (Cambridge: Cambridge University Press, 2014), 145–50, and *Rousseau's Theodicy of Self-Love: Evil, Rationality, and the Drive for Recognition* (Oxford: Oxford University Press, 2008), chaps. 6–7. Similar readings are endorsed in John Rawls, *Lectures on the History of Political Philosophy* (Cambridge, MA: Harvard University Press, 2007), 247–48, and Joshua Cohen, *Rousseau: A Free Community of Equals*

fundamentally rejected this: the desire for riches and greatness, and the admiration of the rich and the great, were primarily motivated not by the seeking of esteem in the eyes of peers at their expense, but the quirk of human psychology that encouraged people to value the means of utility promotion more than utility itself, and via sympathy to take pleasure not in the actual pleasures of the rich, but in the pleasures one imagined that they *ought* to take (even if they in fact didn't) from their possessions.

In turn, Smith had no place for Rousseau's (or Mandeville's) contention that political society was founded on a conscious deception exercised by the few over the many. Insofar as the history of humans' pursuit of utility fundamentally involved a deception, it related not, as Rousseau claimed, to the rich instituting the con trick of property rights to secure themselves from the aggression of the dispossessed, but to the internal processes of human psychology.[35] In certain frames of mind—most typically those of dejection at the end of a life of failed toil, but also when stepping back and considering the psychology of utility seeking in a disinterested philosophical light—people saw for themselves that "Power and riches appear then to be, what they are, enormous and operose machines contrived to produce a few trifling conveniences to the body . . . which in spite of all our care are ready every moment to burst into pieces, and to crush in their ruins their unfortunate possessor."[36] Yet in good circumstances and good humor, normal individuals could keep up neither the "splenetic" outlook, nor the judgments made in an "abstract and philosophical light." For the most part, ordinary people were "charmed with the beauty of that accommodation which reigns in the palaces and œconomy of the great," with the pleasures of wealth and greatness striking "the imagination as something grand and beautiful and noble, of which the attainment

---

(Oxford: Oxford University Press, 2010), 124–27. For doubts that this was in fact Rousseau's view, see Robin Douglass, "What's Wrong with Inequality? Some Rousseauian Perspectives," *European Journal of Political Theory* 14 (2015), 371–74.

35. Smith did think that the invention of property rights and their public enforcement by governmental institutions was, historically, first hit upon by rich shepherd chieftains to protect themselves from the aggression of the poor. But this was a specific claim about the genesis of an idea and its early enforcement, not a claim about the fundamental basis of modern political society. See Adam Smith, *The Glasgow Edition of the Works and Correspondence of Adam Smith: An Inquiry into the Nature and Causes of the Wealth of Nations*, ed. R. H. Campbell and A. S. Skinner (Oxford: Oxford University Press, 1976), V.i.b; cf. Adam Smith, *The Glasgow Edition of the Works and Correspondence of Adam Smith: Lectures on Jurisprudence*, ed. R. L. Meek, D. D. Raphael, and P. G. Stein (Oxford: Oxford University Press, 1978), LJ(A).iv.21; LJ(B).20. I discuss this in more detail below. For a helpful analysis of Smith's conception of deception in human psychology, albeit one that takes a more gloomy overview of the implications, see Griswold, *Virtues of Enlightenment*, 259–66.

36. Smith, *Theory of Moral Sentiments*, IV.I.8.

is well worth all the toil and anxiety which we are so apt to bestow upon it."[37] In any case, the "deception" that Smith posited was of an entirely different type to that supposed by Rousseau. Whereas the Genevan's account posited a process of deception that was interagential, and furthermore the outcome of purposeful orchestration by the dominant as a way of securing political and social advantages, for the Scot the relevant deception was intra-agential, and related to the internal psychological processes of independent agents with regard to their own wants and desires.

Smith not only ran a very different line to that given by Rousseau, but also took a diametrically opposite stand on its normative implications. Smith stated bluntly that "it is well that nature imposes upon us in this manner. It is this deception which rouses and keeps in continual motion the industry of mankind." Deliberately echoing Rousseau's rhetoric from one of the passages of the *Second Discourse* that he had translated for readers of the *Edinburgh Review*, Smith continued: "It is this which first prompted them to cultivate the ground, to build houses, to found cities and commonwealths, and to invent and improve all sciences and arts, which ennoble and embellish human life; which have entirely changed the whole face of the globe, have turned the rude forests of nature into agreeable and fertile plains, and made the trackless and barren ocean a new fund of subsistence, and the great high road of communication to the different nations of the earth."[38] We must not, however, interpret Smith's appropriation of Rousseau's rhetoric as signaling that he shared Rousseau's assessment, or was motivated by the same fundamental concerns regarding the effects of political society on human well-being when combined with increasing material development. Precisely the opposite is the case. For although the "proud and unfeeling landlord" cared not at all for the poor, he "in imagination consumes himself the whole harvest" produced on his acreage. And yet his eyes were always bigger than his belly: "The capacity of his stomach bears no proportion to the immensity of his desires, and will receive no more than that of the meanest peasant. The rest he is obliged to distribute among those, who prepare, in the nicest manner, that little which he himself makes use of." It was the designs of the rich for their own pleasure that originally stimulated much economic activity. Not just the cultivation of

---

37. Ibid., IV.I.9.

38. Ibid., IV.I.10; cf. Ignatieff, "Republic of Needs," 191; Hanley, *Character of Virtue*, 105. Smith's own translation runs: "But from the instant in which one man had occasion for the assistance of another, from the moment that he perceived that it could be advantageous to a single person to have provisions for two, equality disappeared, property was introduced, labor became necessary, and the vast forrests of nature were changed into agreeable plains, which must be watered with the sweat of mankind, and in which the world beheld slavery and wretchedness begin to grow up and blossom with the harvest" (Adam Smith, "A Letter to the Authors of the Edinburgh Review," in *Essays on Philosophical Subjects*, 252).

land and the production of subsistence goods, but of luxuries ("baubles and trinkets"). The production and exchange of such goods delivered of the "necessities of life" to the poorer, who could not expect them as a matter of simple benevolence, but could only hope to obtain them as a result of widespread market exchanges. The effect of the self-interest of the rich—paradoxically, but not less effectively—was thus to improve the lot of all.[39]

Aligning himself firmly with Locke and Mandeville on this matter,[40] and against Rousseau, Smith insisted that the division of the world into unequal propertied holdings was on balance justified, insofar as the result of the economic activity such inequality stimulated made the poorest vastly better off than they could possibly have been if the earth remained owned in common and yet uncultivated:

> The produce of the soil maintains at all times nearly that number of inhabitants which it is capable of maintaining. The rich only select from the heap what is most precious and agreeable. They consume little more than the poor, and in spite of their natural selfishness and rapacity, though they mean only their own conveniency, though the sole end which they propose from the labors of all the thousands whom they employ, be the gratification of their own vain and insatiable desires, they divide with the poor the produce of all their improvements. They are led by an invisible hand to make nearly the same distribution of the necessaries of life, which would have been made, had the earth been divided into equal portions among all its inhabitants, and thus without intending it, without knowing it, advance the interest of the society, and afford means to the multiplication of the species. When Providence divided the earth among a few lordly masters, it neither forgot nor abandoned those who seemed to have been left out in the partition.[41]

This suggests that Smith did not take Rousseau's challenge particularly seriously. Rather than being centrally animated or worried by the Genevan's positions, Smith dispatched them in passing, whilst correcting Hume's account of the role of utility in human psychology (the primary target of part 4). Indeed, this ought to come as no surprise in light of what has been argued in earlier

---

39. Smith, *Theory of Moral Sentiments*, IV.I.10. This fundamental point is reiterated, although applied in a different direction, in the *Wealth of Nations*, with Smith's famous declaration that "It is not from the benevolence of the butcher, the brewer, or the baker, that we expect our dinner, but from their regard to their own interest": *Wealth of Nations*, I.ii.2.

40. John Locke, "Second Treatise," chap. 5, in *Two Treatises on Government*, ed. P. Laslett (Cambridge: Cambridge University Press, 1960); Bernard Mandeville, *The Fable of the Bees, Volume 2*, ed. F. B. Kaye (Indianapolis: Liberty Fund, 1988), 284; cf. Hont and Ignatieff, "Needs and Justice," 394.

41. Smith, *Theory of Moral Sentiments*, IV.I.10

chapters. As well as rejecting both Rousseau's diagnosis of the "deception" men labored under, and his normative assessment of what such deception entailed, Smith in any case needed to put a great deal less pressure upon the role of deception, however conceived, in explaining political arrangements. For Rousseau, once amour propre became pathologically inflamed after contact with economic inequality, and when natural pity was in turn extensively suppressed, human beings became as Hobbes had claimed: creatures of psychological competition who craved recognition and status. From Rousseau's perspective, the only way that such creatures could be induced to accept status inferiority and material inequality was through tricking them into thinking their interests were being promoted when in reality they were being harmed. Although Rousseau predicted that the deception of private property—enforced in modern conditions by the state—would eventually collapse in upon itself, deception perpetrated by the rich was the only explicable means by which the poor had thus far allowed themselves to be economically and politically subjugated. By contrast, Smith had read and absorbed Hume's argument for the possibility of natural authority rooted in sympathy and the operations of opinion. He therefore knew that there was an entirely different mechanism to bring to bear, one that explained why the poor and middling would willfully submit to the rule of the rich and great without any need for deception—and how such rule must necessarily vary in different material and historical circumstances.

The rest of this chapter explores Smith's subsequent taking up of the idiom of opinion, starting with a more developed analysis of the actual psychology of natural authority than Hume had supplied. Before turning to this, however, it is worth appreciating one final aspect of Smith's distancing of himself from Rousseau. Smith noted that a peculiar result of people's preoccupation with the means of promoting utility, rather than with utility itself, was that the best way to inspire individuals to promote the public good was not to appeal to the public good itself, but to the improvement of "a certain beautiful and orderly system" of political administration. History abounded with cases of prominent individuals—Smith gave as an example Peter the Great of Russia—who were devoid of public spirit, and yet via the love of well-contrived and elaborate systems inadvertently promoted the public good when putting those systems into practice. This was more than a little paradoxical. The very systems such individuals became enamored with had no ultimate purpose and justification other than that "they tend to promote the happiness of those who live under them"—and yet this happiness was not what such leaders aimed at, being besotted instead with the elegance of the systems themselves. Nonetheless, and given that this paradox widely obtained, Smith stressed that the best way to motivate people who lack any public spirit to perform works for the public good was *not* to attempt "to implant public virtue in the breast." Rather, "You will be more likely to persuade, if you describe the great system of public police which procures these advantages, if you explain the connexions and dependencies of its several parts, their mutual subordination to one another, and their general subserviency to the happiness of society," and so on.[42] This had direct political import insofar as it entailed rejection of the classical republican, or civic humanist, insistence that a healthy political society necessitated extensive civic participation, with the ruling citizenry motivated to uphold the public good. Yet a version of this republican emphasis, the love of "public virtue," was central to the theoretical apparatus of Rousseau's *Social Contract*, which as we saw in chapter 4 was his attempt to square the Hobbesian circle he had landed himself in. Three years before *The Social Contract* was published, however, Smith casually intimated that Rousseau's republican strategy was fundamentally misguided, even as a theoretical exercise, insofar as it was founded upon a basic mistake about the operations of human psychology, and the effective motivations for political improvement that were therefore worth considering.[43]

Politics and History: The Challenge of Montesquieu

At the close of the *Theory of Moral Sentiments*, and following an extensive survey of Western moral philosophy, Smith remarked that it was only very late in the development of learning that thinkers had attempted any "particular enumeration of the rules of justice." Cicero and Plato, for example, provided only "laws of police, not of justice," despite the reasonable (from a modern perspective) expectation that they might attempt for jurisprudence what they had done for ethics. Instead, "Grotius seems to have been the first who attempted to give the world any thing like a system of those principles which ought to run through, and be the foundation of the laws of all nations." Although "his treatise" (i.e., *De jure belli ac pacis* of 1625) contained many "imperfections," it remained "perhaps at this day the most complete work that has yet been given upon this subject." What Smith promised his readers—something retained in even the sixth and final 1790 edition of the book, when he knew it could not be fulfilled—was his own subsequent intervention: "I shall in another discourse endeavour to give an account of the general principles of law and government, and of the different revolutions they have undergone in the different ages and periods of society, not only in what concerns justice, but in what concerns police, revenue, and arms, and whatever else is the object of law. I shall not, therefore, at present enter into any further detail concerning the history of jurisprudence."[44] This promise has, unsurprisingly, attracted much attention.

42. Ibid., IV.I.11.
43. A sketch of the theoretical matrix fully developed in the *Social Contract* is also supplied in bk. 5 of *Émile*, also first published in 1762. See Jean-Jacques Rousseau, *Émile; or, On Education*, ed. A. Bloom (New York: Basic Books, 1979), 460–66.
44. Smith, *Theory of Moral Sentiments*, VII.iv.37.

We know that the work was not the *Wealth of Nations*, but the manuscript Smith had destroyed shortly before his death. Yet much of what that contained can be pieced together from the historical parts of Smith's second book, as well as the student notes now known as the *Lectures on Jurisprudence*.

There has been some controversy, however, about whether Smith could have achieved a jurisprudence which delineated "those principles which ought to run through, and be the foundation of the laws of all nations," given that his own philosophical approach in the published works appears to commit him to a view of human moral and political practices as necessarily and deeply shaped by local contingent circumstances, belying any hope of universal principles applicable to all times and places.[45] Yet this controversy may turn out to be misplaced. It is worth noting that the "ought" in the crucial passage is ambiguous. Although most commentators see it as expressive of Smith's own ambitions, he may simply be reporting the aims of Grotius, who certainly did have such universal aspirations. When Smith goes on to summarize his own projected work, he talks only of an intervention in the *history* of jurisprudence, and of offering an account of the different revolutions that have affected the general principles of law and government. The question of whether Smith set out to write a definitive theory of jurisprudence valid for all times and places—and the attendant suggestion the he burned his manuscript because he eventually failed in such a project—may simply be a mistake. Smith may have set out to write a history of jurisprudence, not a treatise of prescriptive natural law (a possibility given plausibility by the actual content of the surviving student notes), and had it destroyed because it did not meet his exceedingly high standards by the time that he knew he was dying.[46] In any case, Smith did burn the manuscript, and so we will never know for sure. Regardless of all that, what I wish to show is that we can gain a much richer appreciation of (what we have of) Smith's political thinking when we recognize him as attempting to apply Hume's emphasis on the priority of opinion, generating different instantiations of natural authority, to the history of law and government, which

---

45. Knud Haakonssen has argued in great detail that Smith did achieve such a synthesis, principally by reworking an earlier natural-law tradition, as inherited in particular from Pufendorf: see most especially Knud Haakonssen, *The Science of a Legislator: The Natural Jurisprudence of David Hume and Adam Smith* (Cambridge: Cambridge University Press, 1981). That Smith achieved such a synthesis is forcefully questioned in Fleischacker, *Smith's "Wealth of Nations,"* chap. 8, and Griswold, *Virtues of Enlightenment*, 28–39; 256–58; 352–54. That Smith was working principally in the tradition of natural law is brought into severe doubt by Vivienne Brown, *Adam Smith's Discourses: Canonicity, Commerce and Conscience* (London: Routledge, 1994), 102–11. It should be evident from what has already been said that I do not find the natural-law tradition to be the right, or an illuminating, intellectual context in which to place Smith.

46. Perfectionism was the explanation given by Dugald Stewart: see "Writings of Adam Smith," 327.

thereby itself became a form of political theory.[47] But before seeing how and why this is so, we must bring another important eighteenth-century thinker into the picture.

In the 1766 "report" of his lectures on jurisprudence, Adam Smith is recorded as saying that "monarchy" denotes "where supreme power and authority is vested in one." "Aristocratical government," by contrast, refers to that condition in which "a certain order of people in the state, either of richest, or of certain families, have it in their power to choose magistrates, who are to have the management of the state." Finally, "democratical government" is "where the management of affaires belongs to the whole body of the people together." To this otherwise orthodox typology Smith added a further comment: "These last two forms may be called republican, and then the division of government is into monarchical and republican."[48] This rider is important, because informed mid-eighteenth-century listeners would have immediately recognized it as a reference to the political thought of Montesquieu.

That Smith was aware of, and drawing on, Montesquieu is made explicit in the earlier (albeit less compact) 1762 report regarding regime classifications, where Smith credited the Frenchman with giving the label "executive" power to that which Smith called *"making peace and war."*[49] Smith's contemporaries noted an important intellectual relationship between him and Montesquieu. Smith's pupil John Millar—who would later become professor of civil law at Glasgow—claimed that his teacher had "followed the plan that seems to be suggested by Montesquieu," whilst Dugald Stewart's 1793 obituary, after quoting Millar on this matter, went on to explicitly place Smith in Montesquieu's lineage.[50] More reverentially still, Millar later claimed that Montesquieu "was the Lord Bacon of his branch of philosophy. Dr. Smith is the Newton."[51] Yet we must be alert to a specific, and not just a general, relationship between Smith's and Montesquieu's intellectual projects. This is brought out by focusing on their classification of regimes.

---

47. On Smith's history as a form of political theory, see especially István Hont, "Adam Smith's History of Law and Government as Political Theory," in *Political Judgment: Essays for John Dunn*, ed. R. Bourke and R. Geuss (Cambridge: Cambridge University Press, 2009), 131–71, and also John Pocock, *Barbarism and Religion*, vol. 2, *Narratives of Civil Government* (Cambridge: Cambridge University Press, 1999), chaps. 20 and 21.

48. Smith, *Lectures on Jurisprudence*, LJ(B).18; cf. ibid., LJ(A).IV.I.1–3.

49. Ibid., LJ(A).IV.2.

50. Stewart, "Writings of Adam Smith," 274, 294.

51. John Millar, *An Historical View of the English Government, from the Settlements of the Saxons in Britain to the Revolution in 1688: To Which Are Subjoined, Some Dissertations Connected with the History of Government, from the Revolution to the Present Time* (London: 1818), 429–30, quoted in Pocock, *Narratives of Civil Government*, 327.

According to Montesquieu, forms of government could be classified according to three essential types.[52] "Monarchies" existed where one person held supreme decision-making power, but was checked by the existence of intermediary powers (ideally a body of nobles), and ruled not by arbitrary whim but according to established laws recorded in a historically accreted "depository." This form of regime was best suited to "medium"-sized territories, in modern times characterized by commerce and luxury.[53] (Montesquieu meant that the large states of Europe were best suited to be monarchies, even though these were medium sized when compared with eastern territories like Persia, and especially China.) Furthermore, Montesquieu insisted upon an actuating "spring" or "principle" that animated the political machinery of all regimes. In the case of monarchy, this was "honor," or its functional equivalent "false honor"—i.e., pride and the desire for status and recognition as satiated through a carefully managed system of ranks, meaning that "each person works for the common good, believing he works for his individual interests."[54] "Despotisms," by contrast, were ruled by a single individual, without check or legal constraint, over large (globally speaking) territories, whose principle was "fear," and where all were cowed before the unmatched power of the ruler, who chose favorites from whim rather than according to a system of regular public ranks.[55] The final form of regime was a "republic," wherein the body of the people ruled collectively, but did so according to a principle of "virtue," which as Montesquieu clarified in an appended 1757 foreword denoted "love of the homeland, that is, love of equality."[56] This was an extension of the older civic humanist, or republican, idiom stressing self-sacrifice, frugality, and patriotism as the bonds that held successful political societies together, on the supposition of political and material egalitarianism.[57] Republicanism was suited to relatively small territories, which must exclude luxury as much as possible insofar as its effeminizing and selfishness-inducing tendencies would corrupt the love of equality, without which the republic could neither function properly nor ultimately survive. Republics, however, could be further subdivided into "aristocracies" and "democracies," depending on whether all or a portion of the citizen body ruled, something that ought to be determined in

---

52. For a more detailed overview, Robin Douglass, "Montesquieu and Modern Republicanism," *Political Studies* 60 (2012), 703–19.

53. Montesquieu, *The Spirit of the Laws*, ed. A. M. Cohler, B. C. Miller, and H. S. Stone (Cambridge: Cambridge University Press, 1989), 17–20, 25–30, 55–58.

54. Montesquieu, *Spirit of the Laws*, 27.

55. Ibid., 20, 27–29, 59–67.

56. Ibid., xli.

57. Ibid., 21–25, 35–36, 42–55.

line with the level of economic development and territorial security a given people found themselves in.[58]

Montesquieu's regime classification was a theoretical novelty. On the one hand it was a rejection of the older classical division of regimes—found especially in Aristotle, Cicero, and Polybius—which held that all forms of government were species of a particular genus, *res publica*, delineated simply by numbers: the rule of the one, the many, or the few (although it was typically also suggested that polities exhibiting legal and material inequality ought to opt for some form of mixed constitution to balance competing interests).[59] But Montesquieu's typology also stood against Hobbes's more recent attempt to claim that all forms of government were instantiations of one more fundamental thing, the state, which was constituted by a unitary principle of sovereignty. Hobbes's theory of union insisted that sovereignty was always held by one "artificial" person, whose existence and correlate exercise of absolute decision-making authority gave unity to an otherwise disparate multitude, and in the process created the state, the solution to the human predicament of natural unsociability. This "artificial" person could be borne by any number of "natural" persons: if one, the regime was a monarchy; if many, an aristocracy; if all, a democracy. Hobbes's underlying point, however, was that all of these were at bottom *the same thing*: undivided sovereignty, held by one artificial person. Thus, rather than *res publica* being a genus with three species, it was (so to speak) just one species of thing, with three (and only three) possible breeds, or variations. Montesquieu's typology by contrast posited no underlying unifying principle between the three regime types. They were simply three different forms of government—i.e., forms of organizing human collective endeavor with recourse to public coercive force. These had emerged in different parts of the world owing to different historical causal factors, but each was a localized response to human beings' perennial need to administer the application of power in complex instantiations of group living. Modern monarchy, for example, was a unique form of government that depended upon the prior existence of feudalism, "an event which happened once in the world and which will never perhaps happen again."[60] Another way of putting the point is that Montesquieu had *no theory of sovereignty* in the sense that Hobbes did. Although Montesquieu was fiercely interested in delineating with whom decision-making power should lie in various human locales (not least his own contemporary France), and why and how that should be, he did not believe that any such investigation could be reduced to one category, or one concept, revealed as underlying all forms of human politics, in turn generating

---

58. Ibid., 10–15.

59. For more details, see Michael Sonenscher, *Before the Deluge: Public Debt, Inequality, and the Intellectual Origins of the French Revolution* (Princeton, NJ: Princeton University Press, 2007), 150.

60. Montesquieu, *Spirit of the Laws*, 619.

binding normative conclusions regarding legitimacy and obedience. Although he (like Smith) periodically employed the language of "the sovereign," this had no deeper theoretical import than to denote whichever group or individual happened to hold decision-making authority, particularly with regard to legislative power, at a given time in a given place.[61] In this, Montesquieu did not go back to the ancients, but he also remained firmly apart from Hobbes.[62] Rousseau saw this very clearly, and chastised Montesquieu in the *Social Contract* for having "failed to see that since Sovereign authority is everywhere the same, the same principle must obtain in every well-constituted State."[63]

Whether, of course, it was Montesquieu who "failed" for not following Hobbes, or rather Rousseau for doing precisely that, is a question that this book is centrally concerned with. Whatever the answer, however, Smith sided with Montesquieu (and, as we have seen, Hume) against Hobbes (and Rousseau), in conducting his political thought outside the framework of sovereignty theory. He silently dropped Montesquieu's category of despotism, however, presumably because it was not germane to his purposes. (That classification was in part a product of Montesquieu's French context, and his ongoing attempt to explain to both critics and supporters of the French crown that the regime form of France—even following the absolutism of Louis XIV—could not reasonably be considered a despotism, or even an arbitrary government. France was [and ought to be] a legal monarchy—in need of reform and repair,

---

61. Douglass, "Modern Republicanism," 705. Montesquieu did on one occasion endorse a Hobbesian-sounding view of the state, albeit one he attributed to Gravina: "A society could not continue to exist without a government [gouvernement]. 'The union [réunion] of all individual strengths,' as Gravina aptly says, 'forms what is called a POLITICAL STATE.'" (*Spirit of the Laws*, 8). But this formulation does not in fact indicate a conscious endorsement of Hobbes's theory of union, as is indicated by the fact Montesquieu attributes continued political association with government, rather than sovereignty, and that he speaks of the union of individual strengths, not wills.

62. I thus disagree with Sonenscher's claim that Montesquieu was fundamentally *adopting* Hobbes's doctrine of unitary sovereignty, but inflecting it through his preferred historical framework of the German barbarian tribes and their contact with Roman Law after the fall of the Empire, where Hobbes's personation theory of representation is replaced with one drawn from legal history: Sonenscher, *Before the Deluge*, 150–52; see also "Introduction," in Sieyès, *Political Writings*, ed. M. Sonenscher (Indianapolis: Hackett, 2003), xlv–lix. As Sonenscher himself concedes, Montesquieu rejected both Hobbes's claim that humans were naturally unsociable, and the theory of authorization and representation as generating legitimate authority. But if this is the case, Montesquieu was repudiating the two central components of Hobbes's theory of union—and thus he cannot rightly be said to be a theorist of Hobbesian sovereignty. Rather than trying to force Montesquieu into a Hobbesian framework, I suggest we instead accept the more straightforward conclusion: that he was not a Hobbesian sovereignty theorist at all. Doing so, however, requires us to take Montesquieu out of Hont's "modern doctrine of sovereignty" lineage, in which Sonenscher is attempting to place him.

63. Rousseau, *The Social Contract and Other Later Political Writings*, ed. V. Gourevitch (Cambridge: Cambridge University Press, 1997), 91–92.

but not fundamentally illegitimate.[64]) Smith concentrated his attention instead on monarchies and republics. But in his outlook, Montesquieu's analysis of both these regime types failed, for two main reasons. The first was that Montesquieu's contentions were predicated on an untenable historical account of the origins and rise of modern European liberty. The second was that the content of Montesquieu's account of what made human groupings either monarchies or republics was incorrect, and had to be replaced with a different analysis facilitated by a different historical heuristic.

The fundamental problem with Montesquieu's historical account was that it made all modern European history German in origin, and by extension neo-German in present political arrangement. Smith didn't disagree that the origins of modern European history were in the Germanic destruction of Rome, but he rejected Montesquieu's account of what followed from this politically. Montesquieu's story of the rise of modern monarchies, which he saw as the future of any stable and enduring European state system, identified them as developing out of the feudal settlement that had come to characterize most of Europe (the small enclaves preserving republican government being anomalous exceptions, whose time was anyway nearly over) after the collapse of the Roman Empire, and following its conquest by northern barbarians, originating in the German forests, in the fifth century. The Germanic tribes had spread out and settled on the lands formerly occupied by the Romans, and had over time developed their customs of tribal representation, which governed the inheritance of fiefs, into a binary system of rule whereby royalty and nobility checked each other, in time creating a depository of laws and other "intermediary bodies" (such as the *parlements* in France) to ensure that political power was exercised nonarbitrarily.[65] Modern law-governed monarchies were a localized, historically contingent phenomenon, albeit one to be celebrated insofar as this "moderate government" was a "masterpiece of legislation that chance rarely produces and prudence is rarely allowed to produce."[66] Within this wider account, Montesquieu famously gave a special explanation for the existence of the English constitution, which had taken a divergent post-Germanic path from the rest of continental Europe, although

---

64. On this see especially Annelien de Dijn, "Montesquieu's Controversial Context: The Spirit of the Laws as a Monarchist Tract," *History of Political Thought* 34 (2013), 66–88, and also "Was Montesquieu a Liberal Republican?," *Review of Politics* 76 (2014), 21–41. Montesquieu also thought, however, that most states that had ever existed were despotisms, and so it was important that his typology could cover this, over and above his localized interventions in French political controversy.

65. See Montesquieu, *Spirit of the Laws*, bks. 28, 30, and 31. For summaries, Sonenscher, *Before the Deluge*, 131–49; Iain McDaniel, *Adam Ferguson in the Scottish Enlightenment: The Roman Past and Europe's Future* (Cambridge, MA: Harvard University Press, 2013), 25–32.

66. Montesquieu, *Spirit of the Laws*, 63.

the English had likewise taken "their idea of political government from the Germans."⁶⁷ Montesquieu classified England as a historically anomalous hybrid of quasi-republican and monarchical forms, arising out of Henry VIII's destruction of noble power during the English reformation, and the subsequent rise of parliament, whose essential roots were nonetheless in the Gothic tradition of representation inherited from the German tribes. English liberty was extremely fragile, however, because it was preserved only by constitutional mechanisms that could quickly disintegrate, rather than the robust system of a checking nobility, intermediary powers, and depository of laws, that a stable large-scale state (i.e., what ought to be a monarchy) required for a secure defense of liberty.⁶⁸ In this, Montesquieu was warning his French compatriots not to emulate the English constitution, whose advantages were only illusory.⁶⁹

Smith challenged both Montesquieu's wider story of European feudal history as leading to neo-German politics, and his more specific account of the English constitution.⁷⁰ These aspects of his writings are already well known.⁷¹ But in brief: Smith held that European history was that of liberty first gained in the ancient world through the innovation of urban living amongst enclaves protecting themselves from piratical and shepherd barbarian attack, liberty lost when the luxury of the cities eventually enticed the barbarian tribes of

---

67. Ibid., 166.

68. Hont, "Introduction," 105. See also Anneline de Dijn, "On Political Liberty: Montesquieu's Missing Manuscript," *Political Theory* 39 (2011), 181–204; McDaniel, *Ferguson in the Scottish Enlightenment*, 32–38; Douglass, "Modern Republicanism," passim.

69. On Montesquieu as warning against French imitation of the English system, see Sylvana Tomaselli, "The Spirit of Nations," in *The Cambridge History of Eighteenth-Century Political Thought*, ed. M. Goldie and R. Wokler (Cambridge: Cambridge University Press, 2006), 9–39.

70. Hont explicitly identifies Montesquieu as a main target of Smith's historical account in bk. 3 of the *Wealth of Nations* in "Introduction," 106. The connection is also stressed in Pocock, *Narratives of Civil Government*, 319–29, and Forbes, "Sceptical Whiggism," 188–90.

71. See especially Hont, "Smith's History of Law," 155–71, and also "Adam Smith and the Political Economy of the 'Unnatural and Retrograde' Order," in *Jealousy of Trade*, 354–88. See also Pocock, *Narratives of Civil Government*, chaps. 20–21, and "Adam Smith and History," in Haakonssen, *Cambridge Companion to Adam Smith*, 270–87; Donald Winch, *Adam Smith's Politics: An Essay in Historiographical Revision* (Cambridge: Cambridge University Press, 1978), chaps. 3–4; J. Slater, "Adam Smith on Feudalism, Commerce and Slavery," *History of Political Thought* 13 (1992), 219–41; E. J. Harpham, "Economics and History: Books II and III of the *Wealth of Nations*," *History of Political Thought* 20 (1999), 438–55; John Robertson, "Scottish Political Economy beyond the Civic Tradition: Government and Economic Development in the *Wealth of Nations*," *History of Political Thought* 4 (1983), 451–82. An important extension of the analysis of Smith's theory of history, widened to include his views on China and Tartary, is given by Ryan Patrick Hanley, "'The Wisdom of the State': Adam Smith on China and Tartary," *American Political Science Review* 108 (2014), 371–82.

the European north to dispossess and destroy the complacent and militarily weakened civilizations of the south (principally Rome), and liberty regained when the backward and repressive system of feudal government eventually erased itself in Western Europe thanks to the short-sighted greed of the barons ensuring that they traded real power over their retainers and vassals for the chance to purchase luxury goods. Rather than modern European government emerging gradually from a complex feudal inheritance, it was founded on the rubble of feudalism's total collapse owing to the political consequences of economic progress. Regarding Montesquieu's claims about the English constitution, Smith put forward a different historical account of the rise of English liberty, one continuous with his explanation for the demise of feudalism and which posited that Britain's liberty was much more recent in origin, but also much more robust, than Montesquieu supposed.[72] Indeed, Montesquieu was also extensively answered on this matter by Hume, the Stuart and Tudor volumes of his *History of England* painting a very different picture of the origins of English liberty to that which saw it as an outgrowth of German barbarian political organization.

As Smith's own historical account of liberty gained, lost, and regained is already well studied, I will not focus on it here (although Smith's wider historical story must be engaged with as it is integral to his political analysis). What I examine instead is a second, hitherto largely neglected, aspect of Smith's rejection of Montesquieu.[73] For although Smith superficially took over the classification of monarchies and republics, he viewed Montesquieu's substantiation of the meanings of these categories as inadequate. On the one hand, Montesquieu's discussion of republics drew upon the older civic humanist discourse of patriotism, frugality, self-sacrifice, and, in Smith's phraseology, "public virtue," to explain the operation and functioning of successful small political entities. As we have already seen, in the *Theory of Moral Sentiments* Smith indicated his belief in the erroneousness of such an approach owing to its misunderstanding of human psychology, and more generally he agreed with Hume that civic humanism was a defunct idiom, a nongeneralizable parochial response to the conditions of those statelets that had by chance survived the barbarian holocaust, and briefly prospered in the interim before the rise of modern large-scale states, and hence which predated the emergence of a proper science of politics.[74] Yet disagreement here was somewhat unimportant. The

---

72. Smith, *Lectures on Jurisprudence*, LJ(A).iv.145–79, v.1–12; LJ(B).58–75.

73. A partial exception is Richard Bourke, "Enlightenment, Revolution and Democracy," *Constellations* 15 (2008), 21–23.

74. On this see especially David Hume, "Of Civil Liberty," in *Essays Moral, Political and Literary*, ed. E. F. Miller (Indianapolis: Liberty Fund, 1985), 88, where tellingly he remarks that "Machiavel was certainly a great genius, but having confined his study to the furious and tyrannical governments of ancient times, or to the little disorderly principalities of ITALY, his reasonings especially upon monarchical government, have been found extremely de-

conclusion of Montesquieu's analysis of republics was that their outlook was bleak, their chances of long-run survival slim. They were sure to be squeezed out by large monarchies, in particular because the spread of commerce would introduce luxury and the pacific tendency of trade would erode martial spirit, together fatally undermining the principle of virtue that enabled the viability of small-state territories.[75] The real action was on the idea of modern monarchy as a form of legally ordered rule—i.e., what has since come to be known as the *Rechtsstaat*—actualized in large-scale territories operating commercial economies.

Yet Smith did not accept Montesquieu's account of monarchies, either. This was because the Frenchman's analysis was predicated not only upon a faulty historical account, but on a quasi-Mandevillean contention that complex systems of hierarchy and rank undergirded the viability of stratified rule, meaning that "honor," or more likely "false honor," was the essence of such a society, which could nonetheless be made stable if properly managed.[76] Smith found this analysis—and the diagnosis for how a large modern monarchy should be ordered—implausible. As we have already seen, Smith was hostile to accounts that posited political rule as a function of the deception of humans due to a preoccupation with rank and status, itself predicated on the central psychological pull of amour propre. Montesquieu's was a weaker version of such an account than that of either Mandeville or Rousseau (and tacked with the former not the latter on the question of stability), but from Smith's perspective it was still the wrong analysis.[77] What he sought to put in its place

---

fective; and there scarcely is any maxim in his *prince*, which subsequent experience has not entirely refuted." See also David Hume, "That Politics May be Reduced to a Science," in *Essays*, 14–31, and for substantiation of Hume as decisively breaking with civic humanism (something I take Smith to have followed him regarding), see James Moore, "Hume's Political Science and the Classical Republican Tradition," *Canadian Journal of Political Science* 10 (1977), 809–40.

75. On this see Douglass, "Modern Republicanism," 711–15; Béla Kapossy, "Neo-Roman Republicanism and Commercial Society: The Example of Eighteenth-Century Berne," in *Republicanism: A Shared European Heritage*, vol. 2, ed. M. V. Gelderen and Q. Skinner (Cambridge: Cambridge University Press, 2002), 227–29; Jacob T. Levy, "Beyond Publius: Montesquieu, Liberal Republicanism, and the Small-Republic Thesis," *History of Political Thought* 21 (2006), 50–90; and more generally on the theme of republicanism's chances from the late eighteenth century onwards, in particular following Montesquieu's analysis but also that of Rousseau, Richard Whatmore, *Against War and Empire: Geneva, Britain and France in the Eighteenth Century* (New Haven: Yale University Press, 2012).

76. McDaniel, *Ferguson in the Scottish Enlightenment*, 31.

77. It is worth noting that Hume also rejected Montesquieu's political analysis. Although he credited "The author of *L'Esprit des Loix*" with establishing "a system of political knowledge, which abounds in ingenious and brilliant thoughts," he went on to state that Montesquieu's system "will never be reconciled with true philosophy" insofar as it set out to explain all rights as established on the basis of "certain *rapports* or relations"—i.e., the

was an explanation of both the origins of modern law-governed monarchies, and their continued good functioning and stability, but based upon a more plausible psychological mechanism. That mechanism was human opinion, understood in particular through the intersection of power and property.

Opinion, Authority, and Historical Political Theory

Smith went further than Hume in the detailed analysis of how opinion generated authority. In book 5 of the *Wealth of Nations* he put into print a small portion of his wider theory of authority, the rest of which is at least partially recoverable via the *Lectures on Jurisprudence*. Examining what he says there is crucial for getting an adequate grip on his wider political theory.

Smith reiterated his agreement with Hume that small-scale sociability without government was entirely possible: "Men may live together in society with some tolerable degree of security, though there is no civil magistrate to protect them from the injustice of those passions," such as envy, malice, or resentment, that prompted primitive men to attack the persons and reputations of others. The introduction of property, however, necessitated the innovation of government: "The affluence of the rich excited the indignation of the poor, who are often both driven by want, and prompted by envy, to invade his possessions."[78] There was no doubt that "Civil government, so far as it is instituted for the security of property, is in reality instituted for the defence of the rich against the poor, or of those who have some property against those who have none at all."[79] Accordingly, it was evidently and necessarily the case that "Civil government supposes a certain subordination."[80] What needed to be explained was how that subordination came about. Crucial to Smith's analysis was the insight that because government was bound up with the protection of property, the nature of submission must vary in line with both of those factors.

Smith identified four separate sources for belief in the authority of another. The first was superior ability such as strength, beauty, wisdom, or prudence. Although humans naturally tend to defer to those with superior abilities, these qualities were by definition "invisible," and open to constant judgment and interpretation. Accordingly, "No society, whether barbarous or civilized, has ever found it convenient to settle the rules of precedency, or rank and

---

complex amalgam of considerations to do with territorial size, climate, constitutions, manners, religion, and ultimately the "spring" or "principle" underpinning each form of government. David Hume, *An Enquiry Concerning the Principles of Morals*, ed. T. L. Beauchamp (Oxford: Oxford University Press, 1998), 22.

78. Smith, *Wealth of Nations*, V.i.b.2.

79. Ibid., V.i.b.12; cf. Smith, *Lectures on Jurisprudence*, LJ(A).iv.22–24.

80. Smith, *Wealth of Nations*, V.i.b.3. The early articulation of Smith's theory of authority in the Glasgow lectures is recorded at *Lectures on Jurisprudence*, LJ(A).iv.119–20, and LJ(B).13–14. For further discussion, see Hont, "Smith's History of Law," 150–55.

subordination" on these lines, "but according to something that is more plain and palpable."[81] The second source of authority was age: "a plain and palpable quality which admits of no dispute." Human beings tend automatically to defer on grounds of age, and indeed in humanity's primitive condition superior age combined with superiority of personal abilities determined who wielded authority.[82]

The emergence of property, and therefore inequality, introduced a third ground: wealth. This was for two reasons. The first—as Smith learned from Hume, but as we saw he also modified in important technical respects—was that thanks to the capacity for sympathy, human beings tend to love and esteem the rich and powerful rather than resent and envy them (even if for Smith what they loved and esteemed was what they *imagined* the rich should feel in relation to their wealth, regardless of whether wealth in fact generated the good consequences spectators attributed to its possession). But Smith added a further, material, dimension to the analysis, noting that when property introduced inequality, it also introduced dependency.[83] Those with material assets could make those without resources dependent upon them for their continued livelihoods and prosperity. This was especially true, Smith thought, in the "shepherding" stage of societal development, when property was first introduced and inequality was at its most pronounced. The rich heads of clans had nothing to spend their money on but retaining those who served them. They thus bought the poor into situations of continued dependency and deference, which the poor accepted owing to both the utility gains it afforded them, and the psychological pull of esteem for established superiors. Furthermore, wealth concentrated the authority of the already wealthy, as these individuals were turned to by inferiors to settle disputes. Early judicial arbitration was vested in the rich, who demanded presents as a form of payment from those who sought redress, further cementing inequality, but also authority, insofar as people learned to submit to the decisions of third-party arbiters. The result was that in early societies the poor "must both obey" the orders of the rich "in war, and submit to his jurisdiction in peace. He is necessarily both their general and their judge, and his chieftainship is the necessary effect of the superiority of his fortune."[84] As we shall see, this state of affairs changed over time. Nonetheless, it was for Smith "in the age of shepherds . . . that the inequality of fortune first begins to take place, and introduces among men a degree of authority and subordination which could not possibly exist before."[85] How authority and subordination developed *after* the age of shepherds was crucial to Smith's political theory, as we shall see below.

81. Smith, *Wealth of Nations*, V.i.b.5.
82. Ibid., V.i.b.6.
83. Ibid., V.i.b.7.
84. Ibid., V.i.b.7.
85. Ibid., V.i.b.12.

The fourth source of authority was birth—i.e., being born to a family of high standing. This, however, presupposed existing inequalities and was dependent upon the prior establishment of property, inequality, and rank. Human beings had a powerful and apparently innate tendency to respect lineages, with a preference for the offspring of already-established leaders over those without hereditary credentials. This source of authority went hand in hand with, and augmented that of, wealth, and in the early shepherd societies where wealth inequality was highly concentrated, reverence for lineage was especially intense. As Smith remarked, the self-recorded histories of Tartar (or as we would now call them, Mongol) clans, the archetype of the shepherd stage of group living, consisted almost exclusively of genealogies of descent.[86]

These four sources of authority enabled Smith to analyze the progress of different kinds of government according to the different forms of political and economic organization human beings found themselves in, which he did extensively in his Glasgow lectures. Doing so, however, required a conceptual shift in the mode of analysis. With the question of sociability settled in favor of Smith's modified version of Hume's story of utility seeking, Smith could entirely abandon state-of-nature theories, even of the sort (as employed by Hume) that treated the supposition of such a condition as a pure thought experiment. Smith shifted the register to actual historical development, which he presented as oriented around four "stages" of society: hunter-gatherer, shepherding, agricultural, and, finally, commercial.[87] Two of these stages, how-

---

86. Smith, *Lectures on Jurisprudence*, LJ(A).iv.43–44.

87. For the pioneer study of Smith's "four-stages" theory, Ronald L. Meek, *Social Science and the Ignoble Savage* (Cambridge: Cambridge University Press, 1976). Understanding of Smith's account has advanced since Meek's study, but in fact the stages theory remains relatively underanalyzed. For important exceptions, see István Hont, "The Language of Sociability and Commerce: Samuel Pufendorf and the Theoretical Foundations of the 'Four Stages' Theory," in *Jealousy of Trade*, 159–84, and "Correcting Europe's Political Economy: The Virtuous Eclecticism of Georg Ludwig Schmid," *History of European Ideas* 33 (2007), 390–410; Maureen Harkin, "Adam Smith's Missing History: Primitives, Progress, and Problems of Genre," *English Literary History* 72 (2005), 429–51; Pocock, "Adam Smith and History"; Jennifer Pitts, *A Turn to Empire: The Rise of Imperial Liberalism in Britain and France* (Princeton, NJ: Princeton University Press, 2006), 34–41; Christopher J. Berry, *The Idea of Commercial Society in the Scottish Enlightenment* (Edinburgh: Edinburgh University Press, 2013), chap. 2; Slater, "Feudalism, Commerce and Slavery"; Robertson, "Scottish Political Economy." It is important to remember that Smith's four-stages theory was an analytic framework designed to facilitate understanding, not a strict historical claim about how human progress necessarily occurred, all of a piece. Europe's modern history in particular was "retrograde," owing especially to the clash of civilizations that occurred between shepherding peoples and the advanced superstate of Rome. For helpful discussion, see Hont, "Introduction," 101–11, especially his gloss on the agricultural and commercial stages as being characterized by "the division of labor between town and country" and "foreign and long-distance trade, moving from strictly local existence of early human groups to commercial globalization."

ever, took place in largely pre-recorded history, and thus Smith undertook this part of his analysis in the mode of what Dugald Stewart was the first to term "theoretical or conjectural history."[88] Nonetheless, it is clear that Smith intends his own story as a genuinely historical understanding of how human societies must have been ordered, based on inferences from the North American tribes that European settlers had encountered, and what was known of the Mongol hordes of the Eastern steppe and their various descendants.[89] And we should be careful not to exaggerate the extent to which Smith's history is conjectural: much of his analysis is focused on the ancient and feudal worlds of Europe, about which much was known, and where Smith took his account not to be conjectural at all, but based on hard historical fact.[90] Furthermore, it is worth noting that Stewart's comment about Smith's conjectural method refers primarily to the latter's "Considerations concerning the First Formation of Languages," not the material that can be recovered from the then-unpublished lecture notes. In any case, by introducing history, Smith sought to provide a theory of political regime forms adequately sensitive to the importance of humans' specific material conditions in the determination of forms of political organization, which improved on Montesquieu's ambitious but flawed analysis, and put the interplay of property and power center stage.

Smith divided the functions of government into the three now well-known categories of legislative, judicial, and executive, the latter of which Smith, following Locke, sometimes called "the foederal" power, and made clear pertained principally to "the power of making peace and war."[91] Yet in order to "acquire proper notions of government," Smith insisted, "it is necessary to consider the first form of it, and observe how the other forms arose out of it."[92] The first stage of society was that of hunter-gatherers, where small troops organized around family structures subsisted together. In this most primitive condition "there is properly no government at all," because there was little or no property, and thus no need for its regulation by coercive imposition.[93] In particular, there was no legislative power, which Smith identified as a much later innovation hit upon for the control of what became excessive

---

88. Stewart, "Writings of Adam Smith," 293. On Smith as "conjectural" historian, see Pocock, *Narratives of Civil Government*, 314–15, but also Pitts, *Turn to Empire*, 35–39.

89. On this see especially Hanley, "Wisdom of the State." For an unflattering appraisal of Smith's use of American Indians in structuring his analysis, Christian Marouby, "Adam Smith and the Anthropology of the Enlightenment: The 'Ethnographic' Sources of Economic Progress," in *The Anthropology of the Enlightenment*, ed. L. Wolff and M. Cipolloni (Stanford: Stanford University Press, 2007), 85–102.

90. This point was in fact made very clearly in Meek's early study (*Ignoble Savage*, 230–43), but has not always been well heeded.

91. Smith, *Lectures on Jurisprudence*, LJ(A).iv.2.

92. Ibid., LJ(B).19.

93. Ibid., LJ(B).19.

and rapacious judicial abuse after the age of shepherds.[94] As regards the executive power of making peace and war, hunter-gatherers could only fight successfully en masse: the decision to engage in military adventures had to be taken collectively, and could only be achieved if the majority agreed to it. Similarly, rudimentary judicial power was exercised in most cases by collective sanction—paradigmatically, ostracism or lynching—although sometimes it would be delegated to the heads of clans whose age and superior abilities generated deference. However, as punishment could only be enforced by the will of the group, judicial power remained, at base, popular. As a result, Smith insisted that the stage of hunters was characterized as one of *democratic* government (insofar as there was any government at all), even if prominent individuals had more sway than others owing to the pull of natural authority rooted in superior age and ability.

The next stage of society, that of shepherds, saw the introduction of property, originally in the form of livestock, and thus of government, which was required to regulate material interactions. Shepherd societies were formidable in nature: nomadic because of the need to graze large herds across expansive swaths of terrain, they were necessarily warlike insofar as moving across lands brought them into competition with other groups. The most successful shepherding clans—the "Tartarian" (i.e., Mongol) hordes, descended from Attila the Hun and later Genghis Khan, that spread out from the Eastern steppe and ravaged Asia, Arabia, and Europe for centuries—grew in enormous wealth as conquest brought spoils. This generated extreme inequality: tribal leaders appropriated wealth for themselves and their families, and kept it. But the nomadic nature of their societies meant that the rich had little to spend their wealth upon besides keeping their retainers dependent upon them. Inequality thus cemented hierarchical political status. As noted above, these leaders were also turned to for administering judicial arbitrage, and used this as an opportunity to further augment their wealth through the form of presents and bribes. Yet Smith insisted that these forms of societies, despite their huge material inequality and strict hierarchies of rank, were not what they first appeared. For although "a state of this sort to a careless observer would appear to be monarchical," the truth was that "Tartarian" shepherd societies were at base democratic.[95] This was because, with regard to the executive power, the clan chieftain had to lead all of his adult male (and sometimes much of the female) population into battle. He had no power to conscript or force them to fight, and could wage war only with their willingness to support him. Similarly, although chieftains were appealed to in order to administer justice, this was a solution endorsed by the general population, who wanted to see crimes against persons and property punished, but who could easily break the power

---

94. Ibid., LJ(A).v.108–10.
95. Ibid., LJ(A).iv.33.

of the chieftain if he ruled in a way that displeased the majority, instead coming to the aid of the condemned. Smith's analysis was thus both complex and original. Shepherd chiefs were *primus inter pares*, and their superior wealth and ancestry meant that others were happy to allow them to be entrusted with many decisions. But the population as a whole could take back that power quite easily if belief in the authority of the chieftain faltered. What were at root democracies took on the appearance of monarchies because of the willingness of the majority to submit. In large measure this was because of the influence of hugely unequal holdings in wealth, and the effect of this upon the generation of authority in the opinion of the ruled. With legislative power not yet introduced as a check to judicial rapacity (something Smith identified as a major problem facing shepherd societies), both the hunter and shepherd forms of society, despite appearances, turned out to be democracies when properly calibrated in line with the workings of opinion and with reference to their particular configurations of property.[96]

Smith implies that many centuries, if not millennia, of human history in the Old World must have been spent in the condition of shepherds.[97] But it was as a reaction to the ravages of steppe nomads that new forms of government, and eventually civilization, emerged. The most notable and important example was Attica, a sparse and territorially arid region that possessed the major advantage of being surrounded on many sides by the sea, making it difficult (and anyway unattractive) to attack. Persistent danger from outside groups came only from the sea, via pirate raids. Groups that settled in Attica thus hit upon the innovation of collecting populations within walled conurbations for easy defense from seaborne raiders. The security this brought translated into prosperity, as sedentary agriculture proved a superior way of feeding populations, in turn creating opportunities for other forms of production and exchange thanks to the benefits of the division of labor.[98]

With changes in forms of property came modifications in the form of government. The earliest of these societies, like the shepherd clans, at first glance appeared to be monarchies owing to the influence of the great men who initially directed affairs because of their eminent wealth and descent. But again, appearances were deceptive: these were really democracies, insofar as power still rested with the majority of the people, and were called monarchies only because of the power and authority of great men who benefited from the influence of wealth and hereditary descent. In time, however, that influence and authority faltered. This was because other notable individuals resented the superiority of putative kings: "The authority of the chief would not be at all

---

96. Ibid., LJ(A).iv.31–47; LJ(B).20–27.

97. For remarks on this, see Pocock, *Narratives of Civil Government*, 317–18, but also Pitts, *Turn to Empire*, 269, n. 42.

98. Smith, *Lectures on Jurisprudence*, LJ(A).iv.56–58; (B).32–35.

agreeable to them if it came to be any way excessive, nor would they be so much below him as to be greatly under his power."[99] As a result, these putative early kingships were all at base democracies: "the King, as he was called, was no more than a leading man who had superior influence in their deliberations." And in time, these regimes were replaced with explicitly republican regime forms, as subordinates refused to follow the singular power of one individual. Some of these republics were, as Athens periodically was, constituted officially as democracies, where all the citizens partook in both the executive and judicial functions. Others were formally constituted as aristocracies, because human deference to wealth and lineage meant that notable individuals were repeatedly chosen to rule, even though this was not strictly necessary. Thus, in reality, all these Attican regimes were at base democratic.[100]

What made ancient democracy possible, however, was that these regimes were slave societies. Citizens were freed from the drudgery and time-consuming nature of working to subsist, and were instead possessed of the leisure time required for active participation in political affairs, alongside a material independence enabling them to oppose the will of the richest. Smith viewed slavery as an abomination, whose only redeeming feature was that it allowed small republics to defend themselves for longer than they would otherwise manage, insofar as the free citizenry could dedicate time to effective military training (something later rendered irrelevant by the innovations of gunpowder and professional standing armies).[101] Yet Smith also considered slavery as incompatible with postfeudal European political organization: "Slavery has not been allowed in any of the modern republicks."[102] As a result, the modern republics of Europe differed crucially from those of the ancient world, insofar as the majority of citizens had to labor for their own subsistence, and thus political rule had to be undertaken by a dedicated cadre of professionals—i.e., an aristocracy proper. The clear implication of Smith's analysis is that democracy is not a modern form of government, but fitted only to the first two stages of human society and the early forms of urban living that emerged as a reaction to shepherd aggression in the ancient world. This by itself is a dramatic result of Smith's analysis, at least to twenty-first-century eyes, and we will need to return to it later and ask whether it might nonetheless usefully—albeit with some important modifications—guide our thinking. That task, however, I delay until chapter 6.

99. Ibid., LJ(A).iv.66.
100. Ibid., LJ(A).iv.59–67.
101. Ibid., LJ(A).iv.69, iv.82.

102. Ibid., LJ(A).iv.110. Smith's reasons for thinking that slavery is not just a moral abomination, but also incompatible with the foundations of modern politics, are somewhat puzzling insofar as no clear explanation is given for this latter contention—and in the context of the North Atlantic slave trade (which Smith famously opposed in the *Wealth of Nations*), one would seem rather to be required.

With the emergence of republics in the ancient world explained as a reaction against shepherd aggression, Smith examined the fates that these forms of political organization themselves came to suffer. He here followed the basic dichotomy familiar from Machiavelli, dividing republics into "defensive" and "conquering" types.[103] In both cases, however, Smith concluded that the end point for republics was failure and collapse, and all that differed was the length of time required to bring it about. Defensive republics were doomed to be conquered owing to improvements in military (especially siege) technology, the very economic prosperity their successful existence created leading to a decline in military participation and aptitude: "when a country arrives at a certain degree of refinement it becomes less fit for war."[104] What started as defensive islands withstanding shepherd onslaughts grew in prosperity until they became both an overwhelmingly tempting target for attack, and increasingly incapable of offering effective resistance. Conquering republics had greater longevity, but they too were eventually bound to fail. Smith principally analyzed Rome, although he made clear that Carthage would have met the same fate had it not lost the life-or-death struggle with the Italian power.[105] Rome lost its republican status when the eminence and wealth of its military leaders led to a series of internal power struggles, eventually resulting in the overthrow of the republican government and the imposition of a dictatorship backed by military force. Rome had transitioned to a genuine form of monarchical rule, albeit one that was both brought about, and continuously enabled, by the overwhelming military might of Caesar and his successors, who also took judicial power out of popular hands and made it the function of a puppet senate. However, this form of military monarchy was tolerated by the majority of citizens because although force was used ruthlessly against those who might challenge the superiority of the emperor in Rome, citizens in more far-away provinces, and those without ambitions of power, "lived more peaceable and happily than they ever did under the Republick."[106] This was because provincial governors—always liable to act as petty local tyrants—were now more frequently called to account, as the emperors had direct interest in having laws upheld and justice consistently administered, so as to cement their own position as rulers through securing the support of ordinary people. In this way, although the Roman Empire was a military regime it was "not of the same kind with those of Turky and the east." But because it was still ultimately founded upon brute military power, it was not like the monarchies of modern Europe,

---

103. Smith, *Lectures on Jurisprudence*, LJ(A).iv.75–76; LJ(B).37; Niccolò Machiavelli, *Discourses on Livy* (Chicago: Chicago University Press, 1996), bk. 2, chaps. 1–4; cf. Hont, "Smith's History of Law," 158–59.

104. Smith, *Lectures on Jurisprudence*, LJ(B).37.

105. Ibid., LJ(A).iv.87–88.

106. Ibid., LJ(A).iv.107.

either.[107] In any case, Smith's message was clear: the fate of a conquering republic was ultimately to conquer itself: "there is only one form of government which can take place in a republick subdued by one of its own members. The action of subduing ones country, and (the army) the instrument by which it was performed, necessarily determine it to be a military monarchy."[108] As is well known, Smith's further analysis was that it was luxury—the spoils of war, in particular from the conquest of the Middle East—that eventually destroyed the Roman Empire. Having grown rich upon their victories, Roman citizens increasingly withdrew from active military participation and the power of the empire came to rest not upon disciplined patriotic citizen-soldiers, but mercenaries recruited from the barbarian provinces that Rome had conquered. Yet the dazzling wealth of the capital enticed aggression from the shepherd peoples unconquered in the northern reaches of Europe, and eventually the German tribes overran and destroyed the Western Empire, bringing to a close the long progress of politics in the ancient world.[109]

With the collapse of Rome, Europe's civilizational advancement was set back severely. Nonetheless, the foundations for new, modern, forms of political organization were also laid. Smith insisted that the modern, like the ancient, forms of politics "have taken their rise from the same Tartarian species of government."[110] Yet the expression "taken their rise" is importantly expansive: as with the progress of the ancient world, modern politics was not a straightforward development out of shepherding society, but a complex historical reaction to its legacy.

In beginning his analysis of modern politics, Smith observed that the "government which succeeded" the fall of the Western Empire "was not altogether unlike the Tartar government formerly mentioned," although the German barbarians possessed more developed notions of agriculture and property in land than the steppe nomads of the East, presumably because of contact with the Romans, and the different conditions of living in dense wooded lands.[111] What followed the collapse of the Roman Empire was not, as many mistakenly believed, the immediate imposition of feudalism, but rather of alodial government, which occurred after the barbarian conquerors made an initial division of lands.[112] This system operated on a model of downward economic

---

107. The modern exception, Smith claimed, was the English Protectorate under Cromwell, which was likewise a military dictatorship acquiesced to by the people, but in England's case, this was because the population was exhausted by civil war, whilst Cromwell's firm rule restored order and prioritized the enforcement of consistent rules of justice that the vast majority desired: ibid., LJ(A).iv.97, iv.105.
108. Ibid., LJ(A).iv.96.
109. Ibid., LJ(A).iv.101–4.
110. Ibid., LJ(A).iv.114.
111. Ibid., LJ(A).iv.114.
112. Smith, *Wealth of Nations*, III.iv.8.

dependency, but retained an important element of popular participation inherited from the Germanic forms of tribal organization that involved upward representation to local chiefs, although local lords largely engaged in the oppression of their subject populations. Around the ninth century, however, alodial government in Western Europe gave way to feudalism, although in England this was imposed decisively only after the Norman Conquest. The move to feudalism centrally involved the great lords giving up property in their lands, and holding them only as feuda granted back to them by the king, who then allowed them to do whatever they liked within their domains. The consequence was that this "took away everything like popular government" that had previously existed, as only the great lords were permitted to engage in the management of political affairs, whilst public courts were abolished and judicial functions dispensed only by the barons, at their private whim.[113] Although commonly seen as having been forced upon European kings by powerful barons, Smith insisted that this was a back projection of later states of affairs. Originally, feudalism was forced upon the great lords by opportunistic kings who wanted to solidify their own power at times when they held the upper hand, seeking to play the barons off against each other. This backfired, however, as baronial power became concentrated and was able to stand in opposition to monarchical direction. As Smith put it in the more polished version of the account that made it into book 3 of the *Wealth of Nations*, "After the institution of feudal subordination, the king was as incapable of restraining the violence of the great lords as before."[114] The feudal barons, like the alodial lords before them, ruled their own territories as miniature—and highly oppressive—monarchs. Owing to the real king's need to engage with them so as to extract financial and military support (each baron having a significant private army), whilst also checking them against each other, nationally speaking feudalism was not a form of monarchy, but "fell into a kind of aristocracy with the king at the head of it."[115] The feudal regimes of modern Europe thus followed the basic path of the Attican walled cities: jealous eminent individuals sought to check the power of the leading figure. But in post-Roman Europe, territorial size and population diffusion meant that the king had to be retained, whereas in Greece the republican form took place outright, oscillating between democratic and aristocratic instantiations.[116]

What ultimately destroyed baronial power was the same thing that brought down Rome: luxury. Whereas the great inequality of fortune introduced by alodial government had previously allowed the barons to exercise enormous

---

113. Smith, *Lectures on Jurisprudence*, LJ(A).iv.137; LJ(B).55–56.
114. Smith, *Wealth of Nations*, III.iv.9; cf. *Lectures on Jurisprudence*, LJ(A).iv.130–38.
115. Ibid., LJ(B).56.
116. Ibid., LJ(A).iv.149–50; cf. Smith, *Wealth of Nations*, III.iv.7–9.

power by expending their revenues on thousands of retainers, they traded away this influence by spending their wealth on luxury goods that meant they no longer held individuals in direct financial dependency, and inadvertently stimulated economic activity that enabled individuals to become materially independent by themselves.[117] Yet the outcome of this process, Smith insisted, was in most parts of Europe the emergence of absolute monarchy. Whereas the barons bankrupted themselves, or at least traded away their power and influence, the kings of Europe were sufficiently wealthy that they could absorb the expense of luxury prestige consumption, and still continue to bind their dependents and retainers through economic patronage.[118] Thus the emergence of regular monarchy—where one individual really did rule alone, but not simply by military dictatorship—was a distinctively modern, and relatively recent, development. The power vacuum left by the barons was filled by kings who assumed absolute status, and commanded allegiance from subject populations owing to their vast superiority of fortune, long ancestral descent, and the tolerable (and sometimes even commodious) state of living such rule guaranteed for ordinary people. Whereas Caesar and the Roman dictators had ultimately relied upon military might (as Cromwell would later do in his reign over England), modern European monarchies did not typically rely upon force to secure power in domestic contexts. This was in large measure because absolute monarchy was, for the vast majority of subjects, a great improvement in terms of liberty compared with feudalism. The nobility historically always proved to be "the greatest oppressors and oppressors of liberty that we can imagine," far worse than any absolute monarch for the majority of subjects. After all, "the greatest part of the nation" have "nothing to fear," nor were in very great danger of being oppressed, by a sovereign "who is terrible to those only who were near at hand to the seat of his court," whereas "everyone is in danger from petty lords, who had the chief power in the whole kingdom."[119] An absolute national monarch was thus, to many ordinary people, a more favorable proposition than a local baron. By the sixteenth century, therefore, absolute monarchy had emerged as the natural and legitimate form of rule in nations like France, Spain, Portugal, and England. It successfully combined authority with utility for subject populations, which—as we saw in chapter 3, and will return to below—Smith saw as the basis of all legitimate government, whatever its precise constitutional form. The collapse of feudalism ushered in the first real monarchies in Europe since the Roman Empire, but ones whose form and basis differed significantly from that ancient predecessor.

---

117. Smith, *Lectures on Jurisprudence*, LJ(A).iv.157–59; cf. *Wealth of Nations*, III.iv.10–18.

118. Smith, *Lectures on Jurisprudence*, LJ(A).iv.160–62.

119. Ibid., LJ(A).iv.165–66; Forbes, "Sceptical Whiggism," 192–93.

Smith noted two exceptions to this pattern regarding large states, at least when continued down to the eighteenth century.[120] The first was Germany, whose peculiar geographic situation meant that its feudal lords were not undone by luxury: a giant territory containing enormous estates, which was however relatively sparsely populated, meant that German lords could engage in luxury consumption whilst staying rich, and thus not giving up power over their retainers.[121] The other exception was England, which followed a unique path of development unavailable in the rest of Europe after the sixteenth century. This was the result of geography and a contingent and unique historical event; namely, that when James VI of Scotland succeeded Elizabeth I to become James I of England in 1603, the House of Stuart took rule over the whole of the British Isles. Ending centuries of border conflict, this also removed the need for a standing army because Britain was an island, and thus defended via maritime, not territorial, military power. Smith was forthright in claiming that the Tudors had been absolute monarchs.[122] But English kings had, long before the Tudors, encouraged the erosion of baronial power by introducing the lower ranks to the House of Commons, originally as a check to the power of the great lords (a significant irony, Smith surely wanted his students to notice, given that it was the Commons that would eventually oust Charles I). But British monarchs were also dependent upon parliament for supply, and increasingly struggled to raise adequate funds, which were dependent upon support from both Commons and Lords. Elizabeth I's unwillingness to take hardheaded fiscal decisions at the end of her reign left a time bomb for the succeeding Stuarts. This eventually exploded under Charles I, when his attempt to rule without parliament failed and he was forced to recall it in order to ask for money. Lacking a standing army, Charles could not suppress his opponents via military might (and they certainly would not pay for him to develop such a thing), and when civil war came it turned out to be parliament that was more adept at raising and fielding forces. This set off a process that would culminate in the victory of Cromwell, his ten-year military dictatorship, the restoration of Charles II in 1660, the succession crisis revolving around James II, and ultimately the Glorious Revolution of 1688—the final stage in the emergence of the British constitution as Smith and his contemporaries knew it.[123]

This unique set of events was what made England different from continental Europe. English liberty was a recent and highly localized phenomenon, emerging decisively only after the civil war as a result of the ongoing

120. Smith offered brief examinations of small states still governed as republics, but it is clear he did not consider these to have particularly hopeful prospects in the commercial competitive world of modern Europe: *Lectures on Jurisprudence*, LJ(A).v.45–54; *Wealth of Nations*, V.i.a.10–44.
121. Smith, *Lectures on Jurisprudence*, LJ(A).iv.163–64.
122. Ibid., LJ(A).iv.164.
123. Ibid., LJ(A).iv.170–78.

negotiations between crown and parliament, and the eventual settlement that supreme authority required the two together.[124] English liberties were not fragile, however, as they were extensively secured by the legal system, especially via institutions such as the courts of Chancery and Exchequer, the existence of the jury system and principle of habeas corpus, and the frequency of elections to the lower House, all of which were augmented and strengthened in the settlements of 1660 and 1688.[125] Smith's reply to Montesquieu thus argued that the English constitution was a much more recent, and much less fragile, arrangement than the Frenchman suggested. Rather than being found in the "forests of Germany"—i.e., being an inheritance from the representative practices of the northern shepherd peoples[126]—English politics had, until the seventeenth century, followed the same pattern as the rest of Europe, and took a different path only late in the day. On the one hand, this meant that English liberty was not straightforwardly exportable: other countries could not look to the English constitution and presume to simply apply it to their own states, because they lacked the historical foundations that made such a system functional in England, and which had anyway been achieved only at the cost of bloodshed and upheaval. On the other, the implication of Smith's analysis replicated Hume's. England was unique, but not, by simple virtue of that, superior. Absolute government was received as a legitimate form of rule across Europe by subject populations, not least because it was a considerable enhancement of liberty vis-à-vis the feudal predecessor regimes. English liberty was to be celebrated, certainly, but it was not the only legitimate form of modern rule. For the most part, large-territory politics in eighteenth-century Europe meant monarchical absolutism, which was not defective simply because it wasn't English.[127]

Sovereignty and the Limits of Philosophy

This brings us to the point at which Smith's analysis touches home with Hume's reconfiguration of the normative issues surrounding the question of

124. "In this manner a system of liberty has been established in England before the standing army was introduced; which as it was not the case in other countries, so it has not been ever established in them": ibid., LJ(A).iv.178.

125. Ibid., LJ(A).v.1–43; LJ(B).67–75.

126. Montesquieu, *Spirit of the Laws*, 165–66.

127. Hume, of course, agreed. As he put it in "Of Civil Liberty," 94: "But though all kinds of government be improved in modern times, yet monarchical government seems to have made the greatest advances towards perfection. It may now be affirmed of civilized monarchies, what was formerly said in praise of republics alone, *that they are a government of Laws, not of Men.* They are found susceptible of order, method, and constancy, to a surprizing degree." Indeed, in certain respects absolute monarchies had distinct advantages over republics, although Hume celebrated Britain's hybrid constitution as superior to both; cf. Forbes, "Sceptical Whiggism," 193.

authority and obligation. For Smith, all government was founded on the twin principles of authority and utility. The former was chiefly composed of the four features we examined earlier, whilst Smith noted that a government's authority was also greatly amplified by the quotidian experience ordinary people had of growing up under it, as well as seeing others defer and continuously practicing deference themselves. Ordinary citizens experienced life under government as being in a position of vastly inferior power and importance, and this spontaneously tended to encourage submission, analogous to child-parent relationships: "There is the same propriety in submitting to [government] as to a father, as all of those in authority are either naturally or by the will of the state who lend them their power placed far above you".[128] Utility played an essential role, however, insofar as subjects realized that "the security and independency of each individual . . . cannot be obtained without a regular government." In normal circumstances individuals recognized that even if government was imperfect, it was best to submit to it for the sake of oneself and others, whilst "the naturall modesty of mankind, who are not generally inclined to think they have a title to dispute the authority of those above them" meant that with regard to the promotion of utility, belief in authority made people forgiving of many imperfections.[129]

But although authority was often the foundation for the promotion of utility, the two principles varied in preponderance, depending on the type of regime in question. In monarchies the principle of authority predominated, with individuals automatically granting respect and deference (especially when amplified by hereditary lineage) to established monarchs. In republics, by contrast, and especially those with democratic underpinnings, utility "is that which chiefly, nay allmost entirely, occasions the obedience of the subject."[130] Individuals who became preeminent risked alienating the collective support of the people if not providing closely for their interests, and hence republican regimes with a democratic basis tended quickly to remove powerful individuals, who were automatically perceived as a threat to the common good (as indeed Smith's preceding historical analysis had sought to establish). The principle of authority was not absent in republics, but rather than attaching to individuals it tended to attach "to offices": holding an official position of state carried with it the weight of authority, although this was typically weaker than the respect paid to eminent persons, especially monarchs.[131] Likewise, monarchies were dependent upon the principle of utility as well as authority, even if the weight of emphasis fell on the latter. Yet the interplay of these two principles made the British constitution in particular of especial interest. The presence of the king

---

128. Smith, *Lectures on Jurisprudence*, LJ(A).v.120.
129. Ibid., LJ(A).120–21.
130. Ibid., LJ(A).121.
131. Ibid., LJ(A).122.

and the House of Lords (i.e., an aristocracy of hereditary lineage) ensured that "the principle of authority takes place in a considerable degree." But because "the government is in great part democraticall, by the influence of the House of Commons, the principle of utility is also found in it."[132] This explained the divisions between the Whig and Tory parties: the former were advocates of the principle of utility, the latter of authority, and the competition between them was at base an attempt to make one foundation of government—and the policies that would flow from prioritizing it—predominate over the other.[133] Again, this was at least in part a response to Montesquieu, with Smith offering what he took to be a superior analysis of the foundations and continued functioning of the institutional undergirding of English liberty.

Smith thus followed the essential normative reconfiguration Hume had pioneered, and which we examined in chapter 3. Government was legitimate, whatever its form, if it adequately commanded the assent of subjects by satisfactorily meeting the principles of authority and utility. Of course, what *counted* as an adequate satisfaction would depend upon the opinion of subjects, which varied with prevailing material and historical conditions, and the different forms of government that arose. Smith, like Hume, was in no doubt that government could become illegitimate if it failed to adequately uphold utility and authority: "there are . . . certain abuses which no doubt make resistance in some cases lawful on whatever principle government be founded."[134] He unilaterally rejected the claims of contract theory (naming Locke and Algernon Sidney as his targets), redeploying Hume's arguments and counterexamples to do so.[135] Smith in turn sought to supply a superior analysis for when government became illegitimate, focused on the twin principles of authority and utility.

Authority could be lost if the holders of positions of power (especially monarchs) lacked the capacity to rule—paradigmatically if they were infants, or became insane—in which case decision making was typically put into the hands of overseers, until the regular lineage of descent could be restored.[136] Utility, obviously enough, was compromised by governments excessively attacking or undermining the interests of the people. Unsurprisingly, a loss of belief in the utility of obeying a form of government would in turn rapidly erode any belief

---

132. Ibid., LJ(A).v.122–24.

133. This of course recalls Hume's analysis in "Of the Parties of Great Britain" (in *Essays*, 71): "A Tory, therefore, since the revolution, may be defined in a few words, to be a lover of monarchy, though without abandoning liberty; and a partizan of the family of Stuart. As a Whig may be defined to be a lover of liberty though without renouncing monarchy; and a friend to the settlement in the Protestant line."

134. Smith, *Lectures on Jurisprudence*, LJ(B).93.

135. Ibid., LJ(A).v.112–19; LJ(B).15–18; cf. Forbes, "Sceptical Whiggism," 181, and Hont, "Smith's History of Law," 138.

136. Smith, *Lectures on Jurisprudence*, LJ(A).v.125–26.

in the authority of an office holder, as famous tyrants like Nero and Caligula illustrated.[137] Smith, like Hume, had no doubt that if subject populations were pushed so far as to rebel, then insofar as authority and utility were no longer being adequately upheld, then such rebellion was ipso facto justified. "Absurdity and impropriety of conduct and great perverseness destroy obedience, whether it be due from authority or the sense of the common good."[138]

Yet Smith seems to have felt the theoretical pinch of this position more sharply than Hume. Owing to the fact that all government was imperfect, there was no doubting that subject populations must for the most part treat such an institution on a principle of trust. The rightful default position was to acquiesce to governmental decision-making power even against one's own immediate interests, on the assumption that even apparently utility-harming actions were nonetheless undertaken with the intention of aiding the common weal, and in the parallel knowledge that fomenting rebellion was anyway likely to bring more harm than good. Hence, a considerable degree of inconvenience from the particular policies of government should rightly be tolerated as the necessary cost of having any government at all—which was indeed what most people came spontaneously to see for themselves.[139] This was not, it is worth stressing, an especially new conclusion for Smith when he was delivering his lectures. In the *Theory of Moral Sentiments*, he had already made the point with stark clarity, relying there on the principle of natural authority to explain obedience: "That kings are the servants of the people, to be obeyed, resisted, deposed, or punished, as the public conveniency may require, is the doctrine of reason and philosophy; but it is not the doctrine of Nature. Nature would teach us to submit to them for their own sake, to tremble and bow down before their exalted station, to regard their smile as a reward sufficient to compensate any services, and to dread their displeasure, though no other evil were to follow from it, as the severest of all mortifications."[140] Nonetheless, this did not alter the fact that "whatever the principle of allegiance and obedience of the sovereign, it must have some limits."[141] Yet by adopting Hume's opinion-focused approach, Smith was likewise committed to denying the ability of philosophy to independently specify what those limits were. Although the student notetaker uses the word "sovereign" in recording Smith's analysis of the limits of legitimate power, this is interchangeable in the analysis with both government and, tellingly, "*summa potestas*." Smith, like Hume, had no foundational theory of sovereignty, but instead deployed a theory of the opinion of mankind, which equated sovereignty with whoever controlled government in whatever form it happened to take, seeking to account for the normative

137. Ibid., LJ(A).v.136; LJ(B).94.
138. Ibid., LJ(A).v.127; LJ(B).94–95.
139. Ibid., LJ(A).v.124–26.
140. Smith, *Theory of Moral Sentiments*, I.iii.2.4.
141. Smith, *Lectures on Jurisprudence*, LJ(A).127.

validity of human political practices from within those practices themselves. Yet Smith, more keenly than Hume, realized that this approach generated conceptual complications that the idiom of opinion needed to acknowledge.

The basic problem at issue was familiar enough from Hobbes, and regarded the logic of final decision-making power. Smith noted that it was a plain fact that "The sovereign power is in all governments absolute, and as soon as the govt. is firmly established becomes liable to be controuled by no regular force."[142] This was because final decision-making authority was always needed, or else an infinite regress opened up: "if what we call the summa potestas was liable to be called to account by any man, any body of the people or the whole people, this person would be the summa potestas," and so on, hence, "we must always end in some body who have a power liable to no restriction with regard to legisle., jud., or exec. power."[143] Interestingly, this was not a practical problem in the first two stages of hunter-gatherer and shepherd societies. There, the underlying democratic nature of government meant that abusers of power could always be brought into line, because they were not in fact the summa potestas—the people as a whole were. But for modern governments—both the absolute monarchies of Europe, and the British with their hybrid constitutional settlement—this was impossible. Large-scale modern societies could not be democratic, hence there was no possibility of an inbuilt check to the wielders of power through direct popular sovereignty. There simply was no regular force for modern politics that could be established so as to control the summa potestas. Sovereignty was necessarily absolute owing to the logic of its nature, *and yet* also irreducibly open to challenge and overthrow if it failed in its basic functions, because its entire basis was the interplay of utility and authority in the opinion of the ruled.

Smith indicated that because of this effectively paradoxical situation things would generally go better when the legislative, judicial, and executive powers were separated, a point on which he agreed with Montesquieu. Absolute kings were more prone to abuses of utility (and thus more open to rebellion and overthrow, as the histories of the Turks and Russians proved) than English monarchs or republican councils, because other branches of government, or rival factions and individuals, checked the latter, whereas in the former cases there were no such restraints.[144] By separating powers between different bodies it became easier to control the necessarily absolute nature of the summa potestas, and hence to encourage it to more consistently track the interests of the people. The English constitutional settlement offered a sharp example: because sovereignty rested with the crown in parliament, it was easy to identify when one or the other branch went beyond its constitutional bounds, and

---

142. Ibid., LJ(A).v.140.
143. Ibid., LJ(A).v.140.
144. Ibid., LJ(A).v.133–34, v.138–39.

could in turn be checked by the other. This was certainly a great advantage of the English system. Yet it could only ameliorate, rather than solve, the fundamental problem. For if the crown and parliament *together* made a decision, there was no further independent regular authority to appeal to that could rule on the legitimacy or otherwise of their actions, even though all reasonable people must agree that there certainly existed *some* limits to what the sovereign power could legitimately do.[145] Smith agreed with Hume that Hobbes's solution to this issue—the stipulation that not only must sovereignty be absolute owing to its inherent logic, but that it could also never legitimately be challenged if the sovereign was indeed sovereign[146]—was no solution at all, insofar as it failed to locate the proper basis of legitimate rule in the interplay of authority *and* utility. Hobbes gave too much weight to the former, whilst also mistakenly trying to ground this in pure artifice, specifically the consent of the ruled, when in truth authority was a natural and spontaneously developed phenomenon, albeit one that interacted closely with artifices like justice and notions of allegiance (as Hume had previously maintained). Yet in abandoning the ambitions of sovereignty theory, the opinion of mankind approach had to accept that the predicament could not be solved: "on this branch of public law it is impossible to speak with any degree of precision" owing to the deep theoretical intractability of the issue.[147] Rather than seeing this as a failure of the approach, however, it is better to consider it as a reinforcement of a more fundamental contention: that philosophy cannot settle such matters for us, neither in practice, nor ultimately in theory.

Smith thus came up against the limits of philosophy in relation to politics analyzed in a purely secular mode. Hume's response to this situation had been to largely leave philosophy behind and focus on institutional design as a way of practically ameliorating the potential harms of which governments were capable, whilst providing a detailed historical framework within which

---

145. Ibid., LJ(A).v.138–43. A version of this same problem was put centre stage by Kant when he noted that "man is an animal that needs a master . . . But this master will also be an animal who needs a master. Thus while man may try as he will, it is hard to see how he can obtain for public justice a supreme authority which would itself be just, whether he seeks this authority in a single person or in a group of many persons selected for this purpose": Immanuel Kant, *Political Writings*, ed. H. S. Reiss (Cambridge: Cambridge University Press, 1970), 46. In chapter 6 I will consider Kant as examining exactly the same problems that Smith addressed.

146. It might be replied here that if a sovereign ceased to protect the subjects, then those subjects may, by Hobbes's account, legitimately mount a challenge to the sovereign's authority. This is true insofar as Hobbes is clear that protection is a necessary prerequisite of obedience being owed—but then, a sovereign who does not protect is, for Hobbes, *no sovereign at all*. If the sovereign *does* protect, then no legitimate challenge may be mounted, no matter how badly the utility of the subjects is otherwise being secured.

147. Smith, *Lectures on Jurisprudence*, LJ(B).91.

to understand Britain's situation in particular.[148] Smith followed this example at great length in the *Wealth of Nations*.[149] His "very violent attack on the commercial system of Great Britain" can in large measure be read as an attempt to provide complex institutional remedies for the problems created by bad government, especially as founded upon faulty understandings of the operations of commerce.[150] But at the very end of his life Smith also offered another response to the predicament of human politics in a world where philosophy cannot provide decisive final answers. That response is examined in the final chapter.

148. Most centrally that "it is . . . a just political maxim, that every man must be supposed a knave: Though at the same time, it appears somewhat strange, that a maxim should be true in politics, which is false in fact," with institutions to be designed accordingly, in preemptive efforts at damage control: Hume, "Of the Independency of Parliament," in *Essays*, 42. The Tudor and Stuart portions of Hume's *History of England* can be read as offering the necessary historical background for a proper deployment of the modern science of politics that Hume claimed to be putting forward in the *Essays*.

149. On some of the specific differences between Hume's and Smith's approaches, however, see Robertson, "Scottish Political Economy."

150. Adam Smith, "Letter to Holt," in *The Correspondence of Adam Smith*, ed. E. C. Mosner and I. S. Ross (Oxford: Oxford University Press, 1987), 251. On Smith's *Wealth of Nations* as suggesting careful institutional reform, see especially Pitts, *Turn to Empire*, chap. 2; Sankar Muthu, "Adam Smith's Critique of International Trading Companies: Theorizing 'Globalization' in the Age of Enlightenment." *Political Theory* 36 (2008), 185–212; Hont, "'Unnatural and Retrograde' Order"; Donald Winch, *Riches and Poverty: An Intellectual History of Political Economy in Britain, 1750–1834* (Cambridge: Cambridge University Press, 1996), chaps. 1–3.

CHAPTER SIX

Alternatives and Applications

A Theory of the State?

THERE IS SOMETHING necessarily paradoxical in the claim that Hume and Smith offer theories of the state without sovereignty. This is not, as might be supposed, because theorizing the modern state necessarily requires reference to sovereignty. One of Hume's most penetrating suggestions, adopted by Smith, is that this simply is not the case once we are clear on how to think philosophically in a world governed by opinion. It is instead because they decrease the role of theory itself in the philosophical understanding of politics.

In Hume's phrase, the "established practice of the age" gives both the content, and the conditions of meaning and possibility, for politics in any given time and place.[1] It is only by studying that practice, in particular the form and nature of the opinion that underpins it, that we can come to any worthwhile understanding of politics. The job of the theorist is not to delineate the necessary features of some concept (say, the state) from the armchair, with some allegedly necessary condition annexed to it (say, sovereignty), before adjudicating whether this entity obtains in the world, and praising or impugning actual arrangements accordingly. The job of the theorist is to pay close attention to the forms that politics actually takes, and work from what is given to understand what must—and perhaps might—be in any given context. This vision of political philosophy thereby reverses the typical direction of judgment found in theoretical accounts, in part by elevating the importance of history and practice over that of theory.

But as a consequence Hume's and Smith's theorizations of the state must be reconstructed from what they tell us are the necessary features of the practice of the age, rather than being supplied prepackaged for ready consumption

---

1. David Hume, *The History of England from the Invasion of Julius Caesar to the Revolution in 1688*, foreword by William B. Todd (Indianapolis: Liberty Fund, 1983), vol. 2, 525.

and with minimal judgment on our behalf. Both thinkers believed that organized modern politics is centrally the arrangement by which coercive power is founded upon opinion, and brought to bear for the regulation of property combined with the successful facilitating of large-scale projects—in a word, government. Yet the *specific form* that government can take in modern conditions is variable, and such variability must be acknowledged in understanding the modern state as an inevitably protean entity. Although Hume proclaimed a free government with a mixed constitution of the eighteenth-century English sort to be the best political arrangement, it did not follow that other arrangements thereby fell short of being government proper, something with which Smith agreed.[2] An adequate understanding of the state from a perspective like Hume and Smith's must recognize a plurality of forms of constitutional arrangements as capable of fulfilling the functions of government, each in turn legitimately and successfully claiming the "blind submission" of subjects, as determined by opinion.[3]

Hume and Smith both recognized, however, that the "practice of the age" was in significant transition at the time they were writing. Hume considered his own science of politics as ideally placed to give advice for the improvement of constitutional arrangements in changing times, as well as offering an enhanced understanding of how government could best operate in modern conditions.[4] Most importantly, the age of political virtue was definitively over (if indeed it had ever really obtained, rather than being a series of false conceptions generated by earlier writers' lack of a proper science of politics).[5] Good government depended upon neither the moral character of the citizen body, nor the virtue of its leaders. Instead, the starting point of good political organization should be the assumption—false in fact but true in theory—that every man is a knave. In turn, the central political task was to construct robust institutions sufficiently well designed to control, and ideally redirect, knavish behavior to the good of all, with any virtuous conduct a welcome additional benefit.[6] Likewise, whilst faction and party were inevitable human political tendencies, and the dangers they threw up very real, rather than seeking their

---

2. David Hume, "That Politics May Be Reduced to a Science," in *Essays Moral, Political and Literary*, ed. E. F. Miller (Indianapolis: Liberty Fund, 1985), 18.

3. David Hume, *The Clarendon Edition of the Works of David Hume: A Treatise of Human Nature*, ed. D. F. Norton and M. J. Norton (Oxford: Oxford University Press, 2007), T.3.2.10.2, SBN 554.

4. This, after all, is part of the reason why Hume offered his political ideas to a wider public in the more accessible form of the *Essays*, following the commercial disappointment of the more densely argued and intellectually forbidding *Treatise*.

5. Hume, "Reduced to a Science," 21–23; "Of Civil Liberty," in *Essays*, 88. On Hume's break with the classical republican, or civic humanist, tradition see James Moore, "Hume's Political Science and the Classical Republican Tradition," *Canadian Journal of Political Science* 10 (1977), 809–40.

6. Hume, "Of the Independency of Parliament," in *Essays*, 42–44.

elimination, modern political practice required their being harnessed and controlled for collective benefit and safety.⁷ The foundation of successful modern government was the construction of good institutions capable of balancing the "perpetual intestine struggle, open or secret, between AUTHORITY and LIBERTY," neither of which must "ever absolutely prevail in the contest" or else government would defeat the purpose for which it was ordained—i.e., the promotion of utility.⁸ Theorizing the modern state from Hume's perspective thus requires appreciating the institutional governmental mechanisms by which utility is successfully promoted, authority secured, and liberty protected whilst also limited.⁹ In essence, we can therefore say that for Hume—and after him, for Smith—the modern state is that institutionally ordered human community that (successfully) organizes and coordinates the promotion of utility within a certain territory.¹⁰

As Hume's later essays would make clear, an emphasis on institutions promoting utility in conditions of commercial modernity required an examination of government's role in administering economic affairs, not only as a central domestic political concern, but also under the pressures of international

---

7. Hume, "Of Parties in General," "Of the Parties of Great Britain," and "Of Superstition and Enthusiasm," in *Essays*, 54–63, 64–72, 73–79.

8. Hume, "Of the Origin of Government," in *Essays*, 40.

9. István Hont, "Commercial Society and Political Theory in the Eighteenth Century: The Problem of Authority in David Hume and Adam Smith," in *Main Trends in Cultural History: Ten Essays* ed. W. Melching and W. Velema (Amsterdam: Rodopi, 1994), 78–79. Hume's emphasis on the centrality of institutions passed into political practice via the founding of the United States of America, the victory of the Federalist cause in the post-revolutionary period ensuring that control of faction, the pitting of ambition against ambition, and the imposition of constitutional limits upon government were all made central to American government. Federalists like Alexander Hamilton and (the early) James Madison were close readers of Hume, and it was his emphasis on institutions that they followed. See James Madison, John Jay, and Alexander Hamilton, *The Federalist*, ed. G. W. Carey and J. McClellan (Indianapolis: Liberty Fund, 2001); Mark G. Spencer, "Hume and Madison on Faction," *William and Mary Quarterly* 59 (2002), 869–96; Colleen A. Sheehan, "Madison v. Hamilton: The Battle over Republicanism and the Role of Public Opinion," *American Political Science Review* 98 (2004), 405–24; Alan Gibson, "Veneration and Vigilance: James Madison and Public Opinion, 1785–1800," *Review of Politics* 67 (2005), 5–35.

10. Given Hume and Smith's shared account of how legitimate authority is generated by the successful delivery of utility, this definition is therefore in effect coterminous with the famous definition of Weber's upon which I have modeled it: "a state is that human community which (successfully) lays claim to the monopoly of legitimate physical violence within a certain territory": Max Weber, "The Profession and Vocation of Politics," in *Political Writings*, ed. P. Lassman and R. Speirs (Cambridge: Cambridge University Press, 1994), 310. Analytically speaking (if not historically), this is no coincidence. Weber, like Hume and Smith, is a theorist of opinion, for whom the conditions of legitimate authority are determined internally by the imagination of a thinking citizenry, although Weber emphasized the importance of charisma and demagoguery far more than did Hume and Smith.

competition. "Jealousy of trade" meant that domestic political actors could not simply outlaw economic activity of which they disapproved, owing to the irreducibly cross-border nature of modern commerce. Furthermore, the permanent imperatives of politics—in particular the struggle for international supremacy, as well as the constant need to provide domestic security and prosperity—dominated the logic of economics, with the latter being made subservient to the former.[11] This made for a volatile cocktail of pressures toward bellicosity, with jealous states pressured into undermining their neighbors for short-term advantage rather than opting for the long-term benefits of reciprocal economic exchange that might require loss of relative standing. The innovation of public credit dangerously enhanced the capacity for modern governments to borrow in order to finance aggressive military and economic competition, whilst the cross-generational nature of national debt tied successive administrations together. From the perspective of the twenty-first century, Hume's insistence that "the nation must destroy public credit, or public credit must destroy the nation" may appear misguided.[12] Yet the recognition that public credit lies at the heart of the "practice of the age"—which has become only more international since the eighteenth century—and that our understanding of the modern state must make this fact central, is as vital today as it was then.[13]

Yet although Hume and Smith offer rich resources for coming to understand the practice of our age, we remain separated from their perspective by an unbridgeable historical distance. The practice of our age, here and now, contains at least three central factors that emerged after the eighteenth century, regarding which we cannot look to Hume and Smith for direct guidance.

11. See especially David Hume, "Of Commerce," "Of Refinement in the Arts," "Of the Balance of Trade," "Of the Jealousy of Trade," and "Of the Balance of Power," in *Essays*, 253–67, 268–80, 308–26, 327–31, 332–41; and in contemporary scholarship most centrally István Hont, "Jealousy of Trade: An Introduction," in *Jealousy of Trade: International Competition and the Nation State in Historical Perspective* (Cambridge, MA: Belknap Harvard, 2005), especially 1–37.

12. David Hume, "Of Public Credit," in *Essays*, 360–61. Appearances, however, may be deceptive: see István Hont, "The Rhapsody of Public Debt: David Hume and Voluntary State Bankruptcy," in *Jealousy of Trade*, especially 348–53.

13. This fact has been emphasized by Quentin Skinner, who has called for a revival of Hobbes's theory of state personality as a way of coherently conceptualizing national debt over time, in both political theory and practice. Whether this is a realistic prospect for the current practice of the age is a question those persuaded by Hume will want to press against Skinner. See Quentin Skinner, "A Genealogy of the Modern State," *Proceedings of the British Academy* 162 (2009), 360–64. Regarding the centrality of public debt to the formation of modern politics, see Michael Sonenscher, *Before the Deluge: Public Debt, Inequality, and the Intellectual Origins of the French Revolution* (Princeton, NJ: Princeton University Press, 2009); Isaac Nakhimovsky, *The Closed Commercial State: Perpetual Peace and Commercial Society from Rousseau to Fichte* (Princeton, NJ: Princeton University Press, 2011).

Perhaps most important is the rise of modern mass democracy based on electoral representation. Politics may now be more obviously than ever a function of opinion (though that fact itself is, from a Humean perspective, only a superficial change), but there is nothing obvious about the complexity and importance of democracy's current triumph, both as the only legitimate form of government (at least from a Western perspective) recognized in the world today, and as a paramount moral and political value in its own right.[14] Similarly, Hume's emphasis on government by well-designed institutions may have become widely accepted, in practice if not always in theory.[15] Yet Hume could not foresee the rise of complex modern bureaucracies as integral to the administration of mass government, or the significance of this for the practice of politics. The ideal of the *Rechtsstaat*—of the empire of laws and not of men—may have been an eighteenth-century vision, but it was a nineteenth-century accomplishment, achieved via bureaucratic specialization and the professionalization of governmental functions, the consequences of which are still not particularly well understood in political theory.[16] Finally, the modern state is now intertwined with a concept that postdates Hume and Smith: that of the nation understood in terms of ethnic identity. The idea of the modern state cannot be cleanly detached from that of the *nation-state*, another nineteenth-century innovation, but one with dramatic warnings from the twentieth century regarding its potency and danger.[17]

---

14. John Dunn, *Setting the People Free: The Story of Democracy* (London: Atlantic, 2005), 15–21.

15. Jeremy Waldron has recently called for contemporary political theory to move away from the currently predominant study of values, and return to an emphasis on the central importance of political institutions, with explicit reference to Hume as offering valuable guidance on this matter. Jeremy Waldron, "*Political* Political Theory: An Inaugural Lecture," *Journal of Political Philosophy* 21 (2013), 2–23.

16. Max Weber remains a most useful guide on these matters, especially "Parliament and Government in Germany under a New Order," in *Political Writings*, and "Profession and Vocation of Politics," 130–271, and also "Bureaucracy," in *From Max Weber: Essays in Sociology*, ed. H. H. Gerth and C. Wright Mills (Abingdon: Routledge, 1948), 196–244. But we need to acknowledge not just the impact of bureaucracy upon the processes of "grand" politics, but also the more mundane—yet hugely impactful—features of bureaucracy as the method via which the state implements its directives and decisions in the lives of ordinary citizens. In this regard, recent work on the practicality and difficult demands made of ordinary officialdom is important, especially Mark Philp, *Political Conduct* (Cambridge, MA: Harvard University Press, 2007), chap. 7; Bernardo Zack, *When the State Meets the Street: Moral Agency and Discretionary Power at the Frontlines of Public Service* (Cambridge, MA: Harvard University Press, 2017), as is awareness of more "classic" explorations such as James Q. Wilson, *Bureaucracy: What Government Agencies Do and Why They Do It* (New York: Basic Books, 1989).

17. See especially István Hont, "The Permanent Crisis of a Divided Mankind: 'Nation-State' and 'Nationalism' in Historical Perspective," in *Jealousy of Trade*, 447–528.

[216] CHAPTER SIX

Neither Hume nor Smith can offer direct guidance with regard to these now ineliminable features of modernity, and we will look to them in vain if seeking a prefabricated theory of the state. What we can look to them for, however, is guidance regarding how to think carefully about the facts of the practice of our age as we find it now. Perhaps more than with other political thinkers in the history of ideas, a careful recovery of their writings supports Quentin Skinner's suggestion that "rather than looking for directly applicable 'lessons' in the history of philosophy, we shall do better to learn to do our own thinking for ourselves."[18] Indeed, the suggestion that we do our own thinking for ourselves, albeit for rather different reasons to Skinner's, could serve as a summary of Hume's and Smith's principal practical lessons. In this vein, however, two particular examples of how we can use Hume and Smith's reconfiguration for understanding the state are worth spelling out in terms of the implications for contemporary analysis, which might otherwise be missed or misunderstood, and which may serve as illustrations for how thinking with eighteenth-century texts can improve twenty-first century perspectives.

The first relates to one of the items mentioned above: the place of democracy in modern politics. In chapter 5 we saw that Smith's historically embedded analysis of the rise of modern government out of a collapsed feudal inheritance led him to claim that democracy was a form of rule impossible for the large-scale commercial (and slave-free) states of European modernity. To our eyes this may seem to make Smith immediately irrelevant: Aren't we all democrats now? But the opposite should be true. What we ought to appreciate is that Smith was *right* that democracy, upon his understanding of what that would have to involve, was impossible for the modern world. Accordingly, what we now call democracy is something very different from what Smith believed had ever obtained before. That insight alone should perhaps not be surprising, but what comes in its wake is the suggestion that modern democracy is therefore something *newer* than often supposed, even by those already receptive to the notion that the political systems of the modern West are novel arrangements that share the epithet and label of democracy with ancient forms of government only in name. Modern electoral democracy is of course widely realized not to be ancient democracy, primarily by virtue of the fact that it is representative.[19] But Smith's analysis suggests that not only is modern democracy not some weak aping of an "original" or "pure" premodern

---

18. Quentin Skinner, "Meaning and Understanding in the History of Ideas," in *Visions of Politics*, vol. 1, *Regarding Method* (Cambridge: Cambridge University Press, 2002), 88.

19. As two recent commentators observe, "It is impossible to conceive of political institutions on the scale and power of modern states without making use of the idea of representation": Mónica Brito Vieira and David Runciman, *Representation* (Cambridge: Polity, 2008), 4. Brito Vieira and Runciman go on to argue that rather than seeing representation as a qualification of democracy, representation is the central idea of modern politics, which enables a new and modern theory and practice of democracy, although they trace an in-

direct version—it is something wholly new and to be assessed in its own right on its own terms—but, moreover, neither is it *early* modern in genesis. Smith's analysis suggests that the phenomenon of representation is a practice of the age developed through the contestations of politics that would happen owing to the demographic, economic, and political pressures of complex societal processes in the two centuries *after* he wrote, not as an outgrowth of philosophical and legal theories inherited from earlier periods. In short, if Smith is right in the history he tells, then our present mode of government does not have the long pedigree in philosophical Enlightenment thought that is often claimed for it, but is much more mundanely political in origin, having its origin in the developments of the nineteenth and twentieth centuries. This results in another reason to resist going back to Hobbes in our attempts at political self-understanding. A Smithean view of political history and its contingent evolution allows us to see that the emergence of mass democracy in the Western world had very little (if anything) to do with an early modern legalistic theory of representation, and infinitely more to do with real processes of politics battled and fought for on the streets, as well as in legislatures, law courts, and newspapers, before it eventually, haltingly, became a reality. Hobbes was an outstanding philosophical theorist of representation. But the electoral representation we muddle by with today has an entirely different, and later, provenance. Reading Smith cannot by itself enable us to understand or analyze that later provenance, but it does encourage us to look in more revealing places. If we want to understand how and why what we now call democracy came to be, the nineteenth and twentieth centuries are where we must focus, not the seventeenth or eighteenth, let alone earlier.

The second point of consideration for how Hume and Smith's reconfiguration of the theory of the state has contemporary relevance relates to how we may come to conceive of the normative purposes and possibilities that the modern state encompasses. What follows are, admittedly, polemical claims. The riposte to them will likely be that I fail to distinguish between the grubby reality of how politics happens to be, and the moral imperatives of how it *ought* to be; that even if a Humean or Smithean way of looking at the world ends up being right about how modern politics in fact is, that does not impugn the validity of taking a moral stance for advocating change—and that this change is required and justified simply as it stands, the moral critique legitimate even if any change is impossible. Deep questions are raised here about the relationship of politics to morality, of the nature of practical judgment, and how to bring about real change; in short, of theory to practice. It would be folly to embark upon an attempt to answer such questions here, though they are

---

tellectual lineage for this concept back to Hobbes (and beyond), which I suggest is neither necessary nor helpful.

doubtless connected to the recent development of "realistic" political theory.[20] All I will say in my defense is that insofar as one is genuinely interested in *politics*, and not some idealized moral imagining of how the world might fancifully be, but which we know full well it is never going to be, Hume and Smith can serve as a helpful guides for beginning to get to grips with some of the problems that arise.[21] A more deeply historical understanding of the modern state—which is clearly lacking in a great deal of contemporary political theory, but is one of the main outcomes of Hume's and Smith's analyses—is likely to be a productive way forward for those who wish to return political theory to an emphasis on what is, mundanely speaking, politics.[22]

In that spirit, I suggest that the insistence that the modern state is an outgrowth of commercial sociability, and that its chief function, and ultimate source of legitimacy, is the promotion of utility whilst securing the allegiance of subjects through opinion, stands as a potentially disruptive claim with regard to the majority of normative political theorizing today. To see why, consider the following: It is an irony that the famous opening sentence of John Rawls's *A Theory of Justice* initially looks as though it might capture something akin to Hume and Smith's outlook, whilst in fact introducing a very different philosophical vision. After all, "Justice is the first virtue of social institutions, as truth is of systems of thought" might read like Hume's or Smith's slogan, if by "justice" is understood the coordination of utility seeking via artificial conventions, essential for the maintenance of large and lasting society—in Smith's phrase, the "pillar" that holds up the edifice of advanced civilized living.[23] But by "justice" Rawls meant something different. For him, justice pertained to the structural constraints that a society must operate under if it was to be considered acceptable in terms of a moral judgment derived via a procedure of impartial consideration, which he famously claimed generated specific recommendations regarding the equal shared liberties that were to be afforded to

---

20. See most especially Williams, *In the Beginning Was the Deed: Realism and Moralism in Political Argument*, ed. G Hawthorn (Princeton, NJ: Princeton University Press, 2005), and Raymond Geuss, *Philosophy and Real Politics* (Princeton, NJ: Princeton University Press, 2008), but also William Galston, "Realism in Political Theory," *European Journal of Political Theory* 9, no. 4 (2010), 385–411; Matt Sleat, *Liberal Realism: A Realist Theory of Liberal Politics* (Manchester: Manchester University Press, 2013); Waldron, "Political Theory"; Matt Sleat and Enzo Rossi, "Realism in Normative Political Theory," *Philosophy Compass* 9, no. 10 (2014), 689–701; Edward Hall, "How to Do Realistic Political Theory (and Why You Might Want To)," *European Journal of Political Theory* (forthcoming).

21. I have attempted precisely this in Paul Sagar, "Legitimacy and Domination," in *Politics Recovered: Essays in Realist Political Theory*, ed. M. Sleat (forthcoming). See also Rob Jubb, "The Real Value of Equality," *Journal of Politics* 77 (2015), 679–91.

22. That "realistic" political theory is a *return* to an older approach, rather than a new innovation departing from a post-Rawlsian twentieth-century norm, is helpfully emphasized in Sleat and Rossi, "Realism in Normative Political Theory," 696–97.

23. John Rawls, *A Theory of Justice* (Oxford: Oxford University Press, 1971), 3.

all citizens, and the basic entitlements to material resources (and by extension, correlate permissible levels of inequality) that all were due as a matter of fairness. The central function of the state from a Rawlsian point of view is to act in accordance with these revealed moral imperatives, and attempt as far as possible to uphold them, and thus realize a just (in his specific moralized sense) society.[24] As the second sentence of *A Theory of Justice* made clear, "laws and institutions no matter how efficient and well-arranged must be reformed or abolished if they are unjust."[25] The majority of anglophone normative political theorists after Rawls, even when they disagree severely with Rawls's specific positions, have nonetheless followed this essential vision of the institutions of the state as primarily being for the promotion of specifically moral ends, or whose legitimacy and purpose is centrally conditioned by the extent to which they conform to independent moral constraints, both at home and increasingly (in the ever-expanding "global-justice" literature) abroad.

That Hume and Smith's vision of the state is disruptive of this sort of view is best seen if we put the matter in roughly eighteenth-century terms. If the basis of modern society is commercial sociability—i.e., the mutual pursuit of utility—with the state a contingently shaped historical outgrowth for the coordinating of that utility, then modern large-scale societies are arrangements not of mutual benevolence, but of mutual self-interest.[26] The state's role in this is to facilitate the promotion of utility (still understood in its broad, eighteenth-century, pre-Utilitarianism meaning), whilst stabilizing the domestic arena and facilitating, as far as possible, international security. Insofar as these

---

24. For Rawls's theory as a "structuralist" version of political moralism, see Williams, *In the Beginning*, 1–2.

25. Rawls, *Theory of Justice*, 3.

26. This point stands even if it is replied that from Rawls's point of view, his project may be described as one of mutual self-interest, insofar as his constraints on how institutions may act with regard to the basic structure are supposed to be compatible with moderate scarcity and limited altruism (his famous "circumstances of justice," themselves presented as a gloss on Hume's theory of justice: ibid., 126–30). This is because the *commitment* to justice that Rawls posits is supposed to be an outgrowth of the particular sets of commitments and judgments individuals will develop in a just society. But from Hume and Smith's commercial-sociability perspective, this level of commitment to justice, the ethos of a just society without which Rawls's institutional structures cannot function (e.g. ibid., chap. 8, passim), can be generated only by a sense of what is owed to others, which in practice would require a level of (in eighteenth-century terms) benevolence not in fact exhibited by disparate utility-seeking members of large and lasting associations. So whilst Rawls may be read as in effect criticizing utilitarianism for treating society as effectively one person, and in turn assuming an impossible level of benevolence as regards the institutional ordering of political affairs (ibid., 22–33), essentially the same charge may be leveled at Rawls if one adopts a commercial-sociability perspective. The commitment to justice he demands could only be generated by high levels of benevolence (even if this is presented in the language of duties and rational requirement), and we have good reason to believe that such levels are simply not forthcoming, and never will be.

things are achieved, the agencies of the state may of course pursue goals beyond simply creating a benign environment for the individual pursuit of utility. But these are not essential to its purpose, nor ultimately the conditions upon which subject populations will judge it as succeeding or failing. It is true that in the past six decades the remit of many economically advanced Western states has been expanded to include the provision of more or less basic welfare safety nets and entitlements (varying in extent from country to country) that have done much to alleviate poverty, destitution, and suffering. To a certain extent, the provision of such measures has become a part of the practice of the age, and present opinion confers legitimacy on state institutions insofar as these things are secured to a sufficient degree.[27] But the existence of the postwar welfare state is quite compatible with a Humean or Smithean understanding of the state when put it in its proper historical context. In this, Tony Judt is an instructive voice:

> The twentieth-century "socialist" welfare states were constructed not as an advance guard of egalitarian revolution but to provide a barrier against the return of the past: against economic depression and its polarizing, violent political outcome in the desperate politics of Fascism and Communism alike. The welfare states were thus *prophylactic* states. They were designed quite consciously to meet the widespread yearning for security and stability that John Maynard Keynes and others foresaw long before the end of World War II, and they succeeded beyond anyone's expectations. Thanks to a half-century of prosperity and safety, we in the West have forgotten the political and social traumas of mass insecurity. And thus we have forgotten why we have inherited those welfare states and what brought them about.[28]

Judt's suggestion is that we see Western welfare states as in important measure a response to the external threat of fascism and the internal threat of communism, defensive reactions to prevent a repeat of the horrors of total war born of economic turmoil, and to stifle the growth of domestic subversives feeding on destitution and suffering. That is, political responses to contingent circumstances. Now that those circumstances have changed, and liberal capitalism stands more or less unchallenged in terms of genuinely viable political alternatives in the West, what we see all around us is the dismantling of the welfare state increasing apace, and the general, if not complete, reversion of the state to its function of the promotion of utility in terms of allowing agents to pursue it themselves—i.e., the acceptance of what we now call capitalism as the

---

27. On this see especially Jubb, "Real Value of Equality."
28. Tony Judt, *Reappraisals: Reflections on the Forgotten Twentieth Century* (London: Vintage, 2008), 10.

mode of organizing the economy—but without providing extensive succor for those who come out on the losing end of market competition. This is because what societies built on mutual self-interest lack is, precisely, extensive mutual benevolence: the desire to give up what one has for the good of unknown others in the absence of self-interested pressures (most especially war and the threat of revolution) to do so, whilst also losing the apparently transient socioeconomic infrastructure of the twentieth century that created a sense of shared endeavor and solidarity for leftist reform programs (for example the decline of a male-dominated manual working class that provided an experience of solidarity that social democrats could draw on electorally). Hence popular support for welfare measures fades, whilst peoples who have a strong tendency to sympathize with the (imagined) pleasures of the rich and powerful will tend to defer to their direction thanks to the play-out of the psychology of authority, whilst caring little for the sufferings of less fortunate others so long as they are sufficiently removed from immediate view. A residual welfare state may remain as a minimalist prophylactic against severe social unrest—but that is likely, to put it bluntly, to be more about riot prevention than the realization of an abstract ideal of what distributive justice "demands" or "requires" of us.

This is only a sketch of one way to go about answering what is inevitably a highly complex historical question. And there is no denying that this is a *bleak* answer. My aim is not to celebrate this state of affairs, only to suggest what may unfortunately be true both about where we are, and about where we can realistically expect to end up. What I have supplied above is, of course, only a very basic sketch for explaining modern politics from a commercial-sociability perspective of the sort found in Hume and Smith. Admittedly, one thing that both Hume and Smith teach us is that history is always far more complicated than it seems: these very general claims can only be the start of an analysis, not its conclusion. Nonetheless, looking at matters this way offers potential answers to a particularly striking fact: that since the publication of Rawls's famous and influential (at least, in the academy) book in 1971, in distributive terms Western states have moved ever further away from, not closer to, his ideal of a just society, despite the concomitant explosion of normative anglophone theory, generally calling for vastly more egalitarian arrangements than our societies exhibit at present. The answer may be that Rawls, and those who work in his general mode (even if not in agreement with his specific methods or conclusions), mistake a relatively contingent and transient historical development—the emergence of a welfare state of varying degrees of comprehensiveness in the Western world—for a permanent and central function of the modern state. Taking a longer historical perspective encourages us to see the welfare states of the postwar West as an aberration in the development of commercial society produced by the peculiar upheavals of the mid-twentieth century, now in a process of decay and concomitant downscaling.[29] It does not follow that they will disappear, and indeed may continue to function in more limited capacities for some time to come. But we should not expect them to survive or expand simply because they now exist. On the contrary, under the pressures of severe global economic competition (likely to be exacerbated by climate change), mass movements of peoples, ageing populations, and unwillingness amongst electorates to pay the high levels of taxation required to fund them—i.e., factors that make "benevolence" even weaker in large-scale political arrangements than it would already be—welfare states will require a concerted level of support via recognition of the fact that they are *not* a necessary part of the modern state, and thus will need to be defended precisely because they can be lost. Of course, whether it will turn out to be possible to mount that defense successfully is a question only time will answer. If recent developments are much to go by, there appears little room for truthful optimism. But in any case, Rawls's continued insistence until the end of his life that welfare-state capitalism was not an adequately just arrangement—with either "property-owning democracy" or "liberal (democratic) socialism" being required instead—has something of the Owl of Minerva about it: a vision of a more just society taking flight when the conditions for such a thing were increasingly being lost.[30] By extension, so much recent anglophone political theory emerges as not just obviously ineffectual in terms of encouraging change—something partly due to the innate practical inefficacy of philosophical analysis, as well as misidentification of the central item to be analyzed—but also as *parochial*. Despite characteristic pretensions of appeal to timeless or objective moral values, so much normative political theory of the past four decades may turn out to be the well-meaning, but ultimately misguided, attempts to articulate what societies of mutual benevolence would do if run by appropriately benevolent administrators (to put the matter once more in eighteenth-century terms).[31] As it becomes ever clearer that ours are societies

---

29. For evidence and argument that this is indeed the long-term trajectory, see Thomas Piketty, *Capital in the Twenty-First Century* (Cambridge, MA: Belknap Harvard, 2014).

30. John Rawls, *Justice as Fairness: A Restatement* (Cambridge, MA: Harvard University Press, 2001), 135–38.

31. That defenders of such approaches would object that their proposals have nothing to do with "benevolence" but are demanded by reason, impartiality, fairness, justice, equality, and so on, underlies the parochialism of the perspective as brought out by a comparison with eighteenth-century debates rooted in sociability. For the point is that whatever the putative philosophical *justifications* for moral reforms to politics, the *motivations* that would actually need to be activated in the individuals required to administer and live under such reforms would need to be those of self-sacrifice and generosity to others—in a word, benevolence. Yet if Hume and Smith are right that large and lasting society is held together not by benevolence, but utility, then such projects are doomed from the get-go, in terms of having any real traction on the societies we are compelled to live in.

of mutual self-interest, well-meaning intentions may not be enough to save such approaches from the harsh judgment of later intellectual history.

In what remains of this chapter, however, I leave such difficult matters aside, requiring as they do more detailed treatment in order to yield satisfactory answers than can be achieved here. Instead, I argue for Hume and Smith's approach to the theory of the state as superior to the Hobbesian competitor idiom as exemplified in particular by Immanuel Kant, and examined with specific reference to the question of how to constrain and guide the judgment of rulers regarding the dangers associated with political reform. Kant's writings have been vastly more influential than Hume's and Smith's in both morals and politics, but it is not clear that he had the more plausible vision for how to deal with the difficulties arising from practical political decision making. After considering this, I turn in conclusion to defend Hume and Smith's vision of politics from what might be thought its most pressing philosophical challenge: the charge that their approach leaves us in a position of existential vulnerability, unable to properly account for the demands that we need to make of a fully normative theory of politics. Despair on this score, I suggest, is misplaced.

Political Judgment: Smith vs. Kant

The deeply Hobbesian character of Kant's political theory is widely recognized.[32] It is precisely this feature of his writings that makes putting him into dialogue with Smith in particular especially fruitful. This is because both thinkers tackled the same problems relating to the role of judgment and the need for reform in politics, but did so from alternative philosophical outlooks.[33]

A full-scale analysis of Kant's political theory is beyond the scope of the present work, requiring as it would not just a detailed examination of the "doctrine of public right" as found in the *Metaphysics of Morals*, but an integration of this with Kant's wider metaphysical framework, which undergirds his concept of right and the ability to deduce political conclusions based on a priori considerations, as well as his innovative development of the sovereignty-government distinction, and his complex considerations of the nature of

---

32. Jeremy Waldron, *The Dignity of Legislation* (Oxford: Oxford University Press, 1999), chap. 3; Richard Tuck, *The Rights of War and Peace: Political Thought and the International Order from Grotius to Kant* (Oxford: Oxford University Press, 1999), 207–25; Christopher Meckstroth, *The Struggle for Democracy: Paradoxes of Progress and the Politics of Change* (Oxford: Oxford University Press, 2015), 118–27.

33. Hont has claimed that there is a "tremendous synergy" between Smith's and Kant's work on this score. By contrast, I believe that they finally diverge on crucial matters, and that Smith—not Kant—emerges as the more helpful guide. István Hont, "Adam Smith's History of Law and Government as Political Theory," in *Political Judgment: Essays for John Dunn*, ed. R. Bourke and R. Geuss (Cambridge: Cambridge University Press, 2009), 169.

representation and republican government.[34] Nonetheless, we can usefully compare Kant's essay "On the Common Saying: That May Be Correct in Theory, but It Is of No Use in Practice" with "Of the Order in which Societies Are by Nature Recommended to Our Beneficence," part 6, chapter 2, of the *Theory of Moral Sentiments*, added to the sixth and final 1790 edition. Doing so reveals that Kant and Smith tackled exactly the same problem regarding the judgment of rulers with regard to political reform. What I suggest, however, is that Kant's attempt to give theory a critical edge in the practice of rule cannot get us further than Smith's appeal to the necessity of responsibility in political leadership, and indeed potentially jeopardizes the very real and meaningful measures that Smith put center stage.[35]

In "Of the Order in which Societies Are by Nature Recommended to Our Beneficence," Smith presents what he takes to be the central problem of politics. Firstly, the state is identified simply as the aggregate of "different orders and societies which compose it," with the constitution of any state consisting of "the particular distribution which has been made of their respective powers, privileges, and immunities."[36] Whether a constitution is stable depends upon the capacity for the different orders of society to check each other peacefully, with a constitution being altered "whenever any of its subordinate parts is either raised above or depressed below whatever had been its former rank and condition."[37] Fortunately, this tends to promote stability as each order is partial to its own privileges and inherently suspicious of any changes that might

---

34. As Kant makes clear in the *Metaphysics of Morals*, his view of freedom entails that certain applications of coercion do not interfere with freedom, but in fact enable it, and are thus authorized as a matter of right. This provides the basis for both public right, and the legitimacy of its coercive enforcement. Accordingly, the wider doctrine of right is crucially dependent upon Kant's conception of freedom, and hence his critical transcendental metaphysics: Immanuel Kant, "The Metaphysics of Morals," in *Practical Philosophy*, ed. M. J. Gregor (Cambridge: Cambridge University Press, 1996), 388. Regarding representation and republics, see "Metaphysics of Morals," 478–81. On adaptation of the sovereignty-government distinction, see Immanuel Kant, "Toward Perpetual Peace," in *Practical Philosophy*, 324–25. For a full-scale examination of Kant's political thought as not attempted here, see Arthur Ripstein, *Force and Freedom: Kant's Legal and Political Philosophy* (Cambridge, MA: Harvard University Press, 2009); Elisabeth Ellis, *Kant's Politics: Provisional Theory for an Uncertain World* (New Haven: Yale University Press, 2005).

35. I thus resist Hont's suggestion that Kant's solution is "perhaps superior" to Smith's (Hont, "Smith's History of Law," 169). I here focus only on Smith and Kant with regard to judgment in matters of political reform. For a much more ambitious assessment of the two thinkers' views on judgment—especially in aesthetics and morals—see Samuel Fleischacker, *A Third Concept of Liberty: Judgment and Freedom in Kant and Adam Smith* (Princeton, NJ: Princeton University Press, 1999).

36. Adam Smith, *The Glasgow Edition of the Works and Correspondence of Adam Smith: The Theory of Moral Sentiments*, ed. D. D. Raphael and A. L. Macfie (Oxford: Oxford University Press, 1976), VI.ii.2.8.

37. Smith, *Theory of Moral Sentiments*, VI.ii.2.9.

reduce its standing: "This partiality, though it may sometimes be unjust, may not, upon that account, be useless. It checks the spirit of innovation ... it contributes in reality to the stability and permanency of the whole system."[38] This was particularly important because the question of innovation was central to understanding our most important political predicaments.

Good government, Smith claimed, rested upon two principles. First, a "certain respect and reverence for that constitution or form of government which is actually established." But second, "an earnest desire to render the condition of our fellow-citizens as safe, respectable, and happy as we can."[39] When times were quiet and peaceful the need to preserve the order of society, and the imperative to improve it when possible, harmonized, to the collective good of all. The problem was that "in times of public discontent, faction, and disorder, those two principles may draw different ways." If the existing state of society was "plainly unable to maintain the public tranquility," then some alteration was needed, and it was the duty of statesmen to try to bring it about.[40] Yet innovation, Smith explained, was inherently dangerous. Firstly, and as has long been recognized, Smith was highly skeptical of the capacity for individuals to fully comprehend, let alone safely direct, large-scale reform programs in the complex conditions of commercial modernity.[41] Interference was always prone to do more harm than good because of the sheer number of known and especially unknown variables in play. Human knowledge with regard to social and economic processes was extremely limited, and the scope for inducing bad unintended consequences great. Secondly, and as is also well known, the situation was made especially dangerous because "Amidst the turbulence and disorder of faction, a certain spirit of system is apt to mix itself with that public spirit which is founded upon the love of humanity."[42] When in the mood for introducing reform, the human psyche had a tendency to become enamored with grand schemes to sweep away existing arrangements and introduce wholesale change through the application of a preconceived plan. But the benefits of applying a preconceived system, Smith insisted, were always chimerical: a plan or system could never cope with the difficulties and complexities of the real world, and imposition would usually do more harm

38. Ibid., VI.ii.2.10.
39. Ibid., VI.ii.2.11.
40. Ibid., VI.ii.2.12.
41. Hont, "Introduction," 104–5; Samuel Fleischacker, *On Adam Smith's "Wealth of Nations": A Philosophical Companion* (Princeton, NJ: Princeton University Press, 2005), 233–36.
42. Smith, *Theory of Moral Sentiments*, VI.ii.2.13. For more detailed discussions of Smith's examination of the bad effects of the spirit of system, see Fleischacker, *Smith's "Wealth of Nations,"* chap. 11, especially 229–46; Charles L. Griswold, *Adam Smith and the Virtues of Enlightenment* (Cambridge: Cambridge University Press, 1999), chap. 7, especially 259–66, 301–10; Craig Smith, "Adam Smith: Left or Right?" *Political Studies* 61 (2013), 788–92.

than good. This chimera was particularly dangerous, however, owing to its capacity to enrage party fanaticism and impose policy via the power of faction and the groupthink mentality it fuelled and validated. "The great body of the party are commonly intoxicated with the imaginary beauty of this ideal system," meaning that even individual leaders who were wise enough to appreciate the great difficulties and dangers of introducing reform "dare not always to disappoint the expectation of their followers; but are often obliged, though contrary to their principle and their conscience, to act as if they were under the common delusion."[43]

Human politics faced an unavoidable predicament. At times of disruption and strife reform was necessary. But the introduction of any reform was inherently fraught with danger owing to the general difficulties of introducing beneficial change, and the corrosive effects of the spirit of system. Smith presented two opposed models of political leadership that could emerge in response. The first, which Smith famously condemned, was "the man of system" who "is apt to be very wise in his own conceit; and is so often enamoured with the supposed beauty of his own ideal plan of government, that he cannot suffer the smallest deviation from it." This type sought to treat the different members of a great society "with as much ease as the hand arranges the different pieces upon a chess-board." Such an approach might yield happiness and success if the principles of the "pieces" on the chessboard were fortunate enough to coincide with that of the politician—but if they diverged, "the game will go on miserably, and the society must be at all times in the highest degree of disorder."[44] The other model, which Smith presented as the desirable alternative, was of the "leader of the successful party" who "has authority enough to prevail upon his own friends to act with proper temper and moderation." Such an individual was rare because the spirit of system, combined with the spirit of faction, pushed most individuals into adopting and implementing innovations that put the public safety in jeopardy. But insofar as a leader could resist the spirit of system in both himself and his supporters, then "he may assume the greatest and noblest of character, that of the reformer and legislator of a great state; and, by the wisdom of his institutions, secure the internal tranquility and happiness of his fellow-citizens for many succeeding generations."[45]

What ultimately distinguished the one kind of leader from the other, however, was not simply the capacity to resist the dominating effects of the spirit of system, but the ability to skillfully exercise political judgment. Judgment was necessary for proper political leadership precisely because of the need to make decisions about when to preserve the constitution, and when to innovate: "In such cases, however, it often requires, perhaps, the highest effort of political

---

43. Smith, *Theory of Moral Sentiments*, VI.ii.2.15.
44. Ibid., VI.ii.2.17.
45. Ibid., VI.ii.2.14.

wisdom to determine when a real patriot ought to support and endeavour to re-establish the authority of the old system, and when he ought to give way to a more daring, but often dangerous spirit of innovation."[46] The bad political leader allowed the spirit of system to short-circuit judgment. By imposing a preconceived system of reforms, without regard for the complexity and difficulty of the real world, he avoided the immensely difficult task of thinking for himself and of taking on full responsibility for the dangers and harms he might unleash. The good leader, by contrast, recognized the dangers inherent in what must be done, and that no preconceived plan or system could adequately cope with the difficulties of decisions that must be weighed in their individual and overwhelming complexity.

Smith recognized that it was inherent to the problem of judgment that theory alone could be of no final help. To attempt to offer a theory of how leaders should judge would be to introduce the spirit of system via the back door. Nonetheless, good leaders could adopt certain guiding principles that might help them make better decisions:

> The man whose public spirit is prompted altogether by humanity and benevolence, will respect the established powers and privileges even of individuals, and still more those of the great orders and societies, into which the state is divided. Though he should consider some of them as in some measure abusive, he will content himself with moderating, what he often cannot annihilate without great violence. When he cannot conquer the rooted prejudices of the people by reason and persuasion, he will not attempt to subdue them by force; but will religiously observe what, by Cicero, is justly called the divine maxim of Plato, never to use violence to his country no more than to his parents. He will accommodate, as well as he can, his public arrangements to the confirmed habits and prejudices of the people; and will remedy as well as he can, the inconveniences which may flow from the want of those regulations which the people are averse to submit to. When he cannot establish the right, he will not disdain to ameliorate the wrong; but like Solon, when he cannot establish the best system of laws, he will endeavour to establish the best that the people can bear.[47]

It is not at all anachronistic to say that Smith insisted that good political leadership required a careful balancing act between what Max Weber would later call the "ethic of principled conviction," and the "ethic of responsibility," and on the same grounds that Weber later identified.[48] Yet Smith's arrival at this

---

46. Ibid., VI.ii.2.12.
47. Ibid.
48. Weber, "Profession and Vocation of Politics," 359.

conclusion must be recognized as deeply connected to his acceptance of opinion as the fundamental category of political analysis.[49]

In the first place, it was opinion itself that helped make the predicament of politics especially dangerous. Even those leaders who were themselves resistant to the spirit of system would often be forced to go along with it in order to retain the approval of those—both in their immediate party and in the country at large—who demanded reform as a condition of the principle of utility being met, even if such reform actually put that utility in jeopardy. Furthermore, the preponderant tendency of ordinary people to worship and admire the rich and powerful exacerbated the potential for politicians to inflict harm under the guise of doing good. Even more fundamentally than that, however, we should recognize that Smith's insistence on the importance of judgment, and his condemnation of the man of system, was a direct consequence of the limitations of human political understanding examined in chapter 5. Owing to the fact that philosophical theory was incapable of specifying the limits of legitimate political power, the onus must be placed not on theory, but on practice. The only way to secure good practice was through good judgment—but the only thing that could consistently secure *that* was a deep sense of responsibility in those who held the levers of power. The crucial condition of good statesmanship was that one try to remember to uphold "the divine maxim of Plato": that one was made for the state not the state for oneself.[50] Those enamored with the spirit of system "hold in contempt" this maxim, and for that reason ought never to be trusted or encouraged in their schemes.[51] What one must hope for instead, especially in times of crisis when reform was necessary but also especially dangerous, was the presence of leaders who took upon themselves the true difficulty and severity of what they risked. This was something regarding which a *theory* of sovereignty could offer no help—another reason why Smith, like Hume, chose to do without one.

Kant, by contrast, held out for something more than Smith thought could be had—although whether it is possible to follow him turns upon how much of his enormously ambitious wider system we are willing to endorse. In sociability theory Kant essentially sided with Hobbes on human nature, whilst invoking a novel way of explaining the paradoxical emergence of large and lasting

---

49. Here the symmetry with Weber continues. Weber, after all, was a theorist of authority who located the conditions of political legitimacy in the beliefs of those who submitted to the rule of others, making him likewise a theorist of opinion. See, for example, ibid., 309–14; and also Max Weber, "The Sociology of Charismatic Authority," in *Essays in Sociology*.

50. Compare here with Weber's "windbag," the politician who lacks a true ethic of responsibility and declares "the world . . . is stupid and base, not I," and "The responsibility for the consequences does not fall upon me but upon others whom I serve and whose stupidity I shall eradicate": Weber, *Political Writings*, 367.

51. Smith, *Theory of Moral Sentiments*, VI.ii.2.18.

society amongst creatures who were inherently antagonistic and diffident, a condition he described as "unsocial sociability." As Hobbes had taught, man wanted to live in society because it was only there that he could satisfy the craving for "honour, power or property" that "drives him to seek status among his fellows," and yet these very impulses constantly threatened "to break this society up."[52] The original union of humans was "pathological" and highly combustible, but over time gradually transformed into "a *moral* whole" that could be vindicated by independently verifiable principles. The motor of this long historical process was a teleological tendency built into nature itself: a quasi-theodicy under which humans as a species, but not necessarily as individuals, underwent gradual and continuous progress in an upward trajectory towards ever-more advanced civilized living.[53] The irony of our natural social antagonism was that competition spurred group improvement that would never have been achieved had men been socially sociable: "Nature should thus be thanked for fostering social incompatibility, enviously competitive vanity, and insatiable desires for possessions or even power. Without these desires, all man's excellent natural capacities would never be roused to develop."[54] Kant thereby retained a fundamentally Hobbesian view of humans as capable of building large and lasting society only out of the materials of honor and advantage, but grafted a commercial-sociability outcome on top of this by appealing to a providential teleology. In turn, however, he eschewed Hobbes's and Rousseau's implausible explanatory mechanisms of sovereign dictate, or mass deception, as the mode of transition from savagery to civilization (although whether Kant's historical teleology is any more plausible is, of course, quite a question).

The "moral" union that Kant envisaged as arising out of this historical process, originally founded in a "pathologically enforced social union," was not, however, given *by* that historical process.[55] Kant was a theorist of union in Hobbesian mold, but he innovated by making the idea of the contract that instantiated the union purely hypothetical, "only an idea of reason."[56] It was indubitable that all actual human political associations had come about through force and violence: there never was any original contract in real history.[57] Yet, although it was evident from experience (as Hobbes again taught) that human beings needed to be united under coercive power in order to attain peaceful and productive living, it was not experience that was the true ground of justification

---

52. Immanuel Kant, "Idea for a Universal History with a Cosmopolitan Purpose," in *Political Writings*, ed. H. S. Reiss (Cambridge: Cambridge University Press, 1970), 44.

53. Kant details his views on providence in "Perpetual Peace," 331–37.

54. Kant, "Universal History," 45.

55. Ibid., 45.

56. Immanuel Kant, "On the Common Saying: That May Be Correct in Theory, but It Is of No Use in Practice," in *Practical Philosophy*, 296.

57. Kant, "Metaphysics of Morals," 480.

for the necessity of the state: "however well disposed and law-abiding human beings might be, it still lies a priori in the rational idea of such a condition (one that is not rightful) that before the public lawful condition is established individual human beings, peoples and states can never be secure against violence from one another, since each has its own right to do *what seems right and good to it* and not to be dependent upon another's opinion about this."[58] Recognizing this fact as obtaining a priori, and not just in experience, entailed that humans had an obligation to enter into political society and submit to coercive rule, or to remain under the rule they found themselves with, not merely because it was beneficial, but because it was a duty revealed by reason in accord with humanity's status as a creature equipped with the capacity for freedom. (Hence, the underlying rationale and force of Kant's political system ultimately lay in his "critical" metaphysics.) Granting this, however, it could be concluded that although all actual states came about through violence, nonetheless the legitimacy of existing states could be established by imagining that all individuals had freely submitted themselves to live under public rule, a permissible assumption in Kant's view insofar as freely submitting in this manner was a fundamental obligation for rational creatures.

Kant concluded, however, that sovereignty must necessarily be absolute—and to that extent agreed with Hobbes. A final cite of adjudicating power was required to settle disputes, or else an infinite regress would open up and men would fall into the condition of strife and competition that they were under a rational duty to remove themselves from. The original contract must thus be imagined as stipulating that rulers be invested with absolute sovereignty so as to bring finality to decision making. This however presented a major difficulty. Having granted that man was an "animal who needs a master," the fact could not be escaped that the master must itself be a man (or group of men), and thus liable to the same "misuse of his freedom if he does not have anyone above him to apply force to him as the laws should require it." Sovereignty had to be absolute, but sovereignty was dangerous because always held by human beings, inherently liable to commit abuses. Finding a response to this predicament was "the most difficult of all tasks, and a perfect solution is impossible."[59]

Even if a "perfect" solution could not be had, in "On the Common Saying" Kant did his best to ameliorate the severity of the problem.[60] The aim of this essay was not to deny that there was an ineliminable gap between theory and

---

58. Ibid., 456.

59. Kant, "Universal History," 46.

60. Kant's discussion of the separation of powers in the *Metaphysics of Morals* and his complex ideas about representation are a clear continuation of the attempt to wrestle with this fundamental problem, which as Richard Tuck correctly notes therefore constitutes a very different theoretical enterprise from that undertaken by, e.g., Montesquieu or Madison: Tuck, *Rights of War and Peace*, 211.

practice that could only be filled by judgment: Kant was adamant that such a gap inevitably existed, and perhaps stated it more clearly than anybody else in his *Critique of the Power of Judgment*.[61] Yet Kant did wish to claim that political judgment could nonetheless be stabilized and improved by the very specific application of certain kinds of theory. Working from the claim that the original contract was a hypothetical idea used to establish the necessity and rightfulness of the existence of the coercive apparatus of the state, Kant insisted that this could also provide a "touchstone" for rulers when making decisions about how to conduct political reform. Kant disqualified a regard to the happiness or well-being of subjects as an appropriate ground for deciding what should be done, on the basis that individuals' views of this would necessarily conflict, and that it was the job of the ruler to facilitate the freedom by which individuals could pursue their own welfare, not to try to pursue it for them. Although the state was necessarily charged with securing the *salus populi*, this was a precondition of the protection and upholding of rights, not the final end of political association. Instead, rulers must ask themselves whether a particular reform could *in principle* be endorsed by all individuals subject to it, and universally assented to as such. For Kant, the "undoubted practical reality" of the hypothetical original contract was "to bind every legislator to give his laws in such a way that they *could* have arisen from the united will of a whole people and to regard each subject, insofar as he wants to be a citizen, as if he has joined in voting for such a will."[62] If a law could in principle be so endorsed— even if in practice it was opposed—then the reform could legitimately be applied as in accordance with respect for the rights and freedom of all, and if necessary coercion could legitimately be used to enforce it. Conversely, insofar as a reform met this standard, subjects were under a corresponding duty to refrain from opposing its implementation through active resistance.

Kant subtitled the section of his essay dealing with political judgment "Against Hobbes" because he wished to deny what he took to be Hobbes's proposition that subjects must silently and unquestioningly accept all decisions made by the sovereign. Against this, Kant reserved to subjects the right to oppose and criticize the sovereign's decision in writing and speech—but unambiguously drew the line there, totally prohibiting any right of active resistance or sedition.[63] The point of Kant's appeal to theory was ultimately to introduce a check on the judgment of rulers, whilst opening up a space in

---

61. Judgment, Kant famously there wrote, is "the faculty for thinking of the particular as contained under the universal": Immanuel Kant, *Critique of the Power of Judgment*, ed. P. Guyer, trans. E. Matthews (Cambridge: Cambridge University Press, 2000), 66.

62. Kant, "On the Common Saying," 296–97.

63. Ibid., 297–300; cf. Kant, "Metaphysics of Morals," 642–43. For detailed discussions of Kant's categorical denial of a right of rebellion see Katrin Filkschuh, "Reason, Right, and Revolution: Kant and Locke," *Philosophy and Public Affairs* 36, no. 4 (2008), 375–404; Christine M. Korsgaard, "Taking the Law into Our Own Hands: Kant on the Right

which that judgment could be improved by listening to the objections of the ruled, and simultaneously managing to recognize the absolute nature of sovereignty by denying any right to oppose sovereign-directed reform other than in word. Judgment was ineliminable, but theory could nonetheless stabilize practice.

That, at least, was the grand ambition. But does it really get us any further than Smith? It seems doubtful. Kant, in concluding "On the Common Saying," stated: "If there is not something that through reason compels immediate respect (such as the rights of human beings), then all influences on the choice of human beings are incapable of restraining their freedom; but if, alongside benevolence, right speaks out loudly, human nature does not show itself too depraved to listen deferentially to its voice."[64] The crucial idea being expressed here is that the power of reason can convince human agents of the duties that they owe to each other, and motivate them to act accordingly. And the stakes are clearly high in Kant's estimation: if this is not so, then nothing else will reliably suffice to restrain human wickedness, and we will be cast adrift on the unpredictable and treacherous tides of benevolence—lucky to float happily when the waters are calm, but always at the mercy of their turning murderously violent. The problem is that to share Kant's conclusion that only respect for the moral law can really secure us, one has to endorse his underlying metaphysical commitments regarding humans as free agents who are able to at least attempt to act in accord with the moral law as revealed by reason, even if they can never fully achieve this.[65] Those deeper commitments are, to say the least, controversial. Yet without them, Kant's attempt to stabilize political judgment through theory will fail to deliver what is promised.

What Kant held out for was a kind of existential bedrock: that beneath the turmoil and chaos of politics, standards might be identified that cut through the bargaining of interest, the contest of rival incompatible moral visions, the fluctuating capacity for considering the worth of others, and so on, instead constituting something that is finally and simply good in itself. As a result, whether this bedrock *really in practice* provides a stable foundation for politics— i.e., putting a restraint on the folly of actual political actors—eventually

---

to Revolution," in *Reclaiming the History of Ethics: Essays for John Rawls*, ed. A. Reath, B. Herman, and C. M. Korsgaard (Cambridge: Cambridge University Press, 1997), 297–328.

64. Kant, "On the Common Saying," 304.

65. Immanuel Kant, "Groundwork of the Metaphysics of Morals," in *Practical Philosophy*, 62–63. Kant's claim was not, it should be noted, that our moral duties are based directly on metaphysical suppositions; the point of the moral law was that it involved presuppositions and entailed conclusions that we could not help but adopting insofar as we see ourselves as agents, and to that extent his claims were precisely *not* metaphysical. Nonetheless, adopting his view of rational agency—and how that agency commits us to respect for the moral law—does depend irreducibly upon his transcendental metaphysics for it to have the final force Kant supposes.

transpires not to be the most important ambition in play. What really animates the Kantian impulse is the belief that even if political folly proceeds unabated, the true standards of right conduct will remain regardless, and we can take comfort in knowing that they obtain in principle, even if they are widely disregarded in practice. This, in many ways, is a noble hope, and a seductive moral vision.[66] But if we are being truthful about what it can deliver, it is hard to see it as ultimately anything other than an exaltation of an irrelevance when the question comes of what we are actually to *do* about political situations in which judgment must be exercised. Indeed, the Kantian hope may rapidly start to look not just like the exaltation of an irrelevance, but a form of condemnable negligence, when we recall that politics will stubbornly keep going on, with all the danger and difficulty and harm that entails, regardless of whether or not philosophers believe in an underlying independent standard from which to condemn the failings of the political world that they find themselves firmly stuck within.[67]

If pure respect for the moral law is not to guide political decision making, do we really have nothing else to securely put our faith in, as Kant implies in remarks such as "if justice goes, there is no longer any value in human beings living on earth"?[68] We may well have to give up on the dream of an ultimate standard beyond the contingencies of political rule. But having done that, what is left still standing firm is Smith's emphasis on responsibility. And that is not, whatever Kant implies, nothing. Given what we know about political actors and the pressures that they face, and with the long and ignoble history of human political experience at our disposal, we can be sure that respect for the moral law in a Kantian metaphysic is actually a very bad bet for securing the judgment of our rulers. The irony appears to be that if we want decision makers to apply Kantian maxims in an effort to respect the rights of the ruled, we should rather hope for them to be Smith's responsible politicians, equipped

---

66. For an instantiation of that baseline hope, but alongside an attempt to abandon the metaphysical edifice of Kant's transcendental philosophy—indeed, one advanced in part via a reading of Kant that claims this was to be Kant's own position—see Meckstroth, *Struggle for Democracy*, especially chaps. 1 and 6. As should be clear, I am aligned more closely with the traditional reading of Kant's project in morals than Meckstroth's "elenctic" revisionism, not least because I see Meckstroth's rejection of alleged "foundationalist" readings of Kant as misunderstanding the nature of Kant's arguments from the necessities accruing from rational agency. For a more conventional view of the relationship between Kant's political thought and his critical philosophy, see Ellis, *Kant's Politics*, chap. 4.

67. Interestingly, something like this line of criticism was put forward by Kant's contemporary Friedrich Gentz, although Kant seems to have largely ignored the main thrust of Gentz's critique, despite being aware of it and responding to him in "Perpetual Peace." On this see Jonathan Green, "*Fiat justitia, pereat mundus*: Immanuel Kant, Friedrich Gentz, and the Possibility of Prudential Enlightenment," *Modern Intellectual History* 14 (2017), 35–65.

68. Kant, "Metaphysics of Morals," 473.

with robust motivations and capacities to stick to the principles of good judgment. Insofar as we care about improving our political predicaments and safeguarding the welfare of the states that we have to live in—including respecting the rights of the people subject to their coercive apparatus—an emphasis on responsibility is rather a desirable thing to have. It will not be a feature or standard of judgment beyond contingency, but that is to miss the point of why it is worth having, and why it is worth cultivating or holding on to when we are fortunate enough to be able to do so. Accordingly, we do better to leave Kant aside, and follow Hume on the recommendation that we get on with designing robust institutions able to control even the worst knaves, and which thereby force decision makers to act as responsibly as possible, combining this with Weber's insistence that a good constitution will be one that enables properly responsible leaders to emerge. To be sure, Smith's adoption of the idiom of opinion, and his emphasis on the ultimate irreducibility of judgment and the need for nontheorizable responsibility, leaves us with a picture of human politics as fragile, prone to tragedies both small and great, and of philosophy as basically incapable of making this any less so. This diagnosis of our practical predicament is bleak. But there are ways to try to mitigate, ameliorate, and improve that bleakness, and good reasons to try to achieve this when we can. To deny this is simply to make a mistake about what is at stake.

Part of the impetus behind appeals to Hobbesian state theory, I take it, is that it offers the promise of resolution in certain profound questions. (This perhaps helps to explain the greater appeal that Hobbes and, more recently, Kant have exercised over subsequent political theorists than that enjoyed by Hume and Smith.) The first promised resolution is that we might know, once and for all, what the state, the central unit of modern political analysis, ultimately *is*. The second is that once that foundation is secured, we can build up from it to tackle the normative issues that arise from the intimidating fact that human beings now find themselves arraigned under systems of organized coercion, and that answers are demanded as to how and why this can be an acceptable state of affairs. Yet what Hume and Smith encourage us to abandon is precisely this (endless) quest for foundationalism, or for definite conclusions about what the complex agglomeration of historically inherited institutions we muddle by with must be, and how they might rightfully—and reliably—be controlled. In this regard Hume and Smith emerge as more instructive guides than those in the Hobbesian tradition, insofar as they rightly view the role of the theorist as the modest one of trying to explain the world as it actually is, and how we should conduct and adapt our normative evaluations accordingly, rather than attempting to impose upon it a vision of how we might like it to be for the sake of our moral urges and desires for theoretical finality—urges and desires that we ought by now be disenchanted enough to accept will not be fulfilled.

Commercial sociability is the foundation of our politics. Hume and Smith theorized this fact better than any other thinkers, and their political theories of opinion that are the outgrowth of that more basic commitment in turn represent the most viable frame for conceptualizing the world that we are living in. As a result, we do not need to posit any theorist as having "created" the modern state, or "laid the foundations" for contemporary democracy.[69] We should instead see philosophical theorists as offering competing explanations of the political processes of the world(s) they inhabit, but with different normative ambitions depending on how they view the role of philosophy.

We do not live in Hobbesian states, but Humean ones, and the sooner we recognize that, the better off we will be when it comes to making sense of the rest of our political predicaments. However, it must be noted that this task is (perhaps ironically) made difficult by the fact that our political language is now widely infused with sovereignty talk in a Hobbesian mode. This is unfortunate as such language is ill-equipped to deal with the reality that we face, although its pervasive presence in the political culture of the West, alongside its deep (if permanently unfulfilled) promise of resolution to our political predicaments, helps explain the longevity of its appeal. Political discourse today frequently employs terms like "sovereignty" and "the will of the people" in something like the Hobbesian sense (or Rousseauian or Kantian inflections thereof), even if such language is typically deeply politically charged, and can hardly be regarded as an attempt at dispassionate analytic evaluation. Nonetheless, such ideas have by now become central to our notions of political authority (even if from a Humean perspective they are likely to be confused, lacking the freestanding authority often claimed for them). The language of sovereignty, in other words, is part of the practice of our age. It would be a severe mistake to think that it can therefore simply be thrown away, or disregarded, by those who favor a Humean approach to political theory. To put the point slightly differently: whilst we in fact live in Humean states (whether or not we realize it), there exists a relatively widespread view that what makes present states legitimate is something more like Hobbesian sovereignty theory, albeit updated to

---

69. As, for example, Hont suggests when he credits the French pamphleteer Emmanuel Sieyès with inventing the modern state by synthesizing commercial-sociability theory with Hobbesian state theory, as inherited via Rousseau: Hont, "Introduction," 21, 131–34, and "Permanent Crisis," 487–89; cf. Sonenscher, "Introduction," in Sieyès, *Political Writings* (Indianapolis: Hackett, 2003), lxiii: "In the longer term, however, [Sieyès's] efforts to identify a system of government suitable for what, in the late eighteenth century, was already the modern world, have been broadly confirmed. Representation has become the basis of modern economic and political life... Reading his works is a very good way to find out what this involves and what it might mean for thinking about the nature and future of the system of government that we now call democracy." See also Nakhimovsky, *Closed Commercial State*, chap. 1, for an endorsement of the Hont view.

accommodate modern democratic sensibilities, and with a strong affirmation of popular sovereignty as the basis of all legitimate authority.[70] This is something that any modern theory of opinion must take extremely seriously. But having said that, one of the strengths of treating Hume and Smith as our inspiration is that doing so may help us to demystify much of our often-confused understanding of modern politics.[71]

Existential Angst?

The above analysis indicates a certain bleakness about the practical difficulties and dangers of politics in a world governed by opinion, where we must trust to the judgment of those who hold the levers of political power. Alongside this verdict, however, remains the lurking question embedded in Kant's hope for something more dependable than responsibility as a character trait of the politician: whether there is a fundamentally *existential* bleakness to the worldview that sees no possible foundation beyond the contingencies of opinion. John Dunn has suggested that Hume and Smith, once they make politics a function of opinion, cannot provide us with enough to make coherent sense of our existential situation. Unlike Kant, however, Dunn does not hold out hope that anything better can be brought to bear. Whether we should agree is the final issue to be considered.

Dunn identifies Hume and Smith as moving "to subordinate human practical reason to the contingencies of sociology, seeing history as real causal process, and value for human beings as engendered within this process, and setting themselves to identify the logic of this process."[72] However, a shift to Humean secular sociology, away from a Lockean vision centered on theism and an external grounding for the validity of our normative practices, allegedly brought with it two negative consequences. The first was a relatively naïve optimism about the stability of human societies founded upon self-vindicating and self-regulating opinion: "a certain moral complacency over the social and economic realities of the society in which they were so much at home."[73] This meant that Hume and Smith "distinctly overestimated the long-term prospects for combining the dynamics of capitalist development with the

---

70. For a recent articulation of such a view, Richard Tuck, *The Sleeping Sovereign: The Invention of Modern Democracy* (Cambridge: Cambridge University Press, 2015), especially chap. 3 on Rousseau as the source of transmission of Hobbesian sovereignty theory into modern democratic politics.

71. I am grateful to Robin Douglass for these points.

72. John Dunn, "From Applied Theology to Social Analysis: The Break between John Locke and the Scottish Enlightenment," in *Wealth and Virtue: The Shaping of Political Economy in the Scottish Enlightenment*, ed. I. Hont and M. Ignatieff (Cambridge: Cambridge University Press, 1983), 122.

73. Dunn, "Applied Theology," 133.

deferential socializing capacities of pre-capitalist society."[74] Second, Dunn points to a more philosophically profound worry regarding what we might call the existential inadequacy of trying to make human political practices self-validating in a world without God: "If there is indeed nothing rationally to human existence, individually and socially, but opinion, it will certainly be bad news if opinion ever falters. Locke's serried forty-year defence of theocentrism is a very distant battle. But its purpose, to preserve the rationality for humans of an irrational and heartless world, is disturbingly close. The real anguish which lay behind it is an anguish which we still have coming to us and which will be truly ours when we at last learn to feel what now we know."[75] This book should already have answered Dunn's complaint that Hume and Smith were complacently optimistic about the practical predicaments faced by humans in commercial societies. When we appreciate their vision of the fragility of the politics of opinion, alongside their deep and sophisticated analyses of its foundations and operation as part of a pan-European discourse on sociability, consciously seeking to move beyond the theocentric grounding of Locke, it is simply false to characterize either of them as complacent or naïve.[76]

But what of Dunn's second, existential, complaint: that Hume and Smith failed to grasp the deep normative challenge of making sense of our practices in a world no longer equipped with the sorts of foundations that Locke found in theocentrism (or, we might add, that Kant attempted in his transcendental metaphysics)? Unlike Dunn, Hume and Smith did not feel that the only appropriate response to the fact of what Smith called a "fatherless"

---

74. Ibid., 134.

75. Ibid., 134–35; cf. John Dunn, "What Is Living and What Is Dead in the Political Theory of John Locke?" in *Interpreting Political Responsibility* (Cambridge: Cambridge University Press, 1990), 22–25.

76. On this, including a direct response to Dunn, see also especially Hont, "Commercial Society." The question of Smith's doing without any recourse to God is slightly more complicated than with regard to Hume, as Smith laced his works with allusions to the will of a deity, in a manner that Hume never did. In particular, and with reference to the matter at hand especially, Smith famously remarked that "the very suspicion of a fatherless world, must be the most melancholy of all reflections" (*Theory of Moral Sentiments*, VI.ii.3.I), something that leads Dunn to suppose that late in life Smith became belatedly aware of the existential inadequacy entailed by following Hume. Be that as it may, at no point in Smith's arguments does reference to the divine ever do the intellectual work, and all such instances represent cosmetic adornments not integral to the argument being made. Regarding Smith's stance on religion, I agree with Hanley that we do better to move away from misguided arguments over his being a "theist" or a "skeptic" and understand him as a naturalist about religion: Ryan Patrick Hanley, "Skepticism and Imagination: Smith's Response to Hume's *Dialogues*," in *New Essays on Adam Smith's Moral Philosophy*, ed. W. L. Robison and D. B. Suits (Rochester: RIT, 2012), 173–93. For an insightful related discussion, see Griswold, *Virtues of Enlightenment*, chap. 4 especially, but also 340–41, 356–58, and "Epilogue."

world was "anguish."⁷⁷ Indeed, we can usefully reconstruct what a Humean reply to Dunn's complaint might look like. From a Humean perspective there is something deeply perplexing about Dunn's response of "anguish," the cry of a dispositional Lockean who nonetheless recognizes that what made Locke's outlook coherent is no longer an option for us.⁷⁸ There is something bizarre about accepting that the world we must now live in is a secular one and hence that God cannot resolve our intellectual struggles for us, whilst complaining that the resources available within a secular framework are inadequate to address the existential worries about the lack of justificatory support for human practices that only ever made sense within the theistic worldview that has been renounced.⁷⁹ If it is true that we no longer have good reason to believe in God and make His design central to our political practices and self-understandings, it is bizarre to be troubled by the prospects for a world that does without God, one finding its sources of validation and vindication in less metaphysically discredited locations.

Hume and Smith did not fail to recognize the existential predicament Locke was perturbed by—they simply thought that it was a mistake to be perturbed in that way. But were they right? Whilst much of Dunn's critique of Hume and Smith may be thought off-target, he nonetheless presses the most fundamental challenge that can be issued against their project. We can see this by constructing an appropriate counterreply on his behalf: that simply because it is true that we are now resigned to a secular world, it does not follow that we do—or can—stop having the sorts of existential concerns that properly belong to a world that was not godless. The fact that our world wasn't always disenchanted matters, and arguably in a Humean picture especially so: the "practice of the age," after all, is hardly something invented *ex nihilo*, or that can be replaced overnight. God may be dead, but our inability to truly take that fact on board—to at "last learn to feel what now we know"—may be the source of far more trouble than Hume and Smith appreciated. As Nietzsche put it, we have killed God, but comprehending what this means and acting upon it is a deed "still more remote . . . than the remotest stars."⁸⁰ Dunn's worry, then, is that there is something awfully contingent—something grossly inadequate, and by turns existentially hollow and terrifying—about a world in which the content of moral and political legitimacy, and ultimately the grounds of value

---

77. Smith, *Theory of Moral Sentiments*, VI.ii.3.1.

78. As Dunn himself remarks, once God is removed from Locke's philosophy all that is left is "a somewhat doleful Nietzschean, way before his time": John Dunn, *Western Political Theory in the Face of the Future* (Cambridge: Cambridge University Press, 1993), 42.

79. For a similar reading, relating to Hume's attitude toward questions of God's existence, see Simon Blackburn, *How to Read Hume* (London: Granta, 2008), chap. 8.

80. Friedrich Nietzsche, *The Gay Science*, ed. B. Williams (Cambridge: Cambridge University Press, 2001), 120.

for everything we can and will ever do, are simply the adaptive sentiments, the opinions, of complexly socialized animals who happen to be one way, when they could have been another.

But is this worry well placed? Our situation may not be so bad. In this regard, Bernard Williams is an instructive voice, as well as a fitting one insofar as his later political writings, emphasizing the importance of belief in legitimacy and the contingency of forms of acceptable rule, strongly parallel the opinion-based approaches of Hume and Smith.[81] As Williams urges us to see:

> Precisely because we are not unencumbered intelligences selecting in principle among all possible outlooks, we can accept that this outlook is ours just because of the history that has made it ours.... We are no less contingently formed than the outlook is, and the formation is significantly the same. We and our outlook are not simply in the same place at the same time. If we really understand this, deeply understand it, we can be free of . . . [the] illusion, that it is our job as rational agents to search for, or at least move as best we can towards, a system of political and ethical ideas which would be best from an absolute point of view, a point of view that was free of contingent historical perspective.[82]

As Williams put it, the anguish that Dunn predicts involves a "muddle between thinking that our activities fail some test of cosmic significance, and (as contrasted with that) recognizing that there is no such test. If there is no such thing as the cosmic point of view, if the idea of absolute importance in the scheme of things is an illusion, a relic of a world not yet thoroughly disenchanted, then there is no point of view except ours in which our activities can have or lack significance."[83] We need not be threatened by existential vertigo when we see that the fact that our histories and values are contingently formed does not thereby render them *arbitrary*, and by implication necessarily normatively compromised. Although Hume in particular is famous for being a skeptic, it is important to remember that his skepticism is always localized and targeted, never scatter-gun and general, and indeed in moral matters his central ambition was to vindicate rather than debunk the majority of our normative

---

81. I explore these issues in greater detail in Paul Sagar, "From Scepticism to Liberalism? Bernard Williams, the Foundations of Liberalism, and Political Realism," *Political Studies* 64 (2016), 368–84; see also Edward Hall, "Bernard Williams and the Basic Legitimation Demand: A Defence," *Political Studies* 63 (2015), 466–80, and "Contingency, Confidence, and Liberalism in the Political Thought of Bernard Williams," *Social Theory and Practice* 40, no. 4 (2014), 545–69.

82. Bernard Williams, "Philosophy as a Humanistic Discipline," in *Philosophy as a Humanistic Discipline*, ed. A. W. Moore (Princeton, NJ: Princeton University Press, 2006), 193–94.

83. Bernard Williams, "The Human Prejudice," in *Humanistic Discipline*, 137.

practices. Despite the important differences that exist between Williams's and Hume's final considered views on ethical matters,[84] we can see both Hume and Smith as sharing Williams's belief that "It is the same with skepticism in ethics as it is with skepticism elsewhere, that the more general it is, the more harmless." Ultimately, "more is to be feared and learned from a partial skepticism in ethics, one that casts suspicion on tracts of our moral sentiments and opinions" than a Dunnian belief that, having lost God, when we come to realize the enormity of this truth, we risk losing everything.[85]

Of course, Hume and Smith will fail to convince some who come into contact with their way of looking at things—Dunn with his cry of "anguish" is perhaps proof enough of that, as in a different way is the persistent and widespread tendency towards Kantianism in the contemporary academy. But if so it is not clear that the problem lies with Hume and Smith, rather than with those who insist on wanting something more, when it appears so stubbornly to be the case that more is not to be had.

This book has attempted to bring to the fore a particular style of thinking about politics that has for too long lain overshadowed by its rivals, whilst showing that its power and plausibility is greater than typically supposed. Whilst I have focused on Hume and Smith, these are not the only thinkers who might be appealed to as theorists of opinion, though they are perhaps still the most profound and impressive. As I have hinted in this chapter, Weber and Williams may be considered as fellow intellectual travellers. In the eighteenth century, Montesquieu is a plausible candidate for something like the same, whilst Richard Bourke has recently demonstrated that Edmund Burke's political thought is centrally organized through the opinion-of-mankind idiom he inherited from Hume and Smith.[86] Similarly, the influence of Hume's thought upon the early American Federalists has long been noted, in particular as evidenced in Madison's dictum that "ambition must be made to counteract ambition," a direct echo of Hume's focus on institutional design and the guiding

---

84. For an examination of the similarities and differences between Hume and Williams on ethical issues, see Paul Sagar, "Minding the Gap: Bernard Williams and David Hume on Living an Ethical Life," *Journal of Moral Philosophy* 11, no. 5 (2014), 615–38.

85. Bernard Williams, "The Need to Be Sceptical," in *Essays and Reviews, 1959–2002* (Princeton, NJ: Princeton University Press, 2014), 317.

86. On Montesquieu and opinion, see chapter 5 in relation to Smith. On Burke, see Richard Bourke's magisterial recent study *Empire and Revolution: The Political Life of Edmund Burke* (Princeton, NJ: Princeton University Press, 2015), and also Paul Sagar, "Burke Unboxed," *Political Theory* (forthcoming).

supposition that every man is a knave.[87] But the extent to which defense of the American constitution was refracted through the Federalists' recognition that it was ultimately the support of the opinion of the American people—not any freestanding theory of sovereignty in and of itself—that would secure the fledgling republic, remains an area rich for exploration. It is thus already a strong lineage, and there will likely be further candidates for inclusion. Given the strength of this pedigree as it already stands, however, we might conceive of our own task as that of continuing and deepening the insights and approaches bequeathed to us, albeit appropriately adapted for the changing practices of our age.

I began this study by returning to a set of early-modern questions regarding how it is that human beings succeed in forming large and lasting societies, and what follows from that politically and philosophically. For the most part, political theorists in the early twenty-first century no longer worry much about these matters: Hobbes's most pressing challenges can seem very distant today. What I hope to have shown is that they are really not distant at all, even if we must ultimately leave Hobbes's own answers behind. At any rate, if we no longer feel the force of the questions that consistently animated the most accomplished analysts of the modern political condition, then the failing is more likely to be ours than theirs.

---

87. Alexander Hamilton, James Madison, and John Jay, *The Federalist: With Letters of "Brutus,"* ed. T. Ball (Cambridge: Cambridge University Press, 2003), 252.

INDEX

absolutism, 9, 33, 48, 49, 64–65, 71n17, 79, 80, 86, 112, 133, 137, 156–57, 158, 160–61, 164, 186, 187, 202–4, 208–9, 230, 232
Adam, 142
advantage, 27–33, 37, 41, 48, 51, 54–55, 56, 58–61, 68, 69, 86, 89–93, 95, 96, 109, 114, 117–18, 221, 125–26, 128, 140, 144, 154–56, 176, 179, 182, 214, 229
Africa, 143, 146
agriculture, 153, 194, 197, 200
allegiance, 34, 59, 60, 100, 107, 121, 123–28, 130–31, 133, 135, 202, 207, 209
alodialism, 200–2
America, 33, 76, 99, 114, 117, 119, 195, 213n9, 240–41
amour de soi-même, 142n7, 144, 146, 149
amour propre, 29, 142, 144, 146, 148–51, 153–57, 163, 174, 176, 177, 181, 191. *See also* pride; recognition
apes, 143, 146
Aquinas, 3
Arabia, 196
aristocracy, 64, 161, 186, 198, 201, 206,
Aristotle, 3, 27, 28n3, 68, 81, 83, 186
artificial virtue, 3, 56, 59, 94, 100, 121, 124, 126n93, 130, 170
Asia, 196,
Assyria, 76
atheism, 42n64, 82n48
Athens, 104, 198
Attica. *See* Greece
Attila the Hun, 196
Augustinianism, 42, 49, 50, 157
authority, 8, 10, 23, 59–61, 64–5, 75, 77, 79–80, 85, 87–89, 103, 104, 106–9, 163, 167, 168, 181, 183–84, 186, 187, 192–94, 196, 202, 204–9, 213, 221, 226–27, 235, 236; in Hobbes, 104–6, 135–7; in Hume, 116–38, 140–1, 152n38, 156, 167, 181, 183, 213; in Locke, 106–16; in Rousseau, 163; in Smith, 140–1, 152n38, 168, 181, 183, 184, 192–94, 196, 197, 202, 204–9, 226–27

Bacon, Francis, 14, 184
barons, 119, 190, 201–3
Bayle, Pierre, 14, 42n64, 45
benevolence, 17, 19, 31, 95, 97, 168, 169, 180, 219, 221–22
Berkeley, George, 14
Bodin, Jean, 9, 10, 83n17, 160n63
Bourke, Richard, 138n131, 240
bureaucracy, 215
Burke, Edmund, 240
Butler, Joseph, 14, 39n49, 69, 70

Caesar, Julius, 199, 202
Caligula, 164n71, 207
Calvinism, 5, 50
Cambridge school, 5–6, 25
Campbell, Archibald, 70, 92n86
capitalism, 220, 222
Carmichael, Gershom, 102n110
Carthage, 199
Charles I, 77, 203
Charles II, 203
Charron, Pierre, 6
China, 95, 118, 185, 189n71
Christianity, 17, 41, 47, 90, 136n125
Cicero, 182, 186, 227
civic humanism. *See* republicanism
commerce, 6, 9, 49, 62, 63, 118, 185, 191, 210, 214
commercial sociability, 17–18, 19n41, 61n47, 64, 100, 102n110, 218, 219, 221, 229, 235
commercial society, 9, 10, 46, 174n25, 221
commonwealth, 35–36, 38, 64, 72, 73, 74, 76–80, 88, 89, 104, 133, 179
communism, 220
concord, 33–34, 36, 75–76, 117, 118, 120, 147, 150
consent, 27, 33n28, 57, 65, 75, 79–80, 104–5, 107, 109, 111, 112–15, 117, 120–23, 129, 130n106, 131–2, 136–37, 159, 160, 209
contract, 7, 56, 60, 71–73, 80–81, 87–88, 101, 104n4, 106, 112n35, 120, 121, 123, 133n114, 158–60, 206, 229–31

[243]

[244] INDEX

Cooper, Anthony Ashley, third Earl of Shaftesbury. *See* Shaftesbury, Third Earl of
Cromwell, Oliver, 200n107, 202–3

democracy, 6, 9–10, 64, 78, 79, 88, 101, 157n55, 160, 161, 164, 184–86, 196–8, 201, 205, 206, 208, 215–27, 235, 236
Descartes, René, 14
despotism, 9, 155, 158, 164, 185, 187, 188n64
Dunn, John, 5–6, 20, 24n52, 25, 108n15, 109, 236–40

East Indies, 143
Edinburgh Review, 139, 179
Egypt, 1, 76
Elizabeth I, 203
England, 14, 52, 76, 77, 105n8, 107, 119, 121, 127, 189, 190, 200n107, 201–4, 210n148
Epicureanism, 12n27, 17n38, 25–26, 42, 61n147, 82n48, 88, 91, 101n108
Europe, 9, 14, 22, 38, 76, 90, 95, 101, 112, 118–21, 135, 143, 145, 155–58, 163, 185, 188–90, 194n87, 195, 196, 198–204, 208, 216, 237
executive, 113, 137n130, 160n63, 184, 195, 196, 198, 208

family, 18, 46, 52, 54, 55, 66, 71, 101, 120, 194, 195; in Hobbes, 74–81, 101; in Hume, 93–100; in Hutcheson 91–3; in Locke, 112; in Mandeville, 86–7, 89–91; in Rousseau, 148, 150, 152; in Shaftesbury, 82–6; in Temple, 87–8
fascism, 220
Federalists, 240–41
Ferguson, Adam, 101
feudalism, 90, 119, 157, 186, 188–90, 195, 198, 200, 201–4
Filmer, Robert, 109n21, 112
Forbes, Duncan, 11n27, 121n70
France, 9, 10, 14, 29n8, 76, 107n13, 121n69, 140n2, 142n6, 154n42, 157, 186, 187, 188, 189, 202
freedom. *See* liberty
French Revolution, 9, 138n131, 235n69

Geneva, 140n2, 162n67, 163n70
Germany, 76, 187n62, 188–90, 200–1, 203, 204, 215n16

Genghis Khan, 196
Geuss, Raymond, 7
Girondins, 10
Glasgow, 3, 18, 19n41, 91, 93n91, 102n110, 168, 184, 192n80, 194
Glorious Revolution, 127, 203
glory, 28–32, 34–7, 44, 67, 81, 89, 147
God, 14n30, 35, 36, 39, 40, 46, 108–10, 113, 115, 129, 130, 135, 142, 152n37, 164n71, 237, 238, 240
government, 1, 4n8, 10, 38, 46, 47, 58–62, 64–65, 74, 76, 85, 87–91, 93, 95, 99–100, 107–8, 111–21; 123–29; 131–35, 155, 160–61, 164, 168, 178n35, 182–90, 192, 194–210, 212–17, 223–26, 235
Great Britain, 49, 190, 203, 204n127, 210
Greece, 27, 76, 131, 197–98, 201
Grotius, Hugo, 6, 10, 71n17, 111, 143, 182, 183

Hegel, Georg Wilhelm Friedrich, 3
history, 18, 20–21, 24–26, 36, 37n47, 46–47, 66, 80, 100–2, 107–8, 114–16, 119, 121, 135, 211, 216, 217, 221, 223, 229, 223, 236, 239; in Hobbes, 71–80; in Hume, 93–98, 100, 121, 125, 131, 134, 190, 221; in Locke, 114–16; in Mandeville, 91; in Rousseau, 141, 143–46, 156, 178; in Shaftesbury, 85–86; in Smith, 107–08, 115, 116, 119, 181, 182–83, 188–89, 195, 197, 217, 221
history of political thought, 2–8, 10, 12, 25, 72, 100, 167n4, 216
Hobbes, Thomas, 2, 3, 5–11, 12, 13, 15–19, 22, 27–39, 44, 52–3, 56, 61–66, 67–68, 70, 88, 100–2, 104–6, 107, 136–38, 147, 150, 153, 156, 186–87, 217, 223, 234–35, 241; and authority, 104–6, 135–7; on the family, 74–81, 101; and history, 71–80; in history of political thought, 5–8; in Hont, 9–10, 138n131; and Hume, 15–17, 49–54, 58, 61–66, 67, 69, 93–94, 97, 99–100, 126, 135–37; and Hutcheson, 91–93; and international relations, 28, 37, 62–63, 76n29; and Kant, 100, 223, 228–31; and Locke, 109, 137; and Mandeville, 43–44, 46, 48–49, 68–69, 86–7, 91; and Montesquieu, 186–87; and opinion, 65–66; and Rousseau, 110n23, 141–44, 147, 150, 153, 156, 1159–61, 163–

65, 181, 182, 187; and Shaftesbury, 40–42, 81–86; and Smith, 18–19, 168, 181, 182, 208–09, 217, 223; on sociability, 11, 15–17, 27–34, 71–81, 186; and sovereignty 36–9, 49, 62n150, 63–66, 73, 75, 76n29, 77–80, 99, 103–5, 135–38; and state of nature, 30–37, 54, 73–78; and theory of the state, 5–8, 34–38, 103–5, 135–38, 186, 214n13, 234–35; and Temple, 88
Hoekstra, Kinch, 80
honor, 28–31, 33–36, 41, 44, 47, 56, 67–69, 81, 90–91, 156–57, 185, 191, 229
Hont, István, 6, 9–10, 17–18, 102n110, 106–8, 138n131, 152n38, 154n42, 157n55, 167n4, 187n62, 223n33, 224n35, 235n69
human nature, 13, 14n30, 15, 16n34, 27, 36n40, 37, 45, 50, 55, 56, 63, 64, 67, 80, 91–92, 125, 134, 228, 232
Hume, David, 1–5, 10, 11–13, 21–3, 25, 66, 69–73, 81, 87, 100–2, 103–8, 116–38, 166, 211–23, 228, 234–36, 237–40; and authority, 116–38, 140–1, 156, 167, 181, 183; 152n38, 213; and Hobbes, 15–17, 49–54, 58, 61–66, 67, 69; and family, 93–100; and international relations, 58–59, 62–63; and justice, 54–62, 67, 71, 94–100, 118–20, 124–25, 152–53; and Locke, 103–38; and Mandeville, 49–54, 57, 58; on opinion, 1–2, 10–11, 19, 60–67, 103, 127–38, 167, 181, 183, 192–93; and philosophy, 2, 15, 23; and political theory, 3–5, 11–13; 18–19; and Rousseau, 140–41, 151–53, 155, 156, 164; and Smith, 3–5, 8, 10–13, 18–19, 22–23, 25, 38, 53, 66, 101, 116, 119, 135–38, 140–41, 151–53, 156, 164–65, 166–74, 176, 180–81, 183, 187, 190, 192–94, 204, 206–9, 211–23, 228, 234–36; and science of man, 13–15, 63; on sociability, 11, 15, 17–18, 39, 49–62; and sovereignty, 103–5, 136–38, 204–9; and state of nature, 51–56, 96–100; and theory of the state, 18, 38, 63–66, 93, 99, 103–5, 130n106, 117, 135–38, 211–23, 234–36
hunters, 194–97, 208
Hutcheson, Francis, 12n27, 14, 19, 26, 39n49, 41, 61n147, 70, 81, 91–3, 94, 95, 96, 100, 101n108, 102n110, 140n2

Indians. *See* Native Americans
international relations, 8, 37–38, 49, 58, 62–63, 76n29, 99, 158, 163, 213–14, 219
Ireland, 140n2
Italy, 5, 95, 109n74, 199

James I and VI, 203
James II, 127, 203
judiciary, 113, 137n130, 193, 195–99, 201, 208
Judt, Tony, 220
justice, 2, 3, 53, 54–62, 67, 71, 89, 94–100, 101n108, 107n11, 118–20, 124–25, 128, 140, 151–3, 159, 168–73, 182, 192, 196, 199, 200n107, 209, 218–19, 221, 222n31, 223

Kant, Immanuel, 11, 100, 209n145, 223–4, 228–34, 235, 236, 237
Keynes, John Maynard, 220
kingship. *See* monarchy
knave, 63, 94, 126n93, 210n148, 212, 234, 241

language, 7, 109, 145–46, 148, 195, 235
law, 27, 34, 46–48, 53, 60, 62–63, 64–65, 85, 87, 90, 95, 107, 108, 111, 114–16, 118, 120, 127, 134–35, 136n128, 140, 144, 151–55, 157, 160–62, 164, 168, 171–72, 182–83, 184, 185, 187n62, 188–90, 192, 199, 209, 215, 217, 219, 227, 230–33. *See also* laws of nations; laws of nature; natural laws
lawgiver. *See* legislator
laws of nations, 62, 76n29, 182, 183
laws of nature, 32, 35, 120
legislator, 44–45, 47–48, 57, 64, 97, 113, 137n130, 155, 162, 163, 226, 231
legislature, 159, 160–61, 187, 188, 195, 197, 208, 217
liberalism, 5, 6, 7, 49, 157n55, 220, 222
liberty, 5, 8, 14, 32, 37, 64, 91, 93, 101, 108, 110, 116, 119, 123, 127, 134, 136–37, 154, 157, 160, 188–90, 202, 204, 206, 213, 224n34, 230–2
Locke, John, 2, 3, 4, 5–6, 14, 39–40, 71, 72, 80–81, 82n48, 99n105, 106–16, 118–25, 127, 129, 130–33, 135, 137, 143, 148, 160n63, 180, 195, 206, 236–38
Louis XIV, 187

Lucretia, 44
Lucretius, 74, 88
luxury, 43, 49, 61, 86, 91, 113–14, 116, 119, 149, 157, 162, 185, 189, 190, 191, 200, 201–3

Macedonia, 76
Machiavelli, Niccolò, 199
Madison, James, 213n9, 230n60, 240
magistrates, 58–59, 61, 99, 117–20, 124, 126–28, 161, 184, 192
Malebranche, Nicolas, 14
Mandeville, Bernard, 11, 12n27, 14, 16, 19, 39, 51, 56, 57, 61, 63, 70, 74, 86–91, 93, 98, 100, 101, 139–44, 148, 155, 157, 167, 174, 178, 180, 191; and Hobbes, 43–44, 46, 48–49, 68–69; and Hume, 49–54, 57, 58, 68–69, 93, 98, 100; and Hutcheson, 91–93; and Rousseau, 139–44, 148, 155; and Shaftesbury, 42–43, 45, 46, 86, 157, 180; and Smith, 167, 174, 178, 191; and sociability, 17, 42–9, 68–69, 86–87, 89–91, and state of nature, 44–49, 51, 54, 86–87, 89–91; and Temple, 87–89
Marx, Karl, 3
Middle East, 200
Millar, John, 184
monarchomachs, 5, 9
monarchy, 38, 64, 76–77, 79, 88, 93, 105n8, 112, 115n50, 120, 157, 158, 160, 161, 184–92, 196, 197–204, 205–6, 208
mongols, 194–6. *See also* tartars
Montaigne, Michel de, 6
Montesquieu, 156–58, 161, 167, 182, 184–91, 195, 204, 206, 208, 230n60, 240
moral philosophy, 2n4, 4, 39n49, 40n54, 86n62, 91, 92, 102n110, 182

nation state, 215
Native Americans, 76, 99, 114, 117, 119, 195
natural law, 11n27, 28n3, 35n36, 37, 109, 110, 111n32, 113, 135, 183
Nero, 127, 164n71, 207
Netherlands 41, 49, 140n2, 155
Newton, Isaac, 184
Nicole, Pierre, 29n8, 157
Nietzsche, Friedrich 238
Norman Conquest, 201

opinion, 1–4, 10–11, 18–19, 39, 40, 45, 46, 50, 65, 103, 164, 177, 213n9, 213n10, 215, 218, 220, 228, 230, 234–6, 236–40; in Hume, 1–2, 10–11, 19, 60–67, 103, 127–38, 164, 167, 181, 183, 192–93; in Smith, 141, 167–68, 181, 183, 192, 206–12; in Temple, 87–89
orangutans. *See* apes

parlements, 188
parliament, 77, 189, 203–4, 208–9
Pascal, Blaise, 157
Persia, 76, 185
Peter the Great, 181
Philip II, 127
philosophy, 3, 13, 14–15, 17n38, 19, 20–24, 26, 39–42, 54n117, 61, 78, 80, 82n48, 83n52, 91, 106, 108, 121, 127–29, 131–35, 184, 191n77, 207, 209–10, 216, 233n66, 234–35, 238n78
pity, 55, 68–70, 139, 144–45, 150, 151, 153, 156, 181
Plato, 3, 41, 52, 53, 82n48, 83, 104, 104n5, 182, 227, 228
political philosophy. *See* political theory
political theory, 1–9, 12, 13, 17n38, 18, 19, 25, 26, 36, 39, 66, 71n17, 72, 73, 78, 80, 103, 105, 106–10, 127, 129, 130n106, 131n108, 132, 135, 136n126, 137–38, 156, 157n54, 165, 167–68, 173, 184, 192, 193, 211, 214n13, 215, 218, 222, 223, 235
politics, 3–5, 5–9, 11, 15, 18, 19, 22, 38, 42n64, 49, 64, 87, 106, 115, 120, 122–23, 127–28, 134, 136, 136n125, 137–38, 141, 143, 152n38, 156–8, 158–60, 162, 166, 168, 173, 182, 186, 189, 190, 198n102, 200, 204, 208–10, 211–12, 214–18, 220–21, 222n31, 223–24, 226, 228, 232–36, 236–40; science of, 36–38, 63–65, 74, 78, 80, 97, 137, 156
politician, 44–47, 52, 57, 62, 68, 86, 226, 228, 233, 236. *See also* legislator
Polybius, 186
pongo. *See* apes
Port Royal, 29n8, 157
Portugal, 202
pride, 17, 29, 35–37, 43–45, 48–49, 50–51, 61, 67, 87, 89, 91–93, 98n102, 100, 144, 147, 150, 151, 157, 158, 168, 169, 185. *See also* amour propre, glory; recognition

property, 53, 57, 59–60, 62, 67, 102n110, 110–11, 113–14, 116–118, 128, 140, 145, 147–48, 151, 152–55, 157–58, 177–78, 179n38, 181, 192–97, 200, 201, 212, 222, 229
psychology, 16n35, 37, 44, 67–70, 74, 140, 153, 173, 175, 177, 178, 180–82, 190, 221
Pufendorf, Samuel von, 10, 18, 19, 91, 92, 93, 94n91, 101, 102n110, 143, 183n45

Ramsay, Michael, 14
Rawls, John, 2, 6, 7, 71, 72n19, 218–19, 221–22
rechtsstaat, 157n55, 191, 215
recognition, 15, 29–31, 32n24, 34–36, 41, 44, 47, 50, 52, 56, 91–92, 109, 174, 176, 177, 181, 185, 214, 222, 241. *See also* amour propre, glory; pride
religion, 37, 82n48, 136n125, 162, 192n77, 237n76. *See also* God
Renaissance, 5, 9, 27n3, 49
representation, 5, 6, 9–10, 33, 38, 62n150, 65, 136n126, 147, 158, 161, 187n62, 188, 189, 201, 215, 216n19, 217, 224, 230n60, 235n69
republic, 6, 9–10, 38, 49, 52, 64, 86, 120, 137n128, 138n131, 155, 156, 157n55, 159, 161, 162n67, 163, 182, 184, 185, 188–91, 198–201, 203n120, 204n127, 205, 208, 224, 241
republicanism. *See* republic
revolution, 9, 10, 113–15, 119, 122, 126–27, 138n131, 153, 155–56, 182, 183, 203, 206n133, 213n9, 220, 221. *See also* French Revolution; Glorious Revolution
Rome, 1, 76n29, 131, 187n62, 188, 190, 194n87, 199–202
Rousseau, Jean-Jacques, 3, 9, 10, 11, 12n27, 18, 22, 25, 29, 71, 74, 80–81, 100, 110n23, 138n131, 139–65, 191, 229, 235, 236n70; and Hobbes, 110n23, 141–44, 147, 150, 153, 156, 157–58, 159–61, 163–65, 181, 182, 187; and Hume 140–41, 151–53, 155, 156, 164; and justice, 140, 151–53, 159; and law, 140, 144, 151–55, 160–62, 164; and Mandeville, 139–44, 148, 155, 174; and Smith, 139–41, 144–45, 150–53, 166–68, 174, 176–82, 187; and sociability, 139–158; and

The Social Contract 158–65; and sovereignty, 158–62, 164; and state of nature, 139–58; and theory of the state, 155–57, 159–65
Russia, 181, 208

Scholastics, 28n3, 83
Scotland, 50n107, 203
self-liking, 46–48, 50, 91
self-love, 43, 47, 48, 69n10
Shaftesbury, Third Earl of (Anthony Ashley Cooper), 12n27, 14, 26, 39–42, 43, 45, 46, 53, 61n47, 70, 81–88, 91–6, 100, 101n108
Shepherds, 178n35, 189, 193, 194, 196–200, 204, 208
Sidney, Algernon, 206
Sieyès, Emmanuel, 9–10, 19n44, 138n131, 164, 187n62, 235n69
skepticism, 4n8, 5, 6, 23, 25, 40, 70, 82, 116n52, 127, 166, 236–40
Skinner, Quentin, 5, 21, 24–25, 214n13, 216
slavery, 76n29, 143n10, 162, 179n38, 198
Smith, Adam, 3–5, 7, 10–13, 18–19, 22–23, 25, 53, 66, 101, 106–8, 115–16, 119, 135, 138, 139–41, 144–45, 150–53, 156, 164–65, 166–210, 223–40; and authority 140–1, 152n38, 168, 181, 183, 184, 192–94, 196, 197, 202, 204–9, 226–27; and European history, 190–206; and Hobbes, 3–5, 8, 10–13, 18–19, 22–23, 25, 38, 53, 66, 101, 116, 119, 135–38, 140–41, 151–53, 156, 164–65, 166–74, 176, 180–81, 183, 187, 190, 192–94, 204, 206–9, 211–23, 228, 234–36; and Hume, 3–5, 8, 10–13, 18–19, 22–23, 25, 38, 53, 66, 101, 116, 119, 135–38, 140–41, 151–53, 156, 164–65, 166–74, 176, 180–81, 183, 187, 190, 192–94, 204, 206–9, 211–23, 228, 234–36; and judgment, 223–28, 232–36; and justice, 168–73, 182, 192, 196, 199, 200n107, 209; and law, 168, 171–72; 182–83, 199, 209; and Mandeville, 167, 174, 178, 191; and Montesquieu, 182–92; and opinion, 3, 10–11, 18–19, 141, 167–68, 181, 183, 192, 206–12; and political theory, 3–5, 11–13, 19, 206–10, 211–23; and Rousseau, 139–41, 144–45, 150–53,

Smith, Adam (*continued*)
166–68, 174, 176–82, 187; and sociability, 168–73, 192, 194; and sovereignty, 186–87, 202, 204, 207–9; and stages theory, 194–200; and theory of the state, 38, 166, 168, 181, 184–89, 190, 191, 194n87, 196, 203–4, 205–6, 211–223, 224–28, 234–36

sociability, 11, 15–19, 27–66, 67–102, 186, 192, 194, 218, 219, 222n31, 228–29, 235, 237; in Hobbes, 11, 15–17, 27–34, 71–81, 186; in Hume, 11, 15, 17–18, 39, 49–62, 93–100; in Hutcheson, 91–93; in Kant, 228–29; in Locke 109–16; in Mandeville, 17; 42–9, 68–69, 86–87, 89–91; in Rousseau 139–58; in Shaftesbury, 39–42; in Smith, 168–73, 192, 194. *See also* commercial sociability

social contract. *See* contract

socialism, 220, 222

Socrates, 14, 104

Sonenscher, Michael, 157n55, 187n62, 235n69

sovereignty, 5, 6, 9–11, 36–9, 49, 62n150, 63–66, 73, 75, 76n29, 77–80, 89, 99, 101, 103–5, 135–38, 156, 157n55, 158–62, 164, 186–87, 202, 204, 207–9, 211, 223, 224n34, 228, 229–32, 235–36, 241

Spain, 76, 202

Spinoza, Baruch, 16n34

state, 5–9, 11, 34–35, 38–39, 63–66, 93, 99, 101, 103–5, 130n106, 135–38, 155, 156–57, 159–65, 168, 181, 184–89, 190, 191, 194n87, 196, 203–4, 205–6, 211–22, 223–28, 230–36

state of nature, 18, 70–71, 87–89, 101, 109n21, 177; in Hobbes, 30–37, 54, 73–78; in Hume, 51–56, 96–100; in Hutcheson, 91–93; in Locke, 110–113; in Mandeville, 44–49, 51, 54, 86–87, 89–91; in Rousseau, 139–58; in Shaftesbury, 41–42, 81–86

Stewart, Dugald, 16n35, 168n5, 183n46, 184, 195

Stoicism, 14n30, 25–26, 41, 61n147, 82n48, 83, 101n108

Strauss, Leo, 6

sympathy, 18, 49, 51–52, 54, 56, 61, 67, 70, 93–96, 98, 100, 101n108, 117, 124, 125, 151, 153, 156, 166, 169, 171, 173, 176–78, 181, 193

tacit consent, 67, 81, 114–15, 121–22, 132, 152, 153, 171

tartars, 173, 189n71, 194, 196. *See also* Mongols

Temple, William, 87–89, 91, 100

Thales, 14

theism, 5, 6, 107, 108, 110n27, 115–16, 122–23, 131, 132, 135, 236, 237n76, 238

Tiberius, 164n71

Tuck, Richard, 6, 10, 32n24, 126n93, 138n131, 230n60

Turkey, 191

union, 9, 33–34, 38, 49, 51, 52, 55, 65, 75, 84, 147, 150, 156, 159, 172, 186, 187n61, 187n62, 229

utility, 18, 19, 29n8, 31, 46, 54, 55–58, 60–62, 64, 67, 71, 83, 86, 92–94, 96–97, 99–102, 106, 109, 111–12, 114, 115, 117, 119, 123–28, 133–34, 137, 146, 148, 150, 158, 159, 168–75, 178, 180, 181, 193–94, 202, 205–9, 213, 218–20, 222, 228

vice, 29, 40–41, 50, 56, 69, 82n48, 91, 129, 130

virtue, 3, 40–41, 43, 45–47, 49, 50, 52, 56–59, 69, 69n10, 70, 82, 86, 87, 90, 94, 97–100, 101n108, 103, 113, 121, 124, 126n93, 129, 130, 132n111, 135, 139, 144, 145, 157, 170–71, 174, 181–82, 185, 190, 191, 204, 212, 216, 218. *See also* artificial virtue

Waldron, Jeremy, 7, 22n50, 215n15

war, 9, 32, 47, 53, 58–59, 63, 74, 76–78, 82–83, 85, 88, 90, 99, 105n8, 109n21, 118–20, 147, 150, 155, 184, 193, 195–96, 199–200, 203, 214, 220–21

Weber, Max, 213n10, 215n16, 227, 228n49, 228n50, 234, 240

welfare state, 220–22

whig, 49, 65, 101, 104n4, 120, 121, 127, 131n108, 166, 206

William III, 49

Williams, Bernard, 20, 21n48, 130n106, 239, 240

A NOTE ON THE TYPE

THIS BOOK has been composed in Miller, a Scotch Roman typeface designed by Matthew Carter and first released by Font Bureau in 1997. It resembles Monticello, the typeface developed for The Papers of Thomas Jefferson in the 1940s by C. H. Griffith and P. J. Conkwright and reinterpreted in digital form by Carter in 2003.

Pleasant Jefferson ("P. J.") Conkwright (1905–1986) was Typographer at Princeton University Press from 1939 to 1970. He was an acclaimed book designer and AIGA Medalist.

The ornament used throughout this book was designed by Pierre Simon Fournier (1712–1768) and was a favorite of Conkwright's, used in his design of the *Princeton University Library Chronicle*.

GPSR Authorized Representative: Easy Access System Europe - Mustamäe tee 50, 10621 Tallinn, Estonia, gpsr.requests@easproject.com

www.ingramcontent.com/pod-product-compliance
Lightning Source LLC
Chambersburg PA
CBHW021700230426
43668CB00008B/685